BUYING INTO AMERICA

HOW FOREIGN MONEY IS CHANGING THE FACE OF OUR NATION

MARTIN & SUSAN TOLCHIN

BERKLEY BOOKS, NEW YORK

Grateful acknowledgment is made to The New York Times Company for permission to reprint the following previously published essays by Martin Tolchin: "Russians Sought U.S. Banks to Gain High-Tech Secrets," "Foreigners' Political Roles in U.S. Grew by Investing," "With Lobbies in Full Cry, California Debates . . ." "Foreign Capital Growth in U.S. Causes Concern" and "Some Governors Warn on Foreign Investments." Copyright © 1985, 1986 by The New York Times Company. Reprinted by permission. All rights reserved.

This Berkley book contains the complete
text of the original hardcover edition.
It has been completely reset in a typeface
designed for easy reading and was printed
from new film.

BUYING INTO AMERICA

A Berkley Book/published by arrangement with Times Books,
a division of Random House, Inc.

PRINTING HISTORY
Times Books edition/February 1988
Berkley edition/June 1989

ISBN: 0-425-11610-7

A BERKLEY BOOK® TM 757,375
Berkley Books are published by The Berkley Publishing Group,
200 Madison Avenue, New York, NY 10016.
The name "BERKLEY" and the "B" logo
are trademarks belonging to Berkley Publishing Corporation.

PRINTED IN THE UNITED STATES OF AMERICA

10 9 8 7 6 5 4 3 2 1

For Dorothy

Acknowledgments

This book originated in a conversation with Senator Jim Sasser, a Democrat who had just won reelection as the junior senator from Tennessee. Sasser reflected on a disturbing element in his campaign: His opponent had received political and financial support from American executives of Nissan U.S.A., a wholly owned subsidiary of a Japanese multinational corporation, which had a factory in Smyrna, Tennessee. They acted after consulting corporate executives in Washington and Tokyo, who were angry at Sasser's initial neutrality on a bill that would require a portion of every car sold in the United States to be manufactured in the United States. His Republican opponent, Robin Beard, strongly opposed the legislation.

Nissan's entry into American politics intrigued us. We soon discovered that Nissan was not an isolated case and that foreign investment was beginning to have a profound political, social, and economic impact on American life.

We are indebted to A. M. Rosenthal, former executive editor of *The New York Times* and now a columnist, for encouraging reporting on this trend, as well as to Arthur Gelb, managing editor, for his steadfast support; Bill Kovach, former Washington editor of *The New York Times;* David R. Jones, the *Times*'s former national editor and now editor of the national edition, and Fred Andrews, business editor. A series on this subject was edited by Dan Lewis, the *Times*'s deputy national editor. In addition, we are indebted to colleagues, including David Burnham, Clyde Farnesworth, Barnaby Feder, John Herbers, Robert Hershey, Peter Kilborn, Andy Malcolm, Irvin Molotsky, Claudia Payne, Robert Pear, Philip Shabecoff, William Safire, and Earl Smith. They were a constant source of expertise, advice, and criticism. Monica Borkowski and Nancy Ganahl, librarians in the Washington Bureau, proved endlessly resourceful.

We are grateful for the extensive research support provided by George Washington University. A travel grant from the university's research program provided the resources to do extensive field work throughout the country, while funds for research assistance were expedited by the School of Government and Business Administration and the Department of Public Administration. For their constant support and generosity, we thank Norma Maine Loeser, dean of the School of Government and Business Administration, and Kathryn E. Newcomer, who chairs the Department of Public Administration. Astrid E. Merget, who chaired the department during the first phase of the book, also deserves our thanks for her ongoing friendship and encouragement.

Four graduate research assistants from the Department of Public Administration contributed untold quantities of time, effort, and imagination to this project. We give special thanks to William Vantine, H. Kenneth Garner, Steven Taylor, and Phyllis Shea for the skill with which they checked facts, constructed charts, tracked down leads, surmounted obstacles, and maintained their good humor. Joyce Hopkins, administrative assistant for the department, remains a continual source of help and patience; we also thank department secretaries Karen Kittredge and Martha Engel.

The book has benefited considerably from friends and colleagues who have read portions of the manuscript. For their criticisms and ideas, we thank the following:

Jodie T. Allen, John Boswell, Benjamin J. Cohen, Judy Eggleston, Rod Eldridge, Earl Fry, Dorothy Goldsmith, Warren Greenberg, Phillip D. Grub, Ted Jacobs, Julius Johnson, Jill Kasle, Peter Kilborn, Sar Levitan, Kathryn E. Newcomer, Susan Schwab, George Slover, Charles P. Tolchin, and Karen R. Tolchin.

A significant part of the book is based on original interviews with policymakers and analysts involved in the field of foreign investment. They include representatives from both the public and private sectors: members of Congress, state legislators, economic development officials, government bureaucrats, political appointees, lawyers, trade-association representatives, U.S. business leaders, and executives from foreign multinational corporations. Interviews were conducted between 1984 and 1986; all direct quotes in the text that are not cited in footnotes are taken from these interviews. We thank the following respondents for sharing their knowledge, experience, and insights with us:

Mark Akers, Lamar Alexander, Alfred Alquist, James E. Ammerman, Richard A. Apcar, Bruce Babbitt, Malcolm Baldrige, Harvey E. Bale, Jr., Norman Bangerter, Marion Barry, Lloyd

Bentsen, Jeff Bingaman, Jim Bomkamp, Phyllis Bonanno, Don Bonker, William Boozer, Arnaud de Borchgrave, Quentin Breen, Jeanne Z. Brooks, Donald Brown, Willie Brown, John Bryant, Daryl R. Buffenstein, Michael Butler, Oliver T. Carr, Eugene Casraiss, Marsha Clark, June M. Collier, E. Gerald Corrigan, Frederic R. Dahl, Alphonse M. D'Amato, Mark Dayton, Ron Danielian, J. Peter DeBraal, Robert E. Dillon, Joe DiPietro, David Doerr, George Dubuc, Bob Dugger, Jim Egenolf, Tim Elder, Rod Eldridge, James Elliott, Jr., Dave Flessner, Raymond Flynn, Benjamin Fulgenzi, Kenneth Gibson, John Gornall, Bob Graham, John Griffing, Phillip D. Grub, Mark Guidry, John Gunther, Raj Gupta, Robert L. Haggan, Ricky Halliburton, Stan Hanson, William Hardaman, Thomas E. Harris, Jerre R. Haskew, Tom Hayden, Martin Helmke, Ruth and Bill Holmberg, Leslie Holt, Ned Howenstine, James A. Houpt, Ben C. Huang, Harry R. Hughes, Kazuo Ishikure, Ted Jacobs, Nancy Johnson, Julian Josephs, Jim Joyce, Henry Kaufman, Robert Kerrey, John Kline, Jake Klosterman, Richard D. Lamm, Steve Larson, Patrick J. Leahy, Bartholomew Lee, John Lenkey, III, Jeffrey Lins, William H. Long, Susan MacKnight, David Major, Michael Mann, Ephraim Margolin, Carol Martel, Will Maslow, John McCarthy, John W. McGarry, Reg McGhee, John McClenahen, Steve McSpadden, Ernest N. (Dutch) Morial, Daniel P. Moynihan, David C. Mulford, Jiro Murase, Frank Murkowski, William R. Murray, Jr., Henry Nau, Jack Nelson, Jim Nielsen, Jock O'Connell, Nancy Ordway, Rudy Oswald, Cliff Palefsky, Roger O. Parent, Richard N. Perle, Rudy Perpich, Thomas Pierpoint, Clyde Prestowitz, William Proxmire, Dalton Roberts, (Mayor) Eugene Roberts, Felix Rohatyn, Randy Rose, Denis Rufin, Marvin Runyon, Howard Samuel, Harmut Scheitz, Stephen I. Schlossberg, Charles E. Schumer, Susan Schwab, William L. Seidman, Billy Sellars, John R. Shultz, Muriel Siebert, William Simon, Inez Slayton, George Slover, Richard Smith, Isabel Solomon, James D. Squires, Robert H. Trager, Leonard M. Tyree, John Vasconcellos, Paul Volcker, Frank G. Vukmanic, Ray Waldmann, Dan Walter, Bruce Weindruck, Steven Weiss, Jack Welsh, Peter White, Walter Wriston, Al Zack, and Frank G. Zarb.

We are especially indebted to our editor, Jonathan B. Segal, for his unflagging encouragement and enthusiasm. The book reflects his insights as well as his editorial skill. We also thank Ruth Fecych, Nancy Inglis, Arthur Neuhauser, and Frank Lavena, who provided us with valuable editorial suggestions.

We are also grateful to Steve and Nancy Schlossberg for their involvement, friendship and support.

Most of all, we want to thank our children, Charlie and Karen, who made many substantive suggestions and remain a constant source of pride and strength for us.

Bethesda, Maryland, 1987

Contents

PART I

INTRODUCTION

CHAPTER 1

Foreign Money
The American Challenge

We believe that there are only winners, no losers, and all participants gain from it.

—President Ronald Reagan

Once they own your assets, they own you.

—Senator Frank Murkowski,
Republican of Alaska

Foreign money is changing the face of America, the lives of Americans, and the nature of our political processes. A surge of foreign investment in the United States is rebuilding the nation's cities, reshaping rural America, and building manufacturing and assembly plants that are creating jobs for millions of Americans. Mayors, governors, and cabinet officers are circling the globe in quest of foreign funds, with the intensity of third-world ministers trying to stave off the financial collapse of their shaky governments. Treasury officials have designed securities offerings with a view toward wooing foreign investors, cities and states maintain offices abroad for this purpose, and the U.S. Conference of

Mayors holds semiannual conferences in Asia and Europe to help cities attract foreign money.

For much of our history American businessmen went around the world investing in overseas ventures, exporting their culture, and intervening in foreign governments. During the past decade, however, the trend has steadily reversed. Foreign investors have found a haven on U.S. shores, enriched our lives by bringing us their cultures, and protected their investments by becoming increasingly involved in our political processes.

In the most pragmatic nation in the world, most Americans don't care where the money comes from as long as it provides jobs and stimulates economic growth. Most Americans don't care whom they work for provided their salaries and working conditions are good, and sometimes even when they are not. Most mayors and governors don't care who pours money into their financially beleaguered cities and states to revive their failing economies, and most federal officials don't seem to care who finances the national debt. Under pressure to bring home the bacon, politicians have paid scant attention to the long-term economic, political, and social effects of their country's deepening dependence on foreign money.

Supporters of this trend contend that this nation's greatest strengths, both political and economic, are its openness and diversity. Freedom of expression and opportunity, they note, are the bedrock upon which America was built. They decry xenophobia, hail the global economy, and say that competition will ensure the best results at both the ballot box and marketplace. They note that although total foreign investment is rapidly growing, it amounts to only a small fraction of the nation's wealth. They point out that foreign investment has created three million jobs, buoyed the stock market, heightened real estate values, stimulated art sales, preserved agricultural land, increased the pool of venture capital, lowered home mortgage rates, improved local economies, enabled the nation to sustain record budget deficits, and improved America's balance of payments. Foreign investors bring new technology and new managerial techniques to American firms facing obsolescence, and fresh infusions of capital to dying industries.

The most significant benefit of foreign investment, many believe, is that it furthers the country's historic goal of reducing the restrictions on the free flow of goods, services, and capital throughout the world. Since World War II, the United States has been the leading advocate of free trade and the reduction of tariffs worldwide as well as the prime mover behind the engines that power those goals: the GATT (General Agreement on Tariff and Trade) negotiations, the International Monetary Fund (IMF), and the World Bank. The free flow of investment occupies a vital position in the success of the global economy. The Reagan administration's enthusiasm over foreign investment was expressed in a 1983 statement: "We believe that there are only winners, no losers, and all participants gain from it."[1]

But others are less sanguine. They warn that the United States is becoming "addicted" to foreign capital. They fear that this overdependence has made us vulnerable to the vagaries of foreign investment and that the withdrawal of foreign investment could wreak havoc on the economy. They lament the loss of profits that are taken out of the country and say that some foreign investors treat their American hirelings with the tenderness that imperialist powers reserved for the colonies. Mostly, they fear that the surge of foreign investment is eroding the nation's independence, both political and economic. They warn that major decisions affecting the lives of Americans and, possibly, the security of the nation, are now being made in Tokyo, London, Riyadh, and other foreign capitals.

"They make us dance to a tune played afar," said Richard D. Lamm, former governor of Colorado, adding that Westerners were sensitized to the problems of absentee ownership because they had suffered from Eastern ownership of the West in the last century. "There's all kinds of Faustian bargains made in economic development. Even though you get 250 jobs, the net effect on your community is negative because you've given away the show."

Thoughtful critics do not blame the foreign investors, who are putting their money into a politically safe haven, where they can get the best returns on their yen, francs, pounds, riyals, deutsche marks, and guilders. Instead, these critics blame Americans' own rapacious need for foreign money to finance a standard of living undreamed of in the rest of the world. Paul A. Volcker, former chairman of the Federal Reserve, is one of them:

> In a real sense we have been fortunate that funds have flowed so freely to the U.S. in recent years, reflecting to a considerable extent widespread confidence in our prospects. But it is clearly not healthy for the largest and richest country in the world—in its own interest or that of others—to use up so much of the world's savings to finance a budget deficit.

Most members of the financial community, however, agree with Walter B. Wriston, former chairman of Citicorp, the world's largest bank holding company, who enthusiastically supports foreign investment. "I don't believe in the bogeyman of foreign capital," Mr. Wriston said. "It's painted by folks who don't believe in a global economy." Similarly, Henry Kaufman, an economist and investment banker with Salomon Brothers, says that foreign investment has contributed to the "restructuring of the United States as a service economy," which he sees as desirable, because "over the longer term, societies should do what they're most efficient doing."

Nobody knows the full extent of foreign investment in the United States. Much of it comes across U.S. borders with the stealth and anonymity of illegal aliens. Lax reporting requirements, hidden ownerships, and other circumventions of the laws have made it virtually impossible to keep track of the flood of foreign money.

Most experts agree, however, that more than $1.5 trillion in foreign investment has poured into the United States from around the world, a significant increase from $196 billion in 1974.[2] About 80 percent of this foreign investment is in government and private securities, so-called portfolio investments, with foreign investors now holding more than $200 billion—or one-tenth—of America's $2 trillion national debt. Some experts put the foreign share of the national debt at between $300 billion and $400 billion, or between 15 and 20 percent. In addition, foreign investors own close to $445 billion in U.S. bank assets, more than $300 billion in diversified stocks and bonds, more than $100 billion in real estate, and $200–$300 billion in direct investments of factories, warehouses, and assembly plants.

Foreign companies are buying up American oil and gas companies at a rapid rate and are making significant inroads into the construction industry, machine tools, automobiles, auto parts, and a host of other industries. More than half of the nation's cement industry and four of the nation's top ten chemical companies are foreign owned, while a French company will soon become the leading manufacturer of television sets in the United States. Foreign investors have bought land, skyscrapers, and shopping centers in virtually every state of the union, to the delight of real estate agents and the dismay of some developers and other groups. Foreign governments also play a large role in the investment business, holding 20 percent of all the foreign investment in the United States.[3]

In direct investment, the British have traditionally led the pack of foreign investors. Their efforts date back to the nineteenth century, when their money was crucial to the development of America's infrastructure and industrial might. They are followed by the Dutch, who benefit from their foreign multinational, Royal Dutch Shell. Japan has just overtaken Canada as the third major investor, and if the Japanese continue to invest at their current pace, they will probably overtake Britain and the Netherlands before 1990. After Canada, the other major investors in order of the amount of their investments are West Germany, Switzerland, France, Kuwait, Australia, and Sweden.[4]

The Japanese have emerged as the most active players in this surge of new foreign investment. Now the world's leading capital exporters, they are reaping the benefits of their high rate of savings and commitment to industrial competitiveness. As part of their campaign to increase their investments worldwide, a Japanese-owned Kawasaki motorcycle plant has enriched Lincoln, Nebraska, while thirty Japanese manufacturing plants have brought jobs and prosperity to the state of Tennessee. And in 1986, following approval by the Federal Reserve Board, the Sumitomo Bank bought a $500 million equity stake in the Wall Street firm of Goldman Sachs. If America's debtor status continues along its current course, some economists predict that Japanese investors alone will hold $400 billion of the U.S. debt by 1990.

Foreign capital has flowed into almost every major sector of the American economy. Foreign investors increased their holdings of U.S. bank assets from $32 billion in 1973 to $445 billion in 1986 and now hold more than 16 percent of total U.S. bank assets. Many of their acquisitions had been weak and troubled banks, which they improved with infusions of money and new management policies. Concentrating in California and New York, foreign-owned banks owned 33 percent of the total banking assets in California in 1985 and were responsible for 40 percent of the total business loans made in New York State.

Thus, foreign bankers are playing an increasing role in setting the nation's economic priorities. Foreign investors also have become the new lions of Wall Street. Wertheim & Co. is now Wertheim Schroder & Co., 50 percent owned by Schroders P.L.C. (British). Moseley Securities is 39 percent owned by the Al Mal Group (Middle East investors). Drexel Burnham Lambert is 27 percent owned by a European investor group that includes Pargesa of Switzerland and Groupe Bruxelles Lambert of Belgium. Smith Barney Harris Upham is 22 percent owned by Lama Holdings, an Arab investor group. First Boston Inc. is 21.6 percent owned by Credit Suisse (Swiss). Lazard Frères & Co. is 15.3 percent owned by Lazard Brothers of London and S. Pearson & Son (British). Salomon Brothers is 14 percent owned by Minorco (controlled by Anglo American Corp. of South Africa); Shearson Lehman Brothers is 13 percent owned by Nippon Life Insurance Co. (Japan). Goldman Sachs & Co. is 12.5 percent owned by the Sumitomo Bank (Japan); and L. F. Rothschild, Unterberg, Towbin is 8 percent owned by J. Rothschild Holdings (British).[5]

But while foreign investors have received credit for buoying the stock market, some fear that they could trigger its collapse. James Grant, editor of *Grant's Interest Rate Observer*, a financial newsletter, told the *Wall Street Journal*, ''My pet hypothesis for a blowout is that it will come from Japan. It's the most extreme, the ripest speculative excess in the world.''[6] The theory was that just as the recent surge in the American market had been attributed to buying by foreign investors, especially the Japanese, heavy selling by these same investors would presumably send the market into reverse.

The real estate industry also feels the impact of the influx of foreign capital. By conservative estimates, it is believed that foreign investors have poured more than $100 billion into U.S. real estate, sending real estate prices soaring in some areas and plummeting in others that have suffered from a glut of available office space and housing. The British have amassed $1 billion in real estate holdings in downtown Washington, D.C., and raised real estate prices there, while a Saudi arms dealer deflated prices in Salt Lake City by investing too heavily and creating an overabundance of office space. A Canadian company owns 8 percent of all the office space in Manhattan. The U.S. real estate market has also become a convenient repository for the ill-gotten gains of foreign dictators, including Ferdinand Marcos and Jean-Claude Duvalier.

Americans are constantly surprised to discover that companies that seemed part of the American landscape are now in foreign hands. The familiar hamburger chain Hardee's is Canadian owned; Doubleday & Co., publishers, is German; and Viking Press and E. P. Dutton, British. A British holding company has acquired Smith & Wesson, the 135-year-old firearms manufacturer. Supermarkets across the country have also been sold to foreign owners: A&P is owned by German investors; Grand Union is

French; Red Food, French; Food Lion and Food Giant are Belgian. The resort complex of Kiawah Island in South Carolina is owned by Kuwaiti investors. These investments have revitalized many areas of the country from coast to coast: from the French-owned Michelin truck-radial-tire factory, which has enhanced the economy of Spartanburg, South Carolina, to the Kyocera industrial ceramics plant in San Diego, California.

Similarly, the Nippon Kokan corporation of Japan owns half of the National Steel Corporation; and Nestlé of Switzerland recently bought the Carnation food company for $3 billion. Well-known landmarks are also rapidly being acquired by foreign owners: the Watergate complex in Washington, D.C., is owned by a British pension fund, and the Celanese building in New York City's Rockefeller Center is owned by a foreign oil company.

Much of this investment is an effort to tap into the lucrative U.S. consumer market. When Nestlé acquired Carnation, the company reached its corporate goal: selling to 25 percent of the world market. Some investment is clearly defensive: an immediate response to protectionist winds blowing through the U.S. Congress. Two prime examples are the television industry and the automobile industry; many foreign firms quickly located in the United States directly in response to U.S. protectionist measures. In that sense, foreign investment was deceptive: Foreign industries cornered a substantial part of the U.S. market before anyone realized that foreign investment was an important part of the export strategy of our major trading partners. Japanese auto companies, for example, accelerated their investments in the United States in direct response to voluntary-restraint accords, and many predict that soon there will be more Japanese than American companies making cars in the United States. In rapid succession, these companies lured foreign-owned auto-supply companies to manufacture in the United States, and by 1986, when Toyota started building a plant in Georgetown, Kentucky, the company insisted that foreign contractors do their construction work.

AN AMERICAN HERITAGE

Foreign investors have been part of the American heritage since Peter Minuit, first director general of New Netherland, bought the island of Manhattan from the Indians for 60 guilders—then worth about $24. Since then, foreign investors have helped finance the building of the nation's railroads, canals, factories, mines, and overall industrial capacity, particularly in the last century. "This country was built with foreign investment, Scottish engineers, and Irish labor," said Walter B. Wriston. "Investors put their money here because we have a politically stable government and it's one of the few countries in the world creating jobs. An entrepreneur can make a buck and keep it."[7]

Indeed, the United States often has borrowed to finance investments vital to its national interests—from its early need to industrialize to its periodic need to arm itself for military conflicts. But critics contend that it is one thing to borrow to industrialize and then repay out of a newly industrialized economy, and quite different for the most industrialized nation in the world to go on a borrowing spree to finance its burgeoning budget deficit. Their warnings increased when the United States suddenly became a net debtor nation in 1985 for the first time since World War I. This meant that the value of assets owned by foreigners in the United States exceeded the value of assets owned by Americans abroad. The figure, known as the current-account deficit, widens every year; by the end of 1986, it had reached $263.6 billion.

"The real thinkers around here are concerned about the long-term cost of the capital inflows," said Representative Don Bonker, Washington State Democrat and chairman of the House Democratic Trade Task Force and chairman of the Subcommittee on Economic Policy and Trade of the House Foreign Affairs Committee. "It's subsidizing the present with the hardships of the future."

Critics fear that a growing dependence on foreign investors will inevitably lead to a loss of freedom as foreigners gain economic and political leverage over the lives of Americans. Foreign investors, who now hold more than 10 percent of the outstanding U.S. treasury bills, for example, could exercise this leverage on behalf of a foreign government and shape national decisions. The late representative Benjamin S. Rosenthal, a Queens Democrat, referred to such holdings of U.S. securities by foreign governments as "the money weapon."[8]

Treasury officials panicked in May 1987 when foreign investors temporarily declined to bid on the sale of $29 billion in T-bills, needed to finance the deficit. After two days of nervous waiting, the treasury reduced the price of the thirty-year bills and raised their yield, prompting foreigners to return to the market.

The Japanese alone bought nearly half the $9.3 billion in thirty-year bonds offered to the public.

"The message of the bond sale was clear: Foreigners are our bankers," wrote Jeff B. Copeland and Rich Thomas in *Newsweek*. "The era of American economic independence is gone, thanks to a trade deficit too big to fund ourselves. Foreigners increasingly influence inflation and recession in the United States."[9]

There was mounting evidence, moreover, that private foreign investors were being replaced by foreign governments as major purchasers of government securities. Economist Alan Greenspan calculated that in the first three months of 1987, the central banks of Japan, Western Europe, and Canada provided most of the money needed to finance the U.S. trade deficit. The questions that seem to trouble many policymakers are: What will these governments demand in return? And how long will they continue to bail out the United States?[10]

In April 1987, Paul Volcker disclosed that the Federal Reserve Board had raised short-term interest rates in an effort to stem the plunge of the dollar and make U.S. investments more attractive to foreigners. "Federal policy is increasingly influenced and even dictated by the needs of our foreign creditors," said Norman Robertson, the chief economist at the Mellon Bank.[11]

Questions of national security also emerge from time to time but are quickly dismissed by government officials. The U.S. government's interagency Committee on Foreign Investment in the United States (CFIUS) reviewed the $110 million sale of New Hampshire Ball Bearings to its chief Japanese competitor, Mineoba, on national security grounds and then allowed the sale. CFIUS is known around government circles as a "paper tiger": It rarely meets and has never, to anyone's knowledge, blocked a foreign investment. Considering that CFIUS is the only foreign-investment review mechanism in the executive branch, its inactivity speaks volumes about government complacency toward foreign investment.

There is persuasive evidence that some foreign investors, notably the Japanese, have purchased U.S. companies to acquire their technology and ultimately eliminate U.S. competition in key industries. In this area especially, foreign investment takes on aggressive overtones: a clear attempt to acquire advanced technology in order to dominate industrial markets. The Japanese investment in Boeing, for example, led to widespread alarm about the inevitable loss of the aerospace industry, which many believe to be the last stronghold of American technological superiority.

The announcement of Fujitsu's intended purchase of an 80 percent stake in Fairchild Semiconductor Corp. in the spring of 1987 aroused similar warnings about the nation's future defense capabilities. The impending Fujitsu purchase marked one of the most important foreign investments involving the transfer of cutting-edge American technology, research, and expertise to Japan in decades and created the first major controversy over a foreign investment. Opponents of the sale contended that the investment would make Fujitsu the leading semiconductor firm in the world. (The company already owns half of Amdahl, an American computer company.) The national-security implications of Fujitsu's purchase were also noted by those who are aware of the Pentagon's growing dependence on foreign suppliers: Fairchild's defense electronics subsidiary provides more than $100 million of high-speed circuitry annually to the defense community. (Ironically, Fairchild is owned by a French company, so one foreign investor would merely have replaced another.) Unwilling to continue negotiating in the glare of negative publicity, Fujitsu eventually withdrew its offer.

The Fujitsu effort was notable because it provoked the first major controversy in recent memory over a foreign investment. Until that time, foreign investors could count on a warm welcome from the United States, which regarded almost all foreign investment as good for the country. There are signs, however, that this is changing.

As trade became more of a national issue, policymakers began to notice inequities in investment relationships. An increasing number of congressmen have begun to complain, for example, that America's open-door policy toward investment was not universally reciprocated. Japan was identified as a major offender. In fact, most other nations impose tight restrictions on the investments that may be made by foreigners, and few allow foreign involvement in real estate or communications. Nontariff barriers restricting U.S. investment abroad include phony performance requirements, unnecessary regulations, requirements for joint ventures, restrictions on work permits, lack of cooperation, and a host of others.

Phantom investors abound. Many investments bear few signs of their real foreign owners, as congressional committees discovered when they sought to uncover the U.S. real estate holdings of Ferdinand Marcos. The Marcos investments underscore another criticism: that the United States had become a haven for funds from less developed nations, depriving them of sorely needed capital and making them more vulnerable to communist takeovers. Some suspect that much of this third-world investment in the United States represents the money that the economic elites have skimmed off U.S. foreign aid, sending it abroad for their own personal use.

Nor do U.S. officials always know whether a foreign investor is a legitimate businessman, a front for his government, or a criminal involved in illicit ventures. "A hodgepodge of 16 different federal agencies collects information on foreign investments here," charged Representative John Bryant, a Texas Democrat and sponsor of legislation to stiffen reporting requirements on foreign investment.

> But the information is so limited, hidden in bureaucratic quagmires, or actually kept secret by law—even from Congress—that we often don't know who is investing here or whether they are from friendly nations like Canada or hostile ones like Libya and Iran. Nor do we know whether they are legitimate business people or drug traffickers laundering ill-gotten gains.[12]

Despite such deceptions, complexities, and conflicts, the rivalries between cities and states to obtain foreign investments dwarf the Super Bowl. This has led to a mounting uneasiness about the hidden costs of foreign investment. Some experts fear that the intense competition between mayors and governors has led them to pay too high a price for foreign investment. "Some cities and states made some very extravagant concessions in the sixties, seventies, and early eighties to get plants to move to their areas," said Malcolm Baldrige, secretary of commerce. At the same time, William J. Casey, the director of the Central Intelligence Agency (CIA), warned of the national-security implications of foreign investors acquiring U.S. technology and called Japanese investment in American computer companies "a Trojan horse." Union officials, meanwhile, are just beginning to look closely at the anti-union activities of many foreign companies that build plants in the United States. The message just beginning to emerge is that foreign investment is not a totally free lunch: that the short-term benefits bring long-term costs, which may prove to have a more significant impact on American life than political leaders are ready to recognize.[13]

THE NEW AMERICAN CHALLENGE

Two decades ago, a book on foreign investment sent waves of alarm through the European community. The book was *The American Challenge (Le Défi Américaine)* by the noted French journalist and author Jean-Jacques Servan-Schreiber. The book warned that the invasion of Europe by American multinationals was dominating its economy and destroying its traditional industries. If allowed to continue, argued Servan-Schreiber, "the world's greatest industrial power, just after the United States and Russia, will not be Europe, but American industry in Europe."[14]

Readers today would get an uneasy feeling of déjà vu reading about how American multinationals beat out the Europeans: The "flexibility of the Americans, even more than their wealth, is their major weapon." Hidebound, traditionalist European companies, straitjacketed by social class, were no match for free-wheeling U.S. multinationals, with their sophisticated management techniques and dynamic approach. The question that burned into the European consciousness about U.S. inroads was "Why do they succeed better over here than we do ourselves?"[15]

Servan-Schreiber was criticized as unnecessarily alarmist. Indeed, his scenario never materialized. The oil crisis of 1973 intervened to diminish America's industrial power, and more important, the Europeans rose to meet the American challenge by reorganizing their industries and becoming more competitive. This took concerted government involvement and the recognition that if they did not act, they would ultimately lose a measure of their highly valued political sovereignty. Former colonialists themselves, the Europeans understood all too well the relationship between economic and political power.

Now the shoe is on the other foot. Foreign money has invaded the American economy with an impact that is only beginning to be appreciated. Part of a general shift toward a global economy, foreign investment continues to be coveted by American leaders who are motivated by the need to create jobs and finance the deficit.

Foreign firms that locate in the United States can expect the same political benefits as American businesses—sometimes more. The mayors and governors who have recruited them fight for the same profit-enhancing government grants, tax exemptions, and freedom from regulations that they advocate for domestic companies. In effect, foreign and American investors enjoy equal status in the eyes of the political system, making the United States the only country in the world that practices this form of equality. It is also the only industrialized country that does not keep accurate figures on the extent and origin of foreign investment, lest such disclosure restrict the money flow.

There is little recognition that some of these foreign business-men have hidden agendas, including the destruction of American competitors and the acquisition of American technology. Many of these foreign investors have been motivated by a desire to avoid protective tariffs and view foreign investment as part of their nation's export strategy, to increase their market share.

The challenge for American policymakers is to continue to reap the benefits of foreign investment while minimizing its risks. If they fail to meet this challenge, the threat of losing a measure of political and economic sovereignty becomes a real possibility.

In an ideal world in which free trade and barrier-free invest-ment were the rule rather than the exception, the U.S. position would make sense. In the real world, it raises questions that have been largely ignored by government officials who have focused on their individual short-term needs rather than on the collective long-term effect of the nation's deepening dependence on foreign money.

CHAPTER 2

Trojan Horse or
Gift Horse

Foreign Investors and Political Influence

> I do not think foreign nationals have any business in our political campaigns. They cannot vote in our elections, so why should we allow them to finance our elections? Their loyalties lie elsewhere; they lie with their own countries and their own governments.
>
> —*Senator Lloyd Bentsen,*
> *Democrat of Texas*

> It really is amazing that it took a bunch of Koreans to understand that a two-party democracy cannot function effectively with a one-party press in the nation's capital.
>
> —*Arnaud de Borchgrave,*
> *editor-in-chief,* Washington Times

The emerging debate on the long-range effects of foreign investment has brought foreign investors and their American representatives to congressional hearing rooms as well as financial boardrooms. They have become familiar figures in the corridors of state capitols, city halls, and the U.S. Congress, and there is mounting evidence that their efforts have proved effective. Foreign investors have been a boon to the K Street lobbying firms in downtown Washington. To protect their investments, these investors have become increasingly involved in American politics.

At the behest of their American advisers, Japanese businessmen warned members of Congress in 1986 that the proposed repeal of investment tax credits would lead them to curtail their investments in the United States. Saudi Arabians threatened to divest themselves of their U.S. securities rather than comply with congressional requests to disclose the extent of their substantial holdings. The influence of foreign investors even penetrated a closed meeting of the House Ways and Means Committee, which granted an exemption in the 1986 tax bill to Esselte Pendaflex Corporation, an office-products company in Garden City, L.I., a wholly owned subsidiary of Esselte A.B., a Swedish corporation.

The heaviest price paid by Americans is the loss of a measure of political independence. The political activity generated by foreign investors becomes more visible daily. The Japanese have been the most politically active. "When Japanese companies invest in the United States, in addition to being welcomed on the local level, they would like to see congressmen, senators, the president, vice-president, and secretary of the treasury," said Jiro Murase, a New York lawyer who represents 200 Japanese companies. Mr. Murase is among an army of lawyers who escort foreign businessmen through the corridors of power. His welcome is not harmed by the $24,000 that Mr. Murase contributed to congressional campaigns in 1984, in addition to contributions from his law partners, wife, and son. On the investment-tax-credit issue, Mr. Murase reported that some of his clients had gone to talk to senators and congressmen, adding that "we're not saying that we're not going to invest if the provision is changed, but it's going to make it very hard for us to invest as much as we'd like."[1]

"You get an immediate reaction when you introduce a piece of legislation that affects these foreign investors in the United States," said Senator Lloyd Bentsen, Texas Democrat and chairman of the Finance Committee. "They don't just stop at the Washington level. You hear from their distributors and contractors back home right away."

They can play hardball. Executives of Sony of America, a subsidiary of the Japanese company, threatened both the Florida and California legislatures with cancellation of plans to build facilities in their states unless the unitary tax was repealed. This tax is based on a company's worldwide sales of products manufactured in the state rather than merely the amount of sales within the state. Florida complied in a hastily called session during Christmas week in 1984. Sony contributed $29,000 to the election campaigns of California legislators in 1984 in an effort to repeal the state's unitary tax. They were abetted by a coalition of Japanese investors, who added $108,000 to the coffers, and by European investors and their governments, who also contributed money as well as their considerable political weight. The prime minister of Great Britain, Margaret Thatcher, personally lobbied the U.S. president on the issue of unitary repeal. California finally knuckled under to the pressures in 1986, when the legislature repealed the unitary tax.[2]

The political interests of foreign investors transcend issues of tax and trade. A Japanese-owned pulp mill in Sitka, Alaska, played a leading role in the 1984 congressional defeat of the Clean Water Act. Korean investors opened a newspaper in Washington, D.C., with the stated intent of changing the political climate of the nation's capital.

The campaign activities of foreign investors began to accelerate in the 1980s and continue to increase with no signs of abating. To enhance their lobbying activities, wholly foreign-owned American companies have formed political action committees (PACs); these PACs contributed more than $1 million to congressional campaigns in 1984, twice the 1982 amount. By 1986, almost one hundred PACs controlled by foreign corporations could be identified—a figure that is probably underestimated because of the difficulties in obtaining information. Their activity has been a source of considerable debate, generated by members of Congress, who question the legitimacy of foreign nationals playing such a significant role in American politics.

The Federal Election Commission (FEC) has asked Congress to clarify the legality of these PACs in view of the Federal Election Campaign Act of 1974, which specifically prohibits foreign nationals from contributing to political campaigns. The roots of this act trace back to the late 1930s, when Congress passed the Foreign Agents Registration Act in an effort to prevent foreign governments from pushing the United States into war in Europe. A specific prohibition preventing foreign nationals from contributing to political campaigns was enacted in 1968. It was expanded in the 1974 law, partly in response to the Watergate-related laundering of political funds through foreign banks. Its relevance did not go unnoticed in late 1986 and early 1987, as the growing scandals over insider trading and illegal aid to the Contras also implicated foreign banks.

"I do not think foreign nationals have any business in our political campaigns," said Senator Bentsen, sponsor of the measure, during a Senate debate. "They cannot vote in our elections, so why should we allow them to finance our elections? Their loyalties lie elsewhere; they lie with their own countries and their own governments."

The law states that "a foreign national shall not directly or through any other person make a contribution or expressly or impliedly promise to make a contribution, in connection with a convention, caucus, primary, general, special or run-off election in connection with any local, state or federal public office." The FEC, in a series of divided opinions, has interpreted the law to allow foreign-owned domestic companies to have PACs that contribute to state and federal candidates. The commission ruled that these foreign-owned companies are entitled to the same privileges as any other domestic firms but has asked Congress for clarification on this issue.

Commissioner Thomas E. Harris, the lead dissenter in each of these cases, offered the following argument:

> The PAC is always controlled by the top management of the corporation. By permitting foreign nationals to incorporate in the U.S. and thereby avoid the prohibitions of Section 441(e) [which bars foreign contributions to U.S. political campaigns], the commission does a great disservice to the congressional intention to keep foreign influence out of federal elections in the U.S. The notion that no decisions as to the activities of the proposed political committee will be dictated or directed by foreign nationals strikes me as extremely naive.

Senator Bentsen agreed: "If you have a PAC from a subsidiary of a foreign company, it certainly seems to me that you open the door to foreign influence in our elections. My amendment closed that door. The foreign company will obviously dictate to the subsidiary on how its PAC will be used."

One possible violation of the law occurred in 1982, when American executives of the Nissan Motor Company held a fundraiser in Tennessee on behalf of Robin Beard, a Republican candidate campaigning for the seat of U.S. Senator Jim Sasser, a Democrat. Mr. Beard had opposed the domestic content bill, then pending in the Congress, which Mr. Sasser supported. The bill would require a certain percentage of heavy industrial products sold in the United States to be manufactured in the United States. The violation occurred when the Nissan executives consulted the company's lobbyists for approval of the fund-raiser, said Commissioner John W. McGarry, then chairman of the FEC.

The PACs insist, however, that they are independent. George

Meany, treasurer of the Shell Oil Co. Political Awareness Committee, said that there has never been any corporate involvement in his PAC. "The PAC is made up of 1,000 employees, and they're all American citizens," Mr. Meany said.

The contributions of foreign PACs generally follow the pattern of domestic PACs. Most of the money goes to incumbents and to Republicans. Major PAC contributors to the 1984 campaigns, for example, included Shell Oil, a wholly owned subsidiary of Royal Dutch Shell ($186,000); the Seagram Company, a Canadian-owned company ($162,000); Hoffmann-La Roche (Swiss); Ciba-Geigy (Canadian); Santa Fe International (Kuwaiti); Hardee's (Canadian); and the Budd Co. (West German).

Their political clout filters down to the statehouse and the clubhouse, with PAC contributions to local political organizations and candidates. The PAC of the Shell Oil company, for example, gave $726,000 in contributions and loans to an organization that sought to block a proposed oil tax that was presented in a referendum before California voters. Their investment paid immediate dividends; the referendum was soundly defeated. California law allows corporations to contribute to local campaigns, and the FEC has ruled that in such cases, foreign-owned domestic companies can do likewise. Here, too, the FEC has asked Congress to clarify the law.

Another PAC, maintained by the Revere Sugar Company of New York City, is owned by a citizen of the Philippines, who kept his identity secret and controlled the company through a chain of corporations he owned in the Netherlands Antilles. Corporate records indicate that the owner was Antonio O. Floriendo, a confidant of Mr. Marcos and a business associate of his wife, Imelda. The company's true ownership became widely known upon the collapse of the Marcos government.

Just as many Americans are unaware that the Seagram Company and Hardee's are Canadian owned or that the Revere Sugar Company is Philippine owned, so also have many congressmen been unaware of the foreign connection of what appeared to be domestic PACs. Representative Thomas J. Downey, a Long Island Democrat, would not have accepted campaign contributions totaling $500 from the Revere Sugar Company PAC, his campaign manager said, had he known that the company was owned by a business associate of Imelda Marcos. "We had no idea that they were in any way connected with Marcos," said Isabel Solomon, Mr. Downey's campaign manager. "Had we known, we never would have taken that money. The election laws should be changed to indicate when a PAC represents a foreign-owned company.'' Her suggestion was passed along to Chairman McGarry of the FEC, who agreed, saying, ''I think it's a good idea. The entire thrust of the election-reform law is full disclosure. Nobody knows the extent of either foreign ownership of American companies or their participation in politics.''

THE SITKA MILL

The political influence that foreign investors exert on national policy is underscored by the leading role played by a Japanese-owned Alaskan lumber mill in the defeat of the Clean Water Act of 1984, a measure to protect citizens of all fifty states from the toxic effects of water pollution. The incident provided dramatic evidence that when foreign owners invest in the United States, they enjoy the political benefits awarded their domestic counterparts. Mayors, governors, and congressmen, who work hard to persuade these foreign companies to open manufacturing plants in their cities and states, become vigilant protectors of these firms, sometimes at the expense of American competitors. The Sitka experience shows that foreign owners, like domestic owners, quickly become skilled at threatening drastic action—such as closing their plants—unless they receive various political and economic benefits.[3]

''Alaska is no different from anybody else,'' said Senator Frank Murkowski, Alaska Republican who pressed the case for the Japanese-owned mill in the U.S. Senate. ''We have Japanese capital . . . and we are selfish enough to want to keep it.''

Japanese investment in the Alaskan lumber mill had its origins in the U.S. occupation of Japan in the aftermath of World War II. It was part of the U.S. effort to make our war-ravaged enemy economically independent. To rebuild Japan, General Douglas MacArthur sought to acquire additional resources for Japanese industry. He looked to Alaska, particularly to the Tongass National Forest, to supply timber for Japan's industrial base.

President Eisenhower implemented the plan, which he viewed as a boon to America's economy as well as Japan's. He proposed that the Japanese manufacture their pulp products in the United States and send them back to Japan. The president called upon the Japanese to invest in Alaska and build a pulp mill at Sitka that would process timber into primary pulp products that would then be shipped to Japan.

The Sitka mill was thus the forerunner of a deluge of Japanese investment in the United States. It has flourished with the help of the American taxpayer, operating with the help of federally subsidized timber. According to the Congressional Research Service, the Forest Service loses $171 for every 1,000 board feet sold to the mill. In addition, the mill received $14.9 million from the United States from 1976 to 1981 to help comply with the requirements of the Clean Water Act.

If the United States tried to be a good world citizen by guiding the Japanese toward this investment, the Japanese owners have hardly followed suit. The Sitka mill has been a world-class polluter, resolutely defying the Clean Water Act and threatening to shut down its operations if forced to comply with the law. Sitka, acting in concert with an American lumber company in Ketchikan, prevailed upon Alaska's senators to place a "hold" on the bill, thereby killing it.

"We had a clean water bill on the floor, ready to go, and they [Sitka] wanted a waiver," said Senator John Chafee, a Rhode Island Republican who sponsored the bill. "I wasn't having any part of it. The Alaskan senators put a hold on the bill, and it didn't pass." The senator noted, however, that Alaska's senators were merely trying to preserve jobs for their constituents. "If it had been in my state, I would have fought just as hard," Mr. Chafee said. "You're fighting for the jobs and the investment." Senator Murkowski clarified the stakes. "There were 1,200 jobs in the two mills, plus 2,500 loggers," he said.

Despite Sitka's efforts, the Clean Water Act was renewed in the fall of 1985; to nobody's surprise, the Alaskan mills failed to make good on their threat to shut down. The American-owned Ketchikan mill took immediate steps toward compliance, but the Japanese-owned Sitka mill sought $7 million for a federally subsidized antipollution demonstration project. Alaska's senators took the mill's case to the Senate floor. "Everyone understands that members of Congress pursue special or local interests that sometimes may not lie wholly within the national interest," *The New York Times* editorialized: "But there's a line beyond which a little regional favor-seeking becomes a brazen trial of public patience." Even the *Anchorage Daily News* found the strategy hard to swallow. "From a national viewpoint, there are good reasons for Congress to reject Federal aid to the mill," the paper editorialized.

The Senate did, in fact, reject this ploy by a vote of 70–26 on October 17, 1985, but not until after a ringing debate in the chamber. Opposition was led by senators from other lumber-producing states, notably Washington, Maine, and Vermont. Senator Robert Stafford, a usually mild-mannered Vermont Republican who was chairman of the Environment and Public Works Committee, noted that "other mills of the same type owned by American companies have been forced to install the required technology. They cannot compete fairly with the Japanese mill, which presently enjoys a $30–$40 per ton advantage." Mr. Stafford continued:

> Mr. President, this is one of two pulp mills in Alaska that have resisted the Clean Water Act. A year ago, it was being claimed that both mills would close without immediate relief in the form of an amendment to the Clean Water Act. But statutory relief was not forthcoming. The other mill [American-owned] immediately entered into a consent order and now is on a compliance schedule. The second mill [Japanese-owned] continues to make administrative appeals. Now this body is being asked to reward this mill with a special appropriation to pay for the pollution control it has successfully avoided for a decade.

At last report, the Sitka mill was still operating despite earlier threats, renewal of the Clean Water Act, and defeat of an effort to provide Sitka with a special subsidy.

LOBBYING IN REVERSE

The elaborate mating ritual that culminates in foreign investment begins with intense political negotiations abroad. It begins with mayors and governors circling the globe, financial Lochinvars who woo foreign investors with funds, grants, and tax abatements. These public officials stress that they do not give foreign corporations any benefits not offered to domestic corporations that relocate in their cities and states. Some critics question why U.S. taxpayers should give foreign investors an advantage over domestic competitors.

"Why are we using taxpayers' money to put Komatsu in business in Tennessee?" asked Senator Jim Sasser, referring to the Japanese manufacturer of earth-moving equipment. Komatsu has received state and local tax advantages, as well as funds for training workers, to locate in Chattanooga. "Why are we using taxpayers' money to help Komatsu beat Caterpillar's brains out?"

(Caterpillar is a domestic multinational corporation specializing in earth-moving machinery.)

The competition is intense, with the federal government as anxious to give money away as the states and localities. Foreign investors successfully lobbied for more than $100 million in Housing and Urban Development (HUD) funds to help them set up facilities in the United States. Investors from West Germany and the Netherlands Antilles were among 598 foreign investors receiving more than $7.7 million in agricultural subsidies intended for American farmers. Twenty-one of those investors were foreign corporations.[4]

Funds for foreign investors abound. To name a few examples:

- To lure the Nissan Motor Company to Smyrna, Tennessee, the state provided low-interest loans, job training, and land improvements.
- To lure Kanto Seiki, which manufactures automotive instrument panels, the town leaders of Lewisburg, Tennessee, helped the company obtain an $820,000 Urban Development Action Grant (UDAG), sold them the land, and provided bilingual education in the schools and a tax abatement, whereby the company will avoid its entire tax load for ten years.
- To lure Amkor, a Korean-American joint venture that will manufacture oil filters, Peoria, Illinois, helped the company obtain a $1.8 million UDAG grant, gave the company a forty-two-acre site, and provided a $1 million direct grant and $2 million in long-term, low-interest loans.
- To lure Toyota to Georgetown, Kentucky, the state provided $112 million in new roads, employee training programs, grants and low-cost loans, as well as 1,500 acres of free land.

"We view it as a trade," said Bob Marcusse, president of Peoria's Economic Development Council, referring to the Amkor inducements. "In exchange, we received 400 jobs created by the plant, a $20 million investment, plus subsidiary income." The trade-off for Kentucky is even more dramatic: 3,000 in new jobs. Representative Don Bonker cautions, however, that such beneficence may not be in the national interest. "Mayors and governors are concerned with microeconomics," he said. "The Congress should be concerned with macroeconomics."

Meanwhile, federal officials, hungry for foreign dollars to

finance the budget deficit, parallel local and state politicians in
the rush to attract foreign dollars. They promise anonymity and
tax advantages, while foreign investors take advantage of America's new dependence on their capital with threats to withdraw
funds unless these privileges are granted and expanded.

MEDIA PENETRATION

The political efforts of foreign investors are not limited to issues
of tax and trade. In 1982, the Korean-based Unification Church
began publishing a newspaper, the *Washington Times,* with the
express intention of providing a conservative voice in the nation's capital. Thus far, investors have poured $100 million into
the newspaper, according to its executives, and are spending $1
million a week to keep it afloat. "It really is amazing that it took
a bunch of Koreans to understand that a two-party democracy
cannot function effectively with a one-party press in the nation's
capital," said A naud de Borchgrave, the newspaper's editor in
chief. He added that his conservative views usually matched
those of the newspaper's ownership. "I'm my own man," he
stressed. Some key staffers disagreed. In April 1987, the
newspaper's editorial-page editor and four editorial writers quit
the paper, charging that Mr. de Borchgrave had allowed an
executive of the Unification Church to dictate editorial policy.[5]

Some critics consider the newspaper too ideological. "They're
injecting ideology into news columns, particularly in the play
they give stories and headlines," said Jack Nelson, Washington
bureau chief of the *Los Angeles Times.* He also said that the
newspaper's fund to aid the Nicaraguan Contras "distorts what
journalism is about," because the newspaper has taken the role
of player, not observer.

Similarly, the 1986 sale of United Press International (UPI) to
a Mexican businessman has touched off some uneasiness. "Only
two governments in the world have a good enough press tradition
to have earned the respect of American newspaper editors," said
James D. Squires, editor of the *Chicago Tribune.* "From my
perspective, if it's not British or American, it's going to lose the
kind of faith and confidence that it needs to have." Indeed, less
than a year later, several newspapers, including *The New York
Times,* canceled the service. Times officials said that they preferred to use the money to hire additional staff.

While still an Australian citizen, Rupert Murdoch played a
role in political campaigns in New York, where he owns the *New

York Post, and Chicago, where he owns the *Chicago Sun-Times.* Mr. Murdoch became an American citizen in 1986 in order to purchase radio and television stations, whose ownership is limited to U.S. citizens. Meanwhile, the Thomson chain, a Canadian enterprise, publishes ninety-four newspapers in the United States, mostly in small communities. Each newspaper enjoys "complete autonomy," according to Frank C. Miles, Thomson's senior vice-president and general manager.

More insidious are hidden takeovers. Government prosecutors charged in 1986 that John P. McGoff, a conservative Michigan newspaper publisher, had acted as an unregistered foreign agent for South Africa since 1974 and had purchased an interest in the *Sacramento Union* on behalf of the government of South Africa. The government charged that at the *Union,* Mr. McGoff created an editorial policy "designed to promote a positive and favorable image of South Africa and to support and promote closer cooperation between the United States and South Africa."

The U.S. government also charged that Mr. McGoff had sought to purchase the *Washington Star* to assure that "positive material relating to the strategic and economic importance of South Africa to the United States and the West would be published and disseminated to policy leaders and opinion makers in the U.S. capital." A second goal was to counter what was considered an anti-South Africa position of the capital's other major daily newspaper, the *Washington Post.* Mr. McGoff, a close friend of former President Gerald Ford, was charged with failing to register as a foreign agent under the Foreign Agents Registration Act.

The ease with which foreign investors purchase American newspapers is unique. Most countries recognize the importance of the media to their national well-being and restrict their ownership to their own citizens—or governments. In countries in which the political environment is unstable, the means of communication are heavily guarded; in Cairo, for example, soldiers stand behind shoulder-high sandbags, with their bayonets drawn, in the lobbies of the state-owned radio and television stations.

THE DEBATE

The surge of foreign investments in the United States has touched off a political debate that focuses not merely on their overall merits but also on a host of peripheral issues. These include:

• An acknowledged data gap concerning the extent of foreign investments

• A lack of reciprocity on the part of most foreign governments and foreign nationals who invest here but ban similar foreign investments in their own countries

• Charges that U.S. taxpayers are providing grants and tax advantages that help foreign competitors gain an edge over domestic companies

• Allegations that foreign investors from third-world nations are merely sending our own economic aid back to us rather than investing in their own hard-pressed countries

• The anti-union practices of many foreign investors who enjoy good labor relations in their own countries

• The anticompetitive practices of some foreign investors who purchase American companies to acquire their technology to the detriment of American competitors

• A realization that many foreign firms are merely assembly plants that may actually increase the imports of parts and worsen the trade imbalance

• The loss of U.S. profits to overseas parent corporations

The Reagan administration strongly supports foreign investment. Malcolm Baldrige said that "investment in the U.S. does provide jobs, financing, and helps keep interest rates down. I think socially as well as financially there's much more gain to having an open investment policy throughout the world than the converse, which are barriers that impede capital flows." But he stressed that "foreign investment should be a two-way street to be of overall benefit. Our policy is to encourage investment flows into the U.S., but our policy also is to encourage the same investment freedom throughout the world."

Mr. Baldrige was concerned, however, by the lack of information on the specifics of foreign investment and the ownership of American firms. "We are disturbed by the size of the gap," he said. "I'm not sure tightening up reporting would give us the answer. There's a large, worldwide underground economy, a gray-market economy, that's very difficult to keep track of." He also noted the intense competition for foreign investment and said that some of the inducements offered by cities and states appeared to be excessive.

The real risks, he suggested, were borne by those who invested here. "Suppose you imagine the worst," the secretary suggested. "The Japanese win this [ball bearing] plant in New

Hampshire. The war came. In an emergency, steps would be taken." Was he talking about expropriation? "That depends on the type of emergency," Mr. Baldrige said. "If a war came or a national emergency, we have plans drawn up in general, but I don't know any for expropriation." He also expressed concern about overdependence on foreign investors. "We simply don't want to be dependent on those flows," Mr. Baldrige said. "If we get hooked on them, we will be in trouble at some time in the future."

Felix Rohatyn envisions a stark scenario in which the risks are borne by the United States rather than the foreign investors. The dollar will fall eventually, he notes, and when it does and interest rates decline, in a period of recession, foreign investors would withdraw their portfolio investments, triggering a banking crisis. These foreign investors then could use their inflated portfolios to make direct investments of American industry "at bargain-basement prices," Mr. Rohatyn said. "We will have financed our deficit by putting up permanent assets."

Other gloomy forecasts have come from members of Congress as well as from some western governors whose constituents have long bridled under absentee ownership of their state's resources. Former governor Richard D. Lamm of Colorado raised the specter of what he called "economic colonialism."

"I think America is mainly at fault for its trade deficit," Mr. Lamm said. "I don't think it's fair to say that it's the Japanese or Taiwanese who are doing this to us. But I think (1) there's a degradation of our industrial base going on because of Japanese investment, and (2) there's a phenomenal export of U.S. technology to Japan."

The governor noted that much foreign investment here involved assembly plants and warehouses, both using unskilled labor:

> In the auto industry, those assembly plants that so many of the local people think are so unequivocally great create low-skilled jobs and in fact knock out better-skilled, higher-paid workers. The net effect on our economy, the high value-added segment, is always added in Japan. We are seeing in many places that they keep seventy-five percent of the value-added in Japan. In addition, there has been a fairly substantial technology flow. Here in Colorado, they're coming in and buying companies with the biggest high-tech ideas.

Senator Murkowski added another interesting perspective. "Having been a banker," said Mr. Murkowski, "I know the significance of holding another's debt. There's a tremendous lack of appreciation of that." As for direct foreign investment, he added: "Once they own your assets, they own you. They employ you."

Critics say that the political muscle exerted by foreign investors was suggested by the refusal of treasury officials to disclose the amount of U.S. securities held by Saudi Arabia. The treasury officials refused to divulge the amount when subpoenaed by a congressional committee in 1979 and still refuse to make that information public. They say that the Saudis threatened to sell their U.S. securities rather than acquiesce. "Confidentiality is terribly important when it comes to investment, no matter who the individual is," said William E. Simon, who, as treasury secretary in the Ford administration, promised confidentiality to the Saudis, who had agreed to purchase a "substantial" but undisclosed portion of subsequent issues of U.S. securities. "There is absolutely no good reason why it should be divulged," Mr. Simon said. He noted that the Saudis, like any other investors, could have achieved anonymity by purchasing the securities through foreign banks and said that the United States would have lost their business.

The Saudi threat to sell U.S. securities was conveyed to Congress by Anthony Solomon, then assistant secretary of the treasury for monetary affairs. A request for the data on Saudi investments had been made by the late representative Benjamin S. Rosenthal, a Queens Democrat and chairman of the Consumer Affairs Subcommittee of the Government Operations Committee, who held hearings in 1979–80 on foreign investment.[6] Had the Saudis made good their threat, Mr. Solomon recalled, the effect would have been disastrous: "The dollar at that time was sinking very badly. Anybody switching from dollars to other currencies would have driven the dollar down further. The Saudis had the largest single holding of dollars. U.S. government securities were a large part of their holdings."

But some members of Congress believe that it is as important to know the source of funds flowing into this country as to know the nationality of aliens crossing our borders. "It's not healthy not to know how much foreign investment there is or where it comes from," said Connecticut Representative Nancy Johnson.

At the heart of the debate are questions that remain unanswered. Are foreign investors playing a healthy role in the American economy—and acquiring a stake in its continuing prosperity—or simply gaining undue influence over it? Do foreign investors contribute more new technology to American commerce than they acquire? Is the United States using foreign investment for economic renewal or simply losing control of strategic business sectors and future earnings? And finally, is the United States helping the world economy by providing a productive home for these investments or merely swallowing up capital needed abroad?

PART II

THE STATE EXPERIENCE

CHAPTER 3

The New Wave

Foreign Investment Policy from the States

It's created a lot of jobs in Maryland. We've encouraged it.
            —*Governor Harry R. Hughes of Maryland*

I don't want the Arabs owning our banks or the Japanese owning
our means of production. It terrifies me.
            —*Governor Richard D. Lamm of Colorado*

On the streets of downtown Tokyo, state officials from Virginia, Indiana, California, Florida, New York, Georgia, and a host of other states regularly greet each other. The same people also meet each other in Hong Kong, Singapore, and Brussels, but unlike most reunions of Americans abroad, these encounters are strictly competitive. The officials are prowling the streets of foreign capitals on the same mission: to lure foreign investors to the United States—preferably to their state. As the competition for the foreign dollar heats up, legions of state officials travel the globe, selling the superiority of their state as a home for foreign investment.

All trade-related activities on the state level, including foreign investment, have expanded rapidly over the last twenty years, signaling a new era in business development. As the only non-controversial trade issue, foreign investment has benefited from inattention, emerging virtually untouched by negative publicity or legislative oversight. These factors have combined to make foreign investment a top priority of some of the nation's leading governors, who have recognized the immediate benefits of their states' overseas recruitment efforts and moved quickly to reinforce and expand them. Foreign investment means an infusion of fresh capital and new jobs, in that order, and the message has emerged loud and clear.

The enthusiasm of the governors has made all the difference. With a singularity of purpose uncommon to the public arena, the states moved so quickly and aggressively that they assumed almost total dominance of the issue. No one questions the fact that the states now lead the nation in shaping foreign investment policy—unimpeded and quietly encouraged by the federal government. They earned their new role through sheer tenacity: They provided the leadership, dictated the parameters of the issue, and persuaded their legislatures to allocate resources earmarked for recruiting foreign capital.

This new wave of state activity has revolved around job creation, a theme of such paramount importance that it is sounded repeatedly by governors, mayors, and state development officers. Simply put, foreign companies bring jobs, and jobs are the political bread and butter of state leaders. The linkage between opportunities abroad and jobs at home is forged again and again with concrete actions that are quickly implemented. In fact, when unemployment soared between 1978 and 1980, states responded with the first major expansion of their overseas offices; the next burst of activity followed the recession of 1982.

The search for investment opportunities soon shifted its focus from Western Europe toward Japan and other Far Eastern countries. This turn toward the East was spurred by the increasing difficulty of attracting European firms, particularly from countries whose unions regarded investment in the United States as a threat to their jobs. The Japanese high rate of savings provided a reservoir of available funds, and the U.S. consumer market and high interest rates provided an enviable investment opportunity.

In the quest for investment and the jobs that followed, the states operated as individual entrepreneurs: They competed vigorously, treated other states as enemies, and guarded their secrets closely. Inevitably, bad feelings abounded as one state emerged victorious in the competition for the Honda plant, the Nippondenso distributorship, or the U.S. headquarters of the Bridgestone company. Georgia resents Tennessee, while Virginia accuses her neighbors of "giving away the store."

The results are mixed. The increase in foreign investment has indeed brought jobs and other benefits to many parts of the country and helped many local economies—some of them already flattened by foreign competition—to rebuild. Once foreign multinationals commit themselves to a region, many become ideal citizens: active in community affairs, anxious to integrate socially, and generous contributors to local projects. They make it a point to hire as many Americans as they can and to keep their own foreign nationals to a minimum. (Actually, foreign companies have little choice; the problems they encounter with U.S. immigration law force them to adopt this policy.) Some companies even promote Americans to top executive posts, and in a few rare cases—such as the Yokogawa electronics plant in Georgia—claim they would eventually like to hand their American subsidiaries over to an American chief executive officer (CEO). Yokogawa's record of promoting foreign nationals in other countries indicates the likelihood of their transferring top executive power to American leadership.

Watching states scramble for the foreign dollar raises the question of how this trend fits into a larger context. What are the ultimate consequences for the United States if fifty separate states make their own individual agreements with foreign governments and foreign multinational corporations? Does this put America, the only industrialized country that allows such separatist tendencies to flourish, at a competitive disadvantage in the global economy? As a world power?

In effect, it can be argued that the states are conducting a form of foreign policy on their own, unhampered by either executive-branch leadership or congressional oversight. This is neither a conspiracy nor a ploy; the states are acting honorably and, in their view, in the best interests of their citizens. In many instances, the effects are either positive for the economy of the state or negligible for the country. But what if a state lures a foreign manufacturer whose presence threatens a domestic manufacturer in another state with extinction? What if a foreign government is subsidizing a U.S. investment, sustaining a company's losses until the market is cornered and domestic competitors are driven out of business? Or what if that foreign manufacturer acquires, through its new investment, technology vital to the nation's security or industrial stability? These scenarios are not fantasy; they represent real situations with long-term effects that are uncertain at best and potentially catastrophic. Whatever the outcome, the delicate balance between states' rights and national sovereignty preserved throughout the country's history has been tipped in the direction of the states.

The crux of the matter is that virtually no coordination exists at the federal level, which means there is no serious ongoing assessment of the long-term implications of this important trend. In fact, quite the reverse is occurring, with the federal government—in the spirit of the New Federalism—tacitly encouraging the states to continue their solo flights. The positive side of this new configuration of state-federal power is that it reflects the success of the New Federalism: the federal government in a quietly supportive role, building the capacity of the states to develop their own programs.

Other issues flow from this central question. In the heated competition for foreign investment, the states go head-to-head, offering a smorgasbord of inducements to potential clients—tax holidays, bonds, low-cost loans, free advice, roads, sewers, and other public improvements. The cost to the taxpayer, states argue, is more than justified by the influx of new business. But to what extent are the states giving away too much? Some critics argue that the states would spend considerably less if they coordinated instead of competed with each other. Still others argue that the factors drawing investment to the United States have little to do with incentives. Companies invest primarily to avoid protective tariffs, to corner market share, and to reduce transportation costs. Weighed on that scale, new sewers and tax holidays may be inconsequential to multinational corporations as well as unnecessary expenditures for hard-pressed U.S. taxpayers.

GOVERNORS AS AMBASSADORS

States view foreign markets and foreign investment the way Americans used to view the frontier: as an opportunity for economic expansion as well as an outlet to reverse economic decline. The governors play the role of ambassadors in the effort to open up new frontiers of foreign economic policy, an area once dominated by the federal government. They see themselves as the vital link to a new set of strategies that promise to stave off the devastating effects on their states of imports, job layoffs in the manufacturing and lumber industries, and the country's trade deficit.

Diplomatic and cooperative on the surface, they compete fiercely behind the scenes in a high-stakes game that brings $10 billion and 300,000 new jobs into the United States each year. In New England, for example, 20 percent of all investment activity in the early 1980s was conducted by foreign nationals, most of them in the high-tech field; transactions of at least $6.7 billion took place between 1979 and 1983.[1]

The governors are clear about their new role and the reasons that led them to it. At the annual convention of the National Governors' Association Conference in 1985, Governor John Carlin of Kansas, president of the association, spoke of the "real role for the governors and the state government in the international arena." Indeed, the rapid entry of state governments into international trade and investment activity was regarded as a necessity, since the federal government was doing little to meet their needs. Carlin emphasized that the governors would not be getting into the political quagmire of federal tariffs; the states were too diverse to agree on a common position. What was left, exports and foreign investments, was relatively free from controversy and from federal regulation.[2]

Power loves a vacuum, and the governors took to their new role as international supersalesmen with enthusiasm. Minnesota governor Rudy Perpich, a Democrat, campaigned on a platform in 1982 to improve the state's economy by attracting foreign investment. A former dentist and international businessman, Perpich had the experience and commitment to fulfill his promises; within two years, fifteen foreign companies were involved in setting up plants or sales offices in his state, while serious inquiries from more than a hundred others were discussed.

Perpich branched out on several fronts and penetrated the traditional isolationism of the Midwest. He set up a thirty-member trade office in the state capital, began building a world trade center in St. Paul, held seminars in northern European cities, and traveled the globe seeking investment opportunities. He also restructured the state incentive system to make investment opportunities more attractive to foreign investors. "If they invest in a depressed area, we buy down the interest rate," he said in an interview. The state also subsidizes wages, offering to pay the first five dollars an hour for six months if investors hire the unemployed.

"We had a hard time attracting foreign investment," recalled

Perpich at the annual winter governors' conference in 1985. He analyzed the predicament in terms of the complacency of his constituents. The citizens of Minnesota, lulled into a false sense of security about the economic health of their state, failed to recognize the economic urgency confronting them:

> Nobody cared. Minnesota has a good internal market, its own agriculture, high tech in the cities, the Mayo Clinic medical complex, and abundant natural resources. But now the situation has changed. The strength of the dollar is killing our agriculture; Canadian lumber is hurting us; and the technological drain is returning to haunt us.

In his efforts to bring foreign investment to Minnesota, Perpich found himself forced to make as big a sales pitch to Minnesota as he did to the foreign companies he was trying to attract. What made it easier, he said, was that the cultures of the companies he had targeted were compatible with the ethnic origins of the state. "We concentrate on Scandinavians," said Perpich. "Our people are Scandinavian." Under Perpich's leadership, Minnesota was one of the first states to break free from the isolationist pattern typical of many midwestern states, concentrating on northern Europe, a region that had not, up to that point, been heavily involved in the United States. "We think they feel more comfortable with us," said William Dietrich, director of the Minnesota trade office.

Following the Minnesota pattern, national preferences have played a part in other areas, as well, where, according to Jane Sneddon Little's research,

> some clustering does occur . . . 40 percent of Canadian investments are in the Mid-Atlantic, while 40 percent of Dutch and one-third of German and Belgian investments are in the Southeast. Similarly, about one-third of Italian, Swedish and Japanese investments are in the Mid-Atlantic, the Great Lakes and the Far West respectively.

Geographic proximity also plays a part in site selection—witness the preference of the Far Eastern investors for the Far West— along with previous migration patterns: The "Italians in the Mid-Atlantic, the Swedes and Germans in the Great Lakes, and the Japanese in the Far West," writes Little. Investors also like to hire workers from their own ethnic group and may already have relatives or business contacts in a region.[3]

While cultural affinities may play a crucial role in attracting investors, when domestic companies feel threatened, those ties don't count for much. "Foreign investment was just starting to come in," recalled Governor Perpich, "when I brought a $90 million cheese plant into Little Falls. People are fighting it. The smaller creameries feel it will put them out of business." He also complained that a certain resistance to foreigners put a crimp in the incentives he was able to offer: "As soon as it's foreign, someone blows the whistle, and we can't give them UDAGs."

In Minnesota, foreign investment took another interesting turn: It forced domestic business out of its lethargy, in one case literally to protect its turf—the state racetrack. After several Scandinavian banks began negotiating to buy the racetrack, the state's own banks sat up, took notice, and finally filed their own bids. "They didn't have their act together before the foreign banks started eyeing the track," said the governor.

Ultimately, the key to attracting foreign investment rests with the quality and effectiveness of a governor's leadership. In state after state, the same pattern prevails: The governor persuades the legislature to provide the dollars that fund the state's trade office; it is the governor's clout that impresses foreign investors and the governor's willingness to circle the globe in search of foreign investment that gives a state the edge over other states.

In the race for foreign dollars, some governors stand out for their ability to recruit foreign business. Perpich is one of the nation's most successful, along with Governor Lamar Alexander of Tennessee, who leads the nation in recruiting Japanese business. Before the state's banking crisis occupied so much of his time, Ohio's governor, Richard F. Celeste, traveled extensively in Asia and Europe, bringing home an impressive payload of foreign investment. After attending an international conference in West Germany, he returned with two companies: the Kosmos brewery for Youngstown and Roxane Laboratories for Columbus, an extensive complex that will house the pharmaceutical company's U.S. headquarters and its manufacturing, warehousing, and distribution facilities together in one location.[4] Illinois has also reaped a string of recent successes: Twenty companies from Hong Kong, over thirty from Taiwan, and forty from South Korea have located offices in Illinois.[5]

Encouraged by the success of their competitors, prodded by the political necessity to produce jobs, and reinforced by their

national professional groups, many other governors have directed
their energies to the job of recruiting investment. Governor
Harry R. Hughes of Maryland, who has traveled to Japan—once
with the Baltimore Orioles baseball team—to seek investment,
applauds the results. "It's created a lot of jobs," he said.
"We've encouraged it. With only one exception, all foreign
direct investment in Maryland is in the form of joint ventures
with American companies." Typically, foreign companies investing in Maryland follow a three-step pattern: First the company sets up a sales division, then a service branch, and finally,
a manufacturing plant. Over 440 foreign investors have located
their companies in Maryland, producing over 45,000 jobs. They
are credited with reducing the state's already low unemployment
rate of 5.8 percent by two points.

The governors' contention that jobs result directly from foreign
investment is supported by Commerce Department data, indicating the exact number of jobs traced to foreign-owned property,
plants, and equipment. The top five states are Texas, California,
Alaska, Louisiana, and New York, in that order, with Texas
claiming 172,546 jobs from $22.4 billion in foreign investment.[6]

GOVERNORS AS LOBBYISTS FOR FOREIGN INVESTORS

Recruiting foreign investment is only half the job of the governors; they must also work hard at keeping those companies in the
state. That means protecting them politically from occasional
onslaughts by the federal government as well as challenges from
their competitors in other states. In effect, foreign investors find
themselves in an enviable position, enjoying the same political
benefits as their American counterparts and occasionally, as in
the case of the Japanese company YKK, given preferential
treatment.

YKK, the world's largest manufacturer of zippers, is also
Georgia's largest foreign investor. It has made an investment of
over $200 million and hired a labor force of 1,000 workers at its
Macon plant and 140 at its office in Marietta, according to
George Dubuc, deputy director of the International Division of
the Georgia Department of Industry and Trade.

YKK is thriving in Georgia, thanks to the help of former
governor George Busbee, who interceded with President Gerald
Ford when a complaint was filed against YKK before the International Trade Commission (ITC) by Talon, a domestic zipper

manufacturer, ironically also located in Georgia. Talon argued that foreign zippers were hurting domestic manufacturers. Before filing its petition, Talon executives offered to sell the company to YKK, but the Japanese company refused, fearing such an acquisition would violate the antitrust laws. At that time, YKK had 60 percent of the world market and 60–65 percent of the U.S. market.

The case before the ITC resulted in a tie vote and went to the president for a final decision. At that point, Governor Busbee actively interceded on behalf of YKK. John D. (Jack) Welsh, then director of the Georgia Department of International Trade, went to Washington to read the governor's testimony. "We said YKK were good citizens," he recalled:

> Talon also had a plant in north Georgia. They wrote a letter to Busbee saying they would never vote for him again. He answered them with the statement that their comments were duly noted.
>
> The petition was up before the ITC when Henry Kissinger paid a visit to Georgia and stayed at the governor's mansion. Busbee warned Kissinger that the case would jeopardize foreign investment coming into the United States. The president came down in favor of YKK.

Busbee's intervention in the YKK case showed how far a governor would go to defend a major foreign investor, even at the expense of an American investor in the same state. Clearly, YKK was the larger company, with more jobs at stake, more growth potential, and more to contribute to the state's economic base. Perhaps most important, YKK's experience would influence future foreign investment in Georgia. The governor's decision showed the high priority he placed on foreign investment, a priority shared by many of his fellow governors who would follow his example. It also showed the linkage between recruiting foreign investment and the political vigilance required to ensure that investment's future in the United States. The pattern was set, with the governor in the role of chief lobbyist for foreign investors. It worked well in encouraging foreign investors to locate in the United States; they learned from experiences like that of YKK that they could count on a friendly political environment.

POLITICAL PROBLEMS

The new global-state relationship in investment politics was not trouble-free. Many governors often returned home from foreign travels to face criticism from angry constituents who objected to their tax money spent on "pleasure trips." "States have the problem of the occasional failure in political communication," said Marsha Clark of the National Association of State Development Agencies (NASDA), a national resource and support group for the states. "Governors must defend themselves against charges of junketing. The common perception is that it is a luxury." To a lesser extent, governors also find themselves fielding criticism for spending money for state offices abroad—offices that recruit foreign investment and seek outlets for their products.

When the level of criticism is sufficiently intense, the states respond in a manner often detrimental to their long-term interests. Governor John Y. Brown of Kentucky, caught in the political turbulence, made the mistake of closing his state office, a decision he later regretted. Forced to make large cuts in social programs, Brown pacified his critics by promising to give up "what's nearest and dearest to my heart, international development." Ultimately, "this damages the states," explained Clark. "The continuity of presence is very important."

U.S. governors say that foreign investment has produced political controversy in only one area: farmland. It is ironic that only in agriculture have Americans objected to the threat of foreign domination, while fully accepting foreign investment in manufacturing, banking, urban real estate, and securities. The nation's agrarian heritage, deeply rooted in Jeffersonian democracy, goes further than any other factor in explaining why Americans find the loss of their land more threatening than foreign purchases of their banks or factories. Even today, land remains a symbol of personal ownership: More Americans can identify with owning a farm than owning a bank or a factory.

In Maryland, for example, local residents opposed German land purchases. "We had some political flak several years ago with the foreign purchases of eastern-shore farmland," recalled Governor Harry Hughes. "Germans bought land as working farms and pushed the price of land up. A bill came up in the state legislature requiring 51 percent [by a U.S. citizen] ownership of land. It didn't get anywhere."

The height of the controversy over farmland crested in the late 1970s and early 1980s; with the steep drop in the price of agricultural land, the issue appears to have died down. Nevertheless, many states still restrict foreign ownership: Minnesota, for example, has a law forbidding foreign purchases of land that is vigorously opposed by the governor, who calls it "not rational."

Another dimension of the controversy, according to a state official who lived through it, was simple racism. "My personal judgment," he said, "was that this was not an issue when Europeans were buying, only when non-Caucasians—Japanese, Saudis, etc.—were involved. It was important as an expression of prevailing sentiment."[7]

Any foreign investment that produces radical changes in the market is bound to produce controversy. Initially, agricultural-land purchases created resentment when farmers found the prices so inflated they couldn't afford to buy land for themselves. By 1986, the price of farmland had declined so markedly that many farmers welcomed any investors, foreign or American; in fact, farmers opposed the repeal of a tax break for foreign land purchasers during the waning days of the tax reform bill.

In Utah, a similar controversy surfaced in real estate. "The investment came in too fast," said Governor Norman H. Bangerter, himself a former real estate developer, "faster than we could assimilate it. There are now heavy vacancies which have depressed the inner city and commercial rents in Salt Lake City. There's been too much development, too fast." The city's major developer is Adnan Khashoggi, a Saudi Arabian investor and international arms dealer, whose TRIAD corporation built an industrial park in the city's downtown area. By early 1987, the project had collapsed, and TRIAD faced forty-seven lawsuits from creditors demanding more than $100 million. Khashoggi reportedly refused to pay the company's debts, blaming TRIAD's problems on unfriendly treatment from city officials.[8]

Despite the flooding of Salt Lake's real estate market, Bangerter views foreign investment with cautious optimism. "I have some concern that foreign investment may stop, as well," he continued. "We have to be wary. We shouldn't be overly dependent on foreign investment."

Junketing, inflated property values, and fears of absentee farm ownership seem minor, however, in view of the pockets of political protest that emerge when foreign investors threaten American-owned businesses. Especially when those investors are supported by the American taxpayer. In Wisconsin, dairy farmers lodged a strong protest against an impending investment by an Irish company that planned to build dairies in Georgia with the aid of tax-free industrial development bonds.

The cross-purposes of state and federal policies were never so stark. Under pressure from the federal government to reduce milk surpluses, Georgia dairy farmers agreed to cut their state's milk production by 22 percent, taking 24,000 cows out of production. At the same time, Macon County officials were busy selling $4.5 million worth of bonds to help the Irish company, Masstock International, set up a $35 million operation that would grow to 20,000 cows within a few years. It was a wonderful deal for Masstock: The company benefited from tax-exempt bonds that would reduce their borrowing costs by 2–3 percent; they would pay no tax on income from the bonds; and their investors could look forward to the future protection of their investment by federal price supports, which—thanks to regional differentials— kept Georgia's prices higher than in other parts of the country.[9]

The controversy pitted Americans against one another. Macon County officials, backed by their governor, Joe Frank Harris, a Democrat, argued that it was not fair to discriminate against the Irish investor for a dairy crisis that was twenty years in the making. They claimed that the Irish investment meant jobs for farm workers and benefits for the local economy.

American dairy farmers, led by their representatives in Congress, felt otherwise. "What is happening in Georgia makes absolutely no sense," said Senator Robert W. Kasten, Jr., a Republican from Wisconsin. "We are paying family farmers to leave the dairy industry through the buy-out program at the same time we're paying foreign corporations to get into dairying through tax subsidies and price supports. It's an affront to dairy farmers and to taxpayers alike and must be stopped." Joined by Representative Tony Coelho, Democrat from California and chairman of the House Agriculture Subcommittee on Dairy, Livestock, and Poultry, Kasten vowed to protect American farmers. Although bipartisan, their efforts met roadblocks from the Reagan administration appointees in the Agriculture Department. "We are in favor of free markets," said Richard Goldberg, deputy undersecretary of agriculture. "This administration believes that the federal government should not interfere with an individual's right to open or expand a business."

Faced with such disarray among states and between the federal government and the Congress, foreign investors find it easy to drive a wedge into American markets. By the time policymakers discern a pattern of disadvantage and attempt to remedy it, it is often too late; the investor is solidly established, with all the political protection of an American business.

THE EXPERIENCE OF THE CITIES

Following the example of their governors, mayors of the nation's larger cities have opened ambitious campaigns to lure foreign investors in an effort to offset their domestic economic woes. Increasingly, the mayors are traveling to Europe and Asia to bring foreign capital to their cities, which are often hard-pressed by a loss of jobs and governmental aid. They are promising would-be investors economic, cultural, and social advantages.[10]

Boston recently attracted a Swiss corporation to develop a new hotel, and Newark persuaded Japanese and British manufacturers to build plants that make final preparations on automobiles before delivery. New Orleans successfully wooed British and French investors. A Canadian developer built a shopping mall in Minneapolis, and a West German company built a tire-chain factory in Cedar Rapids, Iowa.

They are among scores of foreign investors that have spent billions of dollars in the nation's cities in a trend that has gained momentum in the last five years. "It's a realization on the part of the mayors that we live in a global economy and there is money to be invested," said New Orleans Mayor Ernest N. (Dutch) Morial, former president of the U.S. Conference of Mayors. The organization has initiated an Invest in America's Cities program—inspired by its creative executive director, John Gunther—and sponsors an annual visit by mayors to Zurich and Hong Kong, where they try to sell their cities' virtues to European and Asian business executives. By embarking on this non-traditional activity, some widely traveled mayors have been criticized at home for ignoring the nuts and bolts of local government, such as repairing potholes, but the mayors say the effort is important.

Many mayors seek foreign investors on their own. Kenneth Lipper, New York's deputy mayor for finance and economic development, visited China and Hong Kong in July 1984 and said that as a result, the National Bank of China planned to open a branch in the city. In addition, the Hong Kong and Shanghai Bank recently located in Manhattan, and several Hong Kong textile companies want to start a joint facility in Brooklyn to avoid limits on textile imports.

The mayors have found that foreign investors are interested in more than merely economic factors. "We talk to them about the quality of life in New Orleans," Mayor Morial said.

> We are an international city. We have an abundance of energy, a port, access to the heartland of America by way of the Mississippi River and its tributaries. We have a good supply of manpower and a city government that's enthusiastic about their coming and will help package their financing. The foreign investor also recognizes the importance of the political climate.

An important factor to some foreign investors is the quality of a city's schools, and their interest can have far-reaching benefits. "The Japanese told us right off the bat that in science and math, if their kids stayed in American high schools and returned to Japan for college, they'd be two or three years behind," said Mayor Roger O. Parent of South Bend, Indiana. Some cities can already report an improvement in their science and math programs as a response to pressure from Japanese investors. One example is the town of Marysville, Ohio, home to the Honda plant, where several teachers with Ph.D.s in mathematics have been hired to teach in the local high school.

The mayors do everything in their power to negotiate for foreign investors. Mayor Marion S. Barry, Jr., of Washington, D.C., said his city recently approved legislation that made it easier for foreign bankers to work there. He stressed that one of his goals was to persuade foreign investors that the nation's capital was more than a one-industry town.

Mayor Raymond L. Flynn of Boston reported that when a new development, Lafayette Place, was being planned, "we put out the word that we were looking for a reputable foreign company to build a hotel. Swissair came over here from Zurich, put up $30 million, and became the developer of the hotel. They were given a lot of attention, a lot of encouragement, a very businesslike approach."

Mayor Kenneth A. Gibson of Newark has journeyed to Hong Kong and Zurich "to reach out to the international financial market to see what kind of interest we can stimulate." Newark's major economic attractions are its airport and seaport, and two automobile manufacturers, Jaguar of Britain and Nissan of Japan, were persuaded to build facilities in the city. In addition, the Maersk shipping company, a European conglomerate, built a major terminal in Newark.

BREAKING RANKS: CRITICS OF FOREIGN INVESTMENT

Moving west across the country, one finds more criticism of foreign investment, ranging from Utah Governor Norman Bangerter's balanced caution to Colorado's Richard Lamm, a firm opponent of the governors' rush to attract foreign capital. The western states have bristled under their prior status as economic colonies of the East and, some say, regard foreign investment as a new form of colonization. In addition, analysts note that the lower unemployment rate in the western states makes the quest for jobs less compelling than the need for jobs felt in the South, Midwest, Middle Atlantic, and Northeast. The western states can afford to be futurists, they say, and take a longer view of what is happening to the country as a whole, in contrast to the more myopic perspective of the majority of the nation's states. The exceptions are California, which tends to view itself closer commercially to the Pacific-rim countries than it does to many parts of the United States, and states like Idaho, whose economies were especially hard hit by the decline in agricultural exports.

Speaking for several of the western governors, Lamm sharply criticized the shortsightedness of the states' new international independence and said he feared where it was leading the country. Lamm identifies himself as one of the only governors who does not recruit foreign investment, although he remarked that his absence—and overt hostility—did not seem to have had any effect in discouraging the rapid incursion of Japanese investment in Colorado. "This is one of the real national mistakes that's going to haunt us for years to come," he warned:

There is a strong sentiment on the part of the western governors that there is something really wrong here. I do not want Japanese coming in and buying up American technology. I do not want them in our state. I don't want the Arabs owning our banks or the Japanese owning our means of production. It terrifies me.

"The governors can play a real role," Lamm continued, "but we're being outnegotiated on everything. The Japanese want it both ways. They're screwing us. They have a different set of values. What's mine is mine, and what's yours is negotiable.'' Lamm argued that his fellow governors' lack of foresight on the issue of foreign investment would haunt the United States for years to come. ''Politicians fight the last war. This is tomorrow's issue emerging.''

Governors Bruce Babbitt of Arizona and Robert Kerrey of Nebraska shared Lamm's concern and agreed to put the issue on their agenda for a 1985 summer meeting in Honolulu. ''Foreign investment is a great concern of mine,'' said Governor Kerrey. ''Technology drain is a major issue. Reciprocity is a major concern. They bring in jobs and money when they come in to invest, but we find ourselves importing their product. The trade deficit creates a major employment problem for us at home.''[11]

Once a consensus develops on foreign investment among the state's top political leaders, the components for a successful program fall into place. An administrative capacity is developed, private-sector resources are mobilized, and efforts can move forward with minimal controversy. The key variable, then as now, is the governor's commitment to foreign investment as well as his effectiveness in convincing others of its benefits.

As a group, the governors have brushed aside warnings that the growing level of foreign investment may restrict domestic production and eventually worsen the budget and trade deficits. For them this scenario reaches too far into the future and is eclipsed by the immediate stimulating effect that foreign investment has had on the economies of their states. With such heady successes, it is reasonable to assume that the states will continue their aggressive campaign for foreign investment, making impressive inroads into the global economy. In that context, the national perspective, national needs, and national interests can expect to remain secondary for a long time to come.

CHAPTER 4

Baiting the Hook

State Incentive Systems and Their Implementation

We're not exactly a giveaway state . . . but we want to make sure companies do well once they're here. . . . We help with tax abatements on buildings or equipment, with infrastructure, water, sewers, roads, and the state gives money to community loans.
—*Mark Akers, director,*
Indiana Department of Commerce,
Industrial Development Division

You people are crazy with incentives. . . . Our company located here and you gave them sewers, roads, and curbs. When the people from the surrounding communities . . . looked around, they said, "We haven't got roads, curbs, and sewers." The resentment gave us a lot of trouble.
—*an executive from Nippon Steel*

Efforts to recruit foreign investment have paid large dividends in a relatively short period of time. Still unsure of what works and what doesn't, states experiment with a variety of strategies in three major areas: increased economic incentives, expanded overseas branch offices, and public policies designed to maintain a favorable business environment. The most common strategy seems to be a combination of all three approaches, at least until more hard data help them figure out more targeted, cost-effective approaches.

Indiana, a good example of a state that has successfully tried everything, considers itself fortunate to begin with a business climate ideal from the point of view of foreign investors: weak unions, a tame legislature, and a governor willing to spend his time and the state's resources on foreign business promotion. Mark Akers, director of the state's Industrial Development Division, talked about what initially attracted foreign investors to Indiana:

> They are concerned about problems with unions. Quit rates are important to them. We have fewer labor problems than Michigan and the surrounding states. The reason is we have a part-time citizen legislature. There is no real lobbying. The labor unions don't control the legislature. We have a prohibition against a state debt. This is a conservative state. The labor-union movement never really took hold here.

The legislature reinforces the state's political philosophy with policies supportive to investors, such as keeping Indiana's taxes and workman's compensation rates among the lowest in the nation. "We used to be fiftieth in the country, but since we raised the sales tax, we're now forty-fifth," boasted Akers. "We're working our way down to forty-seventh or forty-eighth. We use that in our marketing. Indiana also has the lowest workman's compensation premiums in the country. The unions would rather be in Michigan."

Foreign companies that do business in Indiana have learned they can lobby the state quickly and efficiently, a decided advantage in the fast-paced competition for reverse investment. In June 1984, Akio Morita, chairman of Sony of Japan, paid a visit to Indianapolis and met with the governor and the lieutenant governor. "The next day we announced that we would do away with the unitary tax," recalled Akers. "The same day, Morita announced that he would put a video-disk plant in Indiana." The new plant would hire 300 American workers; a second audio-disk plant, already in existence in Terre Haute, employed 200 workers.

Indiana officials take pride in their supine legislature and pitied California for its continuing problems with the unitary tax. In marked contrast to Indiana, the ornery California legislature had resisted annual attempts by the governor and foreign multinational corporations—led by Sony—to repeal the tax. As an object lesson to California, foreign corporations pointedly located plants in states that quickly repealed the tax, but without effect; California held firm until 1986, when the tax was repealed. No state, however, could match Indiana, whose alacrity made headlines in London and Tokyo. Indiana officials proudly pointed to the flow of business following coverage of the issue in the international press.[1]

Indiana's international development agency, a branch of the State Department of Commerce, is one of the busiest in the nation, handling 325 new foreign investments or expansions from 1981 to 1985. The total expenditure for attracting foreign investment for fiscal year 1986 came to $304,110, or 45 percent of the state's total international appropriation. Three foreign offices represent Indiana's interests in Tokyo, Brussels, and London; the state spends 100 percent of its budget in Brussels for investment attraction, 60 percent in Japan, and 80 percent in London.[2]

The state's largest investor is West Germany, followed by the United Kingdom; currently, Japan and Great Britain are the most active investors. Indiana expects Japan to accelerate its investments in the near future, indicated by the recent surge in interest from Japanese companies that supply the auto industry. Indiana's proximity to the Mazda plant in Flat Rock, Michigan; Honda, in Marysville, Ohio; and Nissan in Smyrna, Tennessee, makes it especially attractive to Japanese auto suppliers, who are trying to take advantage of the Japanese preference for doing business with companies from their own country. Indiana officials have also heard from the Japanese electronics industry, which has expressed an interest in expanding its business in Indiana; they are attracted by the high quality of the engineering school at Purdue University, which graduates one out of every twenty engineers in the United States.

In the category of tangible economic incentives, Indiana ranks high for its energy and inventiveness. "We're not exactly a giveaway state, but you can find things that make the difference," said Akers. "We want to make sure companies do well once they are here. Our main focus is job creation and investment in plant and equipment."[3]

The state helps foreign investors with tax abatements on buildings or equipment and with funds for infrastructure—water, sewers, and roads. They also give foreign investors "community loans": The state gives money to the city or locality, the community lends it to the company, and the company then pays back the loan to the community, which in turn uses it for further economic development. The state also offers loan guarantees to foreign firms; research-and-development money (funneled through a private corporation set up by the state); and venture capital, also channeled through a private corporation. Added to these development programs is an institute for new business ventures that does just that: helps to start new businesses. Job-training money is also available to send Americans overseas for training on the condition that the jobs remain in Indiana. State officials emphasize that these incentives, where relevant, are also available to domestic companies.

"There are two phases to attract business," remarked Akers. "Once the incentive phase is over, we work on making [foreign executives] comfortable." Toward that end, the state's Department of Commerce runs a Japanese school in Indianapolis, which meets on Saturdays and teaches culture, language, and English as a second language. Indiana officials hope that quality-of-life efforts such as these will help them add to the sixteen Japanese firms already based in their state.

Akers also credits the state's branch office in Tokyo for its skill in recruiting Japanese investors:

> Our office is manned by an American who speaks Japanese. It is more effective to have an American selling America. Our representative, Larry Ingraham, socializes with the Japanese, is married to a Japanese woman, and has lived there for twelve years. He is very culturally sensitive. It is very important to have good personal relations. They will confide in him.

BRANCHING OUT: OVERSEAS OPERATIONS AND RESOURCE ALLOCATION

Many states followed the Indiana model, quickly learning that they had to spend money to make money if they wished to compete directly for foreign investment. The initial step of setting up branch offices abroad quickly progressed to more direct methods, and states that continued to expand their international operations saw immediate results. "Kentucky showed that for every dollar put into international development, sixteen dollars was returned," said Marsha Clark, of NASDA.[4] Although the data remain uneven, other studies show even more impressive correlations. The Congressional Research Service reported that as early as 1976, state agencies found that for every dollar of state funding there was "foreign direct investment of $667," a relationship that suggested that "$60 in state funding would suffice to attract $40,000 in foreign capital, or enough to create one new industrial job."[5]

Other states quickly recognized this linkage and also increased their expenditures accordingly. "In 1979, the average expenditure for state development agencies for direct investment and trade was $235,000 per year," continued Clark. "In 1982, it was $525,000, with only half a dozen states spending more than half a million; by 1984, the figure rose to $577,000. Meanwhile, we're adding states who are grouping around the average."[6]

By 1986, twenty-nine states had sixty-five field offices throughout the world. Of these, twenty-five states had offices in Asia, twenty-two of them in Tokyo. Illinois runs three offices in Asia—Tokyo, Hong Kong, and Shenyang, China. In all, there are twenty-seven Asian branch offices and twenty-nine in Europe. Three states have field offices in Canada, two in Mexico, one in Brazil, and Ohio plans to open an office in Africa. Investment and export activity takes place at these overseas locations, with a wide disparity among the states in the amounts of money allotted for each activity.[7]

Contrary to expectations, the data show no clear correlation between the size of a state and the extent of its overseas operations. Some of the smaller states run as many or more overseas offices as the states with the largest industrial bases—New York, California, Texas, Pennsylvania, and New Jersey. Alabama, for example, runs five overseas offices—three branches in Asia and two in Europe—while California had no overseas offices until 1986, when it opened branches in London and Tokyo. New York has the largest number of field offices: two in Canada (Montreal and Toronto), two in Europe (Italy and England), and one in Japan. Texas, which has the most foreign investment of any state in the nation, has only one foreign office, in Mexico City, while South Carolina, eleventh on the list, has offices in Tokyo and Belgium. The lesson here is that perhaps smaller states have to try harder to lure the foreign dollar. Arkansas, for example, has developed a six-language capacity in its office in Brussels.

Nor is there a clear connection between a state's success in recruiting investment and the quality or quantity of its branch offices. Tennessee, the state that holds the nation's record for recruiting the most Japanese investment in the shortest period of time, has never opened an overseas office.

States tend to locate their overseas offices with an eye toward current investment and trade patterns. Minnesota, which targeted northern Europe as its major trading partner, put its two overseas offices in Oslo and Stockholm. New York, Georgia, and Vermont, states with strong Canadian ties, opened offices in Toronto and/or Montreal.

Most states identify the percentage of their international development budget that goes to attracting foreign investment, but to retain some flexibility they do not specify exactly where the money is going. There appears to be no pattern in the states' decisions to expend resources to promote foreign investment, their calculations of the levels of funding, or their allocation of the dollars. New Jersey, for example, allots 40 percent of its international budget to foreign investment but has not opened any foreign offices, while New York, with 60 percent of its allocation earmarked for investment, has six offices. Kansas spends 75 percent of its international budget for inward investment and 100 percent of the money in its Tokyo office.

If there is any pattern at all, it is to spend as much money as possible on every strategy in sight. This indiscriminate approach to attracting investment has produced results, but the nagging question of whether the cost is excessive continues to plague policymakers, especially when they look at the dramatic example set by California. That state is a direct challenge to the validity of the argument of the spendthrift advocates. Judging from the data, it appears to allocate absolutely nothing from its $5.7 million international budget for attracting foreign investment, yet has more foreign investment than any other state in the nation except for Texas. Perhaps California found it did not have to spend money. Lured by lucrative markets and other attributes, foreign companies find California attractive enough to continue investing heavily, with or without incentives.[8]

HOW IT WORKS ABROAD: THE VIRGINIA EXPERIENCE

But California is atypical. States without California's natural bounty, enormous population, or skilled labor force find they must work hard and spend a lot of money to compete for foreign investment. They spend a great deal of time determining the right investment strategy for their state, and once that is established, state development officers vigorously lobby their state legislatures for increased funding for overseas offices. Those overseas offices function very effectively, giving considerable attention to detail in terms of the selection of personnel and the management of their activities.

The state of Virginia is a good example of a state that has seen tangible results from allocating resources to attract foreign investment. It was the first state to open an overseas office. In 1955, the Virginia Port Authority established an office in Brussels to promote trade and development; in 1968, the state government set up its own office in Brussels, and in 1980 it opened an office in Tokyo.

Virginia's early start paid dividends. "In 1968, there were 24 foreign firms in Virginia; today there are 289 firms, employing 25,000 people, with a total investment of one billion dollars," reported John Lenkey, III, international director of the Virginia Department of Economic Development. Most foreign investments are fairly small; the state's largest foreign company is the British-owned Imperial Chemical Industries, with 700 employees.

In general, the benefits of foreign investment are measured by the dollars invested, the number of people employed and factories built, and the number of working farms. Typical of state development officers, Lenkey emphasizes job creation as the most visible, politically sensitive benefit of foreign investment. "Our state's mission," he said, "is to increase industrial job-producing assets for Virginia from foreign sources." Since state revenues depend heavily on the personal income tax, Virginia places an even higher premium on job creation than states that depend more heavily on investment for their tax base.

In their overseas offices, recruiters see themselves as supersalesmen for the state. They call on firms, attend conferences, and try to maintain a constant and highly visible presence. Denis Rufin, Virginia's European director for international trade, visits Fortune 500 companies and promotes opportunities in his state for potential investors.

Rufin heads up a small team based in Brussels and reports back to the home office in Richmond. Fluent in French, he has developed an extensive network of key players at the overseas chambers of commerce, embassies, banks, consulting firms, and trade associations. "When we first visit a firm," he reported, "they are not thinking of Virginia, or even the United States. We first have to sell them on the USA. When Jimmy Carter was president, we had a hard time. There were worldwide doubts about the U.S. Things looked unattractive."

After a few years, the successful recruiter learns the most effective approaches. "In Europe, we call on the companies," said Rufin. "Very few come to us. With Tokyo, we use a different approach. No country in the world has Japan's population or its homogeneity." Europeans have to be convinced of the virtues of investing in America, while the Japanese make their decision to invest in the United States long before they have been contacted by a state representative; the Japanese just have to be convinced to locate in one state instead of another. "We didn't have to sell the Japanese on the U.S.," said Lenkey. "There is no consumer market for Japan elsewhere. With Europeans, you need twelve different marketing plans. Japan just has to decide whether the company is big enough to come to the United States."

Officials who deal on a daily basis with disparate styles and traditions would be well served by a degree in cultural anthropology. Lacking that background, officials make their own judgments, based on their subjective professional experiences. Rufin and Lenkey agree that the Japanese researched their investments far more thoroughly than any other culture, while the Europeans function more like Americans—making quick decisions based as often on instinct as research. They considered the Dutch the most perceptive investors, followed by the English, the Germans, and the Scandinavians. The Italians and the Portuguese are prone to make mistakes, while the French tend to be mercurial. Lenkey and Rufin are still smarting over the loss of a French company, ostensibly because the executive in charge of site selection, a weekend sailor, preferred another state's bay to the Chesapeake.

The Japanese fear the famous American "hard sell" and do everything they can to avoid it until they have actually made their decision. As a result, they are perceived by Americans as somewhat oblique, especially in contrast to the Europeans, who are more direct. Japanese multinationals, for example, go to great lengths to erect buffer zones between themselves and the legions of state promoters waiting in the wings. These buffers are thinly disguised as American or Japanese consulting firms, who go around making polite inquiries of local officials. When a firm really wants to throw a state off its scent, another Japanese multinational will act as its stalking horse.

By now, the states are alert to the game. "Before Komatsu located in Chattanooga," recalled Lenkey, "strange companies came at us: Arthur D. Little, Peat Marwick, Sumitomo Research Company. They asked questions about earth-moving equipment. We figured it out. The same with Mazda. There are not that many light-truck manufacturers." A group from Mitsui also approached the Virginia development office without identifying which company was interested in investing in Virginia. Mitsui submitted a thirty-six-page questionnaire, then returned to Japan. "When we see this kind of research, our alerts go up," said Lenkey.

The Europeans come at us more directly. We have to convince a lot more people before the Japanese finally come. When they come, they visit in small blue-chip groups. They make observations, then go home and file a report. Once we get to see the chairman of a company, it is only at the end of the process, at the ceremonial level, when the decision has been made.

By that time, unfortunately, hostilities among the final contenders have usually climbed to a fever pitch. Each state claims the others are not playing fair; that their competitors have given away the store; and that they alone among the fifty states offer incentives purely on the merits. Virginia is no exception and its animus toward Tennessee is typical in this environment. "We have a real fight with other states, particularly with Tennessee," charged Lenkey:

> The Tennessee governor flew over and made Nissan a deal they couldn't refuse. The governor flew four hundred people to Japan for training, and the county bought property and leased it for next to nothing to Nissan. In Virginia, there are no concessions to foreign firms. Our governor and tax commissioner won't play that game. It's not fair to our own companies.

What Virginia offers foreign firms is identical to what it offers domestic companies: the world's largest natural harbor, no unitary tax, no tax on dividends, good transportation, and a desirable location.

The resentment abates, admitted Lenkey, in the case of states whose internal resources put them clearly ahead of the pack. The Volkswagen auto company, for example, wanted an existing auto plant, which Pennsylvania was able to provide. The Japanese asked New York and Virginia if either state would guarantee a minimum number of purchases if they located a bus factory in either state. New York was in a better position to meet that requirement.

In addition to revenue and jobs, foreign investment brings intangible benefits in the form of favorable social impacts. "The image of foreign direct investment bringing jobs changes America's views of foreigners," said Lenkey. This appears to be the case, even when foreign nationals fill the jobs. ODIN, a Swiss-German joint venture in Chesterfield County, Virginia, employs mostly Vietnamese-Americans in the manufacture of high-tech circuitboard connectors. "Vietnamese are now accepted on the streets of Richmond," Lenkey continued. "It has made Virginians conscious of the world."

HIGH STAKES: STATE INCENTIVE SYSTEMS

The states use a variety of weapons to recruit foreign investment, promoting their wares in national and international advertising campaigns. New Jersey ran a full-page ad in *Business Week* featuring a testimonial from Hai-Min Lee, president of Samsung International, a South Korean electronics firm. "We found a U.S. location that wasn't foreign to our business," read the advertisement. "As soon as we spoke to New Jersey, we felt right at home." What it took to make Samsung feel at home was also spelled out—"the willingness of New Jersey to develop an attractive $9.1 million bond and financing program made the decision for us"—along with what Samsung was giving back to the state: "a new $25 million TV and microwave manufacturing plant" in Bergen County, with "a $10 million, 8-year lease on office and warehouse facilities."[9]

The messages are clear and blunt; there is no time for subtlety in the heated competition for foreign investment. North Carolina's promotional material, for example, emphasizes that "North Carolina's percentage of unionized employment is the lowest of all 50 states. . . . A recent productivity study revealed that North Carolina workers produced 22 cents more output per $1 received in wages than workers [elsewhere] in the United States in the same industries." In other words, weak unions, hard workers, and cheap labor.[10]

Behind the promotional campaigns are the goods: a rich panoply of loans, tax exemptions, and other forms of directed revenue. The activity is frenetic, and much of it unrecorded, but about six thousand economic development groups in the states spend hundreds of millions of dollars each year to attract foreign investors. Competition among the states has escalated the offering of incentives, often at great cost to the taxpayer in terms of "lost tax revenue and of revenue disbursement," according to a report issued by David D. Driscoll of the Congressional Research Service.[11]

The major incentives, part of a larger fiscal policy to attract foreign business, fall into five basic categories:

1. Easing the Tax Climate. Depending on the ingenuity of its accountants, all states offer foreign investors some way of reducing the burden of state and local taxes. Compared to the other costs of doing business, however, state and local taxes are relatively insignificant, according to many analysts.[12] Moreover, since tax structures and tax rates change over time and depend so heavily on the political climate, an astute foreign investor would not make a long-term commitment based on tax holidays alone.

2. Specific Tax Concessions. Most localities offer property-tax exemptions to new business—foreign and domestic—ranging up to fifteen years on land and buildings. Since the largest local tax is the property tax, which also includes machinery, furniture, and equipment, states have the most latitude in this area of tax relief. They are also eager to provide accelerated depreciation on plants and equipment.

3. Industrial Development Bonds (IDBs). These are municipal bonds issued by state and local governments to finance industrial projects at low rates of interest. Availability of these bonds is considered a major incentive and is featured in the promotional literature of all states serious about recruiting foreign investment. IDBs are offered in two forms: revenue bonds, repaid from the project's revenues; and general-obligation bonds, which make the locality responsible for repayment. In a typical IDB, a state or municipality purchases or builds a facility, then leases it back to the investor. In this way, the company is freed from property taxes and spared a huge chunk of its initial capital outlay. Since these bonds are capped at $10 million and since their use precludes other forms of financing, larger industries tend not to take advantage of them. Multinationals like Nissan or Toshiba, for example, whose investment may reach the $300–$400 million mark, would not utilize IDBs.

4. Infrastructure and Special Services. The last set of incentives involves a series of efforts to reduce the cost of doing business once the company has located in the state. Rail and highway connections, roads, sewers, and water facilities all help toward reducing operating expenses and capital expenditures. In addition, states offer specific assistance to companies, such as aid in design and layout of new plants, making available research-and-development facilities (i.e., at a local university or government agency), and state-supported job-training programs. It has been suggested that some states are so eager for foreign investment that they offer outright gifts of land.

5. Public-Private Sector Agreements. In California, the state has initiated a cooperative agreement with Japanese banks in which the banks investigate areas of California and analyze them in terms of their investment potential. The banks then alert Japanese firms of their findings and recommendations. New York State has also instituted a similar venture through its Department of Commerce, with the goal of facilitating joint ventures between firms in the state and foreign investors. The state identifies the companies, then puts them in contact with overseas firms with matching interests and assets.[13]

With so many available incentives, foreign investors clearly have the upper hand, using it to squeeze as much as they can out of the states. The classic case of interstate rivalry involved the forty-state competition over the Volkswagen Rabbit plant. Although Ohio came close, Pennsylvania emerged the victor because it offered the most.[14] The specific package included the following:

- A $40 million loan repayable in thirty years to purchase and build on to an unfinished former Chrysler plant. The interest rate averaged 4 percent, dipping down to 1.75 percent for the first twenty years.
- A $20 million bond issue for a road link between the plant and the state highway.
- A $10 million state bond issue for a railway spur linking the plant with a main line.
- A $6 million loan from the Pennsylvania state employees pension fund for fifteen years at 8.5 percent.
- A $3.8 million training program for Volkswagen workers, funded by the federal government but acquired through state efforts.
- A five-year county property-tax abatement worth $200,000.
- State designation of the plant site as a foreign-trade subzone, bringing down the duty on finished cars to 3 percent.

The total value of Pennsylvania's incentive package initially came to more than $51.7 million, or 19.6 percent of the total cost of the plant, according to a report issued by the Northeast-

Midwest Institute. Put another way, the state spent $4,103 for each new job created by the Volkswagen facility.[15] This was a conservative estimate, however; by the time they were through, the figure rose to a cost of over $90 million.

INTERSTATE RIVALRIES

The competition for the Volkswagen plant, while intense, was national, involving so many states that it was conducted in a relatively open, aboveboard manner. In contrast, rivalries between neighboring states often turn bitter and are characterized by misinformation, secrecy, and bad feeling. Every time it loses an investment to Tennessee, Georgia accuses its neighbor of bribing the Japanese with giveaway packages that include everything but the capitol building; the rancor and hostility between the two states have become palpable.

Another bitter head-to-head competition pitted Florida against Alabama over the location of a $16 million Sony plant that manufactures audiovisual tapes. Alabama won, elated with a foreign investment that quickly quadrupled in size to employ a work force of 1,200. Anthony H. Warner, III, of the Alabama development office, explained that his state simply stole the investment from its neighbor. When they learned that Florida was coming close to acquiring the investment, they mounted a last-minute campaign: "We called up Sony in New York and said just give us one day of your time. . . . We'll pick you up in New York in time for breakfast, fly you down in our state jet, and have you home in time for lunch." Alabama also outbid Florida in the area of tax advantages, exempting Sony from property taxes, use taxes on plant equipment, and sales taxes on the building.[16]

The result of the Alabama-Florida bidding war was that Florida became much more aggressive in recruiting foreign investment. The state quickly eliminated the unitary tax, ran ads in the foreign press boasting about its low workmen's compensation rates, and made sure no grass grew under its feet in the next bidding war.

Interstate rivalries are getting worse, not better, and affect export activity as well as investment. "Turf jealousies," in fact, were identified as the most "consistent problem . . . faced across the nation" by Mark Tigan, director of a national group involved in export development.[17]

HOW COMPANIES VIEW INCENTIVES

From the point of view of the investing companies, the incentive packages offered by the states are less crucial than the bidding wars would have us believe. The decision of SAMPO, a Taiwan-based manufacturer of television sets, to locate a plant in Norcross, Georgia, was a typical example of the role of incentives from a multinational's perspective. For SAMPO, incentives played an important part but a very minor one, and only at the very last stage of the process, when the basic decisions had already been agreed upon. Companies like SAMPO invest in two stages: (1) when it makes the decision to invest in the United States and (2) when it chooses the state and locality to site its plant.

At the first stage—and this is true of most foreign investors—incentives played no part at all. The reason, pure and simple, was the imposition of protective tariffs. "Every petition to the ITC impacts investment," said Ben C. Huang, manager of the import and traffic division of SAMPO. "Import quotas on TVs is the reason SAMPO is here. As a result of TV quotas, SAMPO was forced into production here three or four years ago." Huang stressed that there was no other economic advantage in coming to the United States, especially since labor costs in Taiwan were still so cheap: $1.25 an hour in Taiwan versus $6 an hour in the United States. Factoring in "ocean freight, transportation, and insurance costs," continued Huang, "we break even."

A native of Taiwan with an MBA, Huang was interviewed at SAMPO's Georgia headquarters, a compact, immaculate building of 110,000 square feet facing a major highway. Chinese screens on orange carpets decorated the front office, along with twenty-five different types of television sets. MUZAK piped in a pallid version of "When the Saints Go Marching In." Primarily an assembling operation, SAMPO employs 200 people, 15 percent of them Taiwanese. All of the top executives except the accounting manager are from Taiwan.

In choosing a state and county, incentives entered the picture only at the final stages of the process, certainly well after the state had been chosen. And of the five most important factors cited by Huang attracting SAMPO to Georgia, incentives represented one relatively unimportant category, he said. He cited industrial revenue bonds, which the company could easily have obtained in a number of other localities in addition to Gwinnett County, where it finally settled. The other factors, according to Huang, included the following:

1. The Cost of Labor. "Four dollars an hour in Georgia, contrasted to $6 to $7 an hour in Chicago and New Jersey," the leading competitors for the SAMPO plant.

2. The Low Level of Union Activity. "The northern states are 70 percent union; in Georgia, only 14 to 15 percent are unionized."

3. The Weather. "An important factor because it is an economic trend. People are moving south for the weather; the Sunbelt is growing fast."

4. Market. "We are a sales-oriented company, and the South is a growing market with great purchasing potential. In Chicago, the population is decreasing. In Georgia, the transportation was better than other southern states. Tennessee is inland."

Peripheral factors influencing SAMPO's decision included avoiding their competitors, particularly those from other Oriental countries. "We didn't want to go to Tennessee; there are too many Japanese companies there who are our competitors," recalled Huang. "The Koreans are also our competitors: Gold Star, Samsung, and the Lucky Group." Despite his aversion to competition, Huang opened up a television set and proudly displayed its international components:

We buy parts from Sanyo, picture tubes from RCA, Zenith, Sylvania, or Hitachi; the chassis are from Taiwan, but the parts for the chassis come from Taiwan, Singapore, the U.S., and Japan; the cabinets come from the USA, as do the packaging materials. TV is an international product, and the internationalization of resources is a real benefit.

Only after all these factors were sorted out by the company did state and county incentives enter the picture; and at that point the counties began to compete against each other. "The state government helped us find land. We toured the state and compared Rockdale, Newnan, Shenandoah, Fayette, and DeKalb counties," said Huang. "It looks easy, but it isn't. In Fayette, the county taxes were very low, but the problem was the supply of labor; it was too rural." Gwinnett County finally won, offering SAMPO an 80 percent exemption from property taxes and a training program at the local technical school. In the final analysis, these incentives were icing on the cake; an insignificant part of the company's decision making and easily duplicated almost anywhere else.

THE LONG VIEW—INCENTIVES AND THEIR PROBLEMS

As some companies admit, state giveaways can be counterproductive. At a Southeast governors' conference, a representative of Nippon Steel warned Americans to look more carefully at what they were giving away. "You people are crazy with incentives," he lamented:

> Ask a Japanese company what it needs. Our company located here, and you gave them sewers, roads, and curbs. When the people from the surrounding communities working at the plant looked around, they said, "We haven't got roads, curbs, and sewers." The resentment gave us a lot of trouble. This is what causes trouble. When the states fire all the cannons to get foreign companies.

The Nippon response was unusual for a foreign multinational. Most companies regard efforts to bait them with incentives as a reflection of what it can expect from the state in the future as well as an indication of a "pro-business" climate. In this context, foreign companies go for all the incentives they can get, playing the states against each other with resounding success.

The states have figured out the game by now but are rendered powerless by the very rules they initiated. While most accept the status quo, some resentment has escalated along with the emergence of interstate rivalries. Seeing no other way out, one state official offered the unlikely solution of federal legislation to restrict incentives, comparable to Proposition 13, which puts a ceiling on property taxes.

The real problem for states is whether or not they are giving away too much, and if so, how much is too much? Would the company have invested, anyway, without the package of rail links, tax abatements, bonds, roads, and sewers? The problem is that no one knows the answer to that question except the foreign multinationals, and they keep the reasons behind their decisions to themselves. What is known, to some extent, is how much states are spending to attract foreign investment; the data become more exact—as in the Volkswagen case—with respect to incentive packages for specific companies.

But data alone are inconclusive, evidenced by California, which claims to spend nothing on the recruitment of foreign investment, yet is saturated with all the foreign investment it can absorb. At least the state says it spends nothing. A close examination of the activities of international development officers reveals a great deal of investment activity. Another factor offsetting the state's omission of resources for reverse investment is the eagerness of municipalities to spend money to attract foreign investment; and in California, some localities easily outspend many of the nation's states.

The California example also reinforces much of the research in this area, which shows that incentives play a very small part in the overall investment picture; that companies look at a number of other factors before weighing incentives. These include market conditions, labor rates, energy costs, transportation, and the availability of labor. A report on French investment in the southeastern United States by Crédit Lyonnais surveyed sixteen firms and noted that incentives were "weighted relatively low."[18]

A study of foreign investment published in the journal of the Federal Reserve Bank of Atlanta agreed that "despite the recent explosion in promotional activities . . . current research suggests that foreign investors do not consider incentives as important as the overall investment climate in a state."[19] The study suggests that state and local authorities benefit from this research and "examine more carefully their investment climate before going overboard on incentives. . . . Investment is a long-term profit-oriented decision, and virtually no amount of special incentives . . . is likely to attract and keep a firm in an area in which the long-term profitability criteria are not present." In fact, a state would be much better off spending its money on developing its investment climate than on "special incentives."[20]

But the states argue otherwise. They say that incentive packages produce results, and the results are multiples of what they spent. Alabama officials claimed that the Sony payroll generated sales triple its size as well as substantial tax revenues. From the Indiana and Virginia experiences, state officials regarded their money well spent.

Another criticism of incentives is that they are nonselective. Jeffrey S. Arpan singled out the South for "not taking a targeted approach" and for their interest in "attracting any or all investment."[21] States rarely debate whether an investment diversifies their industrial base or whether it competes unfairly with existing industries. In fact, when held up to a less flattering light, state incentive packages look curiously like subsidies; indeed, at one point they were a source of great embarrassment to trade negotia-

tors at the GATT talks, who argued for an end to unfair government subsidies to private business.[22]

No one really knows how much is spent in the aggregate on
these incentive packages and how much they cost the taxpayer.
What is clear is that the cost is substantial and that some inequities are inevitable. Louisiana's ten-year moratorium on taxing
land, equipment, and building improvements cost the state $108
million a year in lost revenues. The problem is that lost revenues
have to be recouped eventually, albeit by a wider pool of corporations and taxpayers who will be paying for incentive packages
that benefit a limited number of people.

Some taxpayers have begun to question the price tag at the
ballot box. Mayor Ted Anders, of Flat Rock, Michigan, was
turned out of office in 1985 after luring a Mazda plant to his
town with a fourteen-year tax holiday. Apparently the voters did
not think the $2.5-million-a-year loss was worth the effort. Signs
of a backlash are beginning to appear in other states, as well,
where recent estimates of how much a state had to spend challenge the earlier optimism of how much it would get in return.
The state of Kentucky, which spent about $112 million in incen-
tives for a new Toyota plant, faced intense criticism from many
constituencies.[23]

Is it worth it? It is hard to tell, especially without adequate
information, which states seem reluctant to gather. Without long-
term data, the benefits and disadvantages will remain a mystery
to policymakers who may wish to evaluate incentives on a more
empirical basis. Only then will incentives be used in an efficient,
targeted fashion instead of the current pattern: scattershot, waste-
ful, and inequitable.

The rush to inundate foreign investors with incentives rests on
the assumption that all foreign investment is beneficial. Otherwise, how could states justify such generosity with the taxpayers' money? This assumption masks larger questions that never
get asked because the answers might force a radical change in
policy. One of these questions is, what is the basic motivation of
the foreign investor and how does this relate to the economic
health of the nation?

Some answers have already been suggested in the trade literature. One of the reasons the Japanese invest, for example, is to
deflect criticism of their trade practices. In other words, Japanese
investment policy is part of their export policy, not separate and
distinct, as analysts often view it. As protectionism heated up in
Europe, the Japanese deflected it the same way they did in the

United States: They built plants in the European Community. To get around tariff barriers on compact-disk players, the Sony Corporation built a production facility in France; Komatsu, Nissan, NEC, and a number of other Japanese multinationals have also located plants in Europe. In fact, Japanese investment in the European Community increased 100 percent between 1982 and 1985, while Europe's trade deficit with Japan doubled. Is investment part of what has been called Japan's "laser-beam export strategy"? And if so, what are the short- and long-term implications?[24]

The longer view always ends in a question mark. State officials are forced to be myopic; it comes with the territory. Their concerns begin and end with jobs and the tax base, allowing them to keep other factors at bay. In effect, their policy has become national policy, since federal officials, supposedly the guardians of the national interest, have abdicated to state leadership. The system of checks and balances has tipped over, landing flat at the feet of short-term needs.

CHAPTER 5

Cherry Blossoms and Lift Trucks

The Coming of Komatsu and the Tennessee Strategy

A plant in the U.S. will make Komatsu part of the local community . . . it should generate at least 250 jobs and annual sales of some $160 million by 1988.

—*Shoji Nogawa, president,*
Komatsu, Ltd.

Why are we using taxpayers' money to help Komatsu beat Caterpillar's brains out?

—*Senator Jim Sasser,*
Democrat of Tennessee

In a sunlit room in the state capitol, Governor Lamar Alexander of Tennessee welcomed a visiting delegation of Japanese television producers and reporters. In an atmosphere that was both formal and congenial, an exchange of gifts took place: The governor presented his visitors with tie pins depicting crossed flags of Tennessee and Japan. He then graciously accepted the group's gift of a painting. As the ceremony continued, the translation slowed the pace of his welcoming remarks and added emphasis to Alexander's message: the strong bonds of culture and geography between Japan and Tennessee.

"In April and May our dogwoods bloom at the same time your cherry trees bloom," he began:

We celebrate the turning of maple leaves to red and yellow about a week or two before the leaves turn in Nikko. We have lots of festivals just like Japan has many festivals. I hope you will see the similarities between the land and the people that we see in Tennessee. That may be . . . why Japanese businesses feel at home in Tennessee.

Governor Alexander had worked hard to bring Japanese manufacturing to Tennessee. His efforts have paid off handsomely. A total of thirty companies, representing 12 percent of the total Japanese manufacturing investment in the United States, have located in Tennessee. These include giants such as Nissan, a manufacturer of small trucks and automobiles, in Smyrna; Sharp (television sets and microwave ovens) in Memphis; Bridgestone (truck radial tires) in La Vergne; and Toshiba (microwave ovens and television sets) in Lebanon. They have created jobs for 7,000 workers, almost all of whom are native Tennesseans. Total Japanese capital investment in Tennessee hovers at the $1.25 billion mark, with more to come as these companies bring over their favorite suppliers.[1]

To recruit investors to his state, the governor made six trips to Japan in six years and met with the prime minister three times. He has coordinated statewide efforts to assure that everything possible was done to cut red tape and to maximize the incentives that often make the difference in a company's final decision about where to locate. During one trip to San Francisco, the state's development officials made 179 visits to foreign and American businessmen in one week's time, trying to convince them to locate a plant in Tennessee.

"When we went to California to see Toshiba, they told us that this was the only governor who had ever visited them personally," said William Long, commissioner for economic development. Even the state legislators participate in the statewide effort to bring foreign investment to Tennessee. "The Japanese know then that what we say will be backed up in the legislature. Nissan told me that," added Long.

Governor Alexander's formula for attracting foreign investors blended superb public relations with well-honed negotiating skills. The public relations dimension, and the care that went into it, emerged at the conclusion of Alexander's speech. "The most interesting thing Tennessee is doing for Japanese companies that have come to our state," he announced, "is the publication of a book called *Friends*, the story of how so many Japanese people and companies came to a relatively small inland state." Alexander said he would write the text and then personally present the book to several hundred Japanese corporations the following spring around cherry-blossom time. The book's photographs, taken by Robin Hood (his real name), heightened the governor's theme of the visual similarities between Japan and Tennessee. Alexander held up two identical color photos of a mountain at sunset; one was taken in Japan, the other in the Smoky Mountains of Tennessee.

Lamar Alexander's enthusiasm for foreign investment reflects the interests of his region. "We are a small, insular state, with low incomes," he explained. "It is important to Tennessee." His efforts mirror those of his fellow southern governors, all of whom compete intensely for the foreign dollar. Most of all, they want the jobs that these plants bring to their state, often the very jobs that have been lost to foreign competition. "If we're complaining now, it is due to our own laziness," said Alexander, responding to critics of foreign investment. "Americans just didn't produce small cars." The American car companies also missed the boat by not locating in Tennessee, an oversight that has since been corrected by GM's decision—perhaps spurred by Japan's discovery of the state—to build its Saturn plant in Tennessee. "We paid visits to GM for nineteen years," said William Long, "and nothing came of it."

Tennessee's success has caused considerable bewilderment among her rival states, since it is one of the few states left in the entire country without its own office in Tokyo. It shows that other factors take precedence in the decision to locate a plant, some of which explain Tennessee's triumphs as well as those of Georgia, North and South Carolina, Alabama, and Florida. To the foreign investor, the attractions of the South include its climate, labor force, availability of land, special tax breaks and financing opportunities, and what the South's promoters call its "pro-business"—sometimes read as antiunion—environment. Governors and mayors openly recruit foreign investors with the promise that the area is union-free and point to the prevalence of right-to-work laws throughout the region that virtually guarantee that the unions will remain weak. "In Tennessee, they have a choice," said Alexander, "but we couldn't guarantee to Nissan that there wouldn't be a union."

The Tennessee environment for foreign investors at the state level set the stage for individual entrepreneurship on the part of the towns, cities, and counties. In cooperation with state officials, they launched aggressive campaigns to recruit foreign companies, meeting with a high rate of success. Faced with the loss of manufacturing jobs, cities like Chattanooga credit their revival to foreign investment: Chattanooga lost 10,000 manufacturing jobs in the last ten years, some of which are now returning with backing from the French, West Germans, and Japanese.

CHATTANOOGA AND THE KOMATSU VICTORY

The city of Chattanooga's success in snaring Komatsu, the world's second-largest manufacturer of construction equipment, showed how the governor's efforts to attract foreign investment played out at the local level. It took a long time and a great deal of effort to bring Komatsu to Chattanooga, a city nestled on the banks of the Tennessee River and surrounded by the state's lush green hills. The largest inland port in the South, Chattanooga is also an important rail link to the Southeast and Middle West. Almost a textbook study in cooperation between business and government, the campaign to lure Komatsu highlighted the unusual ability of the city's power elite—the mayor, county executive, local bankers, development officials, and the Chamber of Commerce—to join forces, abandon their political differences, and compete effectively for an ambitious prize.

The campaign ended with the announcement on March 20, 1985, that Komatsu had negotiated the purchase of a fifty-five-acre abandoned factory, including 355,000 square feet of plant space, and would begin production the following year. "We rebuilt Japan. In effect, they're helping to rebuild us," said Jerre R. Haskew, chairman of the board and CEO of the Commerce Union Bank. The company's initial investment of $3.5 million for the plant was modest, but Komatsu president Shoji Nogawa predicted that "cumulative investment in equipment . . . would reach $18 million by 1988 . . . and generate at least 250 jobs and annual sales of some $160 million."

Why such a major effort for only 250 jobs? Local officials said that company representatives had given them private assurances that their investment and jobs would grow quickly, while astute local businessmen pointed out that the company bought more land and plant space than it needed for only 250 jobs.

This meant that the Japanese company would finally tackle its major rival, Caterpillar, in head-to-head competition on the American company's home turf. It would be Komatsu's first manufacturing facility in the United States and a hedge against possible protectionist measures in the future. Nogawa said there was "no question" that Komatsu's share of the U.S. market would rise gradually.

Like many other Japanese facilities in the United States, it was believed that the Komatsu plant would manufacture its products in Japan and assemble them in Chattanooga. But Komatsu spokesmen remained deliberately vague about the specifics of their plans.

COURTSHIP

Komatsu's decision was anything but casual. The company made at least eight visits before making its final decision, with everyone aware that its site teams were looking at other cities at the same time. Each visit brought a delegation of six to eight company representatives. "I told them it's time we stopped courting and got married," said Mayor Eugene Roberts, a tall, courtly white-haired man who had been an FBI agent and newspaper reporter.

Roberts described the prodigious efforts of the Komatsu officials to acquire information. "The Japanese are meticulous," he said, a word echoed by many Americans who deal on a regular basis with Japanese businessmen. Their decisions are never made casually, and it takes an unusual amount of patience to reach closure. Since they study every business decision with infinitely greater care than their American counterparts, their American hosts are often driven to distraction. "They look at solid waste disposal, availability of loans, marketing, and the nearness to suppliers. They play you off against other cities, but when they come back a second time, you know they're serious."

With each visit the suspense mounted. "We kept seeing different people," said David Major, a civic leader and one of the most important players in the Komatsu drama. "It was hard to know who was running the show. We treated everyone as if he was the decision maker. We knew the decision would be made in Japan." Major is the executive vice-president of Partners for Economic Progress, a business group closely linked to the Chamber of Commerce that specializes in marketing and economic development. The state government took the initiative in introducing Komatsu to "Partners," and the group took over from there. Partners acted as the broker between Komatsu and the owners of the Koehring plant (the plant Komatsu purchased); it also ran the command post coordinating the activities of the city, county, and state governments as well as the local chamber of commerce and other business groups.

As with any courtship, there were communications difficulties, and they were tougher than anyone expected. Bridging the cultural gaps required unusual sensitivity on both sides—more, it seemed, from the Americans. The continually changing composition of the successive delegations of Japanese confused the Americans, who were accustomed to a business environment that stressed individual relationships. Instead, American negotiators were confronted with ever-changing groups of anonymous officials and a process that was highly depersonalized. For the Japanese, the complex checks and balances were expressly designed to avoid the pitfalls of cronyism and to ensure the rationality of final decisions.

"Some were engineers, some were finance people; a representative from their New York law firm and a banker were always with them," explained Major, and there were always Japanese interpreters. "Most of the Japanese we dealt with understood English but spoke poorly. They'd ask you the same question two or three times to be sure they understood the meaning and to find out if you gave the same answers. We knew that."

The communications problem had its humorous side. The Komatsu reps assumed correctly that their Tennessee hosts did not speak Japanese and felt free to comment candidly to each other. During one of the site visits, an attractive young woman, fluent in Japanese, joined the Chattanooga host group. Since the Japanese provided their own interpreter, she spoke English, but she understood all too clearly the sexual references the Japanese visitors—always all-male groups—thought they were making privately about her. Her revenge came at the farewell dinner, where she presented the American group's gift in flawless Japanese, then sat back to enjoy the shocked expressions on the faces of the guests.

The efforts to attract Komatsu preceded the site visits by at least a decade, according to Jerre R. Haskew:

> We were the people to make the first introductions, the first bank to see it coming. We decided in 1972–73 that because of the currency alignments there would be a wave of foreign investment from Europe and Japan. We knew that it would be worth our while to identify the companies looking to locate in the United States and locate them in Tennessee. We assumed these would be financially secure companies, and we had the selfish reason of wanting to get their accounts.
>
> We knew we had to get the state involved. At that time, Tennessee lagged behind South Carolina, Georgia, and Alabama. Moreover, 67 percent of German industry was in South Carolina, and Georgia was out actively soliciting. So was North Carolina because of textiles and tobacco.
>
> We called on Governor Winfield Dunn and on the economic development commissioner, Pat Choate. We stirred up the waters. We took a trip to the Far East and introduced

the State of Tennessee to quite a few Japanese "zaibatsu-type" [conglomerate] companies: Nissan, Komatsu, Mitsubishi, Sumitomo. The state got its name in the hat.

Through its contacts, the Commerce Union Bank was able to reach policymakers in business and industry in Japan. Many of its customers were already dealing with Japan, a factor that gave the bank added leverage. Another factor working for the Chattanooga bank was the willingness of Japanese companies, frustrated with the inefficiencies of the New York and Chicago banks, to expand their business to other states. Realists might add that the Japanese quickly learned the political importance of dealing with local banks if they wished to do business in the region.

Haskew's efforts to create and reinforce an international banking network for his region helped Chattanooga and his own bank, which eventually won the major Komatsu account. On the recommendation of its Japanese banks, Komatsu named Commerce Union to represent the company in Chattanooga. In addition to handling the company's payroll, the bank would provide an assortment of other services. "We will assist their executives, integrate them in the community, make them feel at home, and facilitate the movement of their money," said Haskew. "The role of American banks is deposits and payroll. The financing is done at home to prevent political flak here."

Every courtship has an element of mystery to it, and this was no less true in the case of Komatsu and Chattanooga. No one knew what was going on in Tokyo while local negotiations proceeded, yet officials speculated that Tennessee had to have a key player in Japan operating in the interests of the state. Tennessee remains the only state with a substantial amount of foreign investment without an office in Tokyo, yet it routinely beats its competitors in attracting new Japanese investment. One prominent official surmised that the governor was well represented in Japan and described how he thought it worked:

> The most important ingredient in attracting foreign investment is to have someone who lives in a foreign country, who brings you intelligence. Someone with great big ol' antennae. This person should have a low profile. If you don't have such a person smoking out things, meeting top business leaders, you can't pull it off. He's like a talent scout for football; a good recruiter checks everything out. He tells the governor where to go. He's somebody who uses him right.

THE DOWRY

With the competition for foreign investment intensifying, other states began to discuss what Tennessee was offering foreign investors. Still smarting from the loss of Nissan and a number of other companies, one Georgia official asked: "How much of the state did Tennessee give away? Tennessee gave roads, bridges, and local airport improvements for corporate aircraft." Others accused the state of giving tax holidays to Japanese companies as a way to beat the competition. "Georgia gives no tax holidays and never will," said Carol Martel, of the Atlanta Chamber of Commerce:

> It's a constitutional issue. There was a big fuss when we lost Nissan. We had worked for two to three years. Georgia was one of the two probable sites. Why didn't they choose Georgia? We've never gotten an adequate answer. We lost a gasket manufacturer when we lost Nissan; Japanese suppliers like to be within 150 miles of the main plant. That's why Nissan was such a great loss. It broke our momentum.

Chattanooga vehemently denied the charges leveled against the state and their city, citing other factors for Komatsu's choice. In their case, the list is long. The site visits, for example, convinced the Japanese that Chattanooga's resources met their needs. Mayor Roberts ticked off his city's major assets, leading with the high level of compliance with federal environmental laws—especially important to Japanese heavy manufacturing companies, who fear extensive litigation. "We have made significant strides in air pollution," he said. "We are the only attainment area in Tennessee. This means less hassle and less expense for the company later on." The city also has provided excess capacity in its waste-water-treatment plant, another important consideration for industries trying to avoid potential problems.

There's no denying, however, that a long engagement served Komatsu well, as the package of incentives offered by state and city officials grew fatter with each site visit. By the end of a five-year period, the dowry included tax-free loans, federal grants, property-tax deferrals, employee training programs, the promise of reducing import tariffs by moving Komatsu into a subzone of a foreign-trade zone, and special Japanese educational programs.[2] Even with all these inducements, "Tennessee doesn't have much to give away," according to Dave Flessner, business editor of the *Chattanooga Times*. "There are no property tax abatements and taxes are very low. Tennessee has no income tax, and no venture capital fund. It is a low-wage, right-to-work state."

The most important inducement was announced in 1985, when the Hamilton County Industrial Development Board agreed to issue $20 million worth of industrial development bonds. These low-interest, tax-exempt bonds would be used by Komatsu to buy the plant and the surrounding land, to modernize it, and to finance the purchase of equipment. The advantage of these bonds, backed by two major Japanese banks, is that since the interest is not taxed by the federal government, a borrower's rate runs 3–4 percent lower than rates charged on conventional loans.[3]

Komatsu's expectation that the company would be able to double the $10 million limit on the bonds and still qualify for tax exemptions and property-tax deferrals was based on the expectation of an $800,000 federal UDAG grant. To everyone's surprise, the grant was denied later in the year on the grounds that Chattanooga's economy was too healthy and its unemployment rate too low to qualify for UDAG aid. It was the company's only disappointment and, significantly, the only part of the package outside state and local control. In fact, one of Chattanooga's major attractions for Komatsu was its ability to attract UDAG money; the city had received more UDAGs in the past decade than any other city its size.

The local tax package offered to Komatsu also included property-tax deferrals. The nonprofit county bond board would own the land on which the plant was located and lease it back to the company, thereby exempting the plant from paying property taxes immediately. Normally, companies make payments in lieu of taxes equal to what they would pay if they owned the plant and the land. Komatsu specifically requested that the county board ask for the authority to own property so that the company could defer its tax payments.

County executive Dalton Roberts emphasized that this was a tax deferral, not a tax holiday:

Komatsu was looking for tax incentives to ease the strain of their capital investment. Under Tennessee law, there are no tax holidays. We negotiated a ten-year program. For the first three years there are no taxes; the second three years 100 percent taxes; and the next three years 200 percent taxes. We can give tax deferrals, but not forgiveness.

(Roberts, a former songwriter and special-education teacher, made the Hit Parade in 1972 with the song "Don't Pay the Ransom.")

Chattanooga was attractive to the Japanese for a variety of other reasons cited by key players in the Komatsu effort. The city is home to Chattanooga State, a university famous for its robotics and productivity center. Together with the Baylor School, the university will sponsor job training specifically for Komatsu with state help. "The state offered a half a million dollars for a job training effort," said David Major. "Actually any state would do that for any industry. We just know how to market it better." The city also boasts about its location on the Tombigbee Canal. Considered by many members of Congress an unnecessary boondoggle—Senator Daniel P. Moynihan, New York Democrat, has called it "cloning the Mississippi River"—no one in Chattanooga questions its advantages: It will cut 700 miles off the trip to the Gulf of Mexico, thereby reducing transportation costs for companies dependent on a river network.

Komatsu was also impressed with the city's work force. Chattanooga, formerly one of the country's leading industrial centers, has a skilled work force, recently hit by cutbacks at the local nuclear plant and the Tennessee Valley Authority. Whether or not they were deliberately kept out of sight in deference to the Japanese aversion to organized labor is anyone's guess, but unions were virtually absent from the joint effort to woo Komatsu. "The unions are no longer in a bargaining position," explained Mayor Roberts. "We told the unions, 'You can't organize anybody unless we get jobs here.' "

Quality-of-life considerations are also important to Japanese investors. Members of site-selection teams are usually young and look especially hard at a city's school system and its residential neighborhoods. As a rule, Japanese executives send their children back to Japan after three years in American schools. "They are gentle people," said David Major. "They wanted to talk about golf and the cost of living. The availability of golf is very important to them. They are ecstatic about coming here."

THE FUTURE

In the courtship ritual Komatsu also played the role of suitor, wooing American customers away from Caterpillar, its major competitor. Komatsu had already moved up to second place in its share of the world market and was moving swiftly to close the gap. "Komatsu targeted Caterpillar years ago as its number-one enemy," commented Clyde Prestowitz, the chief adviser on Japanese industry to the secretary of commerce. "Komatsu may well beat Caterpillar in Caterpillar's backyard. Is it appropriate from a national point of view to cheer about that?"

To Prestowitz, it was readily apparent that Komatsu was operating with fewer constraints and decidedly more advantages than its competitor:

> The Japanese government aided Komatsu; Komatsu functions with lower wages, more flexible work rules, and without union labor. Did Tennessee offer Caterpillar the same incentives? Why not? Caterpillar can't build a plant without union labor. Why don't we modify some of our labor laws and enable Caterpillar to compete in the U.S. and worldwide.

For now, Caterpillar is unconcerned. "There is no competitive disadvantage from Komatsu," responded Tim Elder, government affairs representative for Caterpillar, who added, "Komatsu's manufacturing processes are a decade behind ours. They have no technological lead on us. They're just smart business people who control costs; their labor rate is one-half ours; and they have had an undervalued currency." Many industry analysts agree, but warn that while Caterpillar will probably survive, many smaller companies in the industry will fold under the pressure of the increasing number of mergers and acquisitions that inevitably accompany an industry shake-up.

For a number of reasons, the tractor industry ran in the red from 1982 to 1985, Caterpillar lost close to $1 billion and saw its labor force reduced from 89,000 to 54,000. But the company still has the resources to recoup some of those losses. For example, when Caterpillar was forced to cut labor costs, the company began to manufacture overseas. Its lift-truck subsidiary in Mentor, Ohio, which employed 2,700 people as recently as 1979, closed to make way for a new facility to be built in South Korea under a ten-year joint venture with Daewoo Heavy Industries. And in 1986, in a form of turnabout is fair play, the company announced it would expand a joint venture in Japan with Mitsubishi Heavy Industries Ltd., pitting it against Komatsu Ltd. on Komatsu's home turf. In a pattern reminiscent of the auto industry, American companies are moving jobs offshore, while foreign investors move in to take up the slack.

On closer scrutiny, the Komatsu case reveals some of the realities and the ironies of foreign investment. While Tennessee justly cheers the promise of 250 jobs, who is mourning Caterpillar's loss of 35,000 jobs? Few question the enormous effort and substantial public monies poured into the courtship of Komatsu, except for the realization that nothing comparable is going on at the national level to save the American tractor industry. It is a conundrum of the American federal system that the states have taken the lead on the issue of foreign investment while at the national level public policymakers remain curiously inactive.

For its part, Komatsu has been very honest with its American suitors. The company has openly admitted its fear of rising protectionism as one of the major reasons for its decision to invest in an American plant. It was a prudent move; for when a company moves onto American soil, it is treated exactly like an American company—probably somewhat better. Every public official, from the governor on down, supports its activities, lobbies on its behalf, and becomes its personal political protector. Some states are more welcoming than others, and Komatsu was fortunate in its choice of Tennessee.

Komatsu was also politically shrewd in choosing Tennessee. The decision to spread its investment around was a political decision based on the company's knowledge of American politics. At the time Komatsu began its initial forays into Tennessee, the state's senior senator was Howard Baker, then majority leader of the Senate and one of the most powerful men in the country, while Bill Brock, a wealthy industrialist from Chattanooga, was the country's top trade negotiator. A large contingent of Japanese companies in Tennessee, it was felt, would provide an extra insurance policy against federal protectionist legislation, plus added political clout in the quest for government grants. In fact, when he was U.S. trade representative, Brock encouraged the Japanese to produce more of their products in the United States to deflect protectionist pressures.

To a much greater extent than in the United States, Japanese industrial needs take note of political considerations. While Japanese industrialists reach business decisions with scrupulous attention to detail, just as great an effort goes into developing strategies for political stability. The Komatsu decision demonstrated the company's clearly defined sense of planning and how critical that is in ensuring a secure future for a foreign investor.

CHAPTER 6

Succeeding Where
Firestone Failed

Japanese Management at the
Bridgestone Plant

Bridgestone seems to listen. With Firestone you were just a
machine that worked eight hours.
—*Ricky Halliburton, production worker*

We have applied . . . management tools . . . learned from the
Americans. The technology was born in this country. There is
nothing mysterious about it. The Japanese are just more thorough.
—*Kazuo Ishikure, president,*
Bridgestone Manufacturing (U.S.A.), Inc.

In 1980, the 700 workers at the Firestone tire plant in La
Vergne, Tennessee, lived in daily fear of losing their jobs. The
economy was shaky, and the plant, which manufactured truck
radial tires, was struggling to keep its doors open in the face of
enormous obstacles: a labor-management conflict that was doomed
from the start, including a breakdown in communications, energies diverted from production to conflict, senseless battles, and
inevitably, economic defeat for all; a prime rate that hovered
around 13 percent; and a reputation still tarnished from the
"Firestone 500" scandals, recalling the company's manufacture
of defective and unsafe tires.

"We never knew on a day-to-day basis whether the doors
would be locked or not," recalled Ricky Halliburton, a former
Firestone employee who now works in production at the
Bridgestone plant. "Now nothing is guaranteed, but job security
is better than before."

"The Firestone closing was due 90 percent to management
problems and 10 percent the economy," added Billy Sellars,

who has led the 620-member union local at the plant since it was organized in 1979. Muscular and well tanned, Sellars wore a cap with the label "vice-president, Local 1055, United Rubber Workers" and a T-shirt emblazoned with "Howard's Honda" on the front.

Sellars, Halliburton, and another co-worker chatted informally about their lives at Firestone and how it compared with working for Bridgestone, a Japanese multinational corporation that acquired the La Vergne Firestone plant on January 10, 1983.

To Sellars, the difference between the two companies is "the difference between dark and daylight. Firestone didn't know how to build tractor and truck tires," explained Sellars. "Management wouldn't listen to production people; they felt they knew it all."

In contrast, Bridgestone immediately started quality work circles at the plant, encouraging workers to participate in decision making. "Bridgestone's attitude is the more ideas the better," added Halliburton. "The majority of workers are in favor of them when they see something accomplished." Like other Japanese companies, which pioneered in this innovative technique, Bridgestone valued employee involvement; the company knew from experience that it boosted morale and often resulted in money-saving improvements in production. "Bridgestone seems to listen," he said. "With Firestone you were just a machine that worked eight hours."

"It's unbelievable how far we've come," added Leslie Holt, a young department supervisor. "Firestone didn't invest a lot of dollars. We've made remarkable advances. The Firestone 500 case showed what their management was like; they knew those tires wouldn't ride."

The situation under Firestone appeared to have deteriorated rapidly. "The management went through several campaigns to break the union," said Sellars:

> There were hard feelings. The management would hold meetings telling people they'd lose their jobs. Every two, three months there were warnings here about money lost and threats about the plant closing. You didn't know if you'd have a job in a couple of months. We got a plant closure notice when Bridgestone was already in the picture. Morale was very bad.

Plant managers at Firestone operated under a highly centralized management system, with very little power and flexibility to make timely decisions on their own. "With Firestone," said

Halliburton, "everything had to go back to Akron. Even the payroll was in Akron. Bridgestone says, 'As far as we're concerned, this plant is here.' Of course, big decisions go back to Tokyo."

Bridgestone took the lessons of Firestone's union troubles seriously and tried hard to repair the damage. They replaced several unpopular managers, brought in a management consulting firm on a regular basis, tried to mediate conflicts before they exploded, and instituted a job training program at all levels of the company. "We're still not satisfied with a few of the people in management," said Sellars, "but at least they've made changes. It's taken a while, but it's getting done. They put a man in personnel we like to work with."

A sense of accountability and control distinguished the Bridgestone management system. The company controlled the managers, not vice versa, a development that did not go unnoticed by the workers. "Morale has improved, although we still have grievances," said Sellars. "Some still want to run the plant the old Firestone way," but Bridgestone had its subtle methods of dealing with them. "Bridgestone has downgraded some managers to supervisors. They wind up quitting. The Japanese are also big on training. The training is not limited. It is extended to top management, and they ain't got no choice."

The Americans agreed that they also learned patience from their Japanese employers. "The Americans want to get something done today," reflected Ricky Halliburton. "They don't want to think about it. With the Japanese, it takes them a month; they want to make sure it's the right decision. I've learned from them."

The bottom line for the three men was job security, which Bridgestone imported along with other features of the Japanese management style. "There are still only fourteen people left on the street after the initial Firestone layoff," said Sellars, who added that he was committed to bringing them back. "The Japanese do things very slowly. The philosophy in Japan is when we bring somebody back it is a lifetime job. I feel a lot more comfortable today than I did with Firestone."

How the Japanese employees feel about locating their plants and their families in the United States is another matter. "I asked a Japanese adviser here, Isaac Motohashi, how the Japanese felt about Bridgestone taking work out of their country to the United States," recalled Ricky Halliburton. "He wouldn't give me an answer.

"I was glad to see them," added Halliburton. "I'd be without a job. They put food on my table."

DEMING'S LEGACY: THE AMERICAN ROOTS OF JAPANESE MANAGEMENT

In the late 1940s, an American statistician named W. Edwards Deming warned that unless American companies abandoned their obsolete management methods, they would soon go the way of the dinosaurs. Far ahead of their time, Deming's ideas were ignored by the captains of American industry and adopted with enthusiasm by the Japanese. Now in his mid-eighties, Deming is regarded as the man who taught the Japanese quality control, an honor the Japanese acknowledge with an annual Deming Prize, awarded to the Japanese company that has achieved the highest level of quality.[1]

A prime example of Deming in practice is Bridgestone, whose president, Kazuo Ishikure, fully credits the American management expert for his company's success:

> We have applied two management tools, both learned from the Americans: "Management by Objectives," and "Statistical Quality Control." We have total quality control. Since Bridgestone acquired the plant, we have used those tools. It is easier for Americans to understand. The technology was born in this country. There is nothing mysterious about it. We followed what Firestone had been doing. The Japanese are just more thorough.

Interviewed in his office at the Bridgestone plant, Ishikure was enthusiastic about his job and forthcoming about his management philosophy. Flanked by two public relations advisers in tailored suits, he was dressed like his workers in a red-trimmed beige windbreaker jacket, with "Ishikure" on a nameplate pinned to his chest. "He usually wears a suit and tie; the windbreaker was for your benefit," joked one of the workers, out of the president's earshot.

The symbolism of Ishikure's informal clothing reflects the philosophy of many Japanese companies that followed Deming's advice about removing artificial symbols of hierarchy. Gone are the "perks" that erect artificial barriers. Top executives dress to blend in on the shop floor; they also eat in the company cafeteria, wash in ordinary restrooms, and take their chances on a parking spot.

A perfect example of the Japanese philosophy of lifetime employment, Ishikure has been with Bridgestone and its international division since 1952. With a background in marketing and law, he started in the company's export division as a roving salesman in Asia. He was the first Bridgestone representative in Bangkok and was quickly promoted to market director of the first postwar Bridgestone plant in Singapore. Affable and very articulate—he speaks perfect English—Ishikure was in charge of the entire Bridgestone international operation by 1983, when the company bought Firestone. Although his position in production was at Bridgestone, he had worked in over a hundred countries by the time he arrived in Tennessee. The decision to bring in a chief executive of Ishikure's experience and standing showed how high a premium the company placed on its first major American investment.

Ishikure's management strategy relied on experience, plus a painstaking review and reversal of Firestone's mistakes. "We know the differences between us and Firestone," he pointed out. "The tires look alike, but the methods are different. Our survey showed that the Firestone truck radial tires had a poor image. We decided to improve the quality with the five 'Ms':

1. **Machines.** "Machine failures were a target. We changed 530 machines in two years. We've converted to Bridgestone specifications."
2. **Materials.** "We changed the materials to those only approved by Bridgestone in Japan and tested here and in Japan. We send an audit team to the suppliers before the materials are tested here."
3. **Methods.** "We use Bridgestone management methods."
4 and 5. **Manpower and Morale.** "The first year, we sent union executives to Japan. With Firestone, their relationship was not good. We realized the importance of improving it. We noticed a big gulf between staff and management. Supervisors received training from an outside group in human relations, including motivation, communications, and counseling. The company is reviewing the results, and the survey will determine how we will proceed."

Ishikure immediately addressed the plant's major problems: poor communications and lack of accountability. His first move was to tighten procedures by introducing a more systematic and timely reporting system. "I issued a policy/statement/budget for the first half of 1985," he said, pulling out a large red book filled with data. "I make this presentation twice a year, where I explain company policy to all the employees. This book includes production schedules. The managers implement the plan; soon the foremen and supervisors will have implementation responsibilities.''

Accountability has reached new levels of importance under the new management system. Ishikure has fixed goals in mind and expects his subordinates to perform according to those standards. ''I expect managers to improve the material flow,'' he explained, ''to increase machine conversions, and to improve safety. I've attached numbers to these objectives.''

Success in a system like this means that the participants all have to speak the same language, and that doesn't mean Japanese. It means communicating the material in Ishikure's red book to everyone so that misunderstandings are minimized and a shared consensus is reached. ''When I came, there were no uniform measurements,'' recalled Ishikure. ''I thought it was necessary to have uniform measures. If there are no fixed definitions, people are saying different things.''

Communications reach a new level of importance in multinational corporations, where many different subsidiaries are forced to interact with each other and with the home office. ''I decided how many people had to be employed to make one ton of rubber,'' said Ishikure. ''Then we compare it to one of our plants in Japan. For some departments, the measures are how many tires a day; for others, how many tons of rubber they mix. We have to have the same measurements. Now when people talk production, they know the definition.''

The company reached a milestone in early 1985 when it produced its one millionth tire. In two years, the company tripled its volume of production and doubled its productivity; the company produces approximately twenty-two hundred units a day. At a ceremony celebrating the event, the company distributed over a thousand ''Thanks a million'' T-shirts to workers at the plant.

The new system is streamlined but not draconian. Employees do not seem fearful of being fired if their quotas are not reached; in fact, Bridgestone has kept virtually all of the 700 Firestone employees and added 400 more in the first two years of operation. By 1986, the company had rehired nearly all of the 441 workers laid off by Firestone. (Despite the careful attention its leadership had accorded labor-management relations, the company was not immune to labor problems; in December–January 1986, the plant faced a month-long strike by its maintenance workers. Although the strikers picketed the Bridgestone plant, they were in fact employees of the Allied Maintenance Corporation, a subcontractor of Bridgestone.)

Running the plant twenty-four hours a day with four shifts, Bridgestone has increased production by 300 percent and significantly reduced absenteeism, a major problem during the Firestone years. "Professionalism and quality control make the difference" in motivating employees to higher levels of performance, according to Ishikure, who gives managers substantial responsibility for quality control.

Neither does there appear to be any resentment or xenophobia among the workers about working for Japanese managers, perhaps because there are so few and they are rotated so quickly. "Our policy is to reduce the number of Japanese," said Ishikure:

> Initially, we needed more Japanese technicians and engineers. The average stay of a Japanese executive is four years. The top executives of the company will remain Japanese; the executive vice-president is Japanese; so are three other vice-presidents. It is Bridgestone policy to keep the top executives Japanese. The company is 100 percent Japanese owned.

Tight Japanese control is also maintained at the multinational level; the entire twenty-six-member board of directors is Japanese.

THORNS IN THE ROSE BED

As flexible as they've been in adjusting to American practices, Japanese managers have stood firm in certain areas. Their use of incentives is a typical example of a cross-cultural difference that American workers find hard to understand and accept. The Japanese feel that work is its own reward and that monetary incentives are somewhat demeaning. Needless to say, Bridgestone's American employees object strongly, but to no avail; without evidence that it has hurt production, their Japanese employers see no basis for change.

"Firestone would give you $5,000 if you saved them $100,000," said Sellars. "The Japanese give you $100 to $300 if you save them $500,000. They say it's the recognition that's important, not the money. We've had problems with that, particularly when somebody has a real good suggestion. We had one guy who didn't even take the $50 in protest."

The American workers also struggle to understand the Japanese attitude toward work, which stands in marked contrast to their own. "For the Japanese, their jobs are number one. Here religion and family come first," said Sellars, "at least in my family.

"The Japanese don't have much to do after work," he continued. "They live around the plant. Here people have hobbies. Mine is woodwork. At four o'clock, I'm ready to get out. There [in Japan], they stay after work to write suggestions. They learned awful fast about American workers going home."

The Japanese attitude toward work seems heartless at times to Americans. An incident occurred at the plant that accentuated the gulf between the cultures. A Japanese adviser, grief-stricken by the death of a sister, decided to return home to attend the funeral and comfort his family. The company refused to pay his travel expenses and told him if he wished to return home he would have to foot the bill himself. Shocked by the company's callous attitude, the American workers organized a fund drive and collected the money to send him home.

The incident also highlighted the close personal relationships that had developed between Japanese and American workers. Efforts on both sides have continued to produce results: The Americans find the Japanese very friendly, and eager to take part in community life, while traditional American hospitality has made the Japanese feel very much at home in Tennessee.

"It's no bed of roses," concluded Ricky Halliburton. "There's still some thorns. But there's no comparison with regard to the product or the efficiency of the plant."

MAKING IT WORK

Initially, Bridgestone's American subsidiary was just a network of branch offices, headquartered in California. Before the Tennessee acquisition, the company had already cornered a large share of the truck-radial-tire market; with 10 percent of the total market share, the company ranked third in the replacement market. Bridgestone is Japan's leading tire maker and the fourth largest in the world.

From their network of distributorships, Bridgestone's leaders received their first intelligence about impending legislation that threatened to restrict future trade. From feasibility studies initiated in the 1970s, the company also realized that to increase their market share above 10 percent, they would have to acquire their own manufacturing plant in the United States. In the first two years of production they were proved correct, and their share of the market rose to 12 percent.

But the initial impetus was their fear of protective tariffs, and they acted with an urgency that was uncharacteristic of Japanese decision makers. "We heard rumors from our own dealers that protective legislation was forthcoming," said Ishikure. "Cars, electrical goods, were already under control. Tires were not under any restrictions at that time. The dealers were concerned that in the future the government would take action."

Involved with Bridgestone's venture from the outset, Ishikure ensured a continuity that has been important to the company's success. While the company was deliberating the issue of where to locate, its officers received a proposal from Firestone. After checking the plant, Bridgestone decided to purchase the 30-acre building and 163-acre parcel of land.

The conditions imposed on Bridgestone were onerous; accepting them indicated the company's eagerness to consummate the deal. "Firestone concentrated its resources when they sold this plant," explained Ishikure. "One of the conditions of the sale was that Bridgestone was to manufacture Firestone truck radial tires for Firestone under the Firestone brand. Now we manufacture Bridgestone and Firestone, and we sell only to two customers: Bridgestone of California and Firestone. The FTC [Federal Trade Commission] cleared the agreement."

The company soon found itself in the curious position of competing with itself. In effect, said Ishikure, "now our sister company, Bridgestone of California, is competing with Firestone. This was a condition of the purchase and the sale. If either party is not satisfied, then either can with one year's notice back out." Slowly, the company seems to be catching up with itself and working its way out of a bad bargain. "In 1983, we made only Firestone tires. We started Bridgestone tires in March 1984. We gradually increased production. We add on two sizes every month. Now the ratio has changed; we manufacture more Bridgestone than Firestone."

In contrast to Bridgestone, which was saddled temporarily with the Firestone name, some Japanese companies prefer to use the American brand name if they can profit from that firm's reputation. This is true of companies that have acquired outright ownership as well as joint ventures. At the Yokogawa electronics plant in Shenandoah, Georgia, piles of blue-and-white boxes off to the side of the plant floor bear the familiar General Electric label. Part of Yokogawa's deal to buy five GE product lines allowed the company to use the GE name for four years. "The whole industry knows we bought out GE," said James Elliott, Jr., director of employee relations. "Yet the instruments are made by Yokogawa." In this way, the consumer thinks he's "buying American," while the company has a grace period in which to develop name recognition in the United States.

Bridgestone paid Firestone $52 million the first year and lost an additional $45 million in the first three years of operation, according to Mr. Ishikure. "We're not making a profit yet," he said. "The Bridgestone guideline for overseas investment is that there should be some profit from the third year to offset past losses in five years. In the future, 10 percent profit is reasonable for repatriation. In order for the company to grow, we have to grow."

THE ROLE OF THE STATE

There is no question that Bridgestone benefited from extensive cooperation with state government. Informed about the initial negotiations between the two companies in 1981, Tennessee kept in touch throughout Bridgestone's initial site visits that year. In 1982, the governor visited the company and assured its leaders that the state would do everything in its power to help.

The state delivered on its promises, followed by the county, which granted the company low-cost development bonds. On a continuing basis, the state sends advisers to the company and has awarded subsidies for job training that have enabled Bridgestone to send over fifty employees to Japan. Most important, the state acts as an intermediary between the company and the federal government, often lobbying on its behalf. "The state government presents our point of view to Washington," noted Ishikure. "This year [1985] on steel quotas—the company imports some of its materials from Japan—the state went to Washington and explained our situation. State government officials were very helpful."

Ishikure said he was very happy in Nashville, and so was his wife, who was "a traditional Japanese wife, who spoke no English, didn't drive, or even know how to write checks." She has "learned to use money machines," he added, laughing, and has made friends who take her out. His children are grown and live in Japan. "Nashville is one of the best places to live, and I've been in over a hundred countries. The people are friendly and hospitable. The people and the state government were very receptive. Bridgestone came on a white horse and saved jobs. I don't like to live in a big city like Tokyo. It will be sad when I have to leave."

THE JAPANESE MIRACLE

The Bridgestone rescue mission showed how Japanese capital combined with management skill saved a company from extinction and its surrounding region from recession. Bridgestone stands as a typical example of the enthusiasm of Japanese managers for the application of statistical quality-control methods. Japanese executives have been schooled in the Deming method since 1950, when Deming initiated his four-day seminars in Japan, and the results today are readily apparent. Deming's belief that poor quality was 85 percent a management problem and 15 percent a worker problem inspired a highly efficient manufacturing system in Japan that is only beginning to catch on in the United States, especially in troubled industries.

But the Japanese "miracle" goes deeper than sound management and shrewd investment strategy; its success springs from a supportive government environment, known for its vigorous promotion of industrial growth. Japanese companies, which have matured under that system, expect no less when they invest in the United States; in fact, they demand it as a condition of investment. In this, the best of both possible worlds, they now benefit from government support in Japan as well as the United States.

That Bridgestone succeeded where Firestone failed is also noteworthy purely as a corporate achievement. But Bridgestone's success also owed much to active government intervention at critical stages of its development. In Japan, it benefited from the close business-government relationship for which that country is known. The Japanese utilize a variety of strategies to help industries increase their share of the global marketplace, among them: protective tariffs, barriers against foreign investment, research-and-development aid, direct subsidies, and a long-term, pro-business antitrust climate.

Critics of foreign investment credit Japan's methods of financing selected industries for tipping the scales in that country's favor. The Toshiba company, for example, does all of its long-term borrowing back in Japan, according to Robert Trager, vice-president and general manager of the TV division at Lebanon, Tennessee. Trager indicated that since the Japanese prime interest rate was lower than that of the United States, it would not be advantageous to borrow money from American banks. The Japanese government works hard at keeping down the cost of capital; indeed, when the government is really interested in giving a corporation an edge in world competition, it has been known to lower the interest rate for that company down to 2 percent. (Conversely, when interest rates decline in the United States, some foreign multinationals borrow from American banks, leading to charges that they are drying up capital that would otherwise be available to U.S. companies.)

Bridgestone's achievements are also a tribute to government intervention in the United States at the state, local, and federal levels. When tallied up, the pattern of government interventions on Bridgestone's behalf looks as if the United States practices industrial policy for foreign multinationals while preaching free market philosophy at home. The FTC cleared the Firestone-Bridgestone agreement; the state, representing Bridgestone's interests, lobbied the federal government against steel import quotas; and the state and local governments provided a package of local incentives to help the company over its initial hurdles.

Bridgestone brought a myriad of benefits to Tennessee and to the United States. It brought labor-management peace to a company, saved 700 jobs and created 400 more, and eased a community's fears. In almost all respects, the company is regarded as an American one; and certainly in the eyes of the political system, it is treated as American. The only differences are that top management will always be Japanese and that ultimately the profits will go back to Japan. At this point, the company is not making a profit, but when it does, it expects only 10 percent of that profit to be reinvested in the company and 90 percent to return home.

Bridgestone deserves much credit for devoting so much of its resources to better communications and systematic management; Japan also deserves credit for providing the company with a stable financial environment. Americans should look more closely behind the Japanese miracle and compete on all the levels that have made the Japanese companies more competitive.

CHAPTER 7

Rescued by German Technology

The Egenolfs of Indiana

Foreign investment made us more competitive.
                    —*Jim Egenolf, vice-president,*
              Koenig & Bauer/Egenolf Machine, Inc.

Nestled in the heart of a run-down Indianapolis neighborhood stands a factory the size of eight football fields. Koenig & Bauer/ Egenolf, a recently merged West German and American company, fits right into the landscape, almost inconspicuous among the small gray-and-white one-family homes. Symbols at the entrance to the plant proudly display its dual nationality: two flags, German and American, flank the doorway, along with a sign that proclaims, "Working together is winning together." Pictures of the German chairman of the board, Dr. Hans Bolza-Schuenemann, along with the firm's American president and vice-president, Joe Egenolf and Jim Egenolf, also appear at the entrance.

Before merging with Koenig & Bauer in 1979, the Egenolfs ran a small family-owned business that repaired printing presses. The firm was founded in 1900 by their father, George, a remarkable man of German descent who according to his son Jim won an Olympic gold medal for hammer throwing. Of his seven sons, only his twins, Joe and Jim, remained with the family business. The company's present leaders, they alternate the presidency every year.

Merging with the Germans saved the firm from stagnation and revived its technological capacity, say the Egenolfs. In the late 1970s the company had reached a plateau: It was limited to repair work, topped out at forty employees, and was too small to branch out into international markets. Ambitious to expand, the Egenolf brothers began to explore the available possibilities. Money was no problem. "We could have raised the money ourselves," said

Jim Egenolf in an interview on the plant floor. Dressed in the uniform of the plant workers, dark blue pants and a light blue shirt, Egenolf talked as he worked, bent over a machine, hammering away at a steel rod. "We merged more for expertise. Also, this was a small business. There were tax disadvantages. We were not protected. If one of us died, the other would have lost the business."

At the same time Jim Egenolf and his brother were looking for ways to expand, the German firm of Koenig & Bauer was actively seeking a toehold in the United States. It was a perfect match. Like Egenolf, Koenig & Bauer was a family-owned firm, passed on from father to son, and anxious to retain that basic character. In their search for a company to do their U.S. service work, they looked for a compatible counterpart: an old, reliable family enterprise, preferably of German origin.

The oldest printing-press manufacturer in the world, Koenig & Bauer was founded in 1817 by Friedrich Koenig and his partner, Andreas Bauer. Koenig invented the world's first mechanized printing process, the cylinder press. It was hailed as a historic achievement the night it was used to publish several thousand copies of *The Times* of London. It was a genuine technological breakthrough and a vast improvement over the wooden toggle press, a manual method developed 350 years before by Gutenberg and used ever since. In a classic case of well-timed government intervention, Koenig & Bauer moved their business from England to Germany after the Bavarian government helped them find a manufacturing site in the old Oberzell monastery near Wuerzburg.

Destroyed by bombs during World War II, the company recovered to become one of the world's leading manufacturers of monetary presses, sheet-feed presses, and web presses. Its 2,000 employees in Germany make presses for such well-known American publishers as the National Geographic Society and the Times-Mirror Company. In fact, the Times-Mirror Company brokered the merger with the Egenolfs.

"The merger came about when my brother Joe was in California," recalled Jim Egenolf. "The head of the Times-Mirror Company introduced him to the president of Koenig & Bauer, who was also in Los Angeles at the time. The Koenig & Bauer people flew in in August, and we merged soon afterward." The merger split the company's ownership, with the Egenolfs retaining the controlling interest at 51 percent. "We have total autonomy," said Egenolf.

Added resources and new technology gave the company a new lease on life, and it grew rapidly. "We now have seven crews on the road and the largest lathe in Indianapolis," said Egenolf proudly. "The governor says we were the best-kept secret in the United States. Periodically, he brings people in to encourage them and show them how it's done." The new firm jumped from 40 to 115 workers and bought enough adjacent land to expand its plant size to ten times its former capacity.

Their new partners also brought state-of-the-art technology to the company in the form of the "Compacta S," an enormous bright blue printer that enabled the company to assume a lot more business. New business also came along with the merger: the Egenolfs became Koenig & Bauer's U.S. representative and were introduced to their German partner's European clients. The company has also expanded its capabilities from repair to some manufacturing and assembly work. Ten percent of the Compacta S, for example, is manufactured in Indiana.

The new company also shed its union. "The employees decided to decertify in 1980–81," said Joe DiPietro, director of employee relations. "This is a highly overtime shop. It meant $30 to $40 a month in union dues. The men decided they didn't want the union—the International Association of Machinists and Aerospace Workers. They felt they had been pretty well treated by management. We meet with them twice a month."

Reminiscent of Japanese management methods, the company runs on a cooperative, nonhierarchical model in which unions are viewed as obstacles to labor-management relationships. "This company is run on the family idea," said DiPietro:

> It is not a coat-and-tie operation. Joe and Jim wear work shirts; they work with their hands. They work with the men; they know their family problems. The men see the president of the company sweeping around the presses. If Joe comes in from a trip at three in the morning, he may plow out the parking lot. The men know when we hire them that we don't have job classifications.

A former high school principal and football coach, Mr. DiPietro worked for the plant part-time before assuming his present position. "I was filling out a W-2 form one day for a worker who couldn't read or write," he recalled, "and who was making more money than I was as a high school principal. I figured it was time to make a career change."

Only four or five Germans work at the plant at any given time. One of them, Hartmut Scheitz, the assembly supervisor on the

Compacta S, was forthcoming about his experiences since his transfer in 1982. "Things are slower here," he said. "The company only does repair work. The learning process is slow. You have to start from scratch. I had to make special tools; we can't import everything."

Scheitz has been with the company for twenty-six years, an unremarkable statement except for the fact that he is only forty years old. Apprenticed to the company by his mother when he was only fourteen, he illustrates one of the very real differences between Germany and the United States: the lower percentages of students who complete high school and college. Koenig & Bauer trained Scheitz as a machine mechanic and assumed full charge of his future education. This consisted of going to the company school one day a week and working four days a week until he reached the age of seventeen, when he took a government-controlled test that certified him as a trained mechanic. His loyalty to the company is strong.

Scheitz made some hard choices in coming to the United States. To him, the greatest sacrifice was relinquishing the extensive social benefits that come to every employee of a German firm in Germany. These include six weeks' paid vacation, generous unemployment compensation, and medical benefits far superior to those of the United States. But Scheitz says the transfer was worth it. "Before coming here, I set up presses all around the world. I was away from home all the time. The reason I'm here is that I'm home every night. The benefits are not as good, but my salary is higher."

Not all German companies follow the Koenig & Bauer model. The German executives at the Bleyle company in Georgia keep their benefits even when they are transferred to the United States. This makes them happier but creates real morale problems when their American colleagues watch them depart for six-week vacations while they are stuck with the traditional fortnight.

Jake Klosterman, the chief engineer and plant manager, talked about some of the adjustments of the German and American workers. Klosterman, who has a degree in industrial engineering from Ohio State and joined the company right after the merger specifically to work with the Compacta S press, said:

Germans are very apartment oriented. They live in tight groups. We have three German fitters here now. For some, it is their first time away from home. The first week, the staff takes them home for dinner. The second week, the guys in the shop take them home. By the third week, they have a busier social schedule than mine. We actually have more problems with our own people when they go over there. They complain about the transportation. They're used to having their own car, and they're not used to town living. There you have to go home before the last bus leaves. They also complain about the food.

Many of the workers also find it difficult to convert to the metric system, according to Randy Rose, a black foreman who has been with the company for nineteen years. Jim Egenolf agreed that converting to metric was difficult and said the company encouraged the workers to take classes in metric and to learn German. "The only real problem is communication," he added. "There are different names for the same thing. A bevel gear here is a steering wheel in Germany."

The Egenolfs did not seek assistance from the state or the city of Indianapolis when they were looking for ways to expand their plant. After the merger, they received a bond from the city to buy a new building and CETA (Comprehensive Employment and Training Act) money from the federal government to retrain and upgrade their workers. Eager to bring the printing business back to Indiana, the state government provided funds to send workers back to Germany for training on the Compacta S press. "We'll send people overseas for training as long as the jobs remain here," said Mark Akers, director of the Industrial Development Division of the Indiana Department of Commerce.

In the final analysis, the Koenig & Bauer/Egenolf joint venture brought the company and its leaders into the major leagues. "The merger has made a big difference in my life," said Egenolf. "I never thought I'd be a world traveler, dealing in world financing. When you work outside the country you figure out what kind of currency you want to get paid in—deutsche marks, francs, etc. You can make a lot of money that way.

"Foreign investment made us competitive," continued Egenolf with a gleam in his eye. "We're now working on a $25 million sale in North Carolina. We are subcontracting with the Japanese to build small presses. They will be introduced at the newspaper convention in June. Now we will be able to compete with Rockwell, our biggest competitor. We're going to give them a run for their money."

Linking his father's athletic prowess and the firm's success, he concluded: "Selling equipment is like the Olympics. And like the Olympics, there's only one gold medal."

PART III

ISSUES OF
NATIONAL SOVEREIGNTY

CHAPTER 8

The "Juicing" of California
The Influence of Foreign Investors on State Tax Policy

Against the insidious wiles of foreign influence, the jealousy of a free people ought to be constantly awake, since history and experience prove that foreign influence is one of the most baneful foes of republican government.

—*George Washington, Farewell Address*

Everything we do is out in the open. It isn't big wads of money we're throwing around. It's simply to let the legislators know that we appreciate their support and make sure that we at least have an opportunity to talk to them.

—*Robert E. Dillon, executive vice-president, the Sony Corporation of America*

The growing political clout of foreign investors was dramatically demonstrated by the rousing finale of a successful ten-year state-by-state struggle to repeal the unitary tax.[1] This well-financed, heavily lobbied campaign provided ample evidence that foreign investors wielded even more political clout in state capitals than in Washington.

This state tax, based on a corporation's worldwide earnings, was fought by both U.S. and foreign multinationals, but it was the foreign investors who led the battle for repeal. The biggest holdout, California, faced with repeated threats of retaliatory action, repealed the tax in 1986 in a victory for the foreign multinational corporations and for the sixteen governments, led by Great Britain and Japan, that backed them in their long and difficult battle. Their victory showed anew that governors and state legislatures are no match for the massed political might of the foreign multinationals.

Paradoxes abounded. While other states scrambled to replace money lost under the federal budget-balancing bill, California's political leaders supported a measure that they knew could lead to an annual revenue loss of $300–$600 million. They claimed that the money would be replaced many times over by revenues generated by all the new investment that would come into the state after repeal, but that claim was based on nothing more concrete than the promises of the foreign multinationals.

Similarly, while states ordinarily resist outside interference from a neighboring state or from the federal government, California legislators welcomed lobbyists from London, Tokyo, Washington, Paris, and Rome. Those lobbyists swarmed the state capital, inundating legislators with threats, entreaties, and campaign contributions. By the time they declared victory, they had arrayed an impressive list of allies to help them press their cause, from President Reagan to the British Parliament.

"Just as the Japanese have studied our technology and come up with a better version, they've taken our lobbying techniques and used them in a better form," said Assemblyman Tom Hayden, a liberal Democrat who led the opposition to repealing the tax.

Supporters of repeal learned quickly the cardinal rule of winning in America: that whoever controls the formulation of an issue controls its outcome. Lobbyists from the foreign multinational corporations immediately staked out the parameters of the issue and defined its terms. They linked the state-tax issue to world trade, free markets, and future investment and soon convinced mayors and local officials. Ultimately, there was little difference between the arguments of Sony and the entreaties from the mayor of San Francisco. All linked California's economic future to unitary repeal.

Luck played an important part in their success. The complex issue provoked glazed eyes and ready yawns from the electorate, and this public indifference was helpful to the sponsors of the repeal. "There are not 500 people who are concerned about what I do or what the legislature does about the unitary," said State Senator Alfred Alquist, the sponsor of unitary repeal. "That's out of one and one-half million people. It's a wonder democracy works."

Alquist's sentiments were echoed by State Senate Minority Leader Jim Nielsen, who said he supported the repeal to get it over with so that the Senate could get on to other issues: "The reality is that the people don't care; the Republican caucus doesn't care; my constituents don't care. There is no compelling reason to get involved. The issues are not in the top twenty issues in the state, although it is very important." Nielsen tried unsuccessfully to link unitary repeal to greater trade access to Japanese markets.

California was the last major holdout among the six remaining states that still held on to the unitary method of taxation. Other states capitulated much faster, with Indiana holding the championship: Indiana repealed its unitary tax one day after Akio Morita, the chairman of the Sony Corporation, visited the governor and promised to locate two plants in the state if its legislature repealed the tax. In Florida, the governor called the legislature into a special session during Christmas week 1984 to enact the repeal. But Indiana and Florida paled in comparison to the investment dollars at stake in California. With more foreign investment than any other state in the country as of 1986, California was the stumbling block to tax savings that ran into the billions.

To outsiders, the unitary tax issue defied the laws of politics and common sense. But on closer inspection the issue revealed another dimension to foreign investment and its role in state and national politics. It showed that foreign investment wasn't going to be a free lunch; that foreign multinationals imported political influence along with their manufacturing plants and wouldn't hesitate to use that power to protect and enhance their investments—even if it meant controlling local tax policy. For their part, foreign investors learned that the American political system was as open to their influence as it was to their money; they could finally relax and settle comfortably into a new, more potent political role.

ORIGINS OF THE UNITARY TAX

The unitary tax is not a separate tax but a method of computing a corporation's state tax rate. Under this system, taxes are determined by a percentage of a company's worldwide profits, not by the income it earns in the state. If, for example, a company has 10 percent of its combined sales, property, and payroll in California, it would pay state income tax on 10 percent of its worldwide income, regardless of whether the company made any money in California.

The opposite of taxing a company by the unitary method is called "separate accounting"—it is also known as "arm's length" accounting—and it calculates a company's taxes on the basis of its receipts and costs as they apply only to its in-state activities. If a steel company, for example, had a steel factory in Minnesota and a coal-mining operation in North Dakota, "Minnesota would tax only the income reflected in the accounts of the [steel] factory," explained unitary tax expert Robert Tannenwald.[2]

In the early decades of the twentieth century, states preferred separate accounting, but the method soon proved unequal to the ingenuity of fast-developing multistate and multinational corporations. The potential for shifting income was too great, and companies quickly learned to take advantage of the system. A multinational corporation could easily shift numbers to one of its low-tax operations, say, in Zambia or Bangkok, in order to reduce its taxes in California.[3]

California caught on quicker than other states to the chicaneries possible in the separate accounting method. The state learned an object lesson from its experience with the railroads in the late nineteenth century. California discovered that the railroads were evading taxes by basing the income tax on the number of miles of track they ran in each state. In that way, the railroads paid most of their income to low-tax states like Nevada and Utah, where they had long stretches of track but few customers and profits, and less of it to high-tax, richer states like California.

In California, the unitary method was developed almost as a historical necessity, to ensure that the state got its fair share of corporate taxes. In addition to the railroads, which claimed they just ran tracks through the state, the movie industry argued that its profits were earned worldwide, and the oil companies—along with other extractive industries—said they pumped their oil outside the state. They all argued that the state had no right to tax profits that were earned in other jurisdictions.

By 1929, California had applied the unitary method of taxation to all multistate corporations, and eventually to the multinationals, as well. The new method asserted the state's sovereignty over corporations whose range extended well beyond California's borders. In fact, California was the first state to develop the concept and definition of a unitary business. The vast majority of states followed suit, using some version of the unitary method to determine taxable income. The state recognized that it could better deal with the growing "independence among different operations of a corporation by treating the corporation in its entirety as a unit (hence unitary)."[4]

In determining a corporation's tax bill, California used the most controversial form of the unitary method, known as worldwide unitary combination. This meant that the state ignored national boundaries and considered the combined worldwide income of a corporation. In contrast, some states used the "water's edge" approach, in which only the income of related corporations located in the United States was counted. Before repeal, California used a complicated six-step formula to determine a corporation's total property, sales, and payroll and then applied its 9.6 percent corporate tax rate.

By sticking to its guns, California found itself in court time and time again defending the unitary formula. It was not alone; other states were also forced into court to defend the tax. In 1983, following years of legal precedent, the U.S. Supreme Court upheld California's unitary method of taxation.[5] For this reason, foreign multinationals turned to the state legislatures for more fruitful results.[6]

In essence, unitary means "toward a common profit," reasoned Martin Helmke, chief consultant to the Senate Revenue and Taxation Committee.

It involves companies that have common administrative functions; they lend each other money and supply each other with products—like IBM. These companies are *unitary* operations and therefore subject to worldwide combination and formula apportionment.

It is a good taxing system, except that the people hate it too much. The feds don't use it; foreign governments don't use it. People are annoyed that California is successful, and they're afraid that the feds will catch on and start using it. They are also afraid that third-world countries will start using it. Some people out here speculate that if the feds used this method of taxation, they could close the deficit.

OPPOSITION TO THE UNITARY

Indeed, executives from the multinational corporations came to hate the unitary tax with a passion that was palpable to key officials who dealt with the issue. "It's one of those subjects where people have very strong emotions," said Nancy Ordway, chief deputy director of the California Department of Finance and a tax expert. "Hairs stand out on the back of people's necks when you mention it. There is a perceived barrier with respect to the unitary tax issue. That in itself is important; after all, perception is reality in our business."

To foreign multinationals, the unitary system was patently unfair and in their view a form of double taxation. It led to inordinate complexities and was almost impossible to calculate. "Royal Dutch Shell has 900 subsidiaries," said California State Senator John Vasconcellos, president pro tem of the Senate and a supporter of unitary repeal. "How can they keep track of 900 subsidiaries?"

The arguments against the unitary tax sounded very much like the American revolutionaries' "taxation without representation" theme against their British oppressors. Supported by the U.S. Treasury Department, the foreign multinationals argued that the tax produced the following problems:

Exposed multinational corporations to double taxation.

Many companies argued that the unitary tax "causes more of their income to be taxed by California than is justified, given the extent and profitability of their business activities in the state."[7] Others make the outright claim that they pay more in taxes than they made in profits. "I can tell you from our experience in California, unitary creates a tremendous, unbearable tax burden for our company," said William Everitt, vice-president of corporate communication for Kyocera International, a Japanese company that manufactures industrial ceramics:

Over a five-year period, between federal tax and state tax and the excess paid to the unitary system, Kyocera paid 101

percent of its profits. The company paid more in taxes than
it made in profits; you can't stay in business like that. . . .
We're paying double tax. The Japanese government collects
taxes on Japanese profits; California collects the same taxes
on Japanese profits.[8]

Provided an incentive for firms to locate elsewhere.

Now that so many states have abandoned the unitary method,
companies either abandon California altogether or choose nonuni-
tary states for new plant locations. Kyocera and Fujitsu, Japan's
largest computer manufacturer, made this deliberate choice in a
series of widely publicized plant moves, all targeting the stub-
born California legislature. Kyocera International, for example,
deliberately chose a site in Vancouver, Washington, for its new
electronics-component manufacturing plant, although the company was based in California. The company announced that it
planned to create 2,000 jobs at the new plant.[9]

Violated existing tax treaties.

Australia contends that the unitary tax is contrary to the princi-
ples embodied in a double-taxation treaty between the United
States and Australia, enacted in 1983. In a strong statement, the
Business Council of Australia charged that the double taxation
that resulted threatened the viability of its companies in the
international marketplace.[10] Many other countries claim that bilateral trade treaties between themselves and the United States
preclude unitary taxation and ''upset arrangements for international tax harmonization that have taken more than 50 years to
establish.''[11]

Violated the U.S. Constitution.

This is an inverted version of the states' rights argument.
Advocates of unitary repeal contend that the states' resistance
violates theories of federal supremacy. The executive branch has
made it clear that the unitary method is alienating our major
trading partners, posing a distinct threat to U.S. foreign relations. In that light, the states are out of step with federal policy
and should assume a subordinate role.

Saddled taxpayers with unnecessary administrative costs.

Collecting the corporate income tax and ensuring a workable
compliance system led to added expense for the taxpayers.

Saddled corporations with unnecessary costs.

This is a realistic complaint. Under the unitary method, the burden of administrative costs falls to the corporations, which are required to "collect, evaluate, and report information on all phases of their operations, a difficult and expensive undertaking." An additional accounting burden obligates firms to report their income in dollars.

This issue was exacerbated by the fluctuating value of the dollar. The British claimed that their corporate taxes went up when the dollar was strong, shifting more of their income to the United States.

CARROTS AND STICKS: FOREIGN LOBBYISTS IN THE AMERICAN IMAGE

The leading argument, and the one that finally prevailed, was strictly pragmatic: California would lose investment dollars to states that had abandoned the unitary tax. But polite debate and litigation alone were not enough. In 1984, the foreign multinationals became serious about their threat to invest only in states that prohibited unitary taxes and mounted a systematic campaign of carefully orchestrated rewards and punishments.

First the carrot. In 1984, a delegation of Japanese corporate executives organized by the Japan Federation of Economic Organizations—a group comparable to the U.S. Chamber of Commerce—visited the United States to lobby against the unitary tax. Led by Akio Morita of Sony, the group released a survey indicating that ninety-nine Japanese companies were prepared to invest at least $1.4 billion in California if the unitary tax were repealed. The study, which queried 166 of Japan's largest corporations, also indicated that the investments would lead to 11,000 permanent jobs in the state.[12]

Next the stick. Fujitsu had warned repeatedly that it would not build a magnetic-disk-drive plant in California unless the unitary tax were repealed. Finally, the company made good on its threat, and as soon as Oregon repealed its unitary tax in July 1985 (effective January 1, 1986), Fujitsu held a press conference to announce it would build two $170 million computer-parts factories in Oregon despite the fact that four of its subsidiaries were already located in California; California's unitary tax was cited as the major reason for its decision.

Fujitsu's decision shattered Californians, who finally paid serious attention to unitary repeal. Along with Fujitsu, a number of other Japanese investors, including Kyocera, Nippondenso, NEC, and Epson America, also announced they had rejected California in favor of investing in Washington State and Oregon in reaction to the unitary tax. Legislators referred repeatedly to Fujitsu in discussions of unitary repeal; some were resentful, while others were convinced it was time to act. Willie Brown, Speaker of the California Assembly, indicated disbelief that Japanese companies would leave those rich California markets and the superior life-style of the state just on the unitary issue.

"The Japanese have had a great effect because there is a belief they will invest in California," said Brown. "Their proof is that they located a plant in Alabama or Tennessee. I can't believe anyone would want to live in Alabama or Tennessee if he can live here. California is a better place to live."

Jock O'Connell, a consultant with the lieutenant governor's office and the state's leading expert on the politics of the unitary tax, concluded there were other motivations behind Fujitsu's move:

> There are two schools of thought on the unitary issue. Is it a revenue issue, or an investment issue?
>
> Despite the statements by foreign companies that they're not coming to California unless it repeals the tax, there are many other reasons—investment reasons—for not coming to the state. There are high labor costs, high energy costs, and a high cost of living. It is fantastically expensive to locate in Silicon Valley. It is a challenge for the state to convince companies that there are other areas of the state where living costs are cheaper.
>
> There is no real way of telling how truthful companies are, but they are making good PR use of statements about the unitary. Three months after Fujitsu made its announcement, a newspaper in Hillsdale, Oregon, was quoted as saying that Fujitsu's upper management, based in Palo Alto, was comprised of a number of Oregonians who wanted to go home. They didn't like expensive Santa Clara County and put pressure on the executives of Fujitsu in Japan to locate in Oregon. The move by Fujitsu was used for the unitary issue. The Japanese are quite good at this sort of public relations.

The campaign leaders alternated between rewards and punish-ments to avoid public resentment and to keep the legislators off balance. Often it was difficult to differentiate between carrots and sticks, especially in the area of campaign contributions where foreign lobbyists began throwing vast sums of money into legislators' campaigns. A coalition made up mostly of Japanese investors contributed $108,000 to the campaigns of fifty-three legislators, including $22,000 to David Roberti, the Democratic president pro tem of the State Senate. It was money well spent. California races are very costly—an average of $250,000 each, for a total expenditure of $45 million in 1985—and the unitary issue presented an ideal opportunity for attracting new sources of funds.

Stalling action on unitary repeal kept the campaign coffers full, that is, before some contributors caught on to the scam and accused legislators of prolonging the issue because they were fearful of killing the goose that laid the campaign contribution. The bill soon became known as a "juice bill"—appropriate for a citrus-producing state—so named for the hundreds of thousands of dollars that could be squeezed from it.[13] There are no restrictions on the amount of campaign contributions in California or on foreign contributions, but the disclosure laws are strict.

Lobbyists of all persuasions were also charged with a vested interest in prolonging the unitary issue when the bill became known as the Lobbyists Full Employment Act. The most active lobbyist, Chris Wada of Sony of America, had the dubious honor of having the issue referred to as "Wadagate" and one of its compromises as "Wada's edge."

"Chris Wada listened to me after one exchange on my committee when I opposed the unitary tax," recalled Representative Hayden. "He later called and provided tickets for myself and family to go to a Kabuki play. I didn't accept." Hayden went on to describe other forms of gift giving from Japanese lobbyists to his fellow legislators: "Others get trips to Japan. They are provided with 'social amenities' when they get there. They do a sophisticated lobbying operation that makes our companies look inferior."

"Chris [Wada] tried to give us gifts," recalled Steve Larson, an aide to Senator Alquist. "I heard that he tests you. I told him that he can't give me anything; I'd have to report it. The domestic multinationals don't even want to talk to you. They just expect you to roll over for them."

Dan Walter, political columnist for the *Sacramento Bee*, is very well known in Sacramento for his continuing analysis of the unitary issue as well as his criticism of the increasingly overt and crass lobbying. "There's enough grease to fry a dinosaur," he commented:

> Japanese industrialists show up en masse and order every black limousine in town. Representative Pat Nolan was flown up personally in the Sony jet from Los Angeles to cast the deciding vote [one of the prior votes in which unitary repeal failed]. They're spending huge sums of money, and everybody's getting filthy rich.
>
> California is an extremely expensive, money-ridden operation. It is expensive to play. The California state legislature is more like Congress. It is a full-time body, the legislators are professionals, and they deal with big money issues all the time. There are 700 full-time lobbyists in Sacramento. It is a high-rolling operation. If you want to play in the arena politically with a juice bill, you've got to play with juice. High tech has not done that much in the past. Japanese high tech, if not the biggest players, are at least substantial players, putting several hundred thousand dollars into individual legislative races. When legislators are faced with raising over a half a million dollars every two years, they are more susceptible to that kind of money.

Lobbyists also began inundating legislators with visits and information, hoping that they would eventually wear them down. "Any number of consul generals talk to me," said Senator Alfred Alquist, author of the legislation that repealed the unitary tax:

> They make the point that if we don't act, the federal government will. Japan has the most active consul general. I've met with the consul generals based in Los Angeles and San Francisco, with members of the Diet, the Japanese American Chamber of Commerce, and Japanese business groups. I hear regularly from the British consul general, the Australians, Italians, West Germans, French, British, and recently from South Africa. The Japanese and British have the greatest interest.

"I'm lobbied on this issue all the time," added Senator Jim Nielsen. "I have at least three foreign delegations in my office each week. The consul general from Japan is in my office each week; so is the Common Market. They just come to explain their side."

Sony of America, a wholly owned subsidiary of the Japanese corporation, took the lead as the prime mover in the repeal effort. The company contributed $29,000 to the campaigns of state legislators, legal under California law and allowed under federal law provided no foreign nationals are involved in the decisions. With a television factory in San Diego, a warehouse in Compton, a cabinet-making plant outside Los Angeles, a broadcast warehouse in San Jose, a sales office and warehouse in San Francisco, and a research operation in Palo Alto, the company held a major stake in unitary repeal.

A controversy arose as to whether the company violated federal law in its lobbying effort. John W. McGarry, vice-chairman of the FEC and its former chairman, said in an interview in December 1985 that the Sony donations apparently violated federal laws prohibiting foreign nationals from making contributions. Sony officials contended in response to his remarks that the contributions were entirely legal. The company's lobbying effort is directed by Chris Wada, vice-president and assistant to the chairman. Mr. Wada, a Japanese national who is a permanent resident of the United States, is exempted from the ban on foreign nationals because of his permanent-residence status.[14]

Sony officials said that decisions concerning political contributions were solely the responsibility of Mr. Wada and Robert E. Dillon, the executive vice-president, who is an American citizen. If that were the case, said Mr. McGarry, the contributions would be totally legal. He added that if the chairman of Sony of America, Kenji Tamiya, who is Japanese, or the Japanese who comprise a majority of the board members of Sony of America were in any way involved in the decisions to make contributions, the corporate gifts would violate the election laws.

Both Mr. Tamiya and Akio Morita, chairman of Sony of Japan, have lobbied for repeal in meetings with state officials in California and elsewhere. Mr. Dillon admitted: "I was the one who first got Mr. Morita stirred up about the unitary tax. He got involved in '74 and '75, when we first became truly aware of the magnitude of the problem in California.

"When Jerry Brown came to Japan on a goodwill mission," Mr. Dillon said in a reference to the then governor of California, "he met Mr. Morita. As a result, he became interested in the issue." As for Mr. Tamiya, Mr. Dillon continued:

Our chairman, who was president until recently, certainly was aware and remains aware of what's going on in California. Everything we do is out in the open. It isn't big wads of money we're throwing around. It's simply to let the legislators know that we appreciate their support and make sure that we at least have an opportunity to talk to them.

Before Brown visited Japan, he had endorsed unitary taxation. Afterward, he did an about-face and claimed he changed his position because he'd been given inadequate data by the state's Franchise Tax Board.

Mr. McGarry would not characterize the role of Mr. Tamiya and Mr. Morita in making the contributions. Some California legislators who seek to retain the tax say they believe the two men had a key part in the decision. Sony denies this.

The Japanese took such an active lead in unitary repeal that their supporters feared a backlash and advised them to lower their profile. "Last year during the unitary hearings there was a lot of discontent about the physical presence of Japanese lobbyists," recalled an aide. "The joke was that if you held a hearing a bus would pull up and disgorge thirty to forty Japanese businessmen. The only difference between them and tourists was that they weren't carrying cameras. The following year only two or three Japanese lobbyists would appear at the hearings, although at least 100 people were working on the issue."

Supporters of repeal also worried about a potential linkage between the growing nationwide friction over Japanese trade practices and the unitary issue; to a lesser extent, they also feared that racist sentiments toward the Japanese might surface, although this has been much less of a problem on the West Coast than in other parts of the country. "They fall into the same package as women or blacks," said Nancy Ordway, commenting on the disadvantages experienced by Japanese lobbyists. "They can't hide."

Another problem involved bad timing: Unitary repeal reached a serious point the same year that the U.S. trade deficit intensified trade friction with the Japanese. Legislators said they could envision fifteen-second TV ads by their opponents accusing them of "favoring the Japanese." They also feared headlines reading "$500 Million Tax Relief for the Richest Multinationals in the World."

With all these factors in mind, the Japanese broadened their effort into a coalition, and soon diplomats, business executives, and lobbyists from Canada, the Netherlands, Austria, Great Britain, Italy, and West Germany became familiar figures in the corridors of the state capitol. The British, who had been lobbying the unitary-tax issue mostly in Washington, D.C., assumed a more central role in Sacramento. At this point, it became evident that the multinationals and their governments were working in concert.

"We had to convince the Europeans to come to Sacramento and involve their colleagues so that the bill is not regarded as a Japanese bill," said O'Connell, who went to London to advise the British on the politics of the issue. "I pointed out that the conspicuous Japanese presence had endangered the unitary reform effort. The British and the Japanese have central governments themselves and don't understand our system."

The British heeded his advice. They also joined the Japanese with their own version of wielding "threat power." Two hundred and twenty-one members of the House of Commons voted to empower Prime Minister Thatcher to retaliate against American corporations whose headquarters were located in states with a unitary tax. Thatcher followed up by pressing President Reagan to intervene on behalf of foreign governments in California politics. The British also hoped their actions would spur U.S. corporations with affiliates in Great Britain to abandon their ambivalence, take a position, and actively lobby for unitary repeal.

The British involvement in unitary repeal suggested the most important issue in the foreign lobbying effort: Who is the real lobbyist? Is it the foreign multinational corporation or the foreign government standing firmly behind that company? It might be the British-owned Crocker Bank that protested the unitary tax in Sacramento, but the added boost from Prime Minister Thatcher added another dimension to the issue, one that has passed virtually unnoticed. Indeed, the increased involvement of the British and Japanese governments relates directly to their increased involvement in banking. Nearly 33 percent of the bank assets in California are now foreign owned.

"No one resents Thatcher and the parliamentary move," said Senator Alquist. No wonder. If it were portrayed for what it really represented, a foreign government intervening in state tax policy, Americans might react differently. In Japan and Great Britain, industry's relationship with government is closer than it is in the United States; therefore, in those countries, that form of lobbying behavior would be regarded as normal. In the United States, on the other hand, a more arm's length relationship exists between corporations and the government, although the United

States has been known to intervene in the internal politics of sovereign states on behalf of its multinational corporations. In recent years, however, this policy seems to have fallen out of favor; witness the negative public reaction to U.S. involvement in Chile to protect the interests of ITT, the International Telephone and Telegraph Company, and other U.S. investments.

The intensified involvement of foreign governments in unitary repeal reveals the true reason for their involvement: In the end the benefits of repeal accrue to those governments as well as to the multinationals that are based within their borders. With that in mind, the most cogent argument for unitary repeal—that it represents double taxation—takes on another dimension. While it is true that unitary taxation means double taxation for companies who pay taxes to two governments, it also means that in the process of reducing taxes to remove that "inequity," one government will have to step aside and relinquish taxes in deference to the more compelling needs of the other. In other words, one government will gain revenue, while the other will lose. In controlling the formulation of the unitary issue, foreign governments have convinced Americans that the fairness issue is totally on their side; that it is unfair to tax their corporations abroad if they are already being taxed at home.

The lobbyists' effort paid off. When they began in earnest in 1984, there were twelve states that still practiced unitary taxation. In two years' time, only three remained—Alaska, North Dakota, and Montana.

FEDERAL PRESSURE FOR REPEAL

Acting in concert with the foreign multinationals, federal officials weighed in with their own threats against the state of California. Treasury Secretary Donald T. Regan warned in July 1984 that if states with unitary taxes did not repeal the levy by 1985, he would ask Congress to take action. His comments angered members of a federal task force of corporate, state, and federal officials set up by the Treasury Department for the specific purpose of investigating the unitary tax. Regan ignored the group because their preliminary conclusions disagreed with his own: The group specifically advised against federal intervention.

The following year, on November 8, 1985, President Reagan said he would support federal legislation to outlaw the unitary method in any state that still retained the tax. Affected states in addition to California were Utah, Alaska, Montana, Idaho, North

Dakota, and New Hampshire. Mr. Reagan's move was regarded as an attempt to defuse the trade crisis and a bow to Prime Minister Thatcher, who had persuaded Parliament to empower her to retaliate against U.S. corporations. The British government said it would not implement the law if the administration introduced its bill by the end of the year and if it passed before January 1, 1987. The president's action was aimed directly at California; aides said that if California repealed its tax, the federal legislation would be "reevaluated."[15]

In cooperation with the White House, Senator Pete Wilson, a California Republican, introduced a bill to bar the unitary tax; the bill had two dozen co-sponsors. In 1981, similar bills were introduced prohibiting states from using the worldwide unitary method by Representative Barber Conable, Republican from New York, and Senator Charles McC. Mathias, Republican from Maryland.

The president's announcement represented an about-face from the position he took on the unitary tax when he was governor of California. In a letter to a Senate subcommittee in 1973 opposing pending federal legislation to provide tax relief to multinational corporations, Reagan wrote:

> One of the great strengths of the Federal-state system is the freedom of the states to act to meet their own particular needs. Interference by the Federal Government with the states' power to tax would be a major blow to such freedom.
> . . . a close look will reveal that there are very important areas of controversy between the states and the business community. S. 11245 [the bill in question] sets up an unacceptable rule as to organizations doing business in multicorporate form. The adoption of this bill would result in revenue losses to California of up to $100 million a year. Such losses would inevitably have to be shifted to other taxpayers. Federal intervention in the interstate taxation field is both undesirable and dangerous and should only be considered as a last resort.[16]

Recalling Reagan's stance as governor, state leaders reacted angrily to federal pressures, even though there is no doubt they were sufficiently swayed by Washington's interest to accelerate their efforts to repeal the tax. In a joint letter, the leaders of the California State Senate urged President Reagan to refrain from federal action while assuring him at the same time of their progress toward repeal. "We understand that you may be changing your historic policy regarding federal preemption of state tax policy," wrote Senators Roberti, Nielsen, and Alquist:

> . . . we believe that the Leadership of both houses of the Legislature is ready to develop an equitable and acceptable solution when the Legislature reconvenes in January. . . . We request that you defer any consideration of revising your current position until March 1st at the earliest, so that the California Legislature will have an opportunity to act on its pending unitary reform package.

BUYING OFF THE DOMESTIC MULTINATIONALS

What seemed to disturb many Californians most about the Reagan-Wilson measure was that it would also have exempted from state taxation 85 percent of the dividends paid U.S. firms by their overseas subsidiaries. "Enactment of such a measure would cost the State of California between $500 and $600 million per year in lost corporate tax revenue," estimated a report of the Economic Development Commission, which referred to the unitary issue as a "tiresome capital soap opera."[17]

The unitary tax would have been repealed long ago if not for the stalemate created by Governor George Deukmejian's opposition to dividend relief for domestic multinationals and their equally strong insistence that without dividend relief they would oppose unitary repeal. Their lobbyists also used threat tactics, warning that if they didn't get dividend relief they would move more plants offshore.

"U.S. companies are saying that if a water's-edge approach is enacted [taxing only domestic income], the playing field will no longer be level," said Jim Joyce, the major lobbyist for the California Business Council (CBC), a group of ninety domestic multinational corporations including such giants as IBM, Hewlett-Packard, Coca-Cola, and Intel.

The domestic multinationals were no strangers to power politics in the state capital. Their public relations counsel, Dennis Revell, is President Reagan's son-in-law. In the "juice" department, the CBC had spent $354,556 by June 30, 1985, to lobby the unitary issue, compared with nearly $550,000 from the two major advocacy groups for the foreign multinationals ($370,719 from the California Investment Environment Committee and $177,890 from the California Unitary Coalition).

Domestic multinationals feared that unitary repeal would put them at a serious disadvantage in relation to their foreign competitors. They also claimed double taxation: "Such dividends should not be subject to taxation, since the income from which those dividends are paid has already been taxed by either foreign taxing authorities or other states," said Robert Wayman, vice-president of Hewlett-Packard:

> It is a tax that falls exclusively on American business. Foreign multinationals will receive worldwide unitary relief, but will never pay a tax on their intercorporate dividends. This inequity is inexcusable. To grant tax relief to our competitors while refusing to avoid double taxation on American business places us at a serious competitive disadvantage.[18]

In yet another paradox, the domestic multinationals found themselves at a political disadvantage throughout most of the debate, with the foreign multinationals wielding more influence and credibility. "I represent Silicon Valley," the home of many of the leading domestic multinationals, said Senator Alquist. "I just tell them that to give them what they want costs too much. My computer people want a level playing field. They have that now. None of them are required to pay the unitary tax."

Alquist also pointed out that the California business community was divided on the issue, another reason for the weakness of the domestic multinationals' position. "There is a big push to repeal unitary from the California Chamber of Commerce and other California businessmen connected to the promotion of tourism and trade," he said. "Aside from the electronics field, the business community favors repeal."

Alquist's bill was considered a slap in the face of the domestic multinationals. Until 1985, it was assumed that they had an effective veto power over unitary repeal, but somehow they had frittered away that clout. The reasons varied. Initially, observers felt the domestic multinationals were too greedy in their demands and that they had not presented a convincing case for dividend relief to the legislators. If they had cut their dividend-relief demand in half or displayed a willingness to negotiate, they would not have dissipated their strength.

To appease the domestic multinationals, Senator John Vasconcellos, president pro tem of the Senate, submitted an amendment offering dividend relief. "My fear is that if only the Alquist bill passes, the domestics will be in here every year."

"The foreign multinationals work better than the domestic corporations," said Senator Jim Nielsen:

> The domestic corporations are intransigent, they are not unified, and they suffer from not being unified. They send signals you couldn't understand. There were no CEOs involved until this year; the only ones involved were their tax attorneys. I can't deal with tax attorneys. I insisted they involve their CEOs.

As the issue progressed, however, a more compelling reason emerged: a growing animosity toward domestic multinationals for exporting jobs, compared with foreign investors who were bringing jobs to the state. "Hewlett-Packard is opening up a plant in Spain and cutting back in Palo Alto," reported a legislator. "When they come in to lobby against unitary, they don't get much sympathy. Politically, it doesn't help your cause to come begging for tax relief to Sacramento after you've taken jobs away from California."

One irascible legislator from Los Angeles responded angrily to a witness testifying in favor of the CBC position:

> In my district over the last several years a Goodyear plant has closed down leaving 700 workers. Where are the new jobs coming from in my district? From Sony. Kyocera. I can't carry any brief for domestic industries when it is the foreign companies that are hiring my constituents. I've been against unitary reform for years, but this year I'm changing my mind.

Some argued that dividend relief would encourage domestic companies to export jobs; if companies are allowed to repatriate income without being taxed, the state is providing a strong incentive to expand their offshore production. "If we exempt foreign dividends, we give them an incentive to move offshore," said David Doerr, chief consultant to the Revenue and Tax Committee of the California Assembly. "The dividend issue is really the bigger piece. A lot of members object on those grounds. They say taxes don't matter that much."

There was also residual hostility against some of the domestic multinationals who weren't paying part of their taxes. In fact, more than a dozen foreign and domestic multinationals have refused to pay taxes under the unitary method and have either refused to pay or filed appeals with the Franchise Tax Board. Cases have gone on for ten to fifteen years, according to the board. It pays for a company to keep a case on appeal as long as it can in order to pay off its taxes later on in cheaper dollars.

What was significant about the unitary issue was that domestic multinationals were virtually ignored by state legislators in favor of foreign multinationals throughout the debate. Granted, they made many mistakes: they took their representatives for granted, alienated their supporters, were less generous in their campaign contributions compared with the foreign multinationals, and routinely missed some key opportunities. But with all that, it was surprising that they could be ignored with impunity for such a long period of time.

The reason was a significant shift in power that went unrecognized by the domestic corporations: Foreign multinationals as investors had become the political equals of the domestic multinationals. In the eyes of their representatives, foreign companies deserved the same protection as American companies; if they located in a district, they had the same rights to lobby as American companies. In effect, a new playing field was constructed in which domestic companies suddenly found their competitors on their own turf, often on the winning side. On the unitary tax issue, the foreign companies played a better game. By the time the domestics figured out they were at a political disadvantage, it was almost too late.

THE APARTHEID ISSUE

As unitary repeal headed swiftly toward resolution, an unexpected obstacle appeared to block its path. Maxine Waters, a Democratic member of the influential Revenue and Taxation Committee, attached a condition: an amendment that would bar tax relief for corporations doing business in South Africa. Waters enlisted the support of all of her fellow black legislators, including Willie Brown, Speaker of the Assembly. Brown had his own reservations about unitary repeal. "I don't know of any justifiable reason why we should give another tax exemption," he said. "I'm certain they shouldn't get this exemption. Practical aspects dictate that. There is no provable reason for unitary repeal."

The unwillingness of the governor and key legislators to compromise on the issue of apartheid held up unitary repeal for more than a year. But Waters and her supporters also knew how badly the governor wanted repeal and saw this as an ideal way to force the legislature's hand on an issue that meant so much to them. According to Brown, the governor was the key:

> The real lobbying has taken place in the last two to three years because the governor got interested. Also the forces that had stopped the unitary left the scene. Governor Brown made noises but never really designated an author and didn't put it in his state-of-the-state message. This governor makes speeches about it. Also, Brown had close connections with Silicon Valley, and they were dead set against it.

Governor Deukmejian refused to even consider the amendment, and Speaker Brown was just as unyielding. "Why would companies doing business with South Africa get this huge tax exemption? The governor doesn't believe in linkage when it is inconvenient for him."

THE BILL

Eventually Brown relented, and unitary repeal passed the legislature without the apartheid amendment. The bill, SB 85, also known as the Alquist Bill, passed the Senate on June 25, 1986, by a vote of 24–12, and the Assembly on May 15, 57–8. What made the difference was that the Democrats finally backed the bill, once they were given the signal from the Speaker; before 1986, the Republicans supported the bill, and the Democrats were divided. The governor signed the bill on September 5, 1986. In the spirit of compromise, there was something for everyone, and the sacrifices were spread around.

The governor compromised his earlier position of not wanting to give up state revenue. By August 1986, he indicated that he would support revision of the unitary law if the cost did not exceed $300 million, or roughly 1 percent of California's annual budget of $37 billion. This by itself was significant: a governor willingly campaigning for a measure that would reduce state revenues by $300 million without any guarantees of replacing that revenue. Of course, since earlier versions of the bill would have cost the state $600 million, half that amount looked good to a governor whose political party left him no choice on this issue.

"No governor in his right mind is for repeal," noted Steve

Larson, staff director of the Senate Budget and Fiscal Revenue Committee. "Deukmejian just wanted to get rid of foreign pressure from Washington. He wants to play footsy with the president. The president put him on the unitary task force. Then he changed his mind."

The prize went to the foreign multinationals, who finally proclaimed victory in their ten-year struggle to repeal the unitary tax. Those companies were allowed to choose between using the worldwide unitary method, an unlikely possibility, and the water's-edge formula, which excludes overseas profits. With the prize went a price: the water's-edge compromise included a penalty of .03 percent of the value of a company's payroll. The penalty, called an "election fee"—for electing the water's-edge formula— was more like a gift in view of the 9.6 percent tax paid under the original unitary formula. Nevertheless, foreign companies doing business in the state protested the penalty.[19]

In a nod to the public's interests, the bill provided that two-thirds of the proceeds from the election fee be used for state infrastructure (roads, bridges, etc.) and one-third for local infrastructure. Firms earning no taxable income would not have to pay the election fee, while new investments would also get some relief.

The domestic multinationals also came away enriched by the compromise but not totally satisfied. They were able to get dividend relief, not at the 100 percent level they requested but at 75 percent. "No one will get everything he wants in this bill," said Denny Valentine, a lobbyist for the CBC. "All we want is that the pain be distributed evenly among the American and the foreign multinationals."[20]

THE SEMISOVEREIGN STATE

The history of unitary-tax repeal will be remembered for the magnitude of its revenue loss and the paucity of political opponents. At its final stages, the only defenders of the unitary system were a lonely band of state legislators and state tax administrators, who argued that it was the "fairest, simplest and most practical way to tax the often complex and interconnected operations of multistate and multinational corporations." Despite its limitations, the unitary method was still better than allowing companies to use "sophisticated separate accounting techniques to avoid paying their fair share of California taxes."[21]

Aligned against Fujitsu, Shell Oil, and the British Parliament, the tax experts from the state's Franchise Tax Board and their allies faded into political insignificance. Without them, it was easy to conduct a political debate in the absence of data and without a clearheaded look at the real facts. Years from now, when analysts assess the impact of unitary repeal, they might look back and wonder how and why the United States gave away so much for so little.

The answer lies in the axiom that whoever controls the formulation of an issue often controls its outcome. Fujitsu, the British government, and others hammered away at the issue for so long that eventually it was accepted almost universally as the only version of the truth.

Most important was the economic loss. Even with the compromise that closed some of the loopholes, unitary repeal still makes it much easier for companies to engage in "creative bookkeeping" of the kind that enables them to move their profits to Tasmania. That means they can still benefit from the rich markets and superior work force of California while avoiding the taxes that have made the state so desirable in the first place.

The cost to the state, estimated at the nice round number of $300 million a year, is pure guesswork; no one really knows what the real figure is and whether it will be higher or lower than that number. Over a decade, that number will add up to billions of dollars in revenue losses, borne by individual as well as domestic taxpayers. While the economy of the state may be buoyant in 1986, no one knows whether that will continue or for how long the state can sustain those revenue losses. And although California's $37 billion budget makes it the fourteenth largest in the world, the state is not without its fiscal problems: Its citizens led the nationwide tax revolt, Jarvis-Gann's Proposition 13, and one of its school districts, San Jose, almost went bankrupt. It is doubtful that the voters, with their propensity for tax limitations, would care to replenish the hole in the state treasury from their own pockets.

Not everyone in the business community is thrilled by unitary repeal, and the experience of other states is revealing. When Oregonians were debating the repeal of their unitary tax, Ed McKenney, president of Gem Equipment of Oregon Inc., warned: "If we change our unitary tax, there's going to be $30 million [in tax revenue] lost, and that's got to come from somewhere. It's going to come from insiders, and I'm an insider."

The real surprise in the unitary issue is how much was given away without concrete data to buttress the notion that those losses would be replenished. The promise of future investment is a slim reed on which to hang a $300 million annual tax loss. A better approach would be to examine past experience, which indicates that the unitary tax has had a minimal effect on foreign investment.

Indeed, if the unitary tax were the deterrent its opponents claim it is, California would not now lead the nation in foreign investment. Surely, investors deterred by the unitary tax would have gone elsewhere. Moreover, it appears from the early returns that except in cases of individual lobbying by the multinationals—such as Sony in Indiana—states that repealed the unitary tax have experienced no huge influx of foreign investment. Illinois, which repealed the unitary tax several years earlier than California, has experienced no substantial change in its patterns of foreign investment.

It is also incredulous that California gave away the store without extracting a good price for it. The .03 percent election fee and other lagniappes are hardly worth mentioning next to the billions in tax revenue saved by domestic and foreign multinationals. All efforts to include a quid pro quo in the deal were quickly quashed as politically unrealistic. Senator Nielsen, for example, tried to introduce greater trade access in exchange for the repeal of the unitary tax.

"Promises to invest are not enough," he argued:

> Demands for a quid pro quo are happening all over the country. The foreign companies say, "Senator, this is not related to trade." I say, "Investment *is* related to trade. You want a tax change, and we want more access to your markets. When you bargain, you bargain best from strength. We're not asking protection; we're asking reciprocity—in forestry, agriculture, high tech."

Nielsen acknowledged the limitations of state government in negotiating greater trade access: "The action has to come from the federal government. We can only raise the issue." This perception is true at the state executive level, as well. "A quid pro quo is not possible at the state level," said Nancy Ordway. "We're a subdivision of a nation. The election fee is an attempt to get a quid pro quo. The position of the agricultural sector is 'Why should we give Japan a break when they won't buy our citrus products?' We don't have the ability as a state to do anything."

True, but this puts the state at a distinct disadvantage. States are conducting a form of foreign policy by negotiating tax agreements affecting foreign multinationals and their governments, yet are impeded from working in the best interests of their citizens. The federal government and its major trading partners leaned so heavily on the state that it toppled over—without the participants fully appreciating the consequences of their acts. In fact, the same year the federal government began pressing California, it gave foreign investors its own gift: It repealed their withholding tax on treasury notes.

Throughout the conflict over the unitary tax, neither the state nor the federal government collected data on the real issue: the long-term effects on the state and on the nation. The Multistate Tax Commission, an attempt by the Treasury Department to produce an intelligent assessment of the issue, was almost dead on arrival: A combination of experts and political actors struggled with the issue but couldn't agree on a set of recommendations. What they did agree on—stopping federal intervention—was ignored by their creator, the Treasury Department.

"Multinationals don't understand the concept of the semisovereign state," said Martin Helmke. "California is a semisovereign state with taxing powers. They say, 'This is national stuff. What are you guys doing in California?' They don't understand our federalism, and they don't choose to understand it."

Perhaps Californians capitulated because of their ambivalence toward their role in the federal system. Many of them feel closer to the Pacific rim than they do to the rest of the country and argue that they are part of a global, not national or state, economy. "Repeal is a good idea," said Steve Larson. "California has to reshape its view of the world and look more toward the Pacific. The Pacific is more important than the East or Europe." These attitudes parallel recent trade patterns, according to Stuart Auerbach of the *Washington Post,* who writes that California is entering a second gold rush, aiming to "cash in on the booming economies of nations along Asia's Pacific rim, which have replaced Western Europe during the 1980s as America's leading trade partners. . . . California's . . . trade with Japan places it right behind the entire United States as Japan's second-largest trading partner."[22]

If that scenario is true, then the system of governance should conform to that new configuration or Americans will lose out in the long run. Being part of the global economy doesn't have to mean giving up sovereignty either as a state or a nation. Representative Tom Hayden watched the repeal of the unitary tax with a sense of dismay and disbelief. He compared his fellow Californians to a colonized nation:

> This place has mentally been colonized. There's a servility around investment. Some of it is ignorance; some misguided understanding of the marketplace; some of it the power of money. There is intense anti-Japanese feeling around the trade issue. It's a typical colonial mentality. One moment servile, the next angry. The mythology is that if you give up your right to participate in public policy decisions about the taxation of multinationals, then the invisible international hand would bless you by showering investments on California. This is voodoo economics revisited, and we're expected to accept this on blind faith. There is a common phrase that you hear—"Something's got to be done; something's going to happen." It's an attitude that crisis is inevitable. We've got to break that mentality. There is an absence of protest. The legislators can't only hear from lobbyists.

In the end, the multinationals called California's bluff and won. It is doubtful that they would have left the state en masse if the tax were retained; the advantages of the state's population in providing companies with a labor force and rich markets would have far outweighed its taxes, and eventually the companies would have given up.

Tax policy is one of the last bastions of a state's sovereignty. It is significant that one of the blows struck against that sovereignty came from foreign interests. George Washington's warning was forgotten.

CHAPTER 9

Foreign-Owned
U.S. Banks
A Policy Conundrum

It's damaging our banks and our banking system.
—*William L. Seidman, chairman of
the Federal Deposit Insurance Corporation*

Foreign banks are better to work with.
—*Jeanne Z. Brooks, deputy director,
Mayor's Office of Housing and Economic Development,
San Francisco*

Banks are the combined circulatory system and central nervous system of a nation's economy. They wield extraordinary economic power, influence a nation's business priorities, and keep the money flowing. Their leaders enjoy access to the industrial plans and trade secrets of their manufacturing clients, whose influence pales next to theirs. "What you've got, once you own the bank or have control of the bank, is control of a good deal of economic power as far as where and how loans are to be made, and to whom," noted Representative Fernand J. St. Germain, Rhode Island Democrat and chairman of the House Banking Committee. "A manufacturing plant just manufactures whatever the product might be. That's an investment for profit. However, when we talk about the purchase of a bank, that's an investment for power."[1]

Because banks exercise such power, most nations severely restrict the ability of foreigners to own or control their banks, many of which are state owned. "Few overseas countries would permit any of their major banks to be acquired by foreign interests," noted Elmer B. Staats, comptroller general of the United States, in a report to Congress.[2]

119

While most nations regard banking as central to their sovereignty, the United States has no such qualms about foreign ownership of banking assets. The United States stands virtually alone among nations in its absence of barriers and its de facto policy of welcoming foreign banking assets and new acquisitions. Until recently, very few federal officials even raised questions, accepting the premise that international banking is a key component of the global economy. The federal government asks no more of foreign investors than of Americans who seek to own banks—do they have the requisite financial capability, competence, and integrity? Two states, Vermont and Maine, express their reservations by prohibiting any form of foreign banking; this makes very little difference, however, to foreign banks, which are concentrated in the industrialized states.

It soon became evident that the increase in foreign investment in the banking industry was too dramatic to ignore. In addition, the gathering of data uncovered problems that had been hidden from public view. Foreign-owned banking assets in the United States increased nearly fourteenfold between 1973 and 1986, from $32 billion in 1973 to $445 billion in 1986.[3] This meant that by 1986 nearly 17 percent of the nation's total banking assets of $1.7 trillion were foreign owned, compared with 3.8 percent in 1973 and 11.9 percent in 1980.

Of the $445 billion in foreign-owned banking assets, $11.3 billion was represented by foreign bank ownership of U.S. banks, and $23 billion, by foreign individual and corporate ownership of U.S. banks; $310.8 billion represented the assets of U.S. branches and agencies of foreign banks. The total represented a threefold increase since 1979, when foreign investors held $149.6 billion in U.S. banking assets.[4]

Foreign investors generally purchased control of U.S. banks in less than average condition and strengthened them by adding new capital, changing management, improving loan portfolios, and stopping the unsound practice of "sweetheart" transactions. Foreign banks also saved some failing American banks, which were often turned around by infusions of capital and more efficient management practices.

In some localities, foreign banks were regarded as more public spirited than their domestic counterparts for their willingness to loan money to small and medium-sized businesses. Jeanne Z. Brooks, an economic development official with the San Francisco mayor's office, said she preferred working with foreign-owned banks:

Foreign banks are better to work with. They are more competitive on tax-exempt bonds, and they are more aggressive. I look for IDBs [industrial development bonds] from Barclays [British owned]. Barclays looks at deals American banks wouldn't look at. Foreign banks are more willing to finance small business. These people coming in our doors don't have a bank in their back pocket. Over and over, the foreign banks come through.

In one case, I went to the Hong Kong Shanghai Bank. They saw that the deal worked, and they now enjoy working with us. We'll go back to them again. We had an old milk plant, the Spreckles Dairy, owned by a Chinese-American contractor. We decided to convert the site into a contractors' center, with plumbing, heating, etc. It was appropriate for San Francisco. I had a hard time shopping around trying to get an IDB. Barclays is doing it for us. Security Pacific's rates were too high by percentage and fees. Foreign banks are easier also on fees. They're thinking long-term. All of our banks are targeting big corporations and forgetting small businesses.

Initially, there was no pattern to the influx of foreign money. Led by Europeans, foreign investors purchased ninety-three U.S. banks worth $26.4 billion in the 1970s, and the rush to acquire more banks continued throughout the 1980s. California led all the states in foreign investment, with twenty-four acquired banks worth $10.7 billion. In 1985, of twelve bank acquisitions, five were located in New York and four in California. In the largest transaction of 1985, Midland Bank of Great Britain purchased the additional percentage it did not own of Crocker National Bank of San Francisco for $200 million.[5]

Foreign bankers attracted to the U.S. financial market have followed foreign business to the United States and have sought to tap the U.S. market and exploit its investment opportunities. They have concentrated their operations in New York, California, and Illinois, although they operate throughout the United States. Indeed, foreign-owned banks accounted for more than 40 percent of the total business loans made by banks in New York State in 1985. In California, foreign-owned banks have a market share of 32.8 percent of the state's total banking assets.[6]

By the end of 1985, foreign owners controlled two of the nation's largest banks, Crocker National Bank in California ($23 billion in assets; Midland Bank of U.K.), and Marine Midland of

New York ($22.6 billion in assets; Hong Kong and Shanghai Bank Corp.). These banks rank twelfth and thirteenth in the nation, respectively. Foreign investors also control Republic New York ($12 billion; Luxembourg), California First Bank ($5 billion; Japan), and the Union Bank of Los Angeles ($8 billion, U.K.).

A 1985 report by the Federal Reserve Board found that 250 foreign individuals, banks, holding companies, and other organizations owned and controlled 609 bank branches in the United States, with total assets of $411 billion. Japanese investors owned or controlled the lion's share of $170 billion. Other leading investor nations were the United Kingdom ($54 billion); Canada ($39 billion); France ($20 billion); and Hong Kong ($18.5 billion). One surprise: The communist People's Republic of China partook of this capitalist enterprise to the extent of $371 million in two branches in New York City.[7]

HOW U.S. POLICY GAVE FOREIGN-OWNED BANKS A COMPETITIVE ADVANTAGE OVER DOMESTIC BANKS

One reason that foreign investors achieved such a large share of the American market was the indifference of policymakers to laws and regulations that put U.S. banks at a competitive disadvantage. The most curious twist to the laissez-faire policy toward the influx of foreign banking assets was that many of these laws and regulations affected only U.S. banks, to the decided advantage of the foreign institutions. In effect, foreign banks operated in a deregulated environment, while domestic banks struggled to cope with complex and often confusing restrictions; the upshot was that during a crucial period U.S. laws made it easier for foreign banks to expand, while U.S. banks were held back.

The most glaring example was the restriction against interstate banking, which prohibited U.S. banks from operating across state lines while allowing foreign banks to expand freely. Consequently, U.S. banks could not buy other domestic institutions and had to stand by while foreign banks made the purchases. Meanwhile, during the time when U.S. laws and regulations were being modified, foreign-owned banks gained an enormous foothold in the United States and a competitive edge over U.S. banks. The policy was inadvertent—no one ever set out intentionally to put American banks at a competitive disadvantage—but the consequences were nonetheless very real.

One official who recognized that foreign banking posed real problems was William Seidman, chairman of the Federal Deposit Insurance Corporation (FDIC), who noted that the influx of foreign-owned bank assets was spurred by sparing foreign banks from the antitrust laws and other regulations to which domestic banks were subjected. "It's damaging our banks and our banking system," Mr. Seidman said of the surge of foreign-owned bank investments. "They're a factor in the decreasing earnings of our banks. Our banks are going downhill. They're getting less business. They have to compete with people who are less regulated than we are."

Another advantage enjoyed by foreign-owned banks, Mr. Seidman noted, was that they often operated with government subsidies as well as lower capital requirements. Compared with American banks, they often did so in the dark, with their assets, liabilities, and practices well concealed. "It's often very difficult to find out the parent company's financial position," Mr. Seidman said.

The surge of foreign ownership of U.S. banking assets led to warnings by other officials, who also were alerted by the problems identified by improved data gathering. In 1980, the comptroller general urged a moratorium on foreign ownership, and some state banking officials followed his lead. His report to the Congress bore the arresting title "Despite Positive Effects, Further Foreign Acquisitions of U.S. Banks Should Be Limited Until Policy Conflicts Are Fully Addressed."[8]

Congress often ignores or dilutes the General Accounting Office's recommendations, and this was no exception. In this case, Congress enacted only a three-month moratorium, between March and July 1980, on foreign ownership or control of U.S. banks with more than $100 million in assets, unless such acquisitions were necessary to prevent bankruptcy or insolvency. "One concern is that foreign interests may now control or have the potential to control large concentrations of U.S. banking assets and deposits," the report noted. "Also, it has been contended that foreign owners may change the operation of an acquired bank, making it less responsive to the banking needs of the local community or making it less sound. Another contention is that foreign interests have a distinct advantage in purchasing medium- and large-sized banks" because they were freed from the antitrust laws and other restrictions on domestic banks.[9]

A moratorium also was urged by Alan R. Cohen, the New York State Banking Department's acting superintendent, before a

House subcommittee in 1982. Among his concerns, Mr. Cohen said, were the adequacy of financial information provided by foreign institutions and individuals seeking to acquire U.S. banks, whether there would be the same degree of commitment to meeting local credit needs, and whether such acquisitions would promote the public interest. He said that his interest was spurred by the acquisition of a group of Arab investors of the $2.8 billion Financial General Holding Company and the plan of another group of Arab investors to buy a 25 percent interest in the parent company of Smith, Barney, a major investment banking firm. "The Banking Department's fundamental concern regarding foreign bank acquisitions of large American banks is that there are very important long-term issues involved in this acquisition trend," Mr. Cohen said. "These matters should be discussed and debated in Congress and in other public forums so that a national policy can be developed. Up to now, we have merely been proceeding on a case-by-case basis."[10]

The comptroller general found, however, that despite a few well-publicized problems attributed to foreign investors who gained control of U.S. banks, foreign investors generally improved weak U.S. banks and maintained the condition of financially strong U.S. banks that they acquired. Despite these improvements, foreign-owned banks failed more financial test areas than did domestic banks. These tests included capital adequacy, liquidity, the ratio of the asset/liability mix to deposits, loans, dividend policy, loan losses, and profitability. In addition, those banks that failed in these test areas showed less of a tendency to improve than did domestic-controlled banks.

The comptroller general also found that the foreign owners of U.S. banks were not as accessible to U.S. regulators.[11] Legal constraints prevented U.S. regulators from confirming information or making on-site examinations of foreign parent banks overseas; without those examinations, U.S. regulators were unable to judge the strength of the entire banking organization. Similarly, banking regulators are not fully able to assess the qualifications of foreign applicants to purchase U.S. banks because they cannot always verify information submitted to them. There was also the difficulty of recovering damages from foreign nationals.[12]

Ironically, foreign investors benefited most from our laws by being exempt from many of them. They enjoyed freedom from the very antitrust laws and regulations that have barred some takeovers of U.S. banks by U.S. banks. "The issue of domestic versus foreign buyers of U.S. banks involves a basic conflict between existing U.S. policies," the report found.[13] "U.S. policy is to allow relatively free foreign involvement in the U.S. economy, including banking. In many bank purchase circumstances, foreign banks have an unfair advantage over domestic banks. Yet, the laws and regulations which have caused the advantage are instruments of other U.S. policies." The report thus noted that "U.S. law allows some foreign banks the opportunity to buy large domestic banks which U.S. banks are prevented from buying."[14]

Domestic bankers complained bitterly that U.S. laws gave an unfair advantage to foreign buyers of U.S. banks. "U.S. acquisition laws, restrictions on interstate banking, and antitrust laws combine to give foreign banks an advantage over large U.S. banks when it comes to buying medium- to large-sized U.S. banks," the comptroller general noted.[15] Although the International Banking Act of 1978 modified these rules by making foreign bank holding companies subject to the same nonbanking restrictions applicable to domestic holding companies, foreign bank holding companies are allowed to own foreign businesses that conduct U.S. operations, except those engaged in securities underwriting.[16] In addition, antitrust law further restricts the number of potential bank buyers by subjecting purchase transactions to standards contained in antitrust provisions of the Bank Merger Act and the Bank Holding Act.

"A case could be made, then, given the current combination of laws and regulations, that the only possible buyers for some U.S. banks would be individuals or foreign banks and foreign bank holding companies acquiring a U.S. bank for the first time," the comptroller general argued. "We believe that the unfair situation should not be allowed to continue."[17]

In one case, a midwestern transportation conglomerate was required to sell its interest in a medium-sized Midwest bank because of the divestiture requirements of the Bank Holding Company Act of 1956. The sale had to be completed by January 1, 1981. No out-of-state U.S. banks were able to purchase the bank because of the McFadden Act and Douglas Amendment restrictions. Because the state restricts branching, no in-state bank could purchase the bank for the purposes of making it a branch. "The bank, which was in good condition and which was considered by local bankers to be an attractive investment, was purchased in July 1979 by one of the largest foreign banks in the world," the comptroller general reported. "This bank was establishing a subsidiary in the U.S. for the first time."[18]

Providing competitive equality between foreign and domestic banks in the United States was a major stimulus for enacting the International Banking Act of 1978. Prior to this legislation, competitive advantages favored foreign banking activities. In addition, no framework for their federal regulation existed.

As foreign banking continued to increase in the 1970s, these inequalities became more evident, and action was taken to correct them. The new law placed foreign banks under the same general restrictions as domestic banks. But a giant loophole emerged in the form of a "grandfather" provision in the law, which allowed some of the previously existing competitive inequalities to continue. This provision exempted all foreign bank operations existing or applied for on or before July 27, 1978, from the multistate limitations in the act. Consequently, sixty-three foreign banking organizations were allowed to continue such operations, including some of the largest in the world. "Given the number, size and nature of these existing operations, domestic banks will continue to be at a significant disadvantage in the multistate arena," the comptroller general warned.[19]

Foreign banks were also able to gain on their U.S. competitors through yet another twist in public policy, this time through the cooperation of their own countries. It was no surprise to U.S. banks that not all foreign countries extended the same welcome to them that their country extended to foreign banks. U.S. trade negotiators grappled with the issue with varying degrees of success, and finally Senator Jake Garn, Republican of Utah, introduced legislation in 1984 forcing the issue of reciprocity in banking.[20]

Although some of the competitive edge was dulled by raising these issues, negotiating some reforms, and passing corrective legislation, it is important to remember that foreign banking in the United States flourished because of the slack afforded by the intervening years; in the time it took to correct the inequities, foreign investors could operate unimpeded by fair competition. Moreover, as soon as one loophole was closed, another moved in to take its place. The Sumitomo Bank's purchase of part of Goldman Sachs, for example, hit Wall Street and U.S. banks by surprise, since U.S. banks are still barred from the securities business. The Federal Reserve Board approved the purchase on the grounds that Sumitomo would not control the firm. Coupled with the 75 percent purchase of the U.S.-based ABD securities firm by the Dresdner Bank of Germany, it looked as if U.S. policymakers were giving foreign banks yet another head start on their U.S. competitors—right on their own soil. What was surprising was that there was no outcry from U.S. banks or investment firms. Some analysts speculated that no one wanted to offend Goldman Sachs.[21]

THE SECRECY ISSUE

Foreign-owned banks also benefit from exemptions from disclosure requirements. Many foreign-owned banks, for example, chose not to apply for federal deposit insurance, because they were unwilling to disclose the financial information needed to obtain the insurance. As of January 31, 1980, only 14 of 126 U.S. foreign bank branches had filed applications for the insurance. The International Banking Act does not require foreign bank branches not accepting retail deposits to obtain insurance protection, and the FDIC exempts certain foreign bank branches that accept retail deposits from obtaining the insurance.[22]

The secrecy issue also affected the U.S. government's ability to protect its citizens. When these foreign investors made errors of judgment that harmed U.S. banks, it was often difficult to obtain damages. In one lawsuit, the FDIC learned that before its case could even be presented in the foreign country, the law there required a fee equal to 3 percent of the claim. The foreign court refused to disclose the value of assets or say whether they could be removed from the country.

The FDIC also experienced further delays from inefficient mail and telephone systems. Unlike U.S. litigation, the corporation relied entirely on the foreign lawyers it retained, because it had no familiarity with that country's laws. According to FDIC officials, the foreign lawyers charged high hourly fees and spent vast amounts of time resolving minor matters that could have been dispensed with more rapidly in U.S. courts.

THE MONEY WEAPON AND ISSUES OF SOVEREIGNTY

Arab acquisitions of U.S. banks are a matter of concern to those who fear the ''money weapon.'' The longest-established Arab financial institution in the U.S., the UBAF Arabia-American Bank, was opened in New York in 1976. The bank, a consortium of banks from a dozen Arab nations, holds assets of $1.25

billion. (The Libyan Foreign Bank, for example, owns 7.73 percent.) "The trickle of Arab banks in the United States has lately become a flood," the bank reported in a full-page advertisement in the *Wall Street Journal*.

> In the last two years the number of Arab banks there has tripled to 32, as Arab bankers have acted on the general buzz that they should have a presence in the strongest [financial] capital in the world. The mystery is the length of time Arab banks have taken in arriving in New York when they have been well established in London and Paris for nearly a decade.[23]

The advertisement noted that Suleiman Olayan, a Saudi businessman, owned 7.6 percent of First Chicago Corporation. With about 1 percent of the total stock, Mr. Olayan was also the largest shareholder in Chase Manhattan after David Rockefeller. He also has a 24 percent interest in the private Wall Street brokerage firm Donaldson, Lufkin & Jenrette. In 1982, a group of thirty-four investors from Saudi Arabia, Kuwait, and Bahrain paid $40 million for a similar 25 percent share in Smith Barney, a private investment banking house.[24]

"When these strategically placed private investors and their closely related Arab banks start to act in concert, they are likely to take a more activist role in the United States," the advertisement predicted. It did nothing to ease the fears of those who believe that the United States had become far too dependent on foreign ownership of U.S. banking assets and far too vulnerable to the "money weapon."

Another fear is that foreign investors can trigger banking crises as their collective power continues to grow. The failures of two major banks, Continental Illinois in Chicago and Franklin National in New York, have been attributed to the activities of foreign investors. Continental Illinois relied heavily on large depositors and obtained 55 percent of its deposits abroad. Foreign depositors began a run on the bank, touching off a general panic. "It was foreign involvement, on the funding side, that led to the recent crisis," noted *Business Week*.[25]

Others noted that Continental Illinois was already on the brink of failure and that foreign depositors merely alerted regulators to the impending crisis. The real controversy over Continental emerged later, when many realized that federal regulators bailed out Continental and practically bankrupted the FDIC while allowing hundreds of smaller community banks to fail; in effect, saving foreign investors and ignoring Americans—at least that was the perception of many observers. In their defense, regulators feared the repercussions, the loss of confidence in the international banking community that would have accompanied the failure of Continental.

At the moment, however, there is no hard evidence that these investors have used their financial base as a political weapon, despite the occasional advertisement to that effect. Neither is there any hard evidence that foreign banks are more prone to failure than their U.S. counterparts. But the growing dominance of foreign banks, particularly in the country's financial centers, has given rise to concern among the nation's policymakers.

"It's a question of national sovereignty," said John R. Shultz, deputy associate director of the General Government Division of the General Accounting Office. "Do we want assets and businesses in this country controlled by people in other countries who have different agendas?" Rudy Oswald, chief economist for the AFL-CIO, echoed this fear: "If you lose control of banks, you lose control of monetary policy."

Representative Charles Schumer, Democrat of Brooklyn, New York, and a member of the House Banking Committee, also fears the uncertainties of such a radical transfer of financial power. He notes that the increase in foreign investment in banking has been so rapid that it is difficult to predict precisely what the impact has been. "It's uncharted waters," Mr. Schumer said.

> It impacts very broadly but indirectly. The average depositor gets a good rate of interest, and maybe better service with a foreign-owned bank. But the use of the money is no longer in American hands. You're giving non-Americans the decision on where to put the money. That has to affect the American consumer in the long run.

One fear, as yet undocumented, is that foreign-owned U.S. banks, many of which came on the coattails of foreign-owned U.S. industries, will discriminate against American businesses. "Like anyone else, a foreign bank is more likely to invest in people they're familiar with," Mr. Schumer said. Another problem, he noted, was that the greatest advantages will be reaped by those countries with the fewest regulations, who are best able to compete for the U.S. bank deposit. This could lead to cutthroat competition among U.S. banks.

Those who welcome foreign ownership of U.S. banks argue that money is neutral, that the U.S. benefits from an additional reservoir of funds, and that banking investments go where they will reap the highest yield. Furthermore, it is unlikely that investors will organize to use their money as a weapon and destabilize the very country they have used as a safe haven.

But key policymakers warn that it is essential for a nation to control its flow of money and not depend on foreign investors whose national agendas may differ from those of the United States. In addition, they believe that foreign banks operating in the United States should be subject to the same restrictions imposed on domestic banks. Finally, it is important to monitor the money flow more closely so that Americans can more readily track the effect of foreign money in the United States and take swift action should problems arise.

CHAPTER 10

The Kremlin's Banks in America

National Security and Foreign Investment

I always viewed it as a deliberate penetration by the KGB of the American banking system.

—*Bartholomew Lee, San Francisco attorney*

Our relations in the financial field in the U.S. are practically nonexistent.

—*M. Melnikuv, deputy trade representative, Soviet embassy*

The Soviet effort to acquire several banks in California's Silicon Valley, eventually thwarted by the CIA, is a cloak-and-dagger story that illustrates how the United States appears to be so hungry for foreign dollars that it is blinded to problems of national security. It demonstrates how this country has become so desperate for foreign capital that it fails to take appropriate steps to monitor the source of foreign funds and protect itself against hostile incursions until it is almost too late. It also shows how foreign investors sometimes acquire American companies solely to acquire our technology, as well as the key role played by banks in the nation's industrial life. Most important, the case corroborates former CIA director William Casey's view that foreign investment is a "Trojan horse," deceptively friendly and fraught with danger.

U.S. intelligence and military officials say that the object of the Soviet scheme was to obtain critical credit information on companies and individual scientists and engineers in order to apply pressure on those in financial straits. The objective was to learn the entire financial structure of Silicon Valley and thereby obtain access to the boardrooms and individuals most vulnerable to financial pressure. Their secondary goal was to steal American technology, and what better way than through privileged information about company secrets channeled through a bank's loan department.

To these ends, the Soviets acquired control, albeit temporarily, of the Peninsula National Bank in Burlingame, First National Bank of Fresno, and Tahoe National Bank in South Lake Tahoe. In addition, they obtained partial interest in the Camino California bank in San Francisco. Peninsula National had made numerous loans to high-technology companies and, along with the other banks, counted employees and executives of high-technology companies among its clients.

The scheme focused on Amos Dawe, a Singapore businessman now serving time in a Hong Kong prison, who swiftly rose from an obscure postal clerk to become one of the richest men in Asia and a confidant of Ferdinand Marcos and other chiefs of state. Mr. Dawe is the son of a Canadian father and his Malaysian wife, whom he met and married while serving in the Canadian navy. His rapid climb was accomplished with the help of backing from the Singapore branch of the Soviet Union's Moscow Narodny bank. Some speculate that the Soviets first hired him to intercept mail—who would suspect an obscure functionary?—and the money they paid provided him with the capital for initial real estate investments that became the cornerstone of his financial empire.

In fact, the future tycoon was a Singapore postal clerk in the 1960s, when he began to make contacts and to buy property on an island in Singapore harbor. When the Singapore government decided to build a bridge to the island, Mr. Dawe became rich overnight. It is not known whether he had prior knowledge of the decision, but his business career soared thereafter. Mr. Dawe built and sold homes at first, then put his rapidly growing capital into rubber and palm-oil plantations, eventually acquiring fifteen estates covering 9,000 acres. Profits from the plantations went into insurance companies and mysterious companies with such names as Raja Enterprises, Malaysian Wood Wool Products, and South Jahore Amalgamated Holdings. An interlocking group of 200 Dawe companies was known collectively as the Mosbert Group.[1]

Paralleling the growth of Mr. Dawe's financial empire was the growth of the Singapore branch of the Moscow Narodny Bank, the official overseas bank of the Soviet Union. The staid London head office opened the Singapore branch in 1971, and it immediately began making high-risk loans to overseas Chinese, primarily real estate speculators. The bank expanded rapidly from 1971 to 1975, becoming one of the most active banks in the international market, with loans approaching $1 billion. Moscow Narodny, founded at the time of the Russian Revolution, normally handled transactions abroad for state agencies and managed their foreign-currency holdings.

The activities of its Singapore operations manager, P. K. Teo, were something new in its history and gave rise to conjecture that the bank's real motive was to curry favor with influential overseas Chinese at the expense of the Soviet Union's opponents in Peking. Mr. Teo's clients, in addition to Mr. Dawe, included such colorful characters as Eddie Wong, who sold surplus U.S. Army trucks in Burma after the war, facilitated the flight of refugees from China to Hong Kong, and carried pilgrims to Mecca from Indonesia and Malaysia. Another client was Y. T. Chou, a Singapore businessman involved in a $100 million development in Chinatown in Oakland, California, called "Hong Kong/USA." The Soviet bank also helped finance a plan by Mr. Wong for a resort on Lan Tau, an island off Hong Kong. But it did so covertly, since Hong Kong authorities rigidly exclude any overt Soviet presence in deference to their ultimate landlords in Peking.

Early in his business career, Mr. Dawe was introduced to P. K. Teo, and Moscow Narodny began to pour money into his enterprises. "Amos Dawe and Moscow Narodny were working hand in hand way back," said Cliff Palefsky, one of Mr. Dawe's San Francisco attorneys. U.S. military and intelligence officials regard Mr. Dawe as a front for the Soviet bank and the bank itself as a front for the KGB. Moscow Narodny makes no major transactions without the approval of the Soviet intelligence agency, according to U.S. intelligence officials. "There's no way that the Russians do anything involving money and the Moscow Narodny bank that isn't cleared by their intelligece people," Mr. Palefsky said. Moscow Narodny's attempt to acquire three California banks, and an interest in a fourth, was considered an effort to gain access to advanced American technology. It is considered part of a broad Soviet effort to acquire Western technology for military and commercial purposes.

The Soviet scheme was pieced together from interviews with intelligence and military officials, private lawyers familiar with the case, court records, and statements by Mr. Dawe.[2] Moscow Narodny used Mr. Dawe to acquire the three California banks and another intermediary, Y. T. Chou, to acquire a half interest in the Camino California bank in San Francisco. Moscow Narodny selected the banks to be acquired and supervised their acquisition, according to Mr. Dawe's statements. Ephraim Margolin, another of Mr. Dawe's attorneys in San Francisco, said of his client, "There is no doubt in my mind that he was working for the Russians." Cliff Palefsky added:

> There's no question that he was reporting to the Russians. He came over with Russian money, at the suggestion of the Russians, and accompanied by a Russian agent [P. K. Teo, manager of Moscow Narodny's Singapore bank]. It was Mr. Dawe's belief that the Soviets were interested in gaining some access to computer technology.

THE CIA ALERT

The scheme was aborted by a CIA agent, who noted a peculiar lending pattern by the Moscow Narodny bank and released the story to an Asian financial newsletter.[3] Once it was public, the plan fell apart, and the Soviets disavowed any connection or knowledge of the plot to buy American banks. Mr. Dawe acknowledged through his lawyers his role as an intermediary. Efforts to reach Mr. Chou, who is believed to be living in Southeast Asia, were unavailing.

Mr. Dawe, at fifty-two, was then principal owner of the Mosbert Group, a holding company with interests in hotels, real estate, plantations, finance companies, and other properties. The Mosbert Group controlled 200 companies, with $160 million in assets, in Southeast Asia.

The Soviet funds for the bank purchase traveled a circuitous route. According to court papers filed in Federal District Court in San Francisco, Mr. Dawe obtained a $50 million line of credit in late 1974 from Moscow Narodny's Singapore branch for the purpose of purchasing several banks in northern California. Mr. Dawe has contended that the loan was in exchange for some of his property in the Mosbert Group, but the Soviets contested this allegation.

The first installment of funds to Mr. Dawe, $3 million, went from Moscow Narodny to the Pacific Atlantic Bank in Panama to the Commerce Union Bank in Nashville, Tennessee, and finally, by letters of credit, to Mr. Dawe in San Francisco. Hunter Atkins, executive vice-president of the Commerce Union Bank, said that the $3 million transaction was not unusual. "Extending these amounts of money under an international letter of credit confirmed by a major lender such as Moscow Narodny would be normal," he said. The net effect, however, was that it was difficult to trace these funds back to the Soviet source.

In a brief interview with the British Broadcasting Corporation (BBC) in 1983, Mr. Dawe recalled that Moscow Narodny had sent him to San Francisco to study various banks. Upon his return to Singapore, Mr. Dawe said in the interview, he was surprised by how much the Moscow Narodny officials already knew about the California banks. "Lots of things that are centered in the banking institution in San Francisco, and to my surprise they already have all the information under their table. You know, they have the whole map and everything there and which bank is to be acquired, and so on. They have everything; they have all the information on banks, you know.[4]

"I have details; they have already more details," Mr. Dawe continued. "They have more details than I could imagine. They have done their homework. They have all the details of all the banks in the big area." Why did they have all the details? "They were trying to get someone within the group, within the climes of Moscow Bank, that would be suitable for the job," Mr. Dawe said. "To take over the banks in San Francisco."

Mr. Dawe negotiated the sale of the Fresno, Tahoe, and Burlingame banks, which were owned by the Central Bank of California. He was accompanied by P. K. Teo. Mr. Dawe offered to pay a premium price for the banks, three times the book value, but that did not alert Central California to the possibility that things may not have been as they seemed and that the banks may have had some ulterior value. Nor did it lead Central California to believe that Mr. Dawe may not have been the principal in the case.

"We had no reason to suspect that he was not the principal," Robert L. Haggen, the bank's vice-president and counsel, said in an interview. "Based on the limited information we obtained, he was a very wealthy man with operations all over the world."

But Mr. Palefsky said, "There's no question that he was reporting to the Russians and got their approval." To Quentin Breen, another of Mr. Dawe's San Francisco lawyers, "This is Southeast Asia. Nothing is as it appears. It was a matter of mutual use."

Court records reveal that Mr. Dawe purchased the Burlingame bank in December 1974 for $3.05 million, placed $300,000 in an escrow account, and financed the remainder through a letter of credit issued by the Commerce Union Bank of Nashville. Mr. Dawe purchased the Fresno and Tahoe banks in June 1975 for $7.9 million. He placed $808,300 in escrow and paid an installment of $685,266 in October 1975. He also put up the stock in the Fresno and Tahoe banks as collateral for the sale. Mr. Chou meanwhile purchased the half interest in Camino California in October 1975 for about $2 million, according to his San Francisco attorneys, who said he put up about $200,000.

Members of the intelligence community said that a U.S. intelligence officer with a banking background based in Singapore learned of the transactions. "It was one smart CIA guy who noticed a peculiar lending pattern," said Richard N. Perle, assistant secretary of defense for international security policy. "It didn't smell right." American intelligence officers then disclosed the purchases to Raymond Sacklyn, publisher of a Hong Kong financial newsletter, *Target,* according to U.S. officials. Mr. Sacklyn refused to identify the source of the article but denied that U.S. intelligence officials had "fed" him the article. Mr. Sacklyn was asked by the BBC how he thought Moscow Narodny actually regarded Amos Dawe. "A pleasant, adventurous, egocentrical fool, but a useful one," Mr. Sacklyn replied. But no man who rises from obscure poverty to become one of the richest men in the world can be so easily dismissed.[5]

The bank deal collapsed upon publication of the article. So did Mr. Dawe's financial empire. There was apparently no point in a covert effort that had gone public, and Moscow Narodny withdrew its funds, leaving Mr. Dawe and Mr. Chou financially vulnerable. Central California bank foreclosed on its collateral and acquired the stock to the three banks. In time, Dawe's wife, Angela, divorced him and remarried. His son, Kevin, and daughter, Valeria, remained in the United States with their mother.

In July 1977, Mr. Dawe was indicted by a federal grand jury in San Francisco and charged with "the willful misapplication of the money, funds, and credits of the Peninsula National Bank, the First National Bank of Fresno and the Tahoe National Bank, with the intent to defraud said banks." Mr. Dawe returned to San Francisco from Taiwan to face the charges. "Amos came to the U.S. voluntarily, with certain promises by the government," said Mr. Margolin, his attorney. "They promised that if he stood trial, he would be protected and not extradited. The promises were not kept.''

Federal prosecutors denied that any deal had been made. The charges were dismissed in February 1979 at the request of the Justice Department ''in the interest of justice.'' Robert Mueller, an assistant U.S. attorney who prosecuted the case, was asked if the charges were dismissed at the request of the CIA. He replied, ''I have no comment on that.''

A tangle of lawsuits ensued as the Soviet bank tried to get back its money from Mr. Dawe after the bank purchases were scuttled. Since Mr. Dawe had defaulted on the payments, he lost the funds he had committed for the purchases of the banks and could not repay Moscow Narodny. The suits were subsequently dropped.

In 1979, Mr. Dawe was extradited to Hong Kong to stand trial for fraud. ''The Russians wanted him,'' Mr. Palefsky recalled. ''Through the Moscow Narodny bank, they were able to get him indicted in Hong Kong.'' Although he was acquitted in the Hong Kong trial, the government appealed, and the Supreme Court later asserted its authority, convicted Mr. Dawe, and sentenced him to five years. Mr. Dawe was thereafter arrested carrying a fake passport at a London airport. He was extradited to Hong Kong, where he began his prison sentence in 1984.

''A number of different people have told us that there is a basis for suspicion that Hong Kong is really doing the bidding of somebody else, perhaps knowingly, perhaps not, the bidding of the Soviet Union,'' Mr. Margolin told a federal judge at Mr. Dawe's extradition hearing. William Dorward, commissioner for Hong Kong and its senior representative in the United States, responded through a spokesman. ''It is so bizarre that I could not even begin to comment,'' he said. On January 21, 1979, Victor V. Geraschenko, vice-chairman of the Moscow Narodny bank and managing director of the Singapore branch, signed an affidavit declaring, ''I have never exerted pressure on the official receiver, Hong Kong, or any person in Singapore or anywhere else to extradite Amos Dawe to Hong Kong.'' But on March 27, 1981, after Mr. Dawe's extradition had been ordered, Mr. Geraschenko filed an affidavit supporting Mr. Dawe's return.

Unlike Mr. Dawe's three national banks, Mr. Chou's bank, Camino California, was a state bank. John Paulus, California's deputy superintendent of banks, said there was no information available on the sale. ''There's nobody here who was here then,'' Mr. Paulus said. The small bank, at 250 Sutter Street, is now called American California. Mr. Chou sold his interest in the bank to Jack Johansen, the president.

AMERICAN VULNERABILITY TO FOREIGN CASH

The Soviet bank scheme dramatized how the greed of some businessmen blinded them to the ramifications of their actions, said Richard Perle. The episode reminded him of a favorite quotation in which V. I. Lenin, the Russian revolutionary, advised Carl Radek, head of the Polish Communist party, that the capitalists would sell the revolutionaries the rope for the nooses by which the capitalists would hang.

In September 1985, the Department of Defense published a study, ''Soviet Acquisition of Militarily Significant Western Technology: An Update.''[6] Caspar W. Weinberger, secretary of defense, told a news conference:

> This report pinpoints, I think, one statistic that reveals the astounding level of Soviet absorption of Western technology. By their own estimate, more than 5,000 Soviet military research projects each year are benefiting significantly from Western acquired technology.
>
> What it really means is that we are subsidizing the military buildup of the Soviet Union, and the costs have been staggering. By systematically acquiring Western secrets from high-technology manufacturers, research centers, universities, and defense contractors, the Soviets are advancing their military programs by several years and saving themselves several tens of thousands of man years of scientific research each year, and at the same time, they're requiring us to spend far more for our own defense than would otherwise be the case.

The study noted that one of the most effective stratagems used by the Soviets was what it called a ''contract or broker diverter,'' who typically used dummy and front firms to mask his identity. This was the case in the Soviet scheme to acquire the banks in Silicon Valley. U.S. intelligence, military and banking officials, along with some members of Congress, said that the scheme has raised questions about whether banking statutes, even those that have been strengthened since then, are adequate to cope with a threat to national security. If the Soviet Union had managed to take over a bank, the officials said, they could have learned about the confidential finances of American high-technology companies, enabling them to put pressure on executives and companies, or even take them over.

"I always viewed it as a deliberate penetration by the KGB of the American banking system," said Bartholomew Lee, a San Francisco lawyer involved in the case. Senator Daniel P. Moynihan, Democrat of New York, an intelligence specialist, was one of the few on Capitol Hill aware of the Soviet effort. "It's a new form of industrial espionage," he said. "It doesn't involve people stealing blueprints; they own the blueprints."

As expected, the Soviets denied any involvement. M. Melnikuv, deputy trade representative at the Soviet embassy in Washington, said he was not familiar with the takeover attempt. "I never heard this story, and I don't know anyone who has," he said. "Our relations in the financial field in the United States are practically nonexistent." Similarly, officials of the Moscow Narodny bank, which financed the attempt to buy interests in the banks, have insisted that its loans were strictly business transactions. The Soviet scheme underscores a problem in an unregulated system in which the highest bidder can acquire institutions that have access to sensitive information. The incident also highlighted the difficulty of learning the true principals in some financial transactions and of tracking money that has been laundered to hide its source under layers of transactions.

"There is sometimes a real conflict between free trade and national security," said Perle. "It seems to me it is in our national security interest not to give the Soviets any leverage." He noted the problems of disguised ownership and lax data gathering.

"It seems to me that at the very least we ought to have a continuing audit of what is being acquired, and by whom," he said. "We ought to look behind the immediate purchaser and satisfy ourselves that we know who we're really dealing with."

Similarly, Senator Patrick J. Leahy, Vermont Democrat and vice-chairman of the Intelligence Committee, said, "With the enormous flow of foreign capital into the United States, we have to have something that guarantees that the public knows who is buying and running a bank, and why." Senator Moynihan added that "the ownership of banks is not a private affair. If you have to go two or three layers into the system to find out what's happening, go two or three layers into the system."

Banks are an important source of valuable intelligence, said

Representative Charles E. Schumer, a New York Democrat who is a member of the House Banking Committee. "If you wanted to find out about any aspect of American industry, one of the most effective and relatively cheap ways to do it is to get inside a bank. Banks give unfriendly foreign powers a window into things they ought not to see."

"We're really in a public dilemma," said Frederic R. Dahl, associate director of the Federal Reserve Board's Division of Banking Supervision and Regulation. "We've always had a tradition in this country that anyone could start a bank, with the proviso that he had some money and was reputable. Then you come to the question of undesirables getting in. You try to keep them out, but it's easier said than done."

The Soviets' effort in California may not be an isolated one. Mr. Dawe told federal officials that the Soviet Union had succeeded in carrying out similar acquisitions in other parts of the country but declined to specify where or when, according to his lawyers. Mr. Perle agreed. "If the Moscow Narodny bank attempted to acquire banks in Silicon Valley, you can be sure that they made other efforts elsewhere," he said.

Although federal banking laws were toughened in 1978 as a result of several cases of domestic fraud, many experts contend that they remain inadequate to block the kind of takeover attempted by Moscow Narodny. There is no law, for example, prohibiting the Soviets from acquiring U.S. banks, and intelligence officials believe that there are inadequate efforts to discover the true principals of some bank transactions. "As long as we have an inadequate statutory base, we're going to be vulnerable," Mr. Perle said.

Steven J. Weiss, deputy comptroller of the currency, said that under federal laws "the situation has tightened up a great deal, but there are still some problems. It's disheartening." Mr. Weiss noted that his agency has sixty days to approve or reject a proposed bank sale. Such sales can be rejected on any of three grounds: if the purchaser fails to provide the necessary information, lacks financial capability, or is judged to lack integrity or competence. "That's where we get a lot of murky stuff," Mr. Weiss said. "We have a standard procedure of checking with the CIA, the FBI, and Interpol. Those checks frequently produce nothing." At best, he said, they produce gut reactions or background information that cannot provide the basis for rejecting a sale. "There have been cases where the proposal stinks but we don't have the statutory grounds to turn them down."

Congressional critics dispute such excuses and charge federal agencies with timidity. A 1984 report by the House Committee on Government Operations reflected this view. "Even when confronted with evidence of prior misconduct or questionable integrity, the agencies rarely deny change of control applications," the report said.[7] Representative Fernand J. St. Germain, the Rhode Island Democrat who chairs the House Banking Committee, noted the problems of ascertaining the principals of some transactions. "There are many subterfuges used to disguise ownership," he said. But he said that many of these problems could be solved by strict enforcement of existing laws. "The comptroller's office is wearing blinders," Mr. St. Germain said.

The problem of money laundering—when investors attempt to disguise the source of their funds—led the Reagan administration and members of Congress to introduce legislation to make the process a crime. Senator Alfonse M. D'Amato, the New York Republican who serves on the Banking Committee, has introduced legislation that would make money laundering a crime, impose fines for the full amount of the money laundered, and authorize the Treasury Department to subpoena testimony and bank records to enforce the Bank Secrecy Act. "If the institution was liable for forfeiture of the entire amount of money, you'd see how quickly they'd put a system in," he said. Representative John Bryant, Texas Democrat, has introduced legislation that would require the disclosure of the "ultimate, beneficial owner of five percent or $100,000 value of any foreign investment in the United States, including bank deposits and loans."

But there probably is no defense against a determined, well-financed effort. "If you're willing to spend enough time, money, and effort, you can get away with anything," said Dawe's attorney, Quentin Breen. "When you live in an open society, you have to accept the consequences. The question is, can we afford to continue to be such an open society?"

CHAPTER 11

Buying America

Foreign Investment in U.S. Real Estate

Basically, I think we've improved the architecture of the city.
— *Julian Josephs, a British real estate adviser in Washington, D.C.*

Foreign investment is coming in too fast, faster than we can assimilate it. It has depressed the inner city and commercial rents in Salt Lake City.

— *Norman H. Bangerter, Governor of Utah and former real estate developer*

Since land is a finite resource, the vast majority of nations place severe restrictions on a foreigner's ability to buy it. In many nations, such purchases are totally banned, while others allow foreigners to purchase real estate only in partnership with their own nationals. Still others limit foreign purchases to personal use.

In colonial America, such restrictions also applied. "As early as 1635, Watertown passed its order that no 'forreiner' coming into town should benefit by the commonage." Prior to 1659, Connecticut forbade sales to outsiders unless the town gave permission. Despite such early discrimination against outsiders, landholding in the United States has had a history of liberal settlement and sales.[1] Restrictions still exist in many states against foreign ownership of farmland, but they are slowly being phased out for two reasons: Recent court cases have tended to support the claims of foreign investors;[2] and farmland has decreased so much in value from 1980 to 1987 that American farmers would sell to anyone willing to buy.

Today foreign investors favor urban over rural real estate by about ten to one in capital invested. Urban real estate is not monitored; investors are protected by the anonymity of cities; and they can avoid becoming embroiled in controversies stemming from Americans' traditional attachment to their land. Most important is the anonymity: Nobody knows even approximately how much U.S. real estate is owned by foreign investors because so many of these purchases are concealed, but experts agree that there has been a surge in foreign ownership in the last decade. "I would not be surprised if the figure was more than $100 billion," said Richard A. Apcar, director of the investment analysis division of the Office of Trade and Investment Analysis, the U.S. Department of Commerce. Foreign investors purchased $50 billion worth of real estate between 1979 and 1983, according to data gathered by the International Trade Administration of the U.S. Department of Commerce and analyzed by Mahlon Apgar, a specialist in foreign real estate acquisition.[3]

THE ATTRACTIONS OF U.S. REAL ESTATE

U.S. attitudes toward foreign investors in real estate depend largely on whether one is a buyer or seller. Foreign investors often contribute to soaring real estate prices, a boon to sellers but a bane to buyers. That has especially been true of the British, Canadian, and Japanese investors. Occasionally, when foreign investors are faced with economic reversals, such as the Latin American recession of the early 1980s, foreign investors conduct distress sales that take the bottom out of U.S. real estate markets.

Similarly, U.S. investors in Florida, Texas, and Southern California real estate saw the value of their property plummet during the Mexico currency crisis of the early 1980s, when Mexican investors were forced to sell their condominiums and walk away from their commercial properties because they could not pay their mortgages. In some areas, foreign investors have helped drive middle-class residents out of the central city, as the costs of apartments soar beyond their means. Many of the high-priced condominiums and cooperatives sold in mid-Manhattan are purchased by foreign owners who occupy them only a few days, or weeks, a year. While such housing arrangements may improve midtown traffic, they are nevertheless resented by displaced New Yorkers.

As with other foreign investments, it is often difficult to uncover the true owner of real estate. To remedy this problem, Congress passed the Foreign Investment Study Act of 1974, but the results have been disappointing. Monitoring the ownership of real estate—both urban and rural—is complicated by the layering of control over legal entities, such as corporations or trusts. Nominees may obscure the country of origin as well as the real owners and the source of their funds, and their attorneys take full advantage of the available procedural and technical loopholes to mask their identity. In the legal confusion, the task of locating all the land interests of an owner or a class of owners can be a major undertaking, if not downright impossible.

Congressional committees discovered anew the baffling disguises of real estate ownership when they sought to uncover the U.S. real estate holdings of deposed dictators Ferdinand Marcos of the Philippines and Jean-Claude (Baby Doc) Duvalier of Haiti. Mr. Duvalier's five Manhattan apartments, worth $5 million, included a fifty-fourth-floor Trump Tower condominium purchased for $1.65 million. "Based on information we've picked up, we believe there are a lot more Duvalier holdings to be found in the U.S.," said Jules Kroll, president of Kroll Associates, a large investigative firm.[4]

Such inadequate reporting makes it difficult to estimate the amount of foreign investment in real estate. Of the $50 billion estimate for the period 1979–83, only $26 billion had actually been reported. The unreported $24 billion in sales was gleaned by the Office of Trade and Investment Analysis from newspaper articles, journals, research reports, and other published sources. Canadians dominated the real estate market, purchasing 58 percent of all foreign-owned real estate in the United States during this period. Of the remainder, 28 percent of the investors were European, 7 percent came from the Far East, and 6 percent from South America. In reported dollars, Canada provided 64 percent; United Kingdom, 17 percent; Netherlands Antilles, 6 percent; Japan and the Netherlands, 5 percent each; and West Germany, 3 percent. The majority of foreign investors were institutions—developers, corporations, partnerships, and associations whose main business was development.[5]

During the boom years of the late 1970s and well into the early 1980s, Mr. Apgar noted, "foreign investors cropped up everywhere. Canadian developers, with huge bankrolls and organizations, took on some of the premier office and mixed-use projects and extensive residential activity in key U.S. markets. British and Dutch institutions wrote real estate history by paying record-breaking prices for prime downtown property. Arab traders and Asian entrepreneurs often surprised American promoters by their shrewd insights and deal structures. In short order, these newcomers to the U.S. real estate industry made a visible impact and a significant contribution."[6]

Two broad-based economic forces provided the impetus that drove record-breaking amounts of foreign dollars into U.S. real estate. First, investors in major industrial and OPEC (Organization of Petroleum Exporting Countries) countries had large surpluses to redeploy quickly and safely. Second, countries like Britain, the Netherlands, and Saudi Arabia offered limited opportunities for local investment. Enthusiasm declined in 1982, however, as the strength of the dollar began to erode and overbuilding and high vacancies made real estate values less appealing than bullish Wall Street. The real estate market quickly rebounded, however, and has been strong ever since. By 1986, the Japanese entered it as major players, spurred by the pressures of their surplus capital. Mr. Apgar noted the attractions of U.S. real estate:

> Real estate had distinct advantages for many investors from high-inflation economies; it offered a hedge that did not need to be closely watched. The size, diversity, and local structure of U.S. markets provided opportunities to discreetly invest large amounts of capital. A familiar and tangible asset, real property had the added advantage of needing less management than an operating business, appealing to institutions and individuals alike.[7]

Foreign investors also benefited from certain tax advantages not available to Americans. Before June 18, 1980, foreigners could legally avoid capital gains taxes on the sale of their U.S. property. Now they can still do so, but it is more difficult: A tax loophole allows them to sell stock in foreign companies that hold U.S. property and not pay capital gains taxes.

An attempt to give foreign investors back their full tax advantage in the 1986 tax reform act was defeated by Senator Howard Metzenbaum, Democrat of Ohio. Metzenbaum introduced an amendment specifying that the money paid in capital gains taxes by foreign investors be earmarked to liberalize medical deductions and help distressed farmers average their income.

FARMLAND

Agricultural land sales are not as anonymous as urban real estate, thanks to a 1978 law—the Agricultural Foreign Investment Disclosure Act (AFIDA)—requiring the disclosure of foreign ownership of farmland. The law was passed quickly in response to a heated controversy over rumored purchases of U.S. farmland by Arab sheikhs, the Metternichs of Germany, and even the prince of Liechtenstein. As a result, farmland remains the only area of foreign investment that is regularly monitored by the U.S. government.

AFIDA requires all foreign owners of U.S. agricultural land to submit annual reports detailing the amount of acreage they own. The act also directs the secretary of agriculture to file a report annually assessing the impact of foreign ownership on family farms and rural communities.

Despite all the political pressures that led to its passage, the act is flawed in one major respect: It fails to give agency officials the tools to gather comprehensive information. Several giant loopholes in the law make it possible for foreign investors to conceal their identities, thus rendering the aggregate figure inaccurate.

"If you don't want your name disclosed, all you have to do is set up three levels of incorporation," explained J. Peter DeBraal, the Department of Agriculture's top expert in foreign investment in farmland, and the official responsible for compiling and writing the annual report. If you want to hide your identity, "you can substitute anybody—a trust fund, nominee, attorney, another company."

The irony is that AFIDA, which mandates disclosure, restricts agriculture officials from following up phony-looking documents to find out the real owners. Landholders' attorneys can simply conceal their clients' holdings in multiple dummy corporations, which serve the dual purpose of hiding their identity as well as laundering their money.

"We are prohibited from looking beyond the third level of incorporation," reported DeBraal:

> Once we get to the Netherlands Antilles, we don't even bother. It is done out of file drawers: just corporate records; no information and no taxes. The Netherlands Antilles has a favorable tax treaty with the United States. It is also an identity haven; they are prohibited by law from disclosing information on shareholders.

The Netherlands Antilles, not surprisingly, ranks in the top five countries owning farmland in the United States, with "one acre registered to every man, woman, and child who lives on that tiny Caribbean island nation," quipped Representative John Bryant of Texas, a critic of U.S. policy tolerating dummy corporations.

With the loopholes so visible, many wonder why Congress has not taken steps to close them; they seem such an obvious violation of legislative intent. "There is not much you can do about it," said DeBraal. "There are no longer any advocates in Congress."

As expected, the act quieted the controversy over foreigners' buying up U.S. farmland—an irony since the information was known to be incomplete. Nevertheless, the data indicated that foreign ownership of farmland was insignificant. In 1983, foreign investors disclosed that they directly owned 14 million acres of agricultural land, 300,000 more than the previous year, or slightly more than 1 percent.[8] This compared with 5.2 million acres as of October 1979.[9] By the end of 1985, foreign-owned agricultural land appeared to drop by 1.9 million acres, bringing the total acreage down to 12.1 million acres, which was slightly less than 1 percent of the total.[10] The Department of Agriculture study also concluded that there was no evidence that foreigners were taking purchased agricultural land out of production—a common fear associated with absentee owners.

Foreign investors have bought agricultural land in every state in the union except for Rhode Island, with Maine holding the record for the largest percentage—20 percent of all foreign-owned agricultural land in the country and 14 percent of the agricultural land in Maine. Investors from Canada lead in U.S. purchases, with 31 percent of the total, followed by Great Britain, Hong Kong, West Germany, and the Netherlands Antilles. Foreign nationals from Arab nations held very little land—Saudi Arabians, for example, owned only .2 percent. Fears of foreign control over food production were also laid to rest by the Agriculture Department's research: only 38 percent of agricultural land is used for crops, pasture, or other food-related activities; the rest is either forests or land that is not being used.[11]

The act dampened the controversy over foreign ownership of farmland, but the law sanctioned a system of data collection that allowed foreign investors to hide their identity as well as the source of their funds. If there were a problem, it would be very difficult to identify. The final irony was entirely unanticipated: "The AFIDA Act did more to encourage foreign farmland investment," reported DeBraal, "because of the provision that investments be public. We have created an information source for [foreign] industrial people. I've had so many calls from Americans who want to sell and want a list of investors. Members of Congress thought public disclosure would discourage investors. They were wrong.''

THE EFFECTS OF FOREIGN REAL ESTATE SPECULATION

Sparked by their pension funds, the British have been the leading foreign investors in Washington, D.C., having concentrated on what they call the "Golden Triangle," choice downtown real estate bordered by Pennsylvania, Connecticut, and New Hampshire avenues.

The British-owned buildings are modernistic and expensively built. They have a look of solidity, with sweeping setbacks and marble and granite lobbies filled with sculpture and greenery. The British investors also were partial to large, ornate bathrooms. "Basically, I think we've improved the architecture of the city," said Julian Josephs, an American-born Briton now based there, who has advised British pension funds and other real estate investors. "We've been renovating properties for 500 years."[12]

Mr. Josephs, who put together some of the biggest British deals, noted that the surge of British investment reflected the view that "Washington, with government as the preeminent tenant, is not going to go downhill. It's all happened since 1976. There's been a 50 percent increase in the last two years."[13]

The architecture and workmanship of the British-owned buildings have impressed local developers. Vernon Knarr, a local real estate broker who has sold some properties to the British, noted that "they build to hold for a long period of time. The British look to long-term appreciation, not tax benefits. In Britain, it's 100 years, not a five- or seven-year tax write-off."

The British also pay top dollar. "I think they've driven the prices up," said Oliver T. Carr, another local real estate developer. "The British investors have expected lower yields than American investors, so they've affected the market. Local investors traditionally have paid less for real estate and expected higher yields." Donald Brown, another local developer who teaches at the Harvard Business School, said:

It's a good thing for real estate because it drives the prices up. But it's bad for local buyers. There's a real question with the tax rates coming down why prices stay as high as they are. People attribute that to the fact that foreign investors are anxious to own real estate in Washington.

Mr. Josephs acknowledged the criticism. "I'm sure that if we weren't here, it would have been much easier for Americans to develop these properties," he said.

Occasionally, the British have also acted as the conduit for funds from the Middle East. A telecommunications consultant who recently sought to sublease an office in what he thought was a British-owned building was told by his London landlord that the sublease would have to be cleared by a company in Riyadh. "There is a lot of Middle East money coming through London," Mr. Josephs acknowledged.

The British have also invested in New York, Boston, and other cities, but in nowhere the same amount as in Washington. The local developers meanwhile have accepted the British invasion. "It's just like the mumps," Oliver Carr said. "You get used to everything."

The British are pikers in real estate, however, compared with the Canadians. Canadians owned half the eighty-six new buildings constructed in Denver during the 1980s and almost one-third of Minneapolis's downtown office space. Toronto's Reichman brothers, the world's largest owners of office space, own 8 percent of all the office space in Manhattan and control about 30 million square feet of U.S. real estate, worth an estimated $10 billion.

The three Reichman brothers—Albert, fifty-six, Paul, fifty-four, and Ralph, fifty-two—have built an empire worth $18 billion since they fled Austria with their parents during World War II. In 1977, Olympia and York, the development firm founded by the brothers, picked up eight Manhattan skyscrapers at a distress-sale package price of $400 million during New York City's fiscal crisis. Today those buildings are valued at around $3 billion. Their investments include the new $1.5 billion Battery Park City project and the World Financial Center, a complex of skyscrapers described by Mayor Edward Koch as "the new Wall Street." In March 1986, another major Canadian investor, a subsidiary of Vancouver-based B.C.E. Development, bought $1 billion worth of real estate in five U.S. cities, including 13 percent of the office space in downtown Minneapolis.[14]

Spurred by a strong yen and an excess of capital—both resulting from their trade success—Japanese investors also have gone on a real estate buying spree. Since the yen has appreciated at least 60 percent against the dollar from 1984 to 1986, the Japanese can buy American assets for the equivalent of a 60 percent discount.[15] "Right now U.S. real estate is a bargain compared to Japan," said Yoshio Yamashita, vice-chairman of Shuwa Investment Co., which purchased Arco Plaza in Los Angeles for $620 million.[16] When the Japanese invest in U.S. property, they earn about 8 percent on their investment, compared with the 1 percent yield they would earn on similar property in Japan. Total Japanese real estate investments in 1986 are believed to exceed $5 billion.

Adnan Khashoggi, a Saudi Arabian billionaire arms dealer, is another major investor in U.S. real estate. But his biggest investment may have come a cropper: the $650 million TRIAD Center in Salt Lake City. Only partly built, the heart of the center is a large hole in the ground where a thirty-five-story office tower was to be located.

"We don't know what happened," said Ted Wilson, former mayor of Salt Lake City, now director of the Hinckley Institute of Politics at the University of Utah. "One day there was a huge, glittering celebration and ground breaking, and the next day, or so it seemed, they were facing bankruptcy." The problem was that Salt Lake City had a surfeit of office space. Governor Norman Bangerter said that the center had glutted the market, depressing the rentals of office space and leading the parent companies, TRIAD Properties Corporation and TRIAD America, into debts that totaled $163 million in June 1986.[17]

"Foreign investment is coming in too fast," warned Bangerter, a former developer himself. "We have to be wary; we shouldn't be overly dependent on foreign investment. But Utah is capital short and needs the money."

Although Mr. Khashoggi had pledged to channel half a billion dollars into TRIAD America, myriad lawsuits have revealed that he had raised much of his funds in the United States, thereby crowding out local investors at a time of scarce money. Documents in the lawsuits listed $5 million in debts to Zions First National Bank, $69 million to the Travelers Insurance Company, and $20.4 million to the Sheraton Corporation. Another major creditor was the Société Génerale, a Paris-based bank.

Another example of overdependence on foreign investors was provided by the Mexican investors who paid far more than the going rate when they stashed their pesos in U.S. real estate—in Texas, Florida, Colorado, and California—throughout the 1970s and early 1980s, the very years when their own country was accumulating the largest debt in its history. But later, when their country was wracked by currency crises in the mid-1980s and they were unable to make mortgage payments because they could not send money out of Mexico, they sold at far less than the market value and depressed real estate prices in many localities. Experts estimated that Mexican investors held $30 billion worth of U.S. real estate, much of it at high mortgage rates of 17 or 18 percent.[18]

In 1982, for example, Robert N. Pinkerton, president of Real Estate Services, sold a $215,000 three-bedroom condominium on South Padre Island, Texas, a booming resort community on the Gulf of Mexico, to a Mexican investor. A year later he listed the property for resale at $160,000. Mexicans are estimated to own 5–10 percent of the prime residential property in Vail, Colorado, an expensive ski resort. Construction work was stopped on a $1.3 million renovation project in downtown Vail because the Mexican investors, who owned 70 percent of the project, could not pay the contractor.

THE POLICY QUESTIONS

The flood of foreign investment in real estate has produced winners and losers. American developers who compete against foreign investors willing to pay higher prices are not as enthusiastic about foreign investors as real estate agents seeking to sell for prices as high as the traffic will bear. At the moment, hard-pressed farmers anxious to offset their losses by selling off their land at distress-sale prices welcome foreign investors, while some of their neighbors worry about what will happen to their community if too many absentee owners hold on to the property. Meanwhile, under intense legal and political pressure, the states are slowly repealing the crazy quilt of laws restricting foreign ownership.

No one knows the public policy costs of foreign acquisition of U.S. real estate because the information is flawed and the total amount grossly underestimated. On the local level, the reports are mixed. In Washington, British investors have improved their property and shown a sensitivity to design. In Dallas, according to Representative John Bryant, the experience has been different: "A group of Canadian investors bought real estate and got a zoning change. Then they flipped the property. They don't care what happens to a community."

To protect their interests, the real estate industry has emerged as a champion of foreign investment. Their lobbyists vigorously opposed the Bryant amendment to the 1987 trade bill, which required foreign investors buying U.S. real estate and other businesses to register with the federal government. Improved disclosure will discourage investment, their argument ran, following a familiar theme. "It's like playing Russian roulette with all the chambers loaded," said Wayne Thevenot, president of the National Realty Committee. "Foreign investment is what's keeping this country afloat. This is not the time to discourage foreigners from purchasing U.S. real estate."[19]

Real estate illustrates both the benefits and perils of reliance upon foreign investments and the effect of foreign economies on U.S. markets. Those who exulted when foreign investors drove up the prices of real estate in the United States could not very well complain when the reverse occurred and those same investors drove prices back down. Nor is there much the United States can do to ameliorate the economic crises that confront other governments, as the city of Miami learned when its economy suffered in tune with the recession in Latin America.

Whatever happens, Americans must be prepared to meet these challenges, not just react to events; otherwise they will be held hostage to the vagaries of foreign political and economic crises. Their well-being begins with maintaining a certain degree of control over—at the very least—the knowledge of who is buying their skyscrapers and their farmland, knowing how much money is being spent, and examining on a regular basis what impact it is all having on American life.

CHAPTER 12

Capital Flight and Foreign Aid

The Marcoses' U.S. Investments

The question must be asked whether we can justify sending $260 million in aid to the Philippines when the leader of that country is simultaneously investing over $200 million in American real estate.
—*Representative Stephen Solarz, Democrat of New York*

This is all a rumor.

—*Imelda Marcos*

America's hunger for foreign funds, from whatever source, has made the country a major receptacle for the ill-gotten gains of the world's most scurrilous dictators and their allies. Instead of investing in their own lands, creating jobs, and building new housing, hospitals, roads, and canals, these dictators pour their money—much of it U.S. foreign aid—into safe havens throughout the world, especially in the United States. Instead of providing the improved standard of living that could provide a buffer against the criticism and blandishments of communists and other insurgents, they salt the money away in oceanfront condominiums and country estates.

This puts the country in a curious position, at odds with its own ideology. How can America remain a beacon of democracy for the rest of the world while welcoming investments that represent the fruits of tyranny? How can the United States ignore the source of these funds, knowing full well that they have been stolen from societies that live in such abject poverty? The U.S. relationship with the Philippines shows what went wrong in the face of inadequate oversight over the flow of money into the country.

Ferdinand and Imelda Marcos, the deposed Filipino dictator and his extravagant wife, provided a flagrant example of capital flight, investing hundreds of millions of dollars overseas while their people suffered hunger, poverty, and disease at home. Their abuse of the public trust eventually caught up with them, and they were deposed while their nation teetered on the brink of radical revolution. These investments, which the Filipinos call "dollar salting," fueled domestic unrest in the Philippines and led to the rise of a guerrilla movement that still threatens the stability, and very existence, of a valued ally.

The American people and the Filipinos have a special relationship and share a special history. They fought together during World War II. The United States has provided hundreds of millions of dollars in economic and military assistance to the Philippines each year and relies on Clark Air Force Base and Subic Bay Naval Station as an integral part of the national defense.

Such a stake in the Philippines led U.S. officials to become increasingly concerned by the corruption, economic instability, and guerrilla insurgency that became part of that nation's life. A $27 billion foreign debt has imposed severe austerity measures, and as much as 70 percent of the population lives below the poverty line. Reports that U.S. foreign aid, intended to relieve poverty in the Philippines, formed the basis of much of the Marcoses' foreign investment in this country were added irritants. In fact, reports of government corruption and diversion of U.S. aid had become so widespread that in November 1985, on the eve of general elections in the Philippines, Senator Edward M. Kennedy, Massachusetts Democrat, asked the General Accounting Office (GAO), the investigative arm of the U.S. Congress, to study the charges and report back to Congress.[1]

Mr. Kennedy wrote Comptroller General Charles A. Bowsher:

> There have been an increasing number of reports of corruption at the highest levels of the Filipino government leading to my concern that United States aid to the Philippines has been diverted by President and Mrs. Marcos, or by individuals acting on their behalf. I am therefore requesting the GAO to conduct an independent study of the total assistance program to the Philippines, including: a) U.S. Economic Support Funds; b) U.S. security assistance programs; and c) to the fullest extent possible, multilateral assistance to the Philippines.
>
> In instances where diversion of funds for purposes other than those originally intended by the U.S. government has

occurred, I request the fullest possible accounting of who is responsible for the diversion and for what purposes the funds were actually used.

I am aware of the difficulties your office may face in investigating the U.S. supported multilateral assistance provided to the Philippines through institutions such as the World Bank, the International Monetary Fund and others. However, as the U.S. is a major contributor to these institutions, it is important for the Congress to be able to monitor the use of these funds.

The GAO responded on May 2, 1986, advising the senator that the agency could not determine whether U.S. aid had been misused "because the funds were commingled with other receipts in a general fund of the government of the Philippine treasury," according to a report by Frank C. Conahan, director of the agency's National Security and International Affairs Division. The report noted that between 1978 and 1985 the United States gave the Philippines $1.3 billion in economic and military assistance. "The dollar transfers are not tied to any specific purpose, but may be used for repaying the Philippines' foreign debt or financing imported goods or services or for other purposes," the report said.[2]

In requesting the study, Senator Kennedy cited a major investigative report by the *San Jose Mercury News* that found that as much as $30 billion had left the Philippines since the 1950s and that millions had been used for investment in the United States.[3] These were followed by articles in the *Village Voice* and *The New York Times*. "If only these people kept their money here and reinvested it in productive enterprises, our problems would be a lot more manageable," a Filipino senior executive of a multinational oil company operating in the Philippines told the *San Jose Mercury News*. "Let's face it, this country has been ruined by the greed of a few people, and what makes me sad is, we can't say enough is enough. We can't seem to bring ourselves to stop them. We're broke. Where's the money? There's no accounting. It's sickening."

The amount of capital leaving the Philippines surged shortly after the assassination of opposition leader Benigno S. Aquino, Jr., in 1983, according to a 1984 study by the Northern California Interfaith Committee on Corporate Responsibility in San Francisco. The study found that "out of fear of political and economic turbulence, over a billion dollars left the Philippines" in three months after the assassination. Marcos issued a decree making it illegal for Filipinos to export large sums of cash or hold foreign exchange accounts without approval from the nation's Central Bank.

This didn't stop wealthy Filipinos from shipping their money out of the country. A number of instances in which Filipino clients plopped shopping bags stuffed with cash on their desks to be used for investment in U.S. property, no questions asked, was reported by American real estate agents. "It is illegal, and every once in a while, there'll be fines and confiscations," said the San Francisco lawyer who represents Filipinos. "But if the Philippine government really did anything about this, they'd be indicting all their own officials. They're the biggest offenders."[4]

The worst offenders appear to have been the Marcoses themselves. An impeachment complaint filed against Marcos in the summer of 1985 by fifty-six of the fifty-seven opposition members of the National Assembly charged the president with "taking undue advantage of his office and his authoritarian powers" to enrich himself, family members, and close associates. The complaint was defeated when a parliamentary committee rejected the motion.[5]

Among the abuses of power, the complaint charged, were the creation of commodity marketing monopolies, which the president "placed in the hands of trusted cronies," and the confiscation of the businesses of political opponents. The resulting "ill-gotten wealth," the complaint said, was taken out of the country, often in violation of Philippine foreign-exchange laws, and invested overseas, especially in the United States.

The complaint listed a dozen properties that, the opposition said, were owned by the Marcos family, either directly or by proxies. The government denied that President Marcos and his wife, Imelda, have any sizable investments outside the Philippines.

The complaint charged that in 1981 Mrs. Marcos bought the Crown Building in Manhattan, valued at $51 million, under the name of a Netherlands Antilles holding company, Lastura, N.V. Later, the property was transferred to another holding company, the Canadian Land Company, also owned by Mrs. Marcos. In 1981, Mrs. Marcos bought property on Long Island known as the Lindenmere Estate. Among other properties, Mrs. Marcos owns a six-story townhouse in Manhattan at 13 East Sixty-sixth Street and a $104 million high-rise commercial building at Seventh Avenue and Fifty-seventh Street.

The complaint was based on data compiled by the *San Jose*

Mercury News,[6] which broke down the Marcoses' foreign holdings as follows:

> Ferdinand and Imelda Marcos—Lindenmere in Center Moriches, N.Y.; a home on thirteen acres on Princeton Pike, Princeton, N.J., which local police said was used by the Marcos family; three adjoining condominiums at 641 Fifth Avenue, in Manhattan.
>
> Roberto S. Benedicto, close personal friend and former fraternity brother of Marcos—California Overseas Bank in L.A., with total assets of $133 million. The bank owns $7 million worth of real estate, some of it foreclosures on bad loans and some of it bank property, according to the California superintendent of banks. The bank owns two office buildings in Beverly Hills.
>
> Antonio O. Floriendo, business associate of Imelda Marcos—Revere Sugar Company, with refineries in Brooklyn, Boston, and Chicago; a $1 million mansion in a Honolulu suburb; and a condominium at 641 Fifth Avenue.
>
> Geronimo C. Velasco, minister of energy—A $925,000 mansion at 140 Farm Road, Woodside, N.Y.
>
> Eduardo Cojuangco, the Philippines' "Coconut King," one of the nation's wealthiest men and a longtime friend of Marcos—Unicom, United Coconut Planters Bank, in San Francisco; a house in Beverly Hills; and a jewelry store called Jeweler International, in Beverly Hills.
>
> Rodolfo Cuenca, major public highway builder under the Marcos administration—a condominium in San Francisco; a home in San Francisco; a cooperative apartment at 700 Park Avenue, in New York.
>
> Juan Ponce Enrile, Harvard-educated associate of Marcos and later secretary of defense under the Aquino government—San Francisco condo; $1.8 million house in San Francisco.
>
> José Y. Campos, financial adviser to Marcos—president of UNAM Investment Corporation, registered in the Netherlands Antilles, which purchased buildings worth $9 million on a city block in downtown Seattle.

There is little doubt of the real impact of these investments: if deposited in Philippine banks or invested in Philippine industry, the money would have contributed to the revival of the country's economy and provided jobs for its people. Instead, while the majority of the people struggled to survive, a small elite exported its wealth for safekeeping. Although no one knows the correct figure, some economists estimate that $30 billion has been invested abroad since 1950, perhaps $20 billion of that since 1979, when the economy worsened.[7]

Capital flight extracts heavy costs. During the 1970s, the poorest 60 percent of the Filipino population saw its share of national income slip from 25 percent to 22.5 percent. Factories closed or laid off workers because they lacked the foreign currency to buy parts or raw materials. The result? "There is not the slightest doubt that the mind-boggling manipulation of the economy by less than 1 percent of the population has created fertile ground for the Communists' appeal among the 99 percent who are have-nots," a Western diplomat said.[8]

The Marcoses steadfastly denied the charges. "Well, this is really, this is all a rumor," a flustered Imelda Marcos told ABC-TV's "20/20" in a televised broadcast:

> I am amazed, the many places I have been to or have passed through or been invited to that have been called mine. Now it looks like everywhere I go, I must use blinders for fear that every place that I look is mine. This is a bit unfortunate and this just shows that they must surely be bankrupt of issues. But they can go this low, this is understandable. This is part of the political game.

Similarly, a week before Mr. Marcos was voted out of office, his foreign minister told the National Press Club in Washington that there was not an iota of evidence that the Marcoses owned real estate in the United States.

The hidden wealth of the Marcos family in the United States was finally unraveled by Representative Stephen J. Solarz, a Democrat of Brooklyn, New York, who is chairman of the Asian and Pacific Affairs Subcommittee of the House Foreign Affairs Committee. "The Marcoses' vast investments in real estate in this country raise the most serious questions for American policy toward the Phillppines," the congressman said:

> The subcommittee will try to determine whether any of our foreign aid to the Philippines was siphoned off for the purchase of these prestigious properties. But whether or not it is ultimately shown that some of our foreign-aid funds ended in that fashion, the question must be asked whether we can justify sending $260 million a year in economic and

military aid to the Philippines when the leader of that country is simultaneously investing over $200 million in American real estate. At a time when over half the Filipino people live in poverty, when the dismal performance of the Philippine economy stands in shocking contrast to the relative prosperity and growth of its ASEAN [Association of Southeast Asian Nations] neighbors, when the Reagan administration has testified that if present trends continue, the Communist-dominated New People's Army may be able to achieve a strategic stalemate in the Philippines within five years, Ferdinand and Imelda Marcos have secretly led a head-long, multibillion dollar flight of capital out of their country.[9]

Mr. Solarz had to go to the extraordinary length of having the House cite Marcos's U.S. agents for contempt before his committee could get to the heart of their actions, which were concealed by what Mr. Solarz termed "a paper trail." "It soon became clear that the paper trail, which would have enabled us to have determined beyond a shadow of a doubt who was the owner of these properties, was leading nowhere," Mr. Solarz told the House.[10]

It was no accident that the paper trail led nowhere, Mr. Solarz noted, because the ultimate ownership of the properties was in the names of a series of offshore corporations that had been established in foreign entities whose rules of confidentiality and secrecy made it impossible for anyone from the United States to gain access to the records. The congressman determined that the only way he could establish Marcos's involvement was to subpoena the Marcos agents, and put them under oath in subcommittee hearings.

The keys to the puzzle were Joseph and Ralph Bernstein, New York lawyers who headed the New York Land Co., the parent company for the Netherlands Antilles corporations that owned the Marcoses' Manhattan real estate.

The Bernsteins refused to testify, invoking the privileges of the attorney-client relationship, and the committee and then the House cited them for contempt of Congress, on the grounds that they were probing business transactions, not legal advice. Spurred by the threat of imprisonment and the collapse of the Marcos regime, the Bernstein brothers ultimately cooperated. They wove a tale of avarice and intrigue, confirming the Marcoses' ownership of the U.S. real estate.

"You may be interested to know that President Marcos's sole visible and public and legitimate source of income is the $5,700 a year he earns in his capacity as president of the Philippines,"

Mr. Solarz told the House. On that modest salary, Mr. Marcos nevertheless managed to accumulate $350 million in real estate investments in Manhattan alone. Mr. Solarz then discussed the implications of the Marcos holdings:

> There can be no justification for sending hundreds of millions of dollars in economic aid to help the poor people of the Philippines if simultaneously the President and First Lady of that country are siphoning off perhaps even larger sums that would otherwise be available for economic growth and development in other countries into real estate investments in the United States. I simply do not see how we can justify to the taxpayers of my district in Brooklyn, or to the taxpayer anywhere else in our country, sending additional aid to a country in desperate poverty like the Philippines if the leader of that country insists on diverting hundreds of millions of dollars from his nation into the United States.[11]

The Solarz hearings, which were extensively reported in the Philippines, are generally considered to have contributed to Corazon Aquino's victory. The Marcos property was seized by the U.S. government, pending a resolution in the courts. Four prime Manhattan properties have been the subject of extensive controversy and litigation—200 Madison Avenue, 40 Wall Street, the Herald Center, and the Crown Building. The four buildings are worth at least $350 million. The negotiations involved three antagonistic parties: the Philippine government, which needed the cash from the sale of the buildings and would prefer to avoid several years of litigation; the ousted Marcoses, who want to hold on to their wealth; and the Bernsteins.[12]

The Marcos experience was not unique. The United States has become the haven of funds from despots the world over, from Latin America to Africa and Asia, who pillage their poverty-ridden populations and send their profits here.

Government officials who encourage these investments fail to calculate their true cost: in human suffering, in fanning the flames of revolution, and in engendering hostility toward the United States. By looking only at the financial "bottom line," these officials jeopardize the stability of already shaky regimes and of long-term U.S. geopolitical interests.

CHAPTER 13

Unions and
Equal Employment

A Clash of Cultures

Some foreign companies operate much worse than the worst U.S. companies. You'd have to be hard-pressed to find someone worse than Kawasaki.

—*Rudy Oswald, chief economist,*
AFL-CIO

To produce the highest-quality vehicle in North America, we have to communicate directly with our employees.

—*Marvin Runyon, president of*
Nissan, U.S.A.

The shortsightedness of government officials in accepting foreign funds from virtually every source is matched by the provincialism of foreign entrepreneurs who seek to impose their attitudes toward unions on American workers. Often equally perplexing is their attitude toward women, minority groups, and affirmative action programs.

There is little to prepare some of these foreign businessmen for the American union tradition and the recent advances made by women and minorities in the workplace. Those nations that do have a union tradition tend to regard American workers with a sort of colonialist's hauteur and treat them far worse than they treat their own workers back home.

Even in the anti-union atmosphere of the 1980s, union officials contend that many foreign-owned U.S. companies are in a class by themselves. Although some American companies have taken a tough attitude toward trade unions, most operate in an environment in which they acknowledge their employees' right to organize. They are also aware of the public relations risks of appearing anti-union: Union members are customers who should not be needlessly alienated.

By contrast, many foreign-owned companies, even those that work closely with unions in their native lands, challenge the basic concept of unionization of their U.S. employees. Some of these adamantly anti-union, foreign-owned U.S. companies not only build their manufacturing facilities in nonunion states and regions (not unlike some domestic companies) but threaten to close their doors in the event their employees unionize and, indeed, leave the country. In some cases, they consciously hire nonunion construction firms as subcontractors to build their facilities. They are becoming potent political forces in the right-to-work states where they have settled, reinforcing the anti-union attitudes that drew them to those regions in the first place.

In their defense, many foreign companies were wooed by mayors and governors who promised them a free hand in managing their companies and failed to prepare them for the assertive roles played by American unions in the councils of management. The Japanese were especially unprepared for the role played by American unions; there is no comparison between the generally docile unions in Japan and their more confrontational counterparts in the United States. They regard the adversarial relationship characteristic of U.S. labor-management relations as alien to their corporate culture and disruptive to the production process. They also believe that it led to the high wages that made America noncompetitive in automobiles, steel, and other manufactured goods. They were equally unprepared for the assertive role that American women now play in the workplace.

Foreign ownership also has made it difficult for American unions to obtain information about corporate structure, financial conditions, sources and uses of funds, employees, management, market strategies, and ownership. In general, the U.S. labor movement has not made much of an issue of foreign investment, but lately the unions have begun to protest, as witnessed in a recent union-sponsored television advertising campaign:

"Parlez-vous yourself," said Vicki Lawrence, an actress who portrayed "Mama" on the "Carol Burnett Show," in a television commercial produced by the United Food and Commercial Workers:

That's no way to talk to an old woman. Jabber. Jabber. Jabber. All I want is to talk with the owner of this here supermarket. They don't carry my face cream. You got to call Europe, they say. That's where the head honcho is. So I called the number they give me and asked for Mr. Europe, and all I get is more *parlez-vous*. If I wanted to *parlez-vous*, I'd shop on the French Riviera. I ain't setting foot in that store again. This is Vicki Lawrence. Listen to Mama. Be American. Shop American.

The commercial, shown in Augusta, Georgia, Columbia, South Carolina, and Charlottesville and Richmond, Virginia, protested what the union considered the unfair labor practices of foreign-owned supermarket chains. The nonunion Food Lion chain and Cub chain are both owned by Delhaize, a Belgian company. The company owns two unionized chains, Food Giant and Big Apple. In addition, the West German-owned A&P chain and French-owned Grand Union also are unionized.

The union contended, however, that the nonunion Delhaize chain was undermining the unionization of its competition and took to the airwaves, and newspaper advertising, to fight back. "What we don't need is a bunch of rich foreigners sashaying over here and telling us how to run the whole danged supermarket," Ms. Lawrence says in a radio commercial. "I says, stick it in your frozen foods. This is our flag, and it means life, liberty, and the pursuit of happiness. You can't pursue diddly without a job."

In Cincinnati, Biggs, a French-owned food chain, also has been targeted. "They're taking business from our stores," said Al Zack, a spokesman for the United Food and Commercial Workers. "As a result, our members are losing hours, being pressured by other chains to accept concessions. It becomes a never-ending vicious cycle for us."

In the view of union leaders, foreign investors pose a very special problem. Although welcomed when they revive flagging American companies, such as American Motors, or purchase failing companies the way Japan's Bridgestone took over Firestone, many foreign companies are vigorously anti-union. They use their multinational status as leverage: If a plant becomes unionized, they warn, they will simply shift their operations to another plant in another country.

Jiro Murase, a Japanese-American lawyer who represents 200 Japanese companies in the United States, pointed out that the Japanese businessmen are hardly to blame. They are lured to this country by governors, mayors, senators, and other public officials who assure them that there will be no interference with management's prerogatives. "The Japanese especially fear that unions would not only increase operating costs but also decrease managerial flexibility," Mr. Murase said.

Many foreign-owned companies contend that labor unions pose an obstacle between management and employees. Marvin Runyon, president of Nissan U.S.A., a Japanese subsidiary that opened a factory in Smyrna, Tennessee, said, "Our philosophy is that we should deal directly with our employees. We think that to achieve our company objective, to produce the highest-quality vehicle in North America, we have to communicate directly with our employees." Indeed, Nissan executives threatened not to come to Tennessee if the workers chose to be organized by the United Auto Workers (UAW) and later threatened to close their plant if the union took hold. The UAW has not gained a foothold, nor have unions gained ground in many other Japanese automobile manufacturing plants in the United States.

Foreign-owned companies have deliberately located in nonunion states; the South and Southwest have become their haven. "A lot of German and French plants, particularly in South Carolina, came to this country with the incentive of being nonunion," said Rudy Oswald, chief economist for the AFL-CIO. Among Tennessee's major appeals is the fact that it is a nonunion state. Kawasaki, the motorcycle manufacturer, located outside Lincoln, Nebraska, far from the union halls of the UAW.

These foreign-owned companies thus foster a nonunion atmosphere that threatens organized labor. "A very large number come in and are very antagonistic to the rights of workers to join unions and to bargain collectively," Mr. Oswald charged. "In many cases, it's opposite to what these corporations do in their home countries."

In one highly publicized legal contest, the National Labor Relations Board (NLRB) found Kawasaki guilty of unfair labor practices, specifically for dismissing union organizers. Stan Hanson, the plant manager, contends, however, that the employees became union organizers after their dismissals. "They've had two elections here already," Mr. Hanson noted. "Both they've lost. The third they canceled two days before the vote. The UAW has the right to have another election. They've elected not to."

The UAW, in its complaint to the NLRB, charged that Kawasaki had publicized its ability to move to another location and even leave the United States, if necessary, in an attempt to intimidate its workers:

To intimidate its Lincoln [Nebraska] employees from forming a union, Kawasaki has exploited its position as a multinational enterprise producing similar products in other countries. Since 1978, Kawasaki has repeatedly threatened that if the Lincoln employees chose to be represented by a union, it would close their plant and shift production to one of its foreign plants. Particularly in this period of high unemployment for blue collar workers, Kawasaki's threat to shift production to other plants was the most potent weapon Kawasaki could use to intimidate its employees. Kawasaki has never explained to its Lincoln work force that it bargains with unions in other countries where it has threatened to shift their production. In each union campaign, Kawasaki has intimidated and fired many key union supporters. It has used legal counsel with a reputation for thwarting the legal installation of unions. Through all these tactics, Kawasaki has prevented its employees from enjoying a free and fair union election since 1978. It gives no indication that it intends to act any differently in the future.[1]

Similar intransigence was shown by BASF-Wyandotte, a wholly owned West German corporation, which locked out 100 employees rather than negotiate a new contract with the Oil, Chemical and Atomic Workers Union. And Norsk-Hydrò, 51 percent owned by the Norwegian government, refused to recognize the acceptance of an offer by the International Association of Machinists, which was certified as the employees' bargaining agent but could not negotiate a contract.[2]

"In each of these cases," Mr. Oswald said, "the corporations deal with unions in their own countries, which they refuse to do in this country. Some foreign companies operate much worse than the worst U.S. companies. You'd have to be hard-pressed to find someone worse than Kawasaki."

"It's like when people travel," added Mark Anderson, an economist with the AFL-CIO. "They do things away from home that they'd never do at home."

Union officials say that Volkswagen, the West German automobile manufacturer, is a notable exception to the anti-union flavor of many foreign-owned companies. "Volkswagen attempts to deal honestly with its employees," Mr. Oswald said.

One particularly rancorous union dispute focused on the UAW's efforts to organize the 2,500 Honda automobile workers at the plant in Marysville, Ohio. To some, it was the battle of the baseball caps. Supporters of the UAW wore blue caps emblazoned with the union logo. Opponents wore green Honda caps or the blue UAW caps with a red line across the union logo. Those who were undecided wore everything from Cleveland Indian caps to the caps of favorite trucking companies.

The outcome was closely watched by other Japanese firms. Toshio Uchikawa, treasurer and a director of Stanley Electric Co., London, Ohio, which supplies headlights and other equipment to Honda, said, "We are very concerned. We're just trying to keep a union-free environment here."[3]

To head off the union, Honda worked to build worker loyalty. The company's wages are $12 an hour, only $1.40 below the "Big Three" domestic companies—Chrysler, General Motors, and Ford. It opened an employee sports center and set up a credit union and savings plan. It also offered a dismissal review board composed in part of workers, plus the famous morning exercises and quality circles. Honda deliberately located in rural Ohio, where unionism was offset by an independent-minded farm culture. Its employees were young, with an average age of twenty-seven, and given the title of "associate."

The union nevertheless found an issue—the pace of work at the plant:

> On the production line, for example, workers are often closer to a run than a walk as they rush between the parts benches and car bodies moving down the line. One worker jumps into a car, attaches a back-seat catch, wheels around to attach a piece of waterproofing and then, juggling an electric screwdriver, drives several screws into the frame. She then jumps out, dodges other workers, resupplies and jumps into the next car. Her face is tight with concentration.[4]

The union also made an issue of Honda's refusal to grant sick leave as well as the company's refusal to allow employees to bid for specific jobs, as they do at the "Big Three" plants.

Kawasaki, which is located outside Lincoln, Nebraska, remains a special thorn in the side of organized labor. In 1978, when the UAW announced that Kawasaki workers had asked to be represented by the union, company officials threatened to close the plant or move its operations back to Japan if the employees voted in favor of the union. In its complaint, the union documented its major problems with the company: "Over the years, such threats to close have remained a dominant theme in

Kawasaki's anti-union campaign. Such unlawful threats have long been recognized as the most powerful weapon for intimidating and discouraging employees from joining a union.'' The complaint also alleged threats to employees of loss of jobs; threats of loss of benefits (or promotions to permanent status); changes in job classifications (from permanent to temporary and vice versa); establishment of an anti-UAW employee committee to funnel corporate funds into anti-union buttons, insignia, and activity; and, finally, daily meetings with supervisors, "supervisory trainees," and publication of a handbook for supervisors detailing "union avoidance" techniques to be used in combating the organizing efforts of employees.[5]

Nearly 200 of the employees eligible to vote in the elections were temporary workers for whom the threats of loss of jobs in the event of a union victory seemed all too real. Many were told by Kawasaki officials that they would be dismissed if the union won the election because the UAW would not allow "temporary" workers. One employee, Linda Pester, a member of the 1978 organizing committee, said she had been interrogated during her hiring interview as to her union sympathies and told by Kawasaki officials that the union would not be tolerated. Rebecca Chen, a temporary employee, said she had been told that the company would fire all temporary workers if the union won the election. Her husband was also a temporary worker. The UAW lost the election, 257–135.

When the UAW charged unfair labor practices, Kawasaki agreed to have a rerun election, held in April 1979. "It repeated the same threats to close the plant or to remove the work to Japan," the UAW alleged in a second complaint. The company also threatened to reduce benefits if the employees elected a union and threatened that violence would result if the UAW won the election. The union also charged that the company illegally discharged an employee who was a leader of the organizing drive. "The discharge of Daniel Bennett on April 10, 1979, nine days before the election, was precisely timed to place a chill over the pending rerun election," the union charged. Mr. Hanson of Kawasaki contended, however, that the discharge was not connected with Mr. Bennett's union activities.

One month before the election, Kawasaki employees were also subjected to a variety of anti-union activity characterized by the trial judge as showing "virulent hostility to unionization." These acts included a threat to an employee that if she continued to wear her union button, she would be given a "dirty job"; a supervisor's repeated warnings that if the union won, the plant would close; the plant manager's posting of a notice falsely implying that the UAW was responsible for certain alleged bomb threats at the plant; the plant manager's promise to increase wages if the union lost; the personnel manager's distribution of pro-Kawasaki buttons, thereby forcing employees to make known their union sympathies; the plant manager holding a meeting with all employees, shutting down the entire plant, turning off all the machinery, and saying that the silence was the silence of the UAW on strike. The UAW failed to win the second election by a vote of 297–257 and filed new grievances with the NLRB.

The NLRB directed that a third election be held in 1982. Mr. Hanson, the new plant manager, issued a memorandum to all employees warning them not to sign UAW authorization cards. In July 1982, the U.S. Court of Appeals ruled that Kawasaki must cease and desist from its prior unfair labor practices and reinstate Daniel Bennett with seniority and back pay. This decision was subsequently upheld by the Supreme Court. On October 11, 1982, Kawasaki distributed a "newsletter" apparently designed to sow confusion. Its format resembled the UAW newsletter *The Bridge* and contained a list of sixty employees who would be dismissed if the union won the election. "The company's illegal threats had their intended result," the union said. "Employees whose support for the union had been assured became convinced that voting yes was voting for layoffs and a probable plant shutdown." In another tactic, the company showed employees a videotape intended to convey a negative impression of unions generally and the UAW in particular. It pictured and listed plants that had closed during the automotive depression of 1981–82. The accompanying commentary in effect stated that a UAW victory would jeopardize the plant's future. The narrator of the film stated that the UAW had a national goal of making Japanese producers noncompetitive. Support for the union eroded, and the organizing committee asked for an indefinite postponement of the election.

The union has given up, at least temporarily. "We're not actively organizing at the moment," said Reg McGhee, a UAW spokesman, in November 1986. "We're not as active as we were two years ago." The union is still trying to organize the Nissan workers in Smyrna, Tennessee, however, as well as the Honda workers at Marysville, Ohio. The union was able to organize the new Mazda plant at Flat Rock, Michigan, largely because it was a joint venture with Ford, and plans to try to organize Mitsubishi and Toyota, when they open in Illinois and Kentucky, respectively.

CULTURAL DIFFERENCES

There is nothing in Japan to prepare business executives for the union strategies that they find in this country. The four major federations into which most Japanese unions are banded have almost no bargaining ability and little political power. Stan Hanson, of Kawasaki, points out that in Japan unions are far less aggressive than in the United States. They consider themselves part of the corporate management and go through elaborate, formal negotiating procedures before taking the extreme step of going out on strike.

Perhaps nothing better symbolizes the impotence of Japan's labor unions than the rite known as *shunto,* or "spring wage offensive." It has become so inoffensive, some union leaders complain, that it invites unwelcome analogies to highly stylized Kabuki theater. Management clearly has the upper hand, setting limits for pay raises, even before the *shunto* begins, through a cartel representing four key industries—steel, shipbuilding, automobiles, and electrical products.[6]

Every spring the *shunto* is the same. Workers carry red banners, yell ominous slogans, and wear headbands to show solidarity. Some even go on strike. But nearly all the walkouts last only an hour or two, and they are timed carefully to cause as little disruption as possible. In the end, most unions accept wage increases averaging about 5 percent, which the cartel has decided in late winter would be a reasonable settlement. To go any higher, big business argues and labor agrees, would handicap Japan as it competes against low-salary countries like Taiwan and South Korea. Unlike U.S. unions, which are organized around crafts, Japan's 74,000 unions are organized around individual companies. As a result, unions identify with their companies so closely that often they are reluctant to take action that might benefit their members if it also reduces profits.

James D. Hodgson, a former labor secretary and ambassador to Japan from 1974 to 1977, noted the wide cultural gap between American labor and Japanese management. "American unions were created as an adversary of management and have the right to declare economic warfare on the company," Mr. Hodgson said. But Japanese managers espoused consensus management and were "absolutely terrified" of working with adversarial unions.[7]

An even wider cultural gap, if possible, exists between Japanese and U.S. attitudes and laws relating to the rights of women in the workplace. Little in their native experience prepares Japanese business executives for U.S. laws that protect women against job discrimination. In Japan, women are virtually barred from the hierarchies of the business world. An example of the exploitation of women in Japan follows:

> Michiko Watanabe thought that her years of hard work at a Japanese bank had finally paid off when she was transferred to a branch office in the U.S. But she was wrong. Her new monthly take-home salary was $500—less than what she earned in Japan and a third of what her male counterparts made. The bank would not pay her rent, as it did for men. Though university educated, she was made a clerk. In time, she was promoted to loan officer. But then headquarters in Tokyo decided that giving women such lofty jobs set an unhealthy precedent and ordered her demoted. Today, a clerk once again, she shares an apartment with Indochinese refugees in order to help make ends meet.[8]

Unfortunately, Japanese companies in the United States export their country's national attitude toward women, and Japanese business executives here consider our civil rights laws unwarranted interference in their managerial prerogatives. Thus, Sumitomo Shoji America, Inc., a wholly owned subsidiary of a Japanese general trade company, was shocked to find itself the defendant in a class-action lawsuit brought by thirteen female secretaries who claimed that Sumitomo's alleged practice of hiring only male Japanese citizens to fill executive, managerial, and sales positions violated the Civil Rights Act. Without admitting the alleged discriminatory practice, the company claimed that such a practice would be protected under U.S.-Japanese commercial treaties.

The U.S. Supreme Court disagreed. It ruled that:

> The purpose of the treaties was not to give foreign corporations greater rights than domestic companies, but instead to assure them the right to conduct business on an equal basis without suffering discrimination based on their alienage. The treaties accomplished their purpose by granting foreign

corporations "national treatment" in most respects and by allowing foreign individuals and companies to form locally incorporated subsidiaries. These local subsidiaries are considered for purposes of the treaty to be companies of the country in which they are incorporated; they are entitled to the rights, and subject to the responsibilities, of other domestic corporations. By treating these subsidiaries as domestic companies, the purpose of the Treaty provisions—to assure that corporations of one Treaty party have the right to conduct business within the territory of the other party without suffering discrimination as an alien entity—is fully met.[9]

The Sumitomo decision clarified the issue of treaty protection, stating unequivocally that the company did not have absolute protection under the treaty but at the same time left several crucial questions unresolved. The court dealt, for example, only with whether the local company had to abide by federal laws and did not address the issue of what would happen if the company were not locally incorporated in the United States.

The court also left unanswered the question of BFOQs (bona fide occupational qualifications): cases in which, for example, the company argues that for reasons of business necessity, women could not possibly do the job; that the company needs people well versed in the nuances of the culture and business practices of the country. Although BFOQs can be legitimate, they can also serve as handy excuses for discrimination. So do protective practices, where companies argue that women should be barred from working a night shift or a dangerous job "for their own good." Japanese executives, who are used to protective laws in their own country, find it difficult to deal with current American practice that, for the most part, leaves the decision up to the women themselves.

Finally, in 1987, Sumitomo settled the ten-year case by agreeing to spend $2.8 million to train, promote, and pay its female workers. Lewis Steel, the attorney who represented the thirteen New York City women, said that the company's failure to promote women employees "mirrored the history of the way women were treated in Japan."

The U.S. government's position is that for EEOC (Equal Employment Opportunity Commission) purposes, if a company is operating in the United States, even if it is only recruiting in the United States, for Title VII purposes, it must abide by equal opportunity laws. But the EEOC is often no match for foreign firms and their attorneys, who move into uncharted waters where the law offers little guidance. At times, the examples of discrimination are subtle, such as expense accounts and benefits. "When an alien employee is given an expense account for living expenses, in effect, the citizen employee is paid less," explained Raj Gupta, an attorney with the EEOC. "The EEOC tells companies that they have the burden of showing that the alien has more expenses than the citizen, to prove there is no discrimination. Otherwise, this constitutes discriminatory wages and working conditions."

Gupta blames American political leaders and legal advisers for not adequately informing foreign investors about U.S. labor and affirmative action laws:

> We should do more preventive work with the Japanese. We should tell them up front. Their EEO knowledge is rudimentary. The concept of sex harassment is beyond them. If you have a booth in Brussels to sell the state, you don't want to tell them [potential investors] the down side. The attitude is "Why give them the bad news?" That is not a good attitude or good business.

Even when the law is clear, the cultural gap may still be too wide to ensure results. Benjamin Fulgenzi, vice-president and general manager of SMC Pneumatics Inc., a Japanese-owned manufacturer of air cylinders, recounted what happened at his plant after an EEOC lawsuit:

"We lost a lawsuit filed by a lady assembler. She filed a harassment [sexual harassment] suit with the EEOC. It took five years and cost us $20,000. We had to hire her back. I fired the guy that caused it in the first place."

Fulgenzi thought all was well until three Japanese engineers, on loan to the forty-five-worker plant, reported the firing back to their superiors in Japan. "I was overruled," Fulgenzi continued. "The Japanese said 'no.' Once a person has been here a few years, it's hell to get rid of him. The Japanese guys created the turmoil. They didn't understand. I had already fired him." Aside from this one equal employment issue, Fulgenzi's superiors rarely intervene in his personnel or financial decisions. "The Japanese leave us alone," he said. "They provide us with the products, and we set the policies and do the marketing. Every year I give them a five-year forecast. I've never been turned down. They only care if we break even."

In larger, unionized companies, affirmative action problems are smoothed out by liaison people, who initiate their Japanese employers to American customs and laws. Leonard M. Tyree, the manager of industrial and public relations for Toshiba America Inc., in Lebanon, Tennessee, explained how he dealt with this problem:

> In our PC2 operation, we set the purity and convergence of picture tubes. In Japan, there are no females doing the job. One of the Japanese executives asked me, "Why do you have women?" I answered, "In this country, you don't make the difference. We have EEOC, the unions, and the NLRB." Once explained, there is no problem.

THE ISSUE OF SECRECY

American unions also complain of the problems in obtaining financial information concerning the corporate structure of foreign companies whose U.S. employees have voted for union representation. Twenty-five percent of the members of the Oil, Chemical and Atomic Workers International Union, for example, work for companies owned or controlled by foreign investors, according to Calvin Moore, the union vice-president.

"While the sale of these assets to foreign interests is preferable to closure, the character of these types of investments deeply concerns us," Mr. Moore told the House Energy and Commerce Subcommittee on Telecommunications, Consumer Protection and Finance.

> In the first place, many of these refineries and market assets were formerly owned by public companies regulated by the Securities and Exchange Commission [SEC]. This is important to us. The various SEC report forms supply indispensable information on financial condition, sources and uses of funds, employees, management, market strategies, and ownership. Our union purchases a minimum amount of stock in every company that we organize so that we can receive this material and if necessary exercise our rights as shareholders.
>
> Unfortunately, few of the companies involved in buyouts of U.S. refining and marketing assets fall under the jurisdiction of the SEC. As a consequence, it is virtually impos-

sible for us to learn anything about ownership, assets, net earnings, financing, or plans and prospects for the future. Without information such as this, it becomes very difficult for us to properly represent our members.[10]

Mr. Moore said that his members also feared that the infusion of foreign capital into the East Coast refined-products market "may be a prelude to pricing policies designed to drive out competition and enlarge the market for OPEC crude." As for foreign investment in the U.S. chemical industry, Mr. Moore noted that during the last fifteen years, European chemical makers had acquired more than three hundred chemical plants in the United States.

Although the unions regard foreign companies as alien corn, the unions recognize that even alien corn provides some nourishment to those starved for jobs. The unions do not want to be cast in the role of spoilsports who stand on principle as they take food out of the mouths of hungry Americans. But they clearly regard the surge of foreign investment as a threat to the U.S. trade-union movement and are trying to develop a strategy—somewhere between confrontation and accommodation—to cope with what they consider a troubling phenomenon.

PART IV

FEDERAL INVOLVEMENT

CHAPTER 14

Brazil North
America as a Debtor Nation

Foreign capital is becoming an addiction, and a sudden withdrawal could produce convulsions.
—Felix Rohatyn, Lazard Frères

Capital has to go somewhere.
—Henry Kaufman, Salomon Brothers

Debtor nations live on the brink of crisis. They are owned by
foreign investors—by individuals, by nations, and by other
forces beyond their control. Their dependence on foreign capital
means they are constantly subject to the will of foreign bankers,
who set their priorities and decide what they can buy and how
much they can spend. The pace of their industrialization is set
thousands of miles away by people with little stake in the quality
of their lives or the long-term future of their nation. "Debtors"
gradually experience a loss of sovereignty, a diminution of power
in the most basic areas of economic and political development.

Nations in debt worry constantly about their dependence on
international bankers, whose pressure never lets up. "It's very

simple," explained Professor Phillip Grub, an expert in international finance at George Washington University.[1] "You're in bed with the international banker whether you want to be or not. It is like having your mortgage due and not having the money to pay. The banker is always saying, 'Are you going to pay up or default?' "

It is one thing to be an underdeveloped debtor nation, amassing funds to industrialize. It is another to be a highly industrialized nation, a "mature debtor," without much hope of future industrialization to pay off those debts. A nation becomes a "net debtor" when the value of foreign investments in that country exceeds the country's investments abroad.[2]

Debt is deceptive. In Latin America, the debt crisis "culminates a twenty-year boom that tripled the size of the Latin economy," according to economist Robert J. Samuelson.[3] Foreign loans contributed to an annual growth rate of 6 percent and the development of a growing middle class. Unfortunately, this new upper middle class gradually became hooked on foreign consumer goods and foreign property ownership, purchases that did little for its future economic development.[4] In effect, the major Latin American countries found themselves in the curious position of borrowing heavily abroad to finance their own spending spree: The money flowed out of the region and into condominiums in Miami, Florida, Aspen, Colorado, among other U.S. resorts and commercial, and industrial properties, as well as into a variety of U.S. securities.

Capital flight from the Latin American countries is both a cause and effect of political instability. Much of that capital flows north to the United States, primarily because the United States is perceived universally as one of the world's leading safe havens. "The rationale for coming over here is more than economic," explained James E. Ammerman, who oversees portfolio investment at the U.S. Treasury Department and watches the huge infusions of foreign capital. "It is stability. You don't have to worry about confiscation, political change. Whenever the Soviets act up or there is a major crisis in Poland, Czechoslovakia, or Hungary, you get capital flight." As an afterthought, he asked, "Wouldn't you get your money out if you lived in Argentina?"

Debtor countries find themselves in a bind when they face accelerating departures of their capital resources. As a country destabilizes, it loses a huge chunk of its financial base; more political unrest inevitably follows, the outward flow of capital accelerates, and the cycle repeats itself. Even Mexico, long considered a bulwark of political stability in Latin America, now finds itself in jeopardy. "That stability can no longer be taken for granted," wrote Jorge G. Castaneda, a professor of political science at the National University of Mexico. "The causes of Mexico's deepest crisis in modern times are clearly economic . . . a $100 million debt; a five-percent drop in GNP . . . a country disappointed in itself, questioning its direction. . . . The economy's chief bottleneck remains the foreign debt . . . [it] has become an intolerable burden for Mexico."[5]

Even though the banks have not yet forced the issue of default, debtor countries find their economies staggering under the burden of accelerating interest costs. Economic hardships are readily apparent in countries like Brazil—Latin America's largest debtor—which watched its industrial output fall by 15 percent from 1977 to 1985 and inflation rise into the triple digits. In Mexico, wages have dropped drastically, while Chile, Argentina, and Venezuela have also witnessed the decline of their economies along with increasing inflation. It is expected that the total Latin debt will rise to $429 billion by 1990.

Eventually, a nation's foreign debt forces its way out of the boardrooms of the international banks and affects the day-to-day lives of ordinary people. Edward Cody, of the *Washington Post*, described the effect of the debt on the working class of Tlaxcala, Mexico:

> . . . the entire population of Tlaxcala has assumed a debt they did not decide to take on themselves. This . . . town is one spot among thousands where Latin America's mammoth repayments to foreign lenders has begun to weigh heavily. But many here are not sure why. Maria Mendieta, who runs a little lunch counter . . . has fallen heavily into debt and does not know what to do about it. Maximino Gutierrez and Blaz Bich, friends who work at a nearby battery factory, also have slipped into debt beyond their means to pay, or even to comprehend. . . . Subsidies have dropped—and therefore prices have risen—for such necessities as food staples, electricity, gas, train fares and telephones, . . . The price of tortillas jumped in one day from 45 to 80 pesos a kilo, and meat that cost 50 cents a pound jumped to a dollar. Salary raises have fallen far behind and, overall, workers have lost about 40 percent of their purchasing power since 1980.

Debt feeds on itself, and to pay off old loans, Mexico negotiated a $12 billion package of new loans and economic assistance. Hailed as good news at the time, according to Cody, the loans included conditions that brought further austerity, inflation, and unemployment to the country:

> The Bank of Mexico estimated that price rises in basic food products . . . in some cases amounted to 100 percent. Central inflation has reached nearly 100 percent a year, and some economists have predicted it will be 150 percent by the end of the year, straining the government's ability to control it. . . . In negotiations with the banks, the government also has committed itself to selling off unprofitable state-owned businesses, even at the price of throwing people out of work in an economy where unemployment and underemployment has risen to 50 percent. More than 8,000 employees immediately lost their jobs when the Fundidora steel mill in Monterrey closed down last May [1986].[6]

Latin America's experience with indebtedness is typical of third-world economies. Witness the recent case of Sudan. In February 1986, the IMF declared Sudan ineligible for additional funds. Burdened with a foreign debt of $9 billion, the Sudanese government could not produce the $200 million payment it needed to retain its credibility with the international bankers. This action forced the country's new, fragile government to raise taxes and food prices and figure out how to cope with the 650,000 refugees who had fled from famine and war in Ethiopia and Chad. Like its neighbors in sub-Saharan Africa, Sudan is regarded as a "small debtor," posing no real threat to the international financial system. Nevertheless, small debtors receive more stringent treatment by the IMF and the banks; they cannot get their loans rescheduled, and every year their creditors and borrowers must reconvene at the negotiating table to decide their fate.[7]

Debtor countries suffer disproportionately in a variety of other ways, wrote policy analyst Christine Bogdanowicz-Bindert.

> Exports by debtors are beginning to contract . . . huge currency devaluations, and thus increased costs of material, labor and debt, have depleted working capital . . . investments needed to maintain infrastructure, roads, telephones and other services have often been postponed, hampering production efficiency. . . . Within the developing countries,

high inflation and slow growth have become the norm. . . . In Latin America . . . inflation for the area as a whole has more than doubled . . . averaging a staggering 117 percent in 1984.[8]

Ultimately, all of the major debtors—Brazil, Venezuela, Mexico, Argentina, and Chile—have paid for their efforts to refinance their foreign debts with soaring unemployment, severe recessions, and rising inflation. This has meant a significant reduction in the standard of living for all but the wealthiest Latin Americans.

The social costs of debtor status are also high. Economic growth is stymied, unemployment continues to rise, "health and education services have declined dramatically; and malnutrition and infant mortality have increased," continued Bogdanowicz-Bindert. "The average citizen in developing [synonymous with debtor] countries today consumes fewer calories daily than in 1975." Without social security and other safety nets, many "governments of debtor nations are clearly sitting on a social powder keg."[9]

The downward spiral of the debtor nations also threatens the stability of the banks that run their affairs and could ultimately affect the world's financial stability. A provocative book on the world's growing debt crisis, *Debt and Danger,* suggests that since debtor nations are beginning to regard default as the only realistic option, lenders should embark on a "cooperative debt strategy." The authors, Harold Lever and Christopher Huhne, argue that the banking system is vulnerable to default, that major banks have been weakened by debt, and that the internationalization of the banking system has made the banks too susceptible to the weaknesses of its weakest participants.[10]

Always at the mercy of outside interests, the debtor nation comes to resent its subservient status and its dependence on foreign banks and foreign governments. Invariably, these countries manifest their collective feelings through waves of xenophobia, social unrest, rising protectionist pressures, and political instability. When Argentina became a debtor nation, it fueled the country's latent anti-Americanism. Many Argentinians believed that foreigners were taking out more than they were putting in and that perhaps it was a mistake to have allowed "them" in in the first place. An incomplete analysis on their part, to be sure, but a recurring one in debtor countries.

U.S. ENTRY INTO DEBTOR RANKS

In 1985, the United States joined Argentina, Sudan, and a host of third-world countries and became a net debtor nation; that is, the United States owed more money to foreigners than foreigners owed the United States. It was the first time in fifty years that America had crossed the line into indebtedness and the first time in history that "an advanced industrialized nation had gone back to debtor status in peacetime," according to Professor Rod Eldridge of George Washington University, an expert in international finance.[11] The magnitude of the debt is rapidly approaching the $1 trillion mark. If allowed to continue, it will soon far exceed that of Latin America and eventually all of the developing countries. (As of 1986, all U.S. loans to the third world totaled $900 billion to $1 trillion.)

It happened swiftly and definitively, according to the numbers, and caught policymakers off guard. The United States shifted from being the world's largest creditor nation in 1982 to the largest debtor in 1986. In the first six months of 1985, the United States went from a net creditor of $28 billion to a net debtor—in the red for $35 billion. By the end of 1986, the country's foreign debt, rising at $100 billion a year, totaled $263.6 billion. In an eerie resemblance to Latin America, the United States slid into debtor status to feed a consumer boom and to finance its budget deficit. ". . . the money we have been borrowing abroad has been financing everything from high-style fashions to fancy cars," wrote Hobart Rowen, a leading critic of U.S. policies.[12]

If this trend continues at the current rate, America's net debt to foreigners will reach the $1 trillion mark by 1990, surpassing Brazil and Mexico combined.[13] (In contrast, Brazil's debt is $105 billion; Mexico's, $95 billion.) By that time, Japan will be the nation's leading creditor, holding $400 billion worth of U.S. debt. "America and Japan now have balance-of-payments profiles that are virtually mirror images," commented David Hale, chief economist with Kemper Financial Services, "with the United States the biggest borrower and Japan the largest creditor . . . the current global expansion [is] a symbiotic mixture of Anglo-Saxon hedonism and Oriental thrift."[14] At the end of 1986, Japan's current account surplus hit world-record levels of $86 billion for the year, making her the world's leading creditor nation.

Net debtor status is compiled from an index known as the current account, which measures both trade and services. It is, therefore, a broader measure than trade alone, which measures only merchandise. The United States has not had a merchandise surplus since 1975—another way of saying it has had a trade deficit—but its earnings from overseas investments usually compensated for the trade deficits.[15] In the final analysis, debtor status means that Americans pay more on their liabilities than they earn on their assets.[16] And at the current rate of foreign investment in the United States, it will not be long before our net outflow on the investment balance will exceed the trade deficit outflows.

The United States has become the land of the free and the home of the deficits: trade, budget, business, farm, consumer, and now, current account. (Agricultural commodities remain the only category with a surplus, although annual figures have reported declines since 1982.) Although it is not blamed as often as the budget deficit, the trade deficit—an excess of imports over exports—should also take some of the blame for contributing to America's new status as a debtor nation. Each year's trade deficit continues to dwarf the preceding year's: The biggest jump occurred in 1984, when figures showed a deficit of $123.3 billion, compared with $69.4 billion in 1983. At the end of 1986, the trade deficit climbed to $169.8 billion. Protectionism, nontariff trade barriers, the budget deficit, years of the strong dollar, and the resistance of America's trading partners to follow its lead and allow unlimited foreign investment remain the major factors perpetuating the trade deficit. The slow pace of foreign reciprocity in encouraging U.S. outward investment further diminishes the hope of offsetting the current account deficit with more extensive overseas investments in foreign markets.[17]

FINANCING THE DEBT WITH FOREIGN CAPITAL

To finance its budget deficits and prevent them from worsening through higher interest costs, the United States has become increasingly reliant on infusions of foreign capital. Without foreign capital, experts agree, the budget deficit would be higher, the dollar would decline even further, and inflation would soar. In the short term, net foreign capital inflows also add to the supply of savings and keep interest rates lower than they would be without them. What policymakers sometimes forget is that when foreigners increase their holdings in the United States, either in direct investments or securities, a percentage of the money eventually leaves the United States in the form of profits, dividends, or interest.

America was a debtor nation throughout the nineteenth century, when European investment financed the country's expansion and industrial revolution and developed its infrastructure: Canals, railroads, factories, and mines all got their start from European investors.[18] The arrangement suited the Europeans, who earned higher returns than they were getting at home, while Americans benefited from the wealth generated from foreign capital. As an "immature debtor," the United States found that the benefits of developing its own manufacturing capacity far exceeded the burdens of debt.

In the long run, foreign borrowing turned the country into a world power, an industrialized nation instead of a supplier of raw materials, a sovereign nation rather than a subservient colony. By contrast, today's debt serves no such lofty purposes. Most of it is being incurred simply to pay off the excesses of the past and not to build wealth for the future. "We're exporting paper in exchange for goods and services," said William Niskanen, Jr., a former acting chairman of the President's Council of Economic Advisers.[19] Instead of investing in things with a potential for growth and development, U.S. dollars are being spent on interest payments, one of the least productive uses of capital. When the time comes to pay off the debt—with interest—experts predict a drastic decline in the country's standard of living, since there will be less money around for consumption and investment.

The search for the real culprit leads back to the budget deficit: To pay it off, the nation may be forced to offer higher interest rates—as an alternative to raising taxes—which in turn have attracted a surge of foreign capital. As a percentage of gross national product (GNP), both the deficit and the debt have climbed at an alarming rate. According to figures from the Congressional Budget Office (CBO), the U.S. national debt rose from 27 percent of the GNP in 1981 to almost 42 percent in fiscal 1986. Foreign capital has temporarily filled in the budget gap, but at tremendous costs later on. In 1986, for example, servicing the debt came to $67 billion, or $200 subtracted from potential per capita income. "We are frittering it [foreign capital] away on consumption," warned Rudolph G. Penner, former CBO director, and this has already shown up "in our standard of living because over time we have to convey income abroad."[20]

There appears to be substantial agreement on the facts: that the budget deficit is to blame; that the national debt impedes growth; and that dependence on foreign capital poses serious risks for the United States and other world economies. But consensus also exists on the inadvisability of patchwork solutions that some claim would solve the problem through exchange controls, exchange market intervention, expansionary monetary policies, or increased trade barriers, which would at best only obscure the fundamental source of the problem.[21] The only possible solution that everyone agrees on but no one knows how to implement remains reducing the nation's mammoth budget deficit.

RISKS AND BENEFITS: THE DEBATE

A spirited debate has developed in the financial community about the risks and benefits of a huge influx of foreign capital, which at first strengthened the dollar and helped finance the Reagan administration's large budget deficits. In the last decade, foreign investment has quadrupled, helping to create jobs and financial opportunities and, to some extent, to build a stronger U.S. economy that encourages yet more foreign investment.[22]

A number of bankers and economists say that the enormous growth of foreign investment has weakened the national resolve to reduce the federal deficit. They also fear that a sudden withdrawal of funds could lead to a financial crisis. "It's becoming an addiction, and a sudden withdrawal could produce convulsions," said Felix G. Rohatyn, an investment banker with Lazard Frères & Company. His fear is that if the dollar falls and interest rates decline, in a period of recession, foreign investors would withdraw their portfolio investments, triggering a banking crisis. These foreign investors then could use their inflated portfolios to make direct investments (the purchase of 10 percent or more of a company's stock) of American industry at "bargain-basement prices," Mr. Rohatyn said. "We will have financed our deficit by putting up permanent assets." Mr. Rohatyn's fears are not without basis. He recalled that the crisis over the collapse of the Continental Illinois Bank began with rumors that foreign investors were pulling out their money.

Similarly, Paul A. Volcker, chairman of the Federal Reserve Board, has warned that the budget and trade deficits "imply a dependence on foreign borrowing by the United States that, left unchecked, will sooner or later undermine the confidence in our economy essential to a strong currency and to prospects for lower interest rates.'' Senator William Proxmire, chairman of the Senate Banking Committee, agrees about the hazards of increased dependence on foreign capital: ''As time goes on, as foreign investors get a larger and larger share of the national debt, they get into a position where they can impose tough terms or cut off the credit. You lose some part of your sovereignty under those circumstances. You lose your independence.''

Some bankers and economists believe these fears are exaggerated, and at least some of them are saying that the criticism of foreign investment has overtones of xenophobia—and in the case of the Japanese investors, outright racism. Others argue that America's economy is sufficiently broad based to absorb enormous amounts of foreign investment without major effects. They add that foreign capital helped build this country's industrial base in the nineteenth century, created new jobs and financial opportunities in recent years, and thereby has helped produce an economy that attracts still more foreign venture capital. Foreign capital will never be abruptly withdrawn, they say, because the economy will remain strong.

Henry Kaufman, chief economist with the investment banking firm of Salomon Brothers, Inc., noted that ''foreign investment has contributed to the strength of the dollar, which has contributed to the trade deficit.'' A strong dollar has increased the prices of our goods on the world market and has enabled foreign manufacturers to undersell U.S. companies at home. It has contributed, he said, to the ''restructuring of the U.S. as a service economy.'' Unlike those who portray that future in terms of ''our children sweeping up around Japanese computers,'' Kaufman sees a service economy as a desirable development, on the grounds that ''over the longer term, societies should do what they're most efficient doing.

''We're going to become more and more a country in which human knowledge will give us a competitive edge,'' Kaufman continued. ''Our priority ought to be to provide technological value added because of our heightened scientific and technological competence. What do we say to the Brazilians and the Koreans? 'You can't use your labor.' Our edge is technology, but other countries have to have more open markets.''

Kaufman's views of America's slowly replacing parts of its manufacturing sector with a service economy have recently been challenged by observers who argue that service industries rely on industry for their business. Where would the banks and the architectural, computer, and engineering companies that repre-

sent America's future in the global economy be without a manufacturing sector to use their services? Many believe that the
decline of manufacturing also risks a parallel decline among
segments of U.S. service industries, since there are no guarantees that foreign manufacturers will use American services.

The debate has been heightened by an influx of Japanese
capital, at a rate of $25–$50 billion a year; in 1986, 45 percent of
all Japanese investment went to the United States. This money
represents Japan's growing surplus in foreign trade, and much of
it is being invested in treasury securities issued to finance the
Reagan administration's huge budget deficits. Japan's surplus in
trade with the United States was $35 billion in 1984, $49.7 in
1985, and $58.6 billion in 1986.

Another debate involves the effect of foreign investment on
the balance of payments. In the short run, foreign direct investment can help the U.S. balance of payments if funds from
abroad add to the supply of savings and lower interest rates. The
long-term effect on the balance of payments is less certain: To
the extent that payments are made abroad in the form of interest,
dividends, royalties, or fees, or the foreign investment is merely
an outlet for imports, then the effect will be negative; in other
words, if profits are repatriated back to the home country and
exceed the capital invested in the United States, then the balance
of payments turns negative. If foreign investment leads to a net
outflow of dollars, it is harmful to the balance of payments,
since it adds to the supply of dollars on the foreign-exchange
market and causes the dollar to depreciate.

No one knows the full extent of foreign investment in the
United States, and public officials as well as financial experts
caution that the influx is probably significantly underreported.
Ago Ambre, a Commerce Department economist, said a discrepancy of $115 billion was found in reports on the flow of money
into and out of the United States between 1979 and 1983. The
discrepancy was between the overall figures and data on imports,
exports, and transfers. "The suspicion is very strong that this
was capital inflow not properly reported," he explained.

This phenomenon is listed in government documents as "Errors and Omissions." Henry Kaufman warned of its dangers:
"Be careful. The issue of capital flows is dramatic. We can
identify only 50 percent of the current account deficit. Errors and
Omissions may be larger than what we can identify. We also
don't know the source of the capital. Is it hot money? Black-
market money? Laundered money? No one knows."

Unlike Kaufman, top government officials remain unconcerned about the whereabouts of $115 billion. To them, it is comparable to a $10 shortfall in a personal checking account. Stephen J. Canner, an official with the Treasury Department's Office of International Investment, called "Errors and Omissions" a "problem in balance-of-payments accounting" and concluded that it was neither "significant" nor "unusual." Responding to queries by Representative John Bryant at a congressional hearing, he said he based his conclusions on the IMF's formula that as long as the size of a country's Errors and Omissions did not exceed 5 percent of the total exports and imports, it was considered acceptable, and "the United States fell within that standard." The chief economist of the Department of Commerce, Robert Ortner, agreed: "We're dealing with net transactions of goods and services in the trillions of dollars. Errors and Omissions just amount to the fact that the accounts don't add up. Compared with the aggregate, it is not that large."[23]

But while the exact amount of inflow is uncertain, "the reasons for it are clear," according to David C. Mulford, assistant secretary of the treasury for international affairs: "attractive investment opportunities here and an easing by foreign governments of their restrictions on the outflow of capital. There's been great progress made in recent years in what you'd call the freeing up of capital markets around the world. The end result was to make flows easier and more market sensitive." Mulford emphasized that "capital should flow to the best return," and when it does, it should be "regarded as a positive development."

Mr. Rohatyn, who has represented some European and Japanese foreign investors, including Santori whiskey and Unilever, the Dutch-British conglomerate trading company, counts himself among those who see the dangers in the unchecked influx of foreign capital. At the same time, he added that he was well aware of the benefits bestowed by foreign investors. "There's no question that without Renault, American Motors would have gone down and you would have had 20,000 to 30,000 people out on the streets." He was referring to the deal in which Régie National des Usines Renault bought a controlling interest in the American Motors Corporation in 1980.

But while he favors such selective foreign investment, he is concerned by the trend. "I think it's scary. It's very volatile money. To become the biggest financial borrower in the world doesn't strike me as such a hot idea." The key question, Rohatyn added, was whether Japan would someday seek to convert its huge liquidity into direct investment. "Suppose we don't do very much with our budget deficit, and we're looking at a $300 billion deficit. The Japanese yank their money, the dollar falls, and we're faced with a falling dollar and higher interest rates at a time of recession."

"We'd probably have some sort of banking crisis," Rohatyn predicted. "Under those circumstances, the Japanese might well take the money they earned from high interest rates and make direct investments [in American businesses]. In order to finance current operating deficits, you are ultimately going to turn over permanent assets."

Others believe that foreign investors, who generally prefer liquid financial assets, are unlikely to switch to illiquid, fixed assets. They note that much of the Japanese investment is made by insurance companies and other institutions that are uncommonly cautious. Senator Daniel P. Moynihan, who sits on both the finance and budget committees, agrees with this assessment but warns of the instability of high levels of foreign capital in portfolio investment. "If the dollar and interest rates dropped at the same time, the Japanese would be out of here with the flick of a microchip," the senator said. "Then we'd have some good depression movies, like the good old days." By the end of 1986, both the dollar and interest rates had indeed dropped, yet foreign investment continued to pour in at unprecedented rates.

Many analysts scoff at these scenarios, arguing that America's economic strengths would act as a cushion against disaster. Frank G. Zarb, a partner of Mr. Rohatyn's at Lazard Frères, argues that "the likelihood of foreign investment pulling out on an abrupt basis because the dollar is weaker or interest rates fall is a ghost we will never face. There's no place else for the foreign capital to go, nor will there be. The flow of capital to a secure economy that is performing well is not a negative."

This view of America as a safe haven is shared by Walter Wriston, former chairman of Citicorp, who believes that "foreign investors really put their money here because the United States has a politically stable government. It is one of the few countries in the world creating jobs, so an entrepreneur can make a buck and keep it." Wriston continued: "I don't believe that if interest rates were going to fall, and they have been falling steadily, that everybody is going to sell their dollars and go back to German marks or cruzeiros or something else. The safe-haven feature is enormously important."

Although he supports foreign investment, Wriston joins many

American businessmen who complain about a lack of reciprocity abroad, especially with Japan. While foreign investors generally enjoy unimpeded access in the United States, American investors are prohibited in some countries from purchasing banks, real estate, and other holdings abroad. "To permit people to move into this country and block us out of their own markets is wrong," said Wriston.

Whatever their differences, financial experts appear to agree on the problems inherent in becoming overly dependent on foreign capital. The theme of overreliance was sounded by Muriel Siebert, president of Siebert & Co., a discount brokerage firm, and the first woman on the New York Stock Exchange. "This country is hooked on foreign capital," she said. "What will be the effect when they have to sell? What happens if we change the tax structure in some way and we're no longer a haven for foreign capital? . . . Foreign capital has not yet flexed its muscle." Siebert also expressed her concern that American industry had become overly dependent on foreign investors. "There's something going on that scares me," she said. "A Japanese automaker comes to the United States to be a partner of a large automobile company to make cheaper cars. Why can't we do it ourselves? Why do we need the Japanese to show us how?" Similarly, she argued that foreign investors may not be sensitive to the needs of American business. As former New York State superintendent of banking, her concerns about foreign investors led her unsuccessfully to oppose the takeover of Marine Midland Bank by the Hong Kong and Shanghai Corp. She noted that Marine Midland was a dominant bank in several upstate New York cities and feared that those cities would be neglected in the event of a credit crunch. However, there is no evidence, to date, that her fears regarding Marine Midland have materialized.

DISEQUILIBRIUM AND FOREIGN CAPITAL

The debate continues over the advantages and risks of the exponential increase of foreign investment in the United States. Those who agree that foreign investment presents no problem argue that the United States was a net debtor from its founding to 1914 without suffering any visible ill effects. Others point out that from a global perspective the debt held by foreigners represents too small a percentage of the total debt—4.1 percent at the end of 1984; 3 percent in 1983—to cause concern. At the end of 1986, the foreign debt equaled only 6 percent of GNP, indicating to some analysts that the U.S. economy was large enough to absorb the costs of servicing the debt. They also argue that foreign ownership in the United States soared because of the bullish stock market, which should be a cause for celebration, not alarm.

Others who believe that there is no cause for concern point out that the U.S. foreign debt is more complex than that of Brazil or Mexico, whose foreign debts constitute a much larger percentage of their GNPs. In addition, unlike Brazil and Mexico, the United States could—if pressed—theoretically sell off its $1.07 trillion in overseas assets to pay off its debts.

Another positive view was expressed by Federal Reserve Board member Manuel Johnson, who won't even use the word debtor nation. "I prefer to say we're a capital surplus nation," he said. "It doesn't matter if you're a debtor nation, if the money represents investment in American industry that produces economic growth, and much of the money has been spent for those purposes."[24]

Many disagree with Johnson's assessment. Much of the money is not used for productive purposes but to buy treasury bills to finance the nation's debt and to build foreign-owned warehouses or assembly operations. It is the size of the national debt that troubles many analysts. It now rests at 41 percent of the GNP, a startling rise from 24 percent ten years ago.[25] Interest payments to securities issued by the Treasury Department constitute almost 14 percent of all federal spending. This means less money to spend on more productive investment, particularly in sectors of the economy that are suffering: agriculture, manufacturing, and the banks that serve them. It should also give pause to those who have argued up to now that the sheer size of our economy meant that it could easily absorb debts, deficits, and the foreign money that has flowed in to fill the vacuum.

By itself, the inflow of foreign money is not a problem, but rather a positive sign of increased confidence in the future of the American economy. In the context of America's new standing as an international debtor, however, it is a key indicator of trouble. Federal Reserve Board Chairman Paul A. Volcker characterized the seriousness of the problem: "My concern is disequilibrium. A big trade deficit and big current account deficit . . . amounts to gigantic disequilibrium. The bigger it is, the more disturbing the readjustment will be. Foreign capital is just a reflection of the disequilibrium of the system."

Testifying before the Senate Budget Committee, Volcker estab-

lished an even closer link between the flow of foreign capital and
the nation's economic maladies.

> The implications of . . . capital inflow are not all favorable,
> and adverse implications are mounting. The mirror image
> of a capital inflow is the trade and current account deficits,
> with adverse impacts on all those industries that look to
> export markets or that compete with imports. One effect is
> sizable sectors of the American economy have not parti-
> cipated at all fully in the recovery.

Volcker was also concerned about the effect of capital flight and
American disequilibrium on foreign economies. "The drain on
foreign savings and the related depreciation of their currencies
vis-à-vis the dollar seem to be inhibiting prospects for internally
generated growth abroad," he testified.[26]

Volcker's major concern is that American sovereignty is being
compromised by her increasing indebtedness. "Our capital markets and interest rates have become hostage to a continuing flow
of foreign capital," he warned. "Over time, the interest cost of
those foreign borrowings will compound upon themselves."
Interdependence among economic markets is fluid, added Volcker,
who concluded that the United States was becoming more vulnerable as "we've shaken confidence in our economy."

If confidence in the economy is shaken, then the foreign
money that now props up the deficit and sustains the strength of
the dollar will eventually begin to ebb. A 1985 poll by Salomon
Brothers of 161 European investors revealed some signs that the
United States was about to lose its position as the world's
leading investment haven. Although the British still ranked the
United States first, Europeans ranked Japan in the lead, with
Europe second and the United States third.

The effects of America's dependence on the foreign dollar
continue to be felt, like the aftershocks of an earthquake. Whatever the consequences, it is important to remember that foreign
money is not the cause but the effect of laissez-faire policies that
have led the United States to look for quick fixes and more
money than the nation can productively absorb.

CHAPTER 15

Faustian Bargains
Domestic Policy and Foreign Debts

We are vitally dependent on foreign savings flows. Directly or indirectly, [foreign investors] are financing half or more of our budget deficit.

> —*E. Gerald Corrigan, president,*
> *Federal Reserve Bank of New York*

America has been selling off the family jewels to pay for a night on the town.

> —*Representative John Bryant, Democrat of Texas*

The U.S. entry into the ranks of international indebtedness in mid-1985 raised cries of alarm from policymakers, editorial writers, and scholars. The consensus was that this was a serious problem and that it was not a good idea for the United States, once the world's leading creditor, to allow itself to slide further into debt. What to do about it, if anything, was another matter. Solutions, as well as the attempt to reach them, were curiously lacking on any policy level, and given the magnitude of the problem, the absence of leadership was striking. It was laissez-faire run rampant. Government policy took the form of nonpolicy, while inactivity, neglect, and short-term patchwork solutions replaced any serious attempt to deal with the long-term consequences.

The real problem was that White House officials did not regard the nation's foreign debt as a problem, focusing instead on the short-term benefits of foreign investment. After all, foreign money had helped finance the domestic deficit and spared politicians the necessity—at least for a while—of imposing tough, politically difficult spending restrictions on the American people.

Some policymakers who enjoyed more distance from the White House sounded the alarm but absolved their institutions of any role in solving the problem. Federal Reserve Board Chairman

Paul A. Volcker, for example, agreed with many of his colleagues that the trend was unsustainable but did not regard the Fed as central to the issue. "The disequilibrium will have to correct itself," he said. "There is no role for the Fed." Volcker implied that the solution would have to come from the executive branch but was not optimistic about the possibility. "State, Treasury, etc., are not disturbed because they have an ideological position to defend," he explained. Despite his disclaimers about the Fed, Volcker deserved plaudits for speaking out; his credibility added weight to the debate.

Leading officials in the Reagan administration privately expressed their concerns about the increasing U.S. dependence on foreign borrowing but believed that tampering with the forces of the marketplace was undesirable. At first surprised to learn of America's new status as a debtor, President Reagan turned the issue inside out to show the silver lining. "We are the best and safest investment in the world," he argued; "that's why foreigners are investing more in the United States than they are borrowing. In other words, increasing inflows of foreign capital to a "safe haven" in the United States are a sign of the world's rising confidence in America's economy as well as its stable political system.[1]

It is also a sign that the U.S. economy is more flexible than foreign economies, many of which are still saddled with bureaucracies that discourage investment. European investors send funds to the United States when they become exasperated with their own poor growth, high unemployment, government restrictions, and structural rigidities. Who your father was is an important consideration in granting bank loans in some regions of France, while background checks in the United States tend to emphasize creditworthiness.

Others argue that foreign debt is still too small a piece of the pie to justify federal intervention: 10 to 20 percent of a total national debt of more than $2 trillion. They see U.S. foreign debt in a positive light, as part of a global picture, not to be tampered with for fear of unanticipated and undesirable consequences. Any attempt to abandon the administration's laissez-faire policy would drive investment into the arms of other countries, which would welcome it openly. Worse, the loss of foreign investment would signal bad times for the American economy.

"What it takes to have a real outflow is to have a loss of confidence in the U.S. economy," said David Mulford, assistant treasury secretary for international affairs, an advocate of the status quo:

In general, there's been great progress made in recent years in what you'd call the freeing up of capital markets around the world. The end result was to make flows easier and more market sensitive. Theoretically, that should be very good from the standpoint of the use of capital. Capital should flow to the best return. That should be positive.

The optimism of the executive branch reflects a deep faith in the powers of the marketplace to right the debtor imbalance in a few short years. "Does it concern you that we're a debtor nation?" asked Representative Thomas A. Luken, Democrat of Ohio, at a congressional hearing on foreign investment on May 8, 1986. "It doesn't concern me," answered Stephen J. Canner, director of the Treasury Department's Office of International Investment. "The situation will correct itself as the dollar depreciates and the trade balance corrects itself. All it means is that we're buying more than we're selling."[2]

It is not merely blind faith that drives officials to this viewpoint; it is the belief that the marketplace is the only viable alternative. Canner outlined what he considered the only options for dealing with debtor status: "We can sell our gold reserves; we can sell foreign investments overseas; or we can continue to allow foreign investing in the United States and borrowing from abroad." It was clear that Canner considered selling off U.S. gold reserves or foreign investments unreasonable, leaving no choice but to continue the open-door policy that he indicated was articulated in 1983 by President Reagan. Representative John Bryant, Democrat of Texas and chairman of the hearings, expressed his incredulity at the government witness's repeated emphasis on the president's policy statement, noting that events had changed sufficiently in three years to warrant a reexamination.

The president's position was clear in 1983 and has remained consistent:

The United States welcomes foreign direct investment that flows according to market forces [and] . . . opposes . . . government intervention that impedes or distorts investment flows or attempts to shift artificially the benefits of these flows. . . . A world with strong foreign investment flows is opposite of a zero-sum game. We believe there are only winners, no losers, and all participants gain from it.[3]

Although in his statement the president was specifically referring to direct investment, his appointees took his views to include portfolio investment as well.

STRATEGIES TO ATTRACT FOREIGN MONEY: PREFERENTIAL TREATMENT FOR FOREIGN INVESTORS

In reality, U.S. policy shows much more initiative than the public statements of treasury officials and the president would lead us to believe. Far from being passive witnesses to the ebb and flow of market forces, the United States has vigorously recruited foreign investment. While the rhetoric remains deceptively neutral, the real reason for the treasury's aggressive search for foreign capital is to defray the country's mushrooming federal deficit. In a sense, federal policy parallels state efforts in the indiscriminate search for foreign money. "We are vitally dependent on foreign savings flows," said E. Gerald Corrigan, president of the Federal Reserve Bank of New York. "Directly or indirectly, [foreign investors] are financing half or more of our budget deficit."[4]

To ensure the steady flow of foreign money, the government, beginning in the early part of 1984, initiated changes in specific laws and regulations. The new policies were implemented during the president's reelection campaign and produced instant success, showing what can happen when an issue is given top priority and full presidential attention. Limited only by the fall election on the horizon, the goals were clear: to portray the deficit as insignificant, temporary, and soon to be relieved by the economic boom created by increasing flows of foreign capital.

Orchestrated by Treasury Secretary Donald T. Regan, the administration relied on two major strategies: to make the United States a tax haven for foreign investors and to guarantee foreigners' anonymity. Initially, Regan was interested in making the United States more competitive. He told the International Forum of the U.S. Chamber of Commerce early in 1984 that ". . . among the major industrial countries, Belgium, Canada, France and Italy all have long-term government-bond yields higher than ours." Add to that the intense competition made possible by modern telecommunications technology, "immense sums of capital now flow instantaneously around the world—in the form of electronic funds transfers seeking fractional increases in investment yields."[5]

The first policy initiative almost slipped by unnoticed. Buried in the 1984 Deficit Reduction Act was a change in the tax code that allowed foreigners who purchased American bonds or other types of portfolio assets to eliminate the 30 percent withholding tax on interest earned by their investments. This meant that American assets became virtually tax-free to foreign buyers, making the United States the world's largest tax haven.

The idea was to attract more money from overseas to help finance the deficit, hold down interest rates, and rally the stock and bond markets. Without this quick fix, officials feared a rise in interest rates of one or two points—a disaster in an election year. The new policy legalized what used to be a tax loophole, making the United States a new tax haven, hosting what experts predicted would become a $50 billion annual business.

On the surface, administration officials hoped to make America more competitive by removing an obstacle to foreign investment. Before the withholding tax was repealed, foreign investors who wanted to avoid U.S. taxes would buy certificates of deposit issued by subsidiaries of U.S. banks in countries where the tax rates were low. Similarly, corporations wishing to sell bonds to tax-avoiding foreign investors would have to go through the nuisance of setting up subsidiaries offshore in places like the Netherlands Antilles. These subsidiaries would issue Eurobonds, sold in London and other European capitals. The U.S. treasury changed its regulations to allow American companies to issue Eurobonds. It is an understatement to say that investment banking firms and U.S. corporations were delighted with the new policy. It enabled them to compete more effectively with other tax havens and bring some of the money back home.

The Netherlands Antilles was not happy about the new developments. Up until this time, the country benefited from a bilateral treaty, negotiated in 1948, that allowed income paid to "residents" of the Netherlands Antilles to be exempt from most taxes. If an American company paid dividends directly to a German investor, for example, it would have to withhold a certain amount of money for taxes. But if the dividends were channeled through Curaçao, an island in the Netherlands Antilles, most of the money would be tax-free. Hundreds of corporations, including General Motors, Sears Roebuck, and Citicorp, have created subsidiaries in the Netherlands Antilles, costing the U.S. treasury—and American taxpayers—billions of dollars each year. The companies claimed it helped them borrow money from foreign sources more easily.[6]

Government officials argued that the new policies would spell economic and political disaster for their region. "We're facing legislation which will wipe out in one shot a major economic pillar of the Netherlands Antilles," said Prime Minister Felip Martina, referring to what is called the islands' "international financial industry."[7]

Encouraged by having successfully whetted foreign appetites for American securities through tax repeal, the Treasury Department forged ahead in midsummer with a second major step to attract overseas capital: a treasury offering of $500 million to $1 billion in new three-year, eleven-month notes designed especially for foreign buyers. Their special attraction included tax relief and anonymity and was designed specifically for those purposes. The notes were a curious hybrid, a cross between a standard treasury issue and a form of bond known as "bearer bonds," popular in Europe because they provide anonymity for the investor. "Bearer bonds" are the property of the investor, who is paid only after appearing in person to collect his money or his interest. The more common form of bond is a registered bond, where the issuer keeps records of ownership and—more important—the treasury knows where to collect its taxes. Exempted from bearer status were U.S. government–sponsored enterprises, such as securities issues from the Federal National Mortgage Association.

No doubt, Secretary Regan's previous experience as the president of the investment brokerage firm of Merrill, Lynch helped him formulate this package, which he described as both "fair to investors and workable for tax collectors."[8]

"The idea is twenty years old," added James E. Ammerman, a specialist in portfolio investment for the Treasury Department. "The change in policy removed an anomaly. U.S. corporations could always work through the tax-free Netherlands Antilles, or they could set up corporations elsewhere. Also, almost every major foreign country issues bearer bonds."

The Treasury Department worked its way out of the quandary between the two forms of bonds by allowing the new notes to be sold in bearer form, that is, without revealing the names of the purchasers but requiring securities dealers to certify annually that the notes are not owned by Americans. Secretary Regan assured doubters that if the treasury found that a brokerage house was buying securities on behalf of Americans, it would begin withholding 20 percent to cover taxes. Lest foreign investors worry about too much U.S. government intrusiveness, the undersecretary of the treasury, John Niehenke, assured foreign investors that "unless there are cases of abuse," they needn't be concerned.[9]

Niehenke's remark betrayed the truth of the situation: The new regulations were almost impossible to enforce, and the government had chosen to sacrifice tax revenue to attract foreign capital on the grounds that in their judgment increased investment far outweighed the inevitable tax losses. It was obviously a decision that policymakers made with their eyes open, indicated by widespread misgivings on the part of financial analysts. Requiring an institution to certify that the buyer was not a U.S. citizen is "an idea that just won't work," said Richard Watkins, of the British securities firm of Phillips & Drew. "It would be difficult to give such certification over the life of the bond."[10]

There was no question that the new regulations also made life easier for institutional investors. Secretary Regan said that they would allow U.S. corporations to issue bearer bonds overseas directly; they would also allow securities firms to buy securities directly from the treasury, repackage them, and then sell them abroad as bearer bonds. Salomon Brothers, along with a group of other firms, took immediate advantage of the new regulations and repackaged $1.7 billion worth of T-bills to sell to foreign purchasers.[11]

The policies were an instant success. The immediate response was $4 billion in bids from securities firms in Europe and Asia. In the first six months of 1985, foreigners bought $14.3 billion worth of treasury securities, or 17 percent of the total investment of all new issues. In 1984, the net foreign purchases of treasury notes, bonds, and bills totaled $25.5 billion, the most since 1977. Japanese investors purchased 25 percent; British investors, $6.1 billion; investors from OPEC nations, $2.1 billion; and Switzerland and others accounted for $1.1 billion.

Foreigners still hold only a relatively small piece of the pie: 10 to 20 percent of a national debt of more than $2 trillion. Total foreign holdings of treasury notes equaled $201.3 billion as of June 1985, twice the $100 billion held in 1980. During the same time period, the debt soared by $864.7 billion to $1.779 trillion. By the end of 1985, foreign investors held more than 15 percent of publicly held U.S. treasury securities, increasing their holdings that year by $37.5 billion to a total of $230 billion; this meant that foreign investors financed almost 19 percent of the treasury's needs.[12]

There was no doubt that Treasury's actions defrayed the deficit. According to Leonard Silk, economic columnist for *The New York Times,* foreign investment covered more than three-quarters of the net federal, state and local deficit, making it relatively tolerable: "Foreign savings nearly cover the shortfall of domestic savings to finance the deficit and thus prevent a soaring of interest rates that would devastate the securities markets and stifle business capital spending, housing and durable goods purchases.''[13]

In terms of its goals, federal policy was clearly a success. But critics worried about the long-term effects of U.S. dependence on foreign capital and the extent to which this "quick fix" had loosened the country's resolve to reduce the deficit.

SPECIAL BREAKS FOR FOREIGNERS: CRITICISMS

From a global perspective, the most serious outcome of such an aggressive policy is the increase in capital flight. Foreign dictators who need a safe place to hide their wealth from the world's scrutiny find guarantees of anonymity irresistible, while tax breaks are just the icing on the cake. "Our economy has become a haven for capital flight from the third world," charged Representative John Bryant.

> Evidence of the billions of dollars Ferdinand and Isabel Marcos . . . have secretly invested here . . . is coming to light. . . . As the beacon of freedom and democracy in the world, we must not allow our economy to be an unwitting accomplice in this theft from the poorest people in the poorest countries.[14]

Capital flight from third-world countries has been calculated in the hundreds of billions of dollars, and much of it has been invested in the United States. "We in the third world desperately need that capital not only to repay our foreign debt but also to develop our economies," explained Professor George B. N. Ayittey, an economist from Ghana. "Tracking down that capital is often impossible on account of secrecy laws, let alone recover it. . . . For decades, third-world dictators thumbed their noses . . . at the plight of their people with the knowledge that they could always escape with their booty to the U.S. or the West.''[15] Policies that accept and encourage anonymity exacerbate these problems and only serve to accelerate the hostility against the United States from third-world countries.

Stemming capital flight would go a long way toward offsetting the problems of the poorest of the debtor countries. A study issued by the Morgan Guaranty Trust Company of eighteen debtor nations in Latin America, Asia, and Africa showed that of the $450 billion increase in the debts of these countries, $200 billion represented capital flight. Without capital flight, Argentina's foreign debt would be $1 billion instead of $50 billion; Mexico's debt would be $12 billion instead of $97 billion; Nigeria, $7 billion instead of $19 billion; the Philippines, $15 billion instead of $27 billion; and South Africa, with a debt of $24 billion, would be almost debt-free. Without capital flight, interest rates in third-world nations might decline and productivity might increase. "Had the earnings on foreign assets acquired through capital flight been repatriated," the study said, "rather than reinvested abroad, the servicing of existing debts would have been facilitated."[16]

The report noted that "only a fraction of the specific assets accumulated through capital flight can be identified," which means that these figures represent only the tip of the iceberg. "Virtually no data are published on other foreign assets acquired through capital flight, such as currency, securities, businesses and real estate."[17]

U.S. officials, while sympathetic to the plight of third-world countries, show no signs of bearing any responsibility for their own policies. "Of course it hurts other countries," said John McCarthy, head of the Office of Investment Affairs at the State Department, in response to a question on the relationship of offering such attractive issues and the encouragement of capital flight. "It is hurting Latin America. We don't have responsibility for that. [Secretary of State] Shultz made speeches about foreign debt in Latin America. He warned countries that their political instability is frightening away their capital. In the 1960s and 1970s, capital stayed in Latin America."

The effects on the United States of such heavy reliance on foreign portfolio investment are also drawing criticism. There is the question of just how long foreigners will continue to finance our deficit. If the money stopped, chaos could follow: The Federal Reserve Board would have to decide whether to finance the deficit and risk inflation or not finance it and risk a recession. There is also the question of how long Europeans will be willing to finance America's deficit before bowing to political pressures. Cries of the "imperial dollar" have been heard in France and printed in *Le Monde*. "Reagan's economy is playing with our money," charged Erwin Pearlmann, head of the West German printers union, I. G. Druck und Papier. "The U.S. economic boom will go bust when we realize that Reagan is not serious about addressing his budget problem."[18]

Concern in Congress has been bipartisan. In fact, the Senate passed a unanimous voice vote condemning the issuance of bearer bonds, fearing this would lead to more tax evasion. The feeling was that Swiss banks (among other foreign institutional investors) would be able to invest huge sums in bearer bonds and certify that they would not resell them to Americans. But since Swiss banks also maintain a policy of secrecy, there would be no way to verify such claims. Ultimately, the more treasury borrowing that is made tax-exempt, the "more American citizens will have to foot all the bills," contended Hobart Rowen, who called these policies "gimmicks, a Faustian bargain . . . to which the government is driven by the hugeness of the deficit and the need to find help in financing it from abroad." It amounts to a "sleazy partnership with tax evaders . . . and compounds the potential for tax abuse and evasion."[19]

Senator Howard Metzenbaum, Democrat of Ohio, was particularly outraged by the Treasury Department's actions. "I resent what the secretary of treasury is doing," he said. "First, he [Regan] sponsored elimination of the 30 percent withholding tax . . . and now he's compounding the problem by making it possible for institutions to issue bearer bonds. It's upsetting to see that Regan, who should be on our side, has become the enemy." The senator suggested that Congress pass a separate bill, or a rider on a bill, that would reverse Treasury's actions.[20]

Some Wall Street critics charged that the treasury had no choice but to change the tax code and the regulations; they had become so dependent on foreign capital, they no longer controlled how that capital was managed. "The basic fact is that the U.S. Treasury is increasingly dependent on foreign capital and, in the long run, cannot dictate the terms on which it raises capital," said Peter J. Widmer, senior vice-president of Julius Baer & Co., of Zurich.[21]

Like trade, investment also creates conflict, and a series of bidding wars soon followed Treasury's drive to lure investment with "quick fix" incentives. The British were the first to follow the United States in repealing the withholding tax. They issued $1.2 billion worth of government bonds exempting foreigners from 30 percent withholding. Two months later, on October 3, 1984, the French and West Germans also agreed to eliminate their withholding on interest paid to foreign investors. The outflow of European capital to the United States had forced these countries to follow suit; in June 1984 alone, West Germans experienced outflows at an annual rate of $7.2 billion, mostly to the United States.[22]

The real question, and the source of much of the criticism, is the extent to which America's future independence is being compromised by its own policymakers. The freedom Americans enjoy today is partly based on a degree of economic self-sufficiency, a notion that has been sacrificed to the immediate necessity of mitigating the effects of a crippling deficit.

"America has been selling off the family jewels to pay for a night on the town," charged Representative John Bryant. "And all too often, we don't even know who is buying."[23]

INTERDEPENDENCE AND POWERLESSNESS

"Is the U.S. getting as hooked on foreign money as it used to be on foreign oil?" asked Allan Sloane in an article in *Forbes*. Sloane raises a number of questions, all pointing to the loss of American independence engendered by bending so far backward to attract foreign money. The United States, he says, is acting like an underdeveloped country: "Advanced countries typically export capital to the rest of the world, while underdeveloped countries import capital."[24]

Sloane questions the practice of eliminating taxes and guaranteeing anonymity for foreign investors as well as the skewed priorities of bank regulators at the FDIC and the Federal Reserve Board, who allowed dozens of banks to fail in 1984, 1985, and 1986, while bailing out Continental Illinois for fear of offending foreign investors. With billions of foreign investors' dollars at stake, the regulators guaranteed the bank's deposits as well as the bondholders and preferred stockholders of the bank's holding company.

"Why is the federal government so worried about the welfare and tender psyches of foreign investors?" wrote Sloane. "The answer, it would seem, is that megabillion-dollar inflows of foreign money are helping the U.S. finance [huge] federal deficits without running interest rates into the stratosphere. That being the case, it behooves the government to be nice to foreign money. Whose bread I borrow, his song I sing."[25]

Others fear that even slight changes in economic conditions would stanch the flow of foreign money, a thought that should give pause to those who put such faith on maintaining its current levels. "If the dollar weakens while the economy is expanding," explained Henry Kaufman of Salomon Brothers, "then a problem will occur because there will be an outflow of foreign funds."

Signs appeared early in 1985 supporting the view that foreign money was not without its risks and that Kaufman's predictions were not so far-fetched. "Foreign investors are wielding increasing power in the U.S. credit markets, making the markets more vulnerable to outside shocks," reported the *Wall Street Journal*.[26] On Wall Street, anxiety was mounting in some quarters over the growing influence of foreign money and how it had become a source of instability for the domestic bond market. With the decline of the dollar, many feared that foreign investors would dump their U.S. bond holdings as well as reduce the purchases on which U.S. policymakers had come to depend.

"Foreign investments in U.S. credit markets may well be a serious source of uncertainty and volatility," said James J. O'Leary, an economist with the U.S. Trust Co. Foreign investments also make the Fed's task of setting credit policy much more complex. "U.S. interest rates are becoming more exposed to changes in economic policy in Tokyo and Bonn," added David D. Hale of Kemper Financial Services. "Not only are our cars made in Japan, but increasingly so are our interest rates."[27]

As predicted, as soon as the dollar began to plunge against foreign currencies in April 1986, some foreign investors began bailing out of U.S. securities markets, creating fears that their actions would eventually heat up inflation. Japanese purchases of treasury bonds dropped sharply, followed by European investors. The loss of foreign investors is "scary, short-term," primarily because of what it could do to bond markets, said David Williams, the head of Alliance Capital Management Corporation, one of the largest institutional investors in the United States.[28]

In a dramatic turn of events one year later, in May 1987, foreign investors began to show exactly how they would influence the U.S. economy by declining to bid on a $29 billion offering of T-bills until the terms were improved. Treasury officials finally capitulated. Reluctantly, they reduced the price of the thirty-year bills and raised their yield, which served the purpose of bringing foreigners back to the fold. This was no minor event. It further solidified the position of foreign investors, who would henceforth play an even greater role in determining U.S. interest rates and setting the course of the U.S. economy.

A sudden shift of investors was also worth noting at this point: Foreign governments replaced private investors in the first three months of 1987 as the major purchasers of U.S. government securities. This meant that America's dependence on foreign investors now included the central banks of Western Europe, Japan, and Canada. What their governments would demand in return for their capital was anyone's guess, along with how long they would continue to prop up U.S. deficits.

As the U.S. treasury grew dependent on foreign money, private investors began to follow suit. U.S. corporations now rely increasingly on money from abroad to finance new plants. The dependence factor has come full circle: Now the treasury can't cut or raise interest rates without weighing the Japanese and German reaction; and U.S. manufacturers can't plan for the future without evaluating the accessibility of foreign capital.

America's emergence as the world's leading debtor nation has also extracted political costs that are just beginning to surface. At the economic summit in Venice in June 1987, for example, many observed that President Reagan and his aides were negotiating from the weakest vantage point in years due to the country's eroded status as a debtor nation. This was the first sign that other nations had lost some of their respect for the United States, because of the magnitude of the debt and its leaders' inability to reduce it. Arguments about the health of the American economy and its ability to absorb a sizable debt paled next to the reality of the situation: the decline of America's position as a world leader.

THE RISKS OF "LAISSEZ-FAIRE"

The debate over government intervention reveals both a basic philosophical disagreement as well as conflicting interpretations of the same body of information. Reagan administration officials, together with many economists, believe that marketplace solutions have generally proved preferable to government intervention and that market forces will eventually even out what they regard as temporary imbalances.

A deep schism also exists between those who worry about America's indebtedness to foreign interests and those who claim it is beneficial. The increase in foreign-owned capital is a myth, argues economist Paul Craig Roberts. "Official data show no increase in foreign-owned capital inflows. Rather, they indicate a sharp drop in U.S. capital outflows. . . . Foreigners today hold about 15% of U.S. government debt. The figure was much higher during the 1970s (26% in 1978) when foreign central banks were trying to prop up a weak dollar by buying U.S. Treasury securities and when OPEC countries were parking their surpluses in Treasury securities."[29]

David Mulford of the Treasury Department agrees, reflecting the laissez-faire policy of the administration: "Overall, we're no more dependent on foreign capital than we were. Foreigners aren't financing our deficit; they're financing private investment." Mulford regards U.S. debtor status as a "short-term adjustment problem" and believes the solutions should be made at the global level, not unilaterally. "It all suggests to me," he said, "that there has to be better coordination of economic policy in the major nations of the world to offset the short-term distortions of investment flows." What Mulford suggests is intervention at the multinational level, ideal in the abstract, but very difficult to implement. There is also an inconsistency with advocating an interventionist policy for a multinational body and a laissez-faire policy at home.

Those who disagree worry about a debt that is increasing exponentially; they offer analogies from the experiences of Brazil to Great Britain to advocate a more long-range, aggressive government policy. One of the leading proponents of this view, economist Lester Thurow, links America's indebtedness with the overvalued dollar, warning that the country "must develop alternative public policies for maintaining a balance between exports and imports"; otherwise the country will sink deeper into debt and crush its most valuable industries. "What is America doing about this twin disaster?" he asks. "Nothing. What will Monday morning economic quarterbacks say about America? Exactly what they said about third-world indebtedness and Britain's industrial demise."[30]

The philosophical debate over intervention is replete with ironies and paradoxes. It is almost too easy to attach labels of "protectionism," or "industrial policy" on solutions that come from liberal economists like Thurow or from Democratic legislators—whose concerns are easy to dismiss as "political." At the same time, devotees of the "free market" are fooling themselves as well as the public if they honestly believe that they can govern according to free-market philosophies while the rest of the world takes advantage of the policy vacuum. The real irony surfaces when policymakers profess free-market passivity while exercising considerable discretion in controlling market forces. Letting market forces work freely would preclude giving special breaks to foreign investors and perhaps stem some of the capital flight that has resulted from this obvious distortion.

Rhetoric thus becomes not only meaningless but totally out of sync with the realities of the international marketplace. Unfortunately, it has taken the place of intelligent discourse. Most important, in the absence of real debate, policymakers have avoided the central issue: how to reap the benefits of foreign investment, yet protect the country from being buffeted by its negative impacts.

PART V

AMERICA'S OPEN DOOR

CHAPTER 16

The Perfect Host

Reciprocity, Disclosure, and the U.S. Role in Global Investment

Many of the foreigners who so freely invest here come from countries that do not allow Americans to make the same kind of investments.

—*Representative John Bryant, Democrat of Texas*

Threatening to close the U.S. market to investors whose home countries restrict U.S. investment may not cause those countries to relax their restrictions. Indeed, these governments might be pleased to have us prevent their investors from investing in the United States because they want to keep that investment at home.

—*Robert Cornell, deputy assistant secretary for trade and investment policy, Treasury Department*

• In Australia, foreign nationals seeking to invest in the country's media, civil aviation, and mining industries must submit to government approval; and mining companies must have at least 50 percent Australian equity. Companies face rejection if the government finds their investment harmful to the national interest or if there are Australians ready to invest "at reasonable terms and conditions." The government can also intervene in foreign acquisitions and has allowed only five U.S.-owned banks operating licenses.

• In South Korea, more than one-third of the country's private-sector industries are off limits to foreign investors. These include advertising, dairy, livestock breeding, communications, wholesale fruit and vegetables, cigarettes, wholesale liquor, and railroads. All foreign investments are subject to government approval to make sure they are in the national interest.

• In Kuwait, all foreign investment must be through joint venture, with a Kuwaiti partner owning at least 51 percent of the company. No one who does business with Israel is allowed to invest at all. The energy industry is totally government owned, while commercial banking, real property ownership, and participation in the local stock market are reserved for Kuwaiti nationals.

• In Mexico, foreign ownership of a business is limited to 49 percent, and in certain industries—such as auto parts—the percentage is even smaller. Foreign ownership of land is totally forbidden in border and coastal areas.

• In Japan, an elaborate investment approval process—based on formal and informal mechanisms—serves to restrict foreign investment. Only joint ventures are permitted in many industries; foreign ownership of more than 50 percent of its energy companies, or 25 percent of its "technologically innovative companies," is flatly prohibited. Foreign-owned businesses are subject to approval by their potential Japanese competitors. For all practical purposes, investment in the following sectors is closed to foreign investors: agriculture, forestry, fisheries, mining, petroleum, leather, and leather products.[1]

These examples represent a fraction of the thousands of investment restrictions imposed on all foreign nationals by other countries, including America's major trading partners. Eclipsed by unfair trade practices, protectionist investment barriers have largely been ignored; the conventional wisdom rests on the assurance that they will quietly melt away under the heat of market forces.

The only political leader to call attention to the inconsistencies of U.S. policies toward reciprocity was Representative John

Bryant, Democrat of Texas, who points out two cases as particularly blatant. Ownership of the print media is flatly prohibited in Australia, yet Australian Rupert Murdoch's American subsidiary owns some major U.S. newspapers and magazines, including the *New York Post,* the *Chicago Sun-Times,* and *New York* magazine. (In 1986, Rupert Murdoch became a naturalized U.S. citizen in order to purchase television stations.)

"Foreign ownership of Mexican agricultural land and land within 100 miles of a border or 50 miles of the coast is prohibited. . . . Land can be held in trust for up to ten years and renewed, but ultimately must be sold to a Mexican national," noted Bryant. "In contrast, Mexican investors have made major investments in agricultural land and other real property in the United States."

It comes as no surprise to anyone involved in trade negotiations that one of the worst offenders is Japan, America's second-largest trading partner. Their protectionist investment barriers, which operate at many different levels, continue to resist change. The inequities are nowhere more apparent than in the high-tech area. While U.S. citizens cannot own more than 25 percent of these companies, Bryant points out, the Japanese have "invested heavily in our high-tech industries and own more than 32,000 U.S. patents. They are draining us of our technology, while denying us access to theirs."

The best analysis of the subtle investment barriers blocking American investment in Japan comes from Clyde Prestowitz, former adviser on Japan to Secretary of Commerce Malcolm Baldrige. Prestowitz, who ran his own trading company and medical-equipment company in Japan, learned his lesson the hard way. It is a mistake, he claims, to look at the plant alone; "you have to look at the distribution system, marketing, hiring workers," and a host of other factors. Sometimes, the roadblocks emerge after a company has opened for business and tries to sell its product:

> In order to sell, you need salesmen, warehouses, office space, distributors, trucks, secretaries, etc. The warehouses are very hard to get. They are controlled by big trading companies. There is cross-shareholding. The presidents of the twenty or so companies meet and coordinate. They could decide not to give warehouse space to a competitor.
>
> In Japan there is lifetime employment till the age of fifty-five. The pensions are not very good, and they are not

vested, so Japanese workers can't transfer them if they
change jobs. There is also a great deal of pressure from the
company. When I tried to hire away workers, the company
called their wives and parents. The pressures were very
intense. I remember one man crying in my office. They
make them feel as if they are betraying the company. It's
hard to get good skilled Japanese employees.

Then you need distributors. Business in Japan is done on
the basis of personal relationships: ties between supplier
and buyer. Many distributors are retirees . . . and depend
on these jobs; it is really a social-welfare system. These
personal relationships are conducted among Japanese companies. Nippondensu sells to Toyota but not to Nissan.
How can American companies get a crack?

The net result, concluded Prestowitz, is that foreign investment is discouraged: "Americans don't sell many auto parts in
Japan. Why put a factory in if you can't sell? Up until 1975 it
was impossible legally to set up a plant in Japan. If the Japanese
had to produce under the same conditions as the U.S. companies, they would lose."

WHY COUNTRIES RESTRICT INVESTMENT

Every country imposes some limitations on foreign investment;
the United States clearly has the fewest restrictions.[2] In all cases,
restrictions on foreign investment reflect a country's insecurity;
they protect a local industry from competition and, in a broader
sense, allow that country to retain a sense of control over its
economy.

Canada, America's largest trading partner, justified its decision to decrease foreign ownership of the book-publishing industry in terms of its fear of U.S. cultural domination. In 1985, the
government issued new rules restricting foreign ownership, then
took action almost immediately to show it was serious. When
Gulf & Western acquired Prentice-Hall, it was told it had to
divest itself of the Canadian subsidiary within two years. At that
time, Prentice-Hall of Canada reported $23 million in annual
sales.

Third-world countries, where restrictive practices are common, cite their long experience with colonialism to justify policies ensuring their economic independence. They remember that
foreign political domination first appeared in the form of foreign

investment: The East India Tea Company preceded British domination of India; ITT was instrumental in overthrowing the elected government of Salvatore Allende in Chile; and the oil companies were believed to have been involved in the CIA-backed coup in Iran in 1954.

Not surprisingly, there is a lack of comprehensive information on specific barriers to foreign investment.[3] The last systematic inventory was taken by the Bureau of Economic Affairs (BEA) as part of the 1977 benchmark survey, and this report investigated only obstacles to investment experienced by U.S. companies that had already located overseas, not obstacles that prevented companies from investing abroad. Even so, the results were dramatic: Of 23,641 companies surveyed, 3,240, or 14 percent, said they were subject to at least one major government-imposed obstacle that impeded their ability to do business.[4]

These obstacles appear in the form of "performance standards" and are considered by U.S. policymakers to be a distortion of free trade and investment. They include domestic content regulations, where the investor is forced to manufacture his product with a certain percentage of materials that are grown or made locally. A good example is Mexico, which forces local content requirements on foreign investors: 60 percent for cars, 70–80 percent for trucks, and 90 percent for buses. IBM succeeded in establishing a wholly owned facility in Mexico only after agreeing to use 82 percent local content and to export 92 percent of its product. (Competing foreign computer manufacturers, many alleged, were responsible for Mexico's initial resistance to IBM.)

In addition to export requirements, which force producers to export a certain percentage of their goods, there are restrictions on foreign exchange as well as labor rules that require investors to hire local workers. (Labor rules no longer pose any hardship on foreign investors; quite the contrary, since the main attraction of manufacturing offshore is the availability of cheap labor.) All performance standards lead to one goal: reducing competition for local manufacturers. They are regarded as an uneconomical use of resources and detrimental to everyone. The worst offenders at the time of the BEA study were the Latin American countries, with Africa and India following closely behind. The industry most subject to local restrictions was the mining industry.[5]

In the last five years, many third-world countries have relaxed their restrictions on foreign investment. Multinationals no longer seem as threatening, as the colonial experience recedes from the minds of developing countries. Even after the tragedy at Bhopal, India, where an explosion at the Union Carbide plant made countries understandably nervous about foreign investment, India's prime minister, Rajiv Gandhi, continued to recruit foreign mutinationals to his country. Mounting foreign debt has also impelled many developing countries to seek new sources of investment: "We feel it is better to have partners than creditors," said Ecuador's foreign minister, Francisco Swett.[6]

But barriers remain in virtually all countries doing business with the United States. Those barriers are understandable in countries that have suffered the ravages of "economic imperialism" or the political intrusiveness of foreign multinationals and their parent governments. What is not understandable are the barriers erected by industrialized countries—like Japan—who are benefiting enormously from widening trade surpluses.

THE U.S. PHILOSOPHY ON OPEN INVESTMENT

For most of its recent history, the United States could afford the luxury of applying its free-market philosophy to investment. A generosity of spirit, the belief that foreign investment brought only benefits, and the hope that maintaining this posture would give its leaders moral leverage led the United States to ignore other countries' protectionist investment practices.

There is also the belief that free-market forces will encourage countries with restrictive practices to abandon them. To some extent, this has already worked in developing countries, which are beginning to seek foreign investment as a solution to their indebtedness. Their leaders fear the austerity measures of the IMF because the resulting political instability often topples governments. Increasing efforts to privatize national industries have also opened the door to foreign multinationals. In Togo, for example, the government leased a steel mill, which had been losing money, to an American steel entrepreneur, who turned a profit in the first month of operation.

Many believe the free market will also eventually knock down investment barriers in industrialized countries, as well. "If the Japanese acquired a firm with a certain technology, then jacked the price up, someone would blow the whistle, either a competitor or a reporter," said Susan MacKnight, an economist with the Japan Economic Institute. She added that monitoring by the free market is being helped along by U.S. antitrust laws.

The consensus among American policymakers is that any

attempt to force reciprocity from other nations would hurt the economy because it would frighten away foreign investment. "The problem with reciprocity is that you deny yourself the benefits of foreign direct investment [FDI]," argued Harvey E. Bale, Jr., assistant U.S. trade representative for investment policy. Above all, "the government does not want investment blocked. The official U.S. policy on FDI made no reference to reciprocity."

Bale fears the consequences of a strict reciprocity policy in which the United States would prohibit investments from countries practicing protectionist investment policies: "I'm worried about a policy like this. Do we prevent Bridgestone? Nippon Steel? General Motors-Toyota? The French are more restrictive than we are, yet where would American Motors and the autoworkers be without Renault? Where would we draw the line?"

The most compelling argument against reciprocity is the question of how it would be implemented. The screening agency that would enforce the law would become a lightning rod for every protectionist interest as well as management groups seeking another buffer against unfriendly takeovers. The Canadian screening agency, FIRA (Foreign Investment Review Agency), always held up as a bad example by advocates of this argument, routinely rejected at least 15 percent of all foreign investments seeking to locate in Canada. When the Canadian unemployment rate reached 11 percent, the agency was abolished by the new Conservative government of Brian Mulroney. His slogan was "Canada is open for business."

But old habits die hard. The new legislation replacing FIRA, the Investment Canada Act, retains some of its former exclusionary practices. The act provides review procedures for investments involving Canada's cultural heritage or national identity; this means the government can exclude investments involving films, video products, music, recordings, newspapers, magazines, books, and periodicals. Also subject to review are direct acquisitions of Canadian businesses with assets of $5 million or more and indirect acquisitions of Canadian businesses with assets in excess of $50 million.

"One despairs of approaching this with an interventionist approach," concluded Bale. "You'd just substitute one evil for another." Bale is also typical of those who feel that America alone is responsible for her own trade and investment problems and that we cannot blame other countries' barriers. "The automakers screwed up by themselves," he said. "The parts manufacturers were screwed by Detroit, not by Honda. The same with TV. They had no foresight.''

U.S. officials also realize that reciprocity enforcement would be politically infeasible. ''The states wouldn't allow the federal government to get between them and foreign investment,'' said Bale. ''In 1984, the Japanese invested $14 billion here. We invested $8 billion there. Representative Bryant wants to do something about that.''

Actually, the same type of political pressures that prevent federal intervention in investment in the United States remain the only hope for breaking down barriers in other countries. It was pressure from the provinces that led Canada to abolish FIRA. In Japan, local officials are also starting to pressure for relaxed investment policies. ''At the prefecture level, officials are killing themselves to get American investment,'' reported MacKnight. ''At the national level, the official attitude is not accommodating, but in the last couple of years, the bureaucratic attitude has improved. They are catching on fast.''

U.S. officials also operate on the theory that profound cultural differences prevent them from surmounting investment barriers and that as these break down, the barriers will disappear. Japan remains a closed society in which informal networks and clubs reinforce the ''Fortress Japan'' national policy. Investments are screened and analyzed by political leaders in their sixties and seventies, whose memory of prewar Japan dictates their economic policies today. American trade and investment officials are patient, waiting for the new generation to take over.

They are more patient, however, than the American business leaders, who are accused of insensitivity to foreign methods and foreign mores. If they were as skilled as their foreign counterparts, the argument goes, those barriers that are cultural and not formal would not exist. Americans should slow down, have more patience during negotiations, learn the language, spend more time with workers after hours, and take local traditions into account.[7]

In the past, the United States has not taken any major initiatives with regard to inequities in foreign investment practices. The prevailing view is that the benefits outweigh the risks and equity considerations don't matter in the great scheme of things. The free market, working in conjunction with antitrust laws, securities laws, and national-security protections, is far preferable to overregulated, overbureaucratized mechanisms that could work to discourage investment. This theory seems to have worked well so far—especially for other countries.

RESPONSE ON CAPITOL HILL

The executive branch, while well aware of the lack of reciprocity, has traditionally fought efforts to negotiate better terms for Americans abroad. In fact, many officials involved in the trade and investment arena have pressed the White House to take a tougher stance, only to be blocked at the final stages. "The State Department always prevails," explained one Commerce Department official, describing the interagency conflict that has become commonplace. Fearful of international repercussions, a pattern emerged in which political considerations invariably take precedence over even the most blatant economic inequities, with the United States opting time after time in the direction of the most timid response.

But many members of Congress were not as sanguine as the executive branch about the lack of equity in investment relationships. They recognized the relationship between the White House's reluctance to demand that other countries reform their restrictive investment practices and America's declining international investment position. They grew increasingly uncomfortable when they saw the parallels between investment and trade barriers; it was no coincidence that some of the worst offenders in the trade wars were the same countries that excluded investment.

After some effort, Congress finally forced the executive branch to take notice. In the Senate, John Danforth, Republican of Missouri, linked investment to trade issues in Title III of the Trade and Tariff Act of 1984. Initially introduced in 1982 as the "Reciprocal Trade and Investment Act," the bill finally passed in 1984, with Title III renamed the "International Trade and Investment Act." Even though the word "reciprocal" was dropped, the legislation still represented a major breakthrough for U.S. policy toward foreign investment in putting investment on a par—at least in the title—with trade issues. His co-sponsor, Texas Democrat Lloyd Bentsen, shared his views on toughening the U.S. stance.[8] Speaking for himself and the bill's thirty-three co-sponsors, Danforth explained the rationale for the legislation:

The idea is to close the credibility gap created when we consistently refuse to take protective action in spite of the widespread perception that we are the only country practicing what everyone else preaches; namely, free trade. [We] share a conviction that the U.S. must seek . . . the opportunity to compete on an equal footing in world markets.

In developed and developing countries alike, restrictions are being put into place which severely distort access opportunities . . . The administration must move forward . . . to reach bilateral and multilateral agreements destined to reduce, eliminate or prevent restrictions on the flow of investment throughout the world.[9]

In effect, the bill strengthens the president's hand in negotiating trade and investment agreements by suggesting that if the president is not successful through quiet negotiation, then stronger measures should be taken: "Foreign barriers not removed through negotiation or enforcement of the GATT (General Agreement on Trade and Tariffs) could be offset by the U.S. through withdrawal of prior concessions, imposition of duties, and other restrictions available under the present law. . . . Of particular interest is the clarification of the President's authority to impose fees and restrictions on foreign services or suppliers of those services."[10]

A key provision of the bill gives the USTR (U.S. Trade Representative) the authority to block products from entering the U.S. market if foreign performance requirements have been imposed by the host country. In 1986, the USTR used that power to inform the government of Taiwan that if it did not lift performance requirements from the Toyota plant then in progress, Toyotas from that factory would not be allowed to enter the United States.

Most important, the bill puts the machinery in place to identify investment barriers by requiring the USTR to submit annual reports that will "identify and analyze key barriers to U.S. trade in products, services, and investment." These reports must include estimates of the impact of these barriers on the economy and spell out White House efforts to eliminate them. In other words, the bill adds investment barriers as a cause of presidential action. If the same barriers appear in the USTR report year after year and the president has failed to take any action to remove them, then the administration will have some explaining to do before the Congress.

"It is my expectation that the annual reports will be used by this and subsequent administrations to identify the most onerous barriers to U.S. trade and investment," said Danforth.

Despite the clear intent of the Congress, the bill's effectiveness depends largely on how it is implemented. The USTR's office has the option of deciding which countries and which barriers are significant enough to appear in the report, and the 1986 report reveals some startling omissions. One example: In the sections on Japan and South Korea, no barriers to foreign investment are identified. Since such barriers were flagged in the cases of Malaysia, Indonesia, Mexico, and other countries, readers who didn't know better could conclude that no significant barriers exist in Japan and South Korea. Another omission is the absence of any information at all on the OPEC countries, several of whom—namely, Kuwait and Saudi Arabia—do a significant amount of trade and investment business with the United States.[11]

Following the Senate's lead, members of the House of Representatives began to focus more intently on foreign investment. Representative John Bryant, Democrat of Texas, staked his claim early, kept the pressure up, and is now widely acknowledged as the major congressional figure in the field of foreign investment. Two years after the trade bill was passed, in 1986, Bryant submitted the "Foreign Investment Disclosure and Reciprocity Act" to the Energy and Commerce Committee.[12] The real contribution of the legislation was its attempt to reverse through a change in national policy the emerging problems of foreign investment.

The bill would have required foreign investors to register all new investments publicly with the Department of Commerce, to disclose exactly who was behind those investments (specifically, the real owners) and the sources of their financing. Stiff penalties would be imposed on anyone who attempted to hide behind dummy corporations or "official secrecy" excuses. The legislation would also have prohibited any new foreign investment in American land or assets unless Americans were able to invest in the foreign investor's home country on the same terms. "We want Japanese businessmen to go home and complain to their government to let our businesses invest," said Bryant.

Bryant first became interested in foreign investment when he was a state legislator. He noticed enormous purchases of Texas farmland by foreign investors; in one county, this represented almost 10 percent of the available agricultural land. Local farmers began to complain that foreign investors had raised the prices so high they could no longer afford to buy land. "The agricultural business felt that land prices were becoming unreasonably high relative to their profit potential,'' Bryant recalled. The same was true of urban real estate in his home city of Dallas, where problems of absentee ownership and speculation accompanied foreign investment.

What surprised Bryant was the lack of information on the investors; he noticed how easy it was under U.S. law to hide the true identity of the real owners: ''Anyone who wants to remain anonymous can hide behind a dummy foreign corporation. Of the one million acres of foreign-owned agricultural land in Texas—80 percent acquired since 1976—200,000 are registered to Netherland Antilles investors. . . . But it is doubtful that a single islander really owns any Texas land.''

When Bryant got to Congress, he realized that the information gap extended to all areas of foreign investment, not only agricultural land.[13] As many as sixteen different government agencies collect data on foreign investment, including the Departments of Commerce, Treasury, and Agriculture, as well as the SEC, the Internal Revenue Service, and the Comptroller of the Currency. The information is so fragmented, however, that its use is limited, so ''hidden in bureaucratic quagmires as to be of little practical use.'' Some of these agencies, such as the Bureau of Economic Analysis in the Department of Commerce, deal with privileged information: This means that to protect the company secrets of the investor, it is kept confidential even from Congress.

At the Bryant hearings, which took place on May 8, 1986, officials from government agencies argued that current informational efforts were perfectly adequate to the needs of the government and that they saw no reason to systematize their data-gathering efforts.[14] A typical response came from Stephen J. Canner, from the Office of International Investment of the Treasury Department, who expressed the view of the Reagan administration that data gathering represented useless paperwork that could lead to unnecessary regulation. Canner offered the following arguments against legislatively imposed disclosure requirements: The bill would ''make it more burdensome and expensive for foreign persons to invest in the U.S. . . . and would discard confidentiality for many investors. . . . The net effect would be to discourage investment and divert investment to other markets where there is respect for and protection of the privacy of investors.''[15]

Canner's superior at the Treasury Department, Robert Cornell, deputy assistant secretary for trade and investment policy, strongly opposed the reciprocity provision of the bill on the grounds that it would discourage foreign investment and encourage retribution from other countries. He also pointed out that bilateral and multilateral treaties and agreements obligated the United States to accord national treatment—the same legal treatment offered its own citizens—to foreign investors:

"Threatening to close the U.S. market to investors whose home countries restrict U.S. investment may not cause those countries to relax their restrictions. Indeed, these governments might be pleased to have us prevent their investors from investing in the U.S. because they want to keep that investment at home."[16]

Most of the testimony from government officials opposing the bill echoed the view that any attempt to ensure reciprocity would inevitably lead to an enormous, unwieldy, and political bureaucracy. Bryant countered that full disclosure would streamline existing agency responsibilities and that no added bureaucracy would be necessary if the method of simple certification were used to guarantee reciprocity. Foreign investors would certify that the same treatment is accorded American investors in their country that they are receiving in the United States. This would solve the problem, and no prescreening bureaucracy would be involved. Civil fines would be imposed if investors refused to disclose their U.S. holdings.

THE BRYANT AMENDMENT

The Bryant bill was resubmitted with thirty-one co-sponsors on January 7, 1987, as H.R. 312, retitled the "Foreign Ownership Disclosure Act."[17] For political reasons the word "reciprocity" was dropped. It was Bryant's hope that if full disclosure was required and implemented seriously, the public would eventually pressure Congress to demand full reciprocity from the nation's trading and investing partners.

Two months later, Bryant succeeded in attaching a modified version of his proposal to the omnibus trade legislation then under consideration in the Energy and Commerce Committee. It was adopted over the strenuous objections of all the Republicans on the committee, by the narrow margin of 21–20. The White House and the securities industry lobbied vigorously against the amendment. The amendment would require only the most basic information from a foreign investor: identity, nationality, size of the investment, and the purchase price. It would affect only major investors: those with a "significant interest" of over 5 percent in a U.S. business or real estate property with assets over $5 million or annual sales over $10 million and those with a controlling interest of over 25 percent in a U.S. business enterprise with assets or annual sales over $20 million.[18]

By the time a modified version of the amendment reached the floor, the opposition of the White House and the committee Republicans intensified. Norman Lent, the ranking Republican member of the committee, offered an amendment to the Bryant proposal that would have created a loophole large enough to destroy its purpose: It would give the secretary of commerce the authority to exempt entire classes of investors or investments if "necessary to prevent a substantial impairment of foreign investment in the United States." Lent argued:

The Bryant provision is a highly controversial, burdensome, confusing, and inflexible provision that Paul Volcker and others have said could cause a severe outflow of capital and produce a severe, negative impact on our economy and on the present and future jobs of millions of U.S. workers. . . . The Bryant amendment threatens almost $350 billion in foreign investment and millions of jobs. . . . It could hurt foreign-held U.S. companies . . . by forcing them to disclose confidential data to their employees or competitors, when U.S.-owned companies are protected.[19]

Lent's allies dwelled on the jobs issue. Representative Michael G. Oxley, Republican of Ohio, called the amendment a "dangerous precedent" and warned:

"Many of us who represent states such as Ohio have been benefited by foreign investment creating jobs and creating wealth in our particular state. I would hate to see us reach a situation where the foreign investment would seek other places because of the strict requirements under the Bryant amendment."

Bryant characterized the Lent amendment as an attempt to "gut" the disclosure provision and encourage foreign investors to "use their economic clout to extort an exemption by threatening to withhold future investments." He was supported by colleagues who expressed a diverse range of concerns, along with a sense of incredulity that simple disclosure would discourage foreign investors.

One of the most compelling arguments addressed the national security issue. Representative James Florio, Democrat of New Jersey, recalled the administration's concerns over the impending acquisition of Fairchild, a manufacturer of semiconductor equipment, by Fujitsu. Section 703 (the Bryant provision) "could not be used to stop a takeover," said Florio, but "would ensure that our government would know . . . whether a foreign person has a significant or controlling interest in a defense contractor with whom it is dealing."[20]

Representative Marcy Kaptur, Democrat of Ohio, also highlighted the "threat to the nation's defense industrial base":

> At this moment, 25 percent of this country's machine-tool industry is owned by foreign investors, none of which have to register. The bill, as drafted, merely requires basic disclosure to help America know what is happening to it when we are experiencing huge unprecedented flows of foreign investment into our country. The bill does not place any limits on foreign investment; it just allows us to track it. Americans ought to know who is buying and who has the potential to control our business, our industry and our defense industrial base.[21]

The Lent amendment lost by a vote of 230 to 190, and the Bryant amendment survived to make its journey to the Senate, where it went down to a resounding defeat. The Senate defeat climaxed an intensified lobbying effort in the interim that drew upon the combined resources of the White House, foreign ambassadors and foreign multinationals, U.S. corporations, state offices, and such luminaries as Paul Volcker who lent their weight to the issue.

Senators and their trade assistants were deluged with phone calls and visits from foreign and U.S. government lobbyists. One staff aide claimed he spent between six and seven hours a day dealing with lobbyists just on this issue. George Slover, legislative counsel to Representative Bryant, reported that following the defeat of the Lent amendment he received over 100 requests for information from Washington law firms representing foreign lobbyists. "It was more intense than anything I've ever seen," he said. "I have never gotten this many requests for any bill."

The Reagan administration opposed the bill on the grounds that it would undermine its efforts to persuade other countries to relax their investment restrictions at multilateral trade talks. In the Senate debate, John Danforth argued that the amendment was "veto bait" for those who wanted to kill the trade bill; in other words, it would add to President Reagan's arsenal of threats to veto the trade bill. He quoted Paul Volcker in opposing the bill: "Legitimate actual and potential investors would be deterred by the risk of revealing proprietary information and would take their money elsewhere."[22]

Volcker objected to the requirement in the Bryant amendment calling for privately held foreign companies to reveal their balance sheet, income statements, and a statement of sales, assets, operating income, and depreciation. Many felt this provision gave privately held U.S. companies—which do not have to reveal this information—an edge over their foreign competitors and thus discriminated against them. Publicly held U.S. and foreign companies would not be affected by the Bryant amendment, since they file public statements with the SEC.

On the surface, this provision appeared discriminatory, but the labor unions disagreed. "Many of these [privately held] new foreign owners of American industrial companies are publicly traded in their home countries," argued Howard D. Samuel and David Mallino, president and director of legislation, respectively, for the Industrial Union Department of the AFL-CIO, "but American workers and communities are often unable to find out even basic information about these firms' activities in the United States."[23]

The labor unions found themselves among the amendment's few allies in the Senate, primarily because of their unfortunate experiences with some foreign investors. If a community is being pressed by a corporation for subsidies and tax breaks or a union finds itself weighing a request for wage and benefit concessions, there is no way to negotiate intelligently without information. How can a union or a community know, without information, whether a corporation is bluffing when it claims it is in poor financial health? If the corporation is publicly held, there is no problem; the community or the union can go directly to the SEC. In the case of privately held U.S. corporations, pressure can be exerted through the media, community leaders, or the board of directors. Problems arise, however, with privately held foreign corporations, whose owners and balance sheets are more remote from their American hosts and American employees. Therefore, the unions argued, differential treatment is justified.

While everyone expected lobbyists from the foreign multinationals to oppose the bill, it came as a surprise to find key sectors of the American business community, such as the Business Roundtable, the U.S. Chamber of Commerce, and the National Association of Manufacturers, lobbying against the amendment.

The reason: U.S. manufacturers feared retaliation from foreign countries, or what they called "mirror-image treatment." This meant that foreign countries could make their disclosure requirements even more onerous for U.S. companies in retaliation for the passage of the Bryant amendment. Other countries already have more stringent disclosure requirements than the United States, but there is always room for tightening and other forms of petty harassment.

The amendment's sponsor, Tom Harkin, Democrat of Iowa, pointed out the spurious connection between disclosure requirements and the withdrawal of foreign investment:

> There are those who say that this bill will discourage foreign investments. I take issue with that. Business people bring their money here because it is a good place to invest and because they make money on it in this country.
>
> Who is concerned with anonymity? Drug traffickers, the PLO, other foreign investors who do not want us to know how much they are acquiring of certain sensitive businesses in this country? . . . I cannot imagine why a Honda or Toyota or other legitimate businesses would be afraid of disclosing this kind of information, which . . . is no more or less than we require of U.S. publicly owned companies.
>
> The short-term advantages of foreign investment should not prevent us from considering the potential long-term effects on our economy and our national security. Over time, as ownership of our assets is transferred overseas, so is the authority to make important business and economic decisions affecting the prosperity and independence of our nation.[24]

The threat by foreign multinationals and their governments to withdraw their investments or withhold future investments was reminiscent of their successful tactics in the unitary tax issue, when they convinced California legislators to repeal the tax for fear of discouraging foreign investment. Similarly, in the case of the Bryant amendment, there were no data indicating that foreign investment would cease and desist because of disclosure requirements. The reason was simple: No data existed that would bear out that threat. California legislators, like U.S. senators, wanted to believe that argument and forget the real reason foreign investors are attracted to the United States: to make money in the world's richest market. "What proof does Paul Volcker have that if we simply have disclosure that somehow Honda will leave America, or Toyota, or anybody else for that matter?'' Harkin asked. "Indeed," he continued, "if disclosure alone were so onerous, why would U.S. investors continue to invest in Japan despite disclosure, preclearance requirements of joint ventures, and everything else?"[25]

One of Harkin's allies—and there were very few—was Dale Bumpers, a Democrat from Arkansas. Bumpers addressed the real issue behind disclosure: America's dependence on foreign capital. Blaming the Reagan administration for what he called its "riverboat gamble with the economy which has led to the greatest increase in government indebtedness in peacetime in our history," Bumpers predicted that the nation's dependence on foreign money would soon become just as alarming as its former dependence on OPEC. "I foresee a time when . . . our foreign creditors and foreign owners will demand concessions from us just as OPEC has done on several occasions. These concessions will undermine our independence. . . . We are a dependent nation that is beginning to lose control of its fate. We need foreign capital and foreign investments, and we have only begun to learn what this means for our standard of living."[26]

After the debate ended, the Senators voted to table the Bryant amendment by a vote of 83–11. The lopsided vote was not a true indicator of the sentiments of the senators, according to Susan C. Schwab, Senator Danforth's legislative director and the top trade expert on Capitol Hill. The amendment got caught in what she called the "atmospherics" of the trade bill, the vagaries of Senate scheduling, and the concerns of the White House. More than a dozen controversial amendments met a similar fate. Several senators expressed added concerns: No hearings had been held, and they felt they wanted more time to study the issue and determine committee jurisdiction.

The most telling observation about the Bryant amendment was the intensity of the opposition. The list of lobbyists in the coalition against the amendment read like a *Who's Who* of foreign and American multinationals, business trade associations, and blue-chip Washington law firms. They joined forces with the White House and their lobbyists in the federal agencies.

"It was the array of lobbyists that amazed me," said Bryant. "Just for disclosure. It was very thorough lobbying, and even more amazing, it was kept out of the papers.

"What concerns me is whether we're going to legislate in time. If we act now, we can act prudently and plan for the future. If we act later, reactively, it will be too late; the legislation could be clumsy and ineffective. The question is whether we have reached the point I fear the most: that because we are so dependent on foreign ownership, we cannot act in our own interest for fear of offending foreign interests. Are we already at the point that our own Congress can't act?''

EFFECTS OF CONGRESSIONAL ACTION

It was apparent that the barriers American companies faced in Mexico, Taiwan, and other countries did not match the welcome they received from the United States. Those barriers never bothered U.S. policymakers until a record trade deficit—$170 billion by the end of 1986—forced the White House to accelerate its efforts to negotiate the removal of restrictive investment barriers.

Some still argued that the effect of investment barriers on the trade deficit was negligible, but sufficient data were beginning to appear to cause alarm among thoughtful policymakers. One example: Although the United States still ranked first among the world's investors, the rate of growth had dropped considerably. Reagan administration officials blamed investment barriers in Mexico for the fact that U.S. investment in 1984 was only one-tenth of what it had been in 1979. Other indicators followed this low growth pattern: while overseas investment increased by 14.4 percent in the late 1970s, it grew by only 4.5 percent in the 1980s; similarly, the return on overseas investment had declined by 8 percent.[27]

Reagan officials believed that liberalization of foreign constraints to investment would benefit all parties. U.S. exports would increase the same way the Japanese expanded their markets by investing abroad. And U.S. companies would become more competitive internationally as they located closer to cheap labor, markets, and raw materials.

For these reasons, along with Congress's mandate in the 1984 trade bill, the White House elevated foreign investment to a higher priority on its trade agenda, admitting that foreign barriers were having an effect on the loss of U.S. preeminence in the world economy.[28] As a concrete move toward addressing the issue, they tried to include trade-related investment issues on the agenda of the Uruguay round of the GATT talks in 1986. U.S. Trade Representative Clayton Yeutter put the issue in a broader context and argued that all nations would benefit from more liberalized investment rules. ''Nations need foreign investment,'' he said, "for economic growth, to expand foreign trade and for better lives for future generations."[29]

With trade uppermost in negotiators' minds, investment issues receded into the background, and no real gains emerged from the multilateral negotiations, although the United States is negotiating three bilateral investment treaties with Haiti, Egypt, and Turkey. At the same time, the existence of investment inequities on the world-trade agenda served notice that the United States had finally caught on to the unfair investment practices of its trading partners and was on the brink of doing something about them.

OPPOSITION TO RECIPROCITY

What is significant about the country's new investment posture is that it focuses on developing countries and not on the major trading partners where the barriers seem most unfair. One of the reasons is that the developing countries have less political clout and cannot defend themselves as well as the richer nations. There is also a significant body of opinion that argues against reciprocity on the grounds that these barriers do not exist abroad; that they are merely a convenient excuse invoked by American companies too lazy to take the measures necessary to compete in the international marketplace.

Take the case of Japan, for example, whose defenders make some interesting points. Kenichi Ohmae, author and vice-president of McKinsey & Co.'s Japan branch, notes that there are 2,900 large U.S. corporations already operating in Japan, including IBM, Texas Instruments, National Cash Register, and Coca-Cola, which has 70 percent of the country's soft-drink market.[30] A new book by Robert Christopher, *Second to None,* makes the same point about the country's hospitality to foreign investors.[31] So does Robert L. Sharp, president of the American Chamber of Commerce in Japan, who says American investment is growing fast, with $3 billion invested. With the average return on investment at 18 percent, American firms are more profitable than their Japanese counterparts in the United States.

Sharp says things do move smoothly and that the Japanese government is cooperative. "MITI [Ministry of International Trade and Industry] Director General Fukukawa said to me that MITI is not only ready to receive complaints, but . . . if the problem cannot be solved, MITI will explain why not." He admits that there "still remain undue burdens of red tape and regulation to new investment" and that the "uncertain status of foreign accountants and lawyers created difficulties for investors."[32]

Although many agree Japan has removed some of its investment barriers in the last five years, serious problems still continue to plague American companies seeking to invest. One recent example involved the attempt of Cargill, Inc., an agribusiness from Minnetonka, Minnesota, to build a livestock feed plant in the town of Shibushi in southern Japan. Cargill found itself in the middle of a classic runaround: the company couldn't buy land without a permit from local officials; local officials said they couldn't sell the land without a license from the Japanese government. The situation would have remained permanently mired in bureaucratic doublespeak were it not for the intervention of Senator Danforth, followed by heavy pressure from the U.S. Trade Representative. The plant finally went forward in 1986. Other companies with less political clout might not have fared as well.

The real difficulty with reciprocity as a political tactic is that as a theory it has problems. It has problems because it has been associated for a long time with trade theory, where it becomes mired in bilateral and multilateral agreements and treaties. Strict tit-for-tat reciprocity means, to its critics, that the United States would be forced to take actions against countries with whom it is bound in treaty relationships and that to do so would violate laws and destroy our credibility in the international community. It would also force the nation to take protectionist-type actions, using tariffs and punitive measures to back up its reciprocity policies.

Others oppose trade reciprocity for fear that foreign nations would retaliate. "The danger of aggressive reciprocity is that foreign nations would respond in kind," wrote William R. Cline, an economist with the Institute for International Economics.[33] This could conceivably occur in an investment action, as well; foreign countries could react quickly by imposing tariffs, increasing their content requirements, or taking other retaliatory measures.

With reciprocity identified so closely with trade policy in the scholarly and popular literature, reactions against it are almost automatic. Most people think it means demanding that Japan buy an amount of U.S. goods equal to the goods the United States buys from Japan in order to reduce the growing trade deficit between the two countries. Columnist Hobart Rowen attacked this concept as unworkable, primarily because "the burden of solving the trade problem would rest entirely on Japan . . . [and] makes no allowance for the fact that the American deficit is also a global problem," created in part by the huge domestic budget deficit.[34]

SOLUTIONS

With only trade theory as a model, it is no wonder that congressional efforts to force investment reciprocity have hit such formidable roadblocks. Advocating reciprocity, economist Ron Danielian said, is "as dangerous as talking about school busing in the United States." The view of reciprocity should be broader, he added. "The policy is one that should be used to maintain an open market, with free competition. It should not be equated with 'tit-for-tat' type restrictions. [It] means balanced opportunities to trade."[35]

The difference between investment and trade is that investment isn't bogged down in multilateral treaties and agreements; in fact, 1986 is the first year it was mentioned formally at the GATT talks. In one sense, America could force the reciprocity issue in investment, primarily because the United States retains the high ground with its open investment policy. In fact, the U.S. remains the perfect host, often in the position of offering foreign investors more benefits than it offers its own investors. "Incredible as it seems," Representative Bryant pointed out, "it is now possible for foreign investors to borrow 100 percent of the cost of acquiring U.S. securities and corporations, while American investors may not borrow more than 50 percent of those costs." This loophole has facilitated hostile attempts by foreign investors to take over U.S. companies and harmful securities speculation. Many analysts expect to see far more hostile take-over attempts from foreign investors in the future—such as Sir James Goldsmith's unsuccessful attempt to acquire Goodyear, which left the company $93 million in the red, the price for buying him off—as the United States grapples with the problem of what to do about them.

Another example of the U.S. welcome mat is the establishment of foreign trade zones, which allow foreign investors and exporters to avoid protective tariffs. Needless to say, the guests generally don't extend the same hospitality: "Japan no longer has any free-trade zones or free ports," stated a report from the U.S. embassy in Japan.[36]

Retaliation, the great fear of trade reciprocity, would not be as easy with investment issues because so many barriers exist already that countries would be unlikely to threaten to impose any more. The real threat is that countries will curtail their investments in the United States, a tactic the Japanese use to great advantage. Every time a news story appears that is critical of foreign investment or legislative efforts begin to churn, Japanese companies get nervous. Their American executives get to work assessing their welcome, calling the Commerce Department, and lobbying political officials at all levels to quiet the controversy. They make it clear that any restrictive legislation will cause them to rethink their American commitment.

Quiet negotiation, the preferred tactic of White House officials, has worked to liberalize investment barriers, but it has worked too slowly to be useful as a long-term strategy. While U.S. policymakers massaged their foreign counterparts, foreign industries investing in the United States gained a considerable edge over their U.S. counterparts. This was particularly true in the banking industry, which was held back from establishing branches abroad while foreign banks cornered large shares of the U.S. market.

The United States has practiced quiet negotiation; it is now time for tougher measures. And they work, as even the most ardent devotees of foreign investment admit. "The Japanese consensus—the excuse they give for not coming quickly to decisions—is all crap," observed a Washington lawyer familiar with investment issues. "They check the airlines and know when you're leaving. Then they get down to the serious stuff." He added that contrary to the theory of foreign investors pulling out, investment actually gave the United States some leverage. "The Iranians didn't sit up and take notice in the hostage crisis until we seized their assets."

One example of how reciprocity works can be found in the experience of the Foreign Missions Bill, which provides for strict reciprocity in the treatment of U.S. missions abroad. The bill was inspired by an incident in the People's Republic of China, in which the Chinese refused to allow the United States to buy property for the embassy or to lease it. In return, the United States imposed the same restrictions on the Chinese, who capitulated very quickly. They allowed the United States to lease the embassy for 100 years, and the United States allowed the People's Republic of China to lease their embassy for 100 years. The legislation says that "the assistance to be provided to a foreign mission in the United States shall be determined after due consideration of the benefits, privileges and immunities provided to missions of the United States in the country or territory represented by that foreign mission.'' Other countries changed their policies within a matter of days.[37]

Lengthy negotiations may be useful for complex trade issues, for arms control, and for a variety of other policy matters. In fact, countries prefer lengthy negotiations when it works to their economic advantage. But for foreign investment, the issues are clear, the inequities transparent, and the solutions obvious. U.S. trading partners must understand that if they can invest freely in the United States, the United States must enjoy similar privileges in their countries. Plainly put, investment barriers are no longer acceptable, and only when they are removed will we practice a more realistic version of the free market in which everyone, not only the United States, participates. But U.S. representatives must speak a language that other countries can understand; it must speak the language of effectiveness, back up its rhetoric with action, and remove itself once and for all from its habit of capitulation, which only leads to a loss of respect in the community of nations.

CHAPTER 17

Coals to Newcastle

*Reciprocity in Reverse,
or How Kuwait Came to Pump Oil
on U.S. Land*

Because we are committed to free trade that works in both directions, we cannot condone practices that shut out Americans.
—*James Watt, former secretary of the interior*

If Kuwait Petroleum acquired a good portion of U.S. oil assets, then we'd get concerned.
—*Harvey E. Bale, Jr.,
Office of U.S. Trade Representative*

One of the greatest paradoxes of America's open-door policy on foreign investment occurred in 1985 when the Kuwaiti government won the right to drill for oil on U.S.-owned land. Kuwait, a country awash in oil, prohibits foreign nationals from conducting similar enterprises on its own soil.

It was a classic case of the United States turning the other cheek. It all began when the Kuwait Petroleum Company bought Santa Fe International, an American multinational corporation specializing in oil exploration, among other ventures. The Kuwaiti company, which paid $2.5 billion for its acquisition, is a state-owned enterprise, a wholly owned subsidiary of the government of Kuwait.

After the purchase, the Department of the Interior undertook a review to determine whether the newly constituted Kuwaiti multinational could apply for leases to drill for oil on federal land. At issue was whether such a lease would violate the Mineral Lands Leasing Act of 1920, which requires foreign governments whose citizens or companies seek U.S. mineral rights to grant reciprocity to American companies seeking mineral rights abroad. In other words, if Kuwaiti nationals can drill for oil on American soil, then Americans should be able to engage in oil exploration in Kuwait. Thus, the participation of foreign nationals is tied to the willingness of their countries to grant similar privileges to Americans. The key clause states: "Citizens of another country, the laws, customs or regulations of which deny similar or like privileges to citizens or corporations of this country, shall not by stock ownership, stock holding, or stock control, own any interest in any lease acquired under the provisions of this Act."[1]

Initially, the Department of the Interior authorized the lease. Acting on the advice of a staff review conducted by the Bureau of Land Management and with the concurrence of the solicitor, the assistant secretary for land and water resources issued a statement on December 29, 1982, declaring Kuwait reciprocal. This meant that Interior would have to proceed on Santa Fe's applications for mineral leases.

The agency decided that Kuwait's laws, customs, and regulations did not in fact "discriminate against investment by U.S. citizens"; that American citizenship alone did not result in discrimination. Indeed, Kuwaiti citizens, just like American citizens, are not allowed to invest in the Kuwait Petroleum Company. As precedent, the department drew on the decision of Great Britain in 1974 to nationalize its coal industry. Citizenship was irrelevant in that case because no private persons or corporations could invest in Britain's coal resources.

A week later on "Meet the Press," Secretary of the Interior James Watt defended the decision to allow Kuwaiti investors to lease federal lands for energy and mineral development. It was the position of the Reagan administration, said Watt, that granting such leases would benefit the United States by creating jobs and developing additional oil and other energy resources for American consumers. Although the final decision was yet to be announced, observers concluded that the administration had decided in principle that Kuwait should be given access to federal lands and that no distinction would be made between individual Kuwaiti investors and government-owned corporations.[2]

The decision evoked a storm of protest. In letters to members of Congress, the president, and the Department of Interior, Jewish organizations, led by the American Jewish Committee, protested Watt's decision. On Capitol Hill, Senator Bill Bradley, Democrat from New Jersey, queried Watt in disbelief:

How could a corporation that was 100 percent owned by a foreign government that excluded any U.S. participation qualify under the law? . . . In other words, there is no opportunity, absolutely no opportunity, for an American citizen to invest in mineral development within Kuwait.

In view of these facts, could you tell me how you could possibly find Kuwait as a reciprocal nation under the Mineral Act of 1920?[3]

Two months later, Watt reversed himself and declared Kuwait nonreciprocal on the grounds that the Persian Gulf state was discriminating against U.S. citizens and U.S. corporations:

Because we are committed to free trade that works in both directions, we cannot condone practices that shut out Americans while allowing access to citizens and corporations of other nations. No U.S. citizen or corporation currently holds or may under current [Kuwait] policy acquire a beneficial interest in the petroleum resources of Kuwait, although corporations of another country are currently allowed to and do hold such an interest. This discrimination against U.S. interests constitutes a denial of similar or like privileges under Section 1.[4]

Watt's ruling, that Kuwait was guilty of *de facto* discrimination, prevented Santa Fe from acquiring future leases and halted pending applications. He explained that during the 1970s Kuwait had nationalized most petroleum development, buying and forcing the buyout of American companies' concessions. By the end of 1977, no U.S. company held a petroleum concession in Kuwait. However, Japanese, British, Dutch, and Spanish companies were not nationalized, and the Japanese-owned company continued to operate in Kuwait under its concession.

Another flood of protest greeted Watt's change of heart; this time over a thousand letters and postcards came from members of the National Association of Arab Americans and their supporters. "I can only surmise that the administration gave in to the pressures of the American Jewish Committee," wrote G. J. Deasy of Dallas. "Secretary Watt's arbitrary decision . . . is totally unfair and specific discrimination against an Arab state," said another letter from Raymond Jallow, Ph.D. from Los Angeles. "Kuwait, for its size, has done more for the West and the

U.S. than any other country in the world in providing an oil supply and investment funds over the years.''

On another level, Kuwait Petroleum mobilized a campaign involving an impressive array of powerful supporters. In Kuwait, officials began to visit the American ambassador, whose cables alerted the State Department. The company retained former transportation secretary William Coleman to lead the legal challenge and attracted blue-ribbon expert witnesses such as former treasury official Marc Leland. The newly constituted Santa Fe corporation included former president Gerald Ford, Brent Scowcroft, a top aide to Henry Kissinger, and Roderick Hills, an influential Republican attorney, whose wife, Carla Hills, was HUD secretary during the Ford administration.

Except for the American Jewish Committee and its allies, support for Watt's position was minimal. According to Mark Guidry of the Interior Department's public affairs office, community pressure on the issue of reciprocity was nonexistent:

> The first time we asked for comments, in 1982, there were lots of expressions of public concern, but none of any substance. They ran along the lines of "I don't like foreigners, the good old USA, etc." There was a letter-writing campaign encouraged by a competing company in North Carolina, but they were all the same and didn't address the reciprocity issue.

Congress reflected the public's disinterest. In 1980, a House subcommittee chaired by Representative Ben Rosenthal, Democrat from New York, investigated the pending Santa Fe acquisition for its national-security implications. (One of Santa Fe's subsidiaries, C. F. Braun & Co., was involved in extensive government contracts in facilities utilized for nuclear weapons materials.) Rosenthal died shortly afterward, and with his death, congressional interest in the issue waned.

THE LEGAL CHALLENGE

The official Kuwaiti protest followed swiftly on the heels of Watt's decision. The Kuwaitis contended that the department's decision was based on shaky legal ground and could destroy their investment if allowed to stand. Santa Fe owned 275 oil and gas leases worth approximately $14 million on 252,950 acres of government land; pending leases covered an additional 219,000 acres.

Santa Fe brought the case to court and in a move designed to boost their chances of success, the company's lawyers filed suit in the Delaware federal circuit—known in legal circles as the businessman's court for its tendency to rule in favor of corporate interests. Well aware of the Delaware court's reputation, Interior Department attorneys sought a change of venue, which was denied.

The company claimed that in the areas in which they had legal authority to nationalize, all nations were treated alike. Watt's ruling had pointed to a discrepancy that he said had given the Japanese favored treatment, but the Kuwaitis contended that the Japanese concession was located in an area under dispute between Kuwait and Saudi Arabia and was therefore not under its jurisdiction. Santa Fe also charged Watt and the agency with arbitrary and capricious behavior based on political pressures and *ex parte* communications between Watt and the leaders of Jewish groups. As evidence, their lawyers pointed to a luncheon held three days before Watt's decision between Watt and representatives of the American Jewish Committee.

The court agreed. Judge Murray M. Schwartz held that Secretary Watt departed from "clear legislative purpose underlying the alien provision" of the act and "deviated without adequate explanation from longstanding agency procedures."[5] Judge Schwartz's decision rested on the department's sixty-year history of implementing the act, and on the status of the Japanese concession.

Watt abused his discretionary power, said the court, by deviating from the enabling statute and from standard agency practice. First the statute:

Secretary Watt did not (and under DOI precedent could not) disqualify Kuwait simply because Kuwait had nationalized its oil and gas industry. . . . Rather Secretary Watt relied on a coincidental difference in treatment between U.S. and Japanese citizens.

Secretary Watt did not . . . conduct an inquiry into whether Kuwait allowed the Japanese interest to remain in private hands for legitimate, objective reasons unrelated to Japanese or American citizenship. His analysis was therefore erroneous. The MLLA [Mineral Lands Leasing Act] . . . allows disqualification of a foreign nation only if that country discriminates against U.S. citizens BECAUSE OF their citizenship. A mere difference in treatment will not suffice.

A legislative history of the act supports the court's view. The "alien qualification" provision of the act was intended to prevent discrimination and retaliation against American citizens doing business abroad. It was not intended to "erect artificial barriers" against alien participation in foreign mineral leases. In fact, restrictions similar to Kuwait's were found in Canadian law, yet Canadian investors were not prevented from pumping oil on American land.[6]

The agency had taken a relaxed view of the law since it was enacted, allowing foreign investors wide latitude in their U.S. activities. The alien provision was implemented from 1920 to 1982 without written guidelines; decisions were reached without conflict after consultation with State and the Interior Department's solicitor's office. Interior had no policy regulating the initiation of reciprocity reviews and no fixed method for looking into the laws, customs, and rules of foreign countries.

Finally, new procedures were initiated on May 7, 1982, that, if anything, further relaxed the department's approach to reciprocity by eliminating the potential for discretion. It was under this new set of guidelines that Interior initiated its review of Kuwait, along with similar reviews of Sweden and Cyprus.[7]

Secretary Watt had originally reversed his decision on the basis of the new reciprocity test, concluding that the "actual custom" of Kuwait was to discriminate "against U.S. citizens and corporations." After the court reversed Watt, the case was remanded back to Interior for a new ruling based on the court's decision. At this time, when the department asked for public comment on the issue of Kuwait's intent to discriminate against U.S. citizens based on nationality, it received only two responses, both upholding the Kuwaiti position: one from Santa Fe and one from the American Petroleum Institute, which includes Santa Fe as a member! The political opposition was nonexistent.

By the time the case came up for a final ruling, Secretary Watt had resigned under pressure for injudicious public statements unrelated to the Kuwaiti case. His successor, William Clark, overturned the decision on February 7, 1985, with a statement reflecting the court's reasoning:

The record reflects that Kuwait did in fact have legitimate . . . business reasons for allowing the Japanese company retention of its interest, while nationalizing those concessions with interests owned by U.S. corporations. There is no evidence of a nationalization policy directed at U.S.

citizens and corporations because they were American. . . .
Therefore, citizens and corporations of Kuwait may . . .
own interests in federal mineral leases issued under that
Act.[8]

THE POLITICAL CHALLENGE

The Kuwait incident showed that the discretion of cabinet secretaries is limited: They must govern within the boundaries of
existing statutes and, when those laws prove inadequate, lobby
the Congress for change. In the case of the Mineral Act, it was
not really the language of the law but the way the law had been
interpreted that made the case against Watt so strong. Watt's
decision correctly pointed out that foreign interests were eliminated from Kuwait not by written law but from the "discretionary actions of Kuwaiti officials." Just as correctly, the court
soundly rejected Watt's decision as "arbitrary and capricious,"
while it declared the Kuwaitis' discretionary actions equitable. If
the U.S. law had been enforced from the beginning with a
stricter interpretation, perhaps Watt's action would have been
judged fair—not "arbitrary and capricious."

It was a convoluted view of reciprocity that turned out to be
the standard interpretation: that as long as a country treats everyone the same, it is considered "reciprocal"; or, as long as the
Kuwaiti government discriminated against everyone equally, this
meant that its policies were nondiscriminatory. And if the rule of
law in Kuwait was expressed through administrative fiat, then
the rest of the world would just have to accept that as standard
practice.

In effect, this puts the United States in the curious position of
being bound by the rule of law, while Kuwait and selected other
countries were allowed to operate by administrative fiat. Unlike
the United States, Kuwait was not tied to a sixty-six-year legislative and administrative history governing its minerals: Quite the
contrary. Its leaders reversed their history by decisively eliminating the last vestiges of colonial rule—foreign ownership of natural resources. Oil resources are not the only industry under lock
and key in Kuwait. Foreigners may only participate in commercial activities through joint stock companies and partnerships,
provided that 51 percent of the capital holdings are owned by
Kuwaiti citizens. No one who does business with Israel is permitted to invest at all. In some circumstances, foreign companies

may participate more directly in commercial activities, but they would most likely be required to employ a foreign agent.

Nationalization—or the elimination of foreign investors—is viewed with a greater degree of indulgence when practiced by less developed countries and when accompanied by adequate compensation. Many believe that these countries are entitled to redress past colonial exploitation and turn a profit on their own for a change. Former colonies appreciate the importance of controlling their own resources; they know that money is not neutral and that imperialism first appeared under the guise of investment.

It is interesting that while the United States has no problem with developing countries that nationalize, its leaders are greatly concerned about industrialized countries engaging in "hegemonic schemes of oil importers, such as Great Britain, to entice oil-exporting nations to discriminate against U.S. interests in favor of their own interests," according to the court.[9] It might make sense to tolerate nationalization and cartelization schemes from countries throwing off the shackles of imperialism as long as this tolerance keeps up with changing times. What happens when the former colony becomes a capital exporter and can no longer claim the status of a poor, deprived third-world nation? As always, attitudes change more slowly than events.

Even more ironic is the status accorded all countries that nationalize under current interpretations of the law. Kuwait is not alone: Other countries—excluding the OPEC nations—whose oil interests are either partly or wholly owned by the state or have been accorded special protective status by the state include Mexico, Venezuela, Brazil, Israel, Austria, Japan, Malaysia, the Netherlands, Norway, the Philippines, Spain, and Sweden. The United States appears almost alone in the world community in retaining a free-enterprise system toward its mineral resources.

The official position of the executive branch is that U.S. leaders will become concerned only if the motive for the investment is political, the issue of government versus individual investors. "You have to go back to motivation," explained Harvey E. Bale, Jr., assistant U.S. trade representative for international investment policy:

Why are those people here? If a Saudi prince or a French banker comes in and invests, we're not concerned. We interpret that as a sound investment. If the investment is government connected, the U.S. government wants to be notified. We don't believe governments make investments the same way people make investments. Governments have political objectives. Kuwait Petroleum was reviewed. If KP acquired a good portion of U.S. oil assets, then we'd get concerned.

Not surprisingly, in the period following the pro-Kuwaiti court ruling, U.S. mineral resources look even more attractive to foreign investors. Almost 44 percent of U.S. gold-mining capacity, for example, is owned by foreign companies, with Canadian and South African firms playing a major role.[10] "We've been getting lots of calls from Santa Fe branches asking for maps," said Mark Guidry. "They are stepping up their operations. Kuwait wants to go into the oil business in this country to reduce their operating costs."

At the same time, European and Japanese companies are rapidly increasing their interests in the U.S. oil and gas industry—no doubt encouraged by Santa Fe's legal and political success. The Europeans have added to their holdings by investing in U.S. reserves, while the Japanese firms have formed joint ventures with American oil companies. No one has questioned whether these countries grant Americans the same privileges.

PART VI

FUTURE STRATEGIES

CHAPTER 18

Nine Myths That
Govern Policy

(And What We Can Do About Them)

> When the history of this period is written, historians are going to
> marvel at a great economic power surrendering its economic
> might with so little resistance.
> —*Professor Carol Greenwald, Harvard Business School[1]*

> Japan's investment . . . is a challenge to us. If we can't meet it,
> we deserve to work for the Japanese.
> —*Edward Lincoln, The Brookings Institution[2]*

Foreign investments have become too important to the nation's
economy to remain in the shadows of its economic consciousness. Foreign money now finances a substantial amount of all
new direct investment and for the last several years has under-
written half the offerings of treasury bills, thereby financing the
U.S. budget deficit.[3] Foreign investments in autos, chemicals,
and a variety of other industries have created almost three million jobs.

These benefits have so captivated mayors, governors, and treasury officials that many ignore the troubling ramifications, which are now becoming apparent. The most serious threat is America's increasing loss of economic and political independence. Decisions that used to be made in Sacramento, Albany, and Washington, D.C., are now being made in Tokyo, London, and Riyadh. And although the United States has entered the global economy, where all nations sacrifice a measure of independence, America seems to have gone overboard.

The real problem is that policymakers are still wedded to a host of myths about foreign investment. Some of these myths are perpetuated by political entrepreneurs who have a vested interest in maintaining the status quo. Others are based on economic data alone and ignore the political and social forces that impact on events. What all myths have in common is that they engender resistance to change, which can paralyze public policy.

Myth 1: History shows that foreign investment built America by providing the capital to industrialize. Foreign capital in the twentieth century will help America rebuild its industrial capacity.

In the nineteenth century, European investors put their money in railroads, canals, factories, mines—projects that enabled the United States to create its own economic miracle. The benefits far outweighed the risks, which were borne by the foreigners; indeed, several states defaulted on their European loans.

The Fallacies: While it is true that as a young nation the United States borrowed extensively, remaining a debtor nation until World War I, it borrowed to build for the long haul, to create infrastructure and factories. The situation is different today: Much of the foreign borrowing is not for reindustrialization but to pay for the country's habits of overconsumption. In 1985, America again became a net debtor nation, with the value of foreign investment in the United States exceeding the value of American investment abroad. This time, America frittered away the creditor status it enjoyed for seventy years for a different reason: to pay off the interest on loans borrowed to sustain its record budget deficit, and otherwise living above its means.

Myth 2: Foreign investment is separate from trade policy.

Behind this myth is the view that foreign investors locate in the United States primarily for economic reasons, leading only to benefits for everyone. The efforts to invest are seen as a sign of goodwill and an indication of commitment to the United States. This view still predominates despite evidence to the contrary. Senator John Danforth modified it by elevating investment barriers in principle to the level of trade barriers in the trade bill of 1984.

The Fallacies: Like it or not, other countries' investment policies are linked to their export strategies. Firms locate in the United States for four major reasons: to avoid protective tariffs, gain access to the rich U.S. market, acquire technology, and make a profit. Some investors build manufacturing facilities to deflect criticism and to stave off the growing protectionist sentiment in the U.S. Congress. This happened in steel, autos, and the television industry, where the lines became blurred and investment often masked export strategy. Whenever the threat of protectionism loomed on the horizon, investors flocked to the United States. The strategy worked: Foreign investment blunted protectionist policies and confused the issue of whether or not America was becoming an economic target.

The Japanese experience in Europe mirrored their American strategy. As protectionism gained support in Europe, the Japanese rapidly expanded their investments there—so much so that by 1985 they had increased by 100 percent in three years. During the same period, Europe's trade deficit with Japan doubled.[4]

There was nothing secret about these strategies: The Japanese encouraged their companies to invest abroad as enlightened policy, designed to stave off protectionism and save jobs. A Japanese government survey of 300 major Japanese corporations revealed the widespread acceptance of their government's policy to expand beyond exports: 87.5 percent of the companies said they had already made investments abroad.[5]

Myth 3: Investment policy exists apart from foreign policy.

A corollary of the myth that investment policy functions in isolation from trade policy, this myth rests on the notion that anything goes when it comes to luring foreign money to the United States. That means tax breaks, guarantees of anonymity, and any other bait that works to sell T-bills to foreign investors and apartment buildings to anyone with spare cash. Whatever it takes to attract capital is acceptable; after all, this money has kept the deficit at bay, made huge profits for investment bankers and real estate agents, and spared the country's leaders the effort of solving its budget problems. It has helped the country's rich foreign friends who live in politically unstable countries by providing a safe haven for their money until things straighten out. After all, if the United States doesn't compete for this money, it will go to other countries.

The Fallacies: It is hard to see how the national interest is served by an open-door policy that fails to discriminate between dictators and criminals, on the one hand, and legitimate investors on the other. It is also hard to justify policies that encourage capital flight from poor nations that desperately need the investment capital to feed their people, build their economies, and pay off their crippling foreign debts. How did Filipinos benefit from the Marcoses' millions, siphoned off from U.S. foreign aid and corrupt governance and invested in U.S. real estate?

Despite short-term benefits for the economy, the U.S. role in encouraging capital flight cannot be ignored much longer. In the long run, capital flight destabilizes nations, foments revolution, and encourages governments that are hostile to the United States.

Myth 4: Foreign investments are a sign of America's economic health.

This myth was especially popular with President Ronald Reagan, who linked foreign investment to America's economic upturn and to the country's political stability.

The Fallacies: While this is partly true, it neglects the other side of a very clear picture—the United States as the world's biggest financial borrower, the only wealthy, industrialized nation to incur debtor status in modern times. In that context, debtor status is a reflection of decline, not economic health. Dollars spent on interest payments, and not on productive growth, mean a heavily mortgaged future.

The risks go deeper. "You lose some of your sovereignty," warned Senator William Proxmire, Democrat of Wisconsin. "You lose your independence."

Being guided by this myth means, in effect, selling off the roof of the house in order to pay the mortgage. Can America continue to sell off its financial resources, as it is selling off its natural resources, to investors who may not have the country's interests at heart in the long run? Besides, once foreign investors perceive that the United States is not a stable economy, they will leave as quickly as they came.

America's debt to foreign investors is surely a sign that its assets are attractive, and in that sense its economy looks healthy; but the geometrically increasing foreign debt is also a sign of economic distress.

Myth 5: Money is neutral, not political. Investors are interested in profit, not power.

America has entered the global economy, goes this line of reasoning, and the country must move with the times. It doesn't matter if we are dealing with deutsche marks, francs, or yen or if companies are run from Bonn or Tokyo. It is all the same; companies want to make a profit, and they couldn't care less about the country's politics.

The Fallacies: Money is rarely neutral, as any former colony can tell you. Firms must protect their investments, and America is no more immune from their influence than Brazil. As American multinationals threw themselves into foreign politics to protect their investments, as in the days when ITT overturned the government of Chile and United Fruit ran Guatemala, foreign multinationals are doing the same to America, with all the resources they can muster. Backed by their governments, foreign companies have plunged into American politics: They have entered U.S. elections, formed their own PACs and contributed to political candidates, changed state tax policies, and successfully lobbied Congress for a range of grants and tax abatements.

Foreign investment also has compromised the political independence of officials on all levels of government. It has affected the national debate on the trade deficit, for example. Senator Jeff Bingaman, a New Mexico Democrat, noted that a senator from a state with substantial foreign investments could hardly play a vigorous role in curbing the trade deficit.

Foreign companies take their politics seriously. Political considerations play a big part in where they invest and how much they invest. Their executives are highly skilled at playing politicians off against each other to get the best deal in tax abatements, subsidies, and low-cost loans. Most attractive are states with right-to-work laws, tame legislatures, and low taxes.

When all that doesn't work, companies bring on the heavy artillery. The most dramatic case of foreign intervention in American political decisions was the fight to repeal the unitary tax, whose survival stood no chance against the combined clout of the prime minister of Britain, President Reagan, and a host of multinational companies with extensive political resources.

Myth 6: U.S. policymakers and the American people have enough information on which to base intelligent decisions.

Sixteen separate federal agencies collect information on foreign investment. How much more do we need? Moreover, collecting more data would inexorably lead to regulation, which might in turn lead to restricting foreign investment, and nobody wants that.

The Fallacies: Sixteen separate agencies might gather information on foreign investment, but the result falls far short of what is needed. Information on foreign companies is often restricted by the laws of their nations; this makes it difficult, for example, to obtain financial data on foreign-owned banks. Successful companies in the private sector wouldn't dream of making decisions without adequate information; why should the public sector?

Myths take on a life of their own, and this one has survived in remarkably good health. During the debate over the Bryant amendment to the 1987 trade bill, members of Congress were warned that any effort to improve disclosure would lead to drastic reductions in foreign investment. The proof? Only the fact that legions of lobbyists said it was so. No one has seen any data to back up this myth, but few have questioned its legitimacy.

"We are witnessing the largest transfer of wealth the world has ever known," said the late representative Ben Rosenthal.[6] Why is the United States so complacent about not knowing exactly what is happening? By 1986, many analysts were describing foreign investment in the terms that Rosenthal had the foresight to use in 1980, when his committee identified the problems that will continue to baffle Americans into the twenty-first century. "Direct investment will be a tidal wave, but it's only starting now," noted Eugene Atkinson, managing director of the Tokyo office of Goldman Sachs.[7] "It is awesomely different from anything experienced in the past," remarked Arthur Burns, quoted on capital inflows in a *New York Times* article headlined "A Nation Hooked on Foreign Funds."[8]

Most experts believe that at least 50 percent of all foreign investment goes unreported. Areas most in need of improved, systematic information include:

- The technology drain. Where are foreign investors investing to acquire American technology? What effect does this have on the national defense and on American industry? What will Japan's investment in Boeing, for example, do in the long run to America's lead in the aerospace industry—the last high-tech industry in which the United States is still predominant?
- The money drain. Where are the profits going? Is foreign investment as good for the American economy as it's

cracked up to be, or do most of the profits return abroad, worsening the trade deficit? Some data suggest that profits of U.S. subsidiaries of foreign firms were being increasingly repatriated to the parent company instead of being reinvested in the U.S. companies. In 1984, 55 percent of the profits of foreign-owned U.S. firms were repatriated back to the foreign parent, whereas in 1985 the figure increased to 79 percent.[9]

• The preemptive strike. What U.S. industries are being driven out of business by unfair competition from foreign investors? Is there a level playing field, or are some companies subsidized by their governments?

• The industry drain. What industries can the nation afford to lose? Can the United States afford to lose the aerospace or computer-chip industry to foreign interests? Can it afford to sell off its natural resources as rapidly as foreign investors can buy them up?

• The government connection. What is the difference between individual foreign investors and foreign governments? Should government records differentiate between them?

• The information gap. Just how much foreign investment is there in the United States, where is it, and how much are local governments spending to recruit it?

Myth 7: We don't need any changes in the current U.S. laissez-faire policy toward foreign investment. Since most of the activity occurs on the state level, federal intervention would be superfluous and unnecessarily intrusive.

Also known as the "hunky-dory syndrome," this theory also postulates that current laws are adequate to deal with the problem areas of foreign investment.

The Fallacies: The states are engaged in economic fratricide. They vie with each other to see who can offer the most tax abatements, grants, real estate, and loans, while the foreign multinationals sit back and wait for the best bargain. While other industrialized nations carefully coordinate and control their own policies toward foreign investment, the United States has embarked on a free-for-all that can only make it less competitive in the long run if it continues to dissipate its resources in this way.

Other areas in which the nation's patchwork quilt of laws and policies clearly works against its interests include real estate, antitrust, and banking. Before the banking laws addressed the inequities, foreign banks moved in and cornered a large part of the market share away from American banks. Salt Lake City surely didn't benefit from arms dealer Adnan Khashoggi's real estate investments, which glutted the market and left his creditors empty-handed when his firm filed for bankruptcy protection.

Myth 8: Foreign investment and free trade are the same thing.

This is the justification for a hands-off policy on foreign investment. The conventional wisdom argues for a laissez-faire policy toward foreign investment on the grounds that market forces are preferable to government intervention, that market forces will correct distortions and inequities, and that intervention in investment issues constitutes an abridgement of free trade.

The Fallacies: Even the Reagan administration modified its views in this area, and started to toughen its stance on trade as well as investment. In 1986, the administration actively sought to include investment policy on the agenda for the GATT talks on multilateral trade negotiations. In this and other international settings, U.S. policymakers keep trying to convince their trading partners that market forces work better when barriers to investment are reduced.[10]

Quiet persuasion has not, unfortunately, proved adequate to the task of addressing the complex problems that have accompanied the surge of foreign investment. When they work, market forces are surely preferable to government intervention, but when they don't work, U.S. policymakers must be prepared to step in without fearing the wrath of Adam Smith's ghost. The failure to deal with foreign investment now will make it more difficult to deal with in the future.

Myth 9: Foreign investment helps American business.

There is no question that foreign investment has breathed new life into many American companies by injecting new capital, new technology, and new management skills. Joint ventures, such as the General Motors-Toyota "NUMMI" plant in California, have benefited all three of America's troubled auto companies, and there is no doubt that American Motors would have gone out of business without Renault as a partner.

The Fallacies: Recently, a closer look at joint ventures and other foreign investments has revealed that there is a price tag on these benefits. A study of joint ventures with Japan in the *Harvard Business Review,* for example, concluded that the price tag was so high that they were "giving away America's future." In exchange for a few lower-skilled and lower-paying jobs, American companies are sacrificing their competitiveness to a Japanese strategy that keeps higher-value, higher-paying jobs in Japan; the American plants were primarily assembly plants, with investors gaining the engineering and production process skills that "underlie competitive success." All three auto joint ventures, argued the authors, reflect this pattern: Auto assembly takes place in the United States, and in each case the "U.S. automakers delegated all plant design and product engineering responsibilities to their Japanese partners. . . . Under the Chrysler-Mitsubishi agreements, the joint venture will import the engine, transmission, and accelerator from Japan." Ultimately, if the higher-value items remain in Japan, the lion's share of the profits will also revert to Japan.[11]

Another challenge to this myth involves the preference of Japanese investors to deal with their own suppliers. When the Japanese automakers first came to the United States, domestic companies hoped to benefit by selling them parts. The reverse occurred: Nearly fifty Japanese suppliers have located in the United States since 1979, with the figure expected to rise to 300 by 1990. "The Japanese are trying to colonize the U.S. auto industry," complained Dan Moore, a parts manufacturer. "The problem is partly our laziness and partly their cultural preferences. But they're also doing some orchestrating." The Japanese argue that American products are not competitive. "Many of their factories are filthy, and their controls are inadequate," said A. Darrell Shown, a Honda manager.[12]

Known as the "group method of doing business," this pattern has been noticed throughout the country, particularly in the South. Nissan, for example, not only used many Japanese suppliers, who followed Nissan to Tennessee, but retains a large interest in many of those companies.[13] The Japanese have extended this policy beyond suppliers to other satellite industries: When Toyota decided to locate a plant in Georgetown, Kentucky, the company insisted on using a Japanese construction firm to build the factory. Things would have gone smoothly if not for the loud protest of the construction trades union, which publicized this practice and identified the more than $100 million worth of U.S. government grants and incentives earmarked for Toyota.

It is probably no coincidence that the only citizens group to protest foreign investment, Citizens Against Foreign Control of the United States, was founded by the president of a company that produces electrical systems for automobiles. June M. Collier, president of National Industries, Inc., advocates legislation restricting foreign investment. "We're transferring control out of this country," she argues. "The global economy would work if we lived in the Garden of Eden. Japan is taking advantage of us. They're keeping just this side of the trade laws."

THE FOREIGN CHALLENGE: NATIONAL SOVEREIGNTY IN THE GLOBAL ECONOMY

Americans are faced with the real challenge of foreign investment: to bury the myths once and for all and get on with the job of enjoying its benefits and reducing its risks. Policymakers must shield citizens from the negative impact of foreign investment and assert some control over its future direction.

The first step is to understand it. Where is it coming from, who really owns what assets, and what are the true figures on the extent of foreign investment? Members of Congress have expressed their concern at the lack of reliable data, and Representative John Bryant's bill calling for full disclosure became a major issue in the debate over the 1987 trade bill. Congress, which spent a great deal of time in 1985 and 1986 enacting legislation intended to secure U.S. borders from illegal aliens, is beginning to recognize the need to know the extent and origins of the influx of foreign funds. Without adequate data, it is impossible to know the dimensions of this phenomenon or begin to formulate a national policy.

A policy of full disclosure would mean the end of flying blind on foreign investments. It would lead to a national perspective that would address not merely whether specific foreign investments were good for Tennessee, Nebraska, Connecticut, or California but for the entire nation. Is it good national (rather than regional) policy, for example, to give a foreign company tax breaks so that it beat the brains out of an American-owned firm? Is it good for the national security of the United States to have the country's supercomputer capability in foreign hands? What about mineral reserves? Machine tools? Is it good for the United States to have foreign banks control loan policies in New York and California? Is it good national policy to have foreign interests purchase half of the treasury bills issued in recent years? Is it good national policy for foreign companies to be involved in local and national elections?

There are no clear-cut answers, but at least these questions must be raised in an open forum. Policymakers must be prepared to be accountable not just to their own narrow constituencies but to the broad national interest. The only way to achieve that accountability is to deal with some of these issues on the national level and to make national policy where it is needed to protect the long-term interests of the American people. Some suggestions for a modest beginning include the following:

IDENTIFY THE BENEFITS OF FOREIGN INVESTMENT AND REINFORCE STATE EFFORTS TO MAXIMIZE THOSE BENEFITS.

Investments like the Bridgestone rescue mission in Tennessee, in which a Japanese company stepped in and succeeded where Firestone had failed, should be applauded and encouraged. Fourteen-hundred workers kept their jobs, the union flourished and worked closely with management, and the region was spared the devastating effects of a factory closing. The revival of Kaiser Steel in Fontana, California, by a joint venture of Japanese, Brazilian, and American interests is another case of healthy international cooperation in action.[14]

TAKE A HARD LOOK AT WHERE FOREIGN INVESTMENT WEAKENS U.S. NATIONAL SECURITY AND TAKE MEASURES TO CURB THOSE INVESTMENTS.

"Much is wrong with letting any country get control of businesses vital to the U.S. defense," wrote the astute *New York Times* columnist William Safire on the impending acquisition of Fairchild Semiconductor—already controlled by Schlumberger, Ltd., a French firm—by Fujitsu, Japan's largest computer company. Fairchild makes the components for the supercomputers that make or break codes and target nuclear weapons and are a vital part of Star Wars research. Only the National Security Agency is concerned about this—since it is their supercomputer world monitoring efforts that are at risk—recalling former CIA director William Casey's warning about foreign investment as a "Trojan horse." America's trust is misplaced, Safire points out, reminding his readers that "Japanese businessmen were accused of stealing secrets from IBM and are suspected of technology diversions through Hong Kong."[15] Stunned by opposition to the sale, Fujitsu withdrew its offer on March 16, 1987.

TAKE A HARD LOOK AT FOREIGN INVESTORS AS EMPLOYERS AND IDENTIFY THEIR FLAWS ALONG WITH THEIR ASSETS.

While the superiority of Japanese management techniques has received wide attention, there are serious flaws in their employment policies that deserve more attention. For one thing, Japanese employers discriminate against women and minorities, and their attitudes show no signs of moderating. Prime Minister Yasuhiro Nakasone's now famous remarks in 1986 equating the low level of intelligence of its black population to America's economic problems were greeted with horror in the United States and with embarrassment in Japan; the Japanese were not embarrassed by their leader's views but by the U.S. reaction to them.

DON'T BE AFRAID TO CONTROL FOREIGN INVESTMENT WHERE IT CONSTITUTES AN UNFAIR THREAT TO AMERICAN BUSINESS OR AMERICAN INTERESTS.

This should not be attempted for frivolous reasons but only in exceptional cases. There is no reason, for example, for the United States to add to its current problems with hostile takeovers by keeping the door open for foreign investors. It is hard to see who benefited from Sir James Goldsmith's attempted raid on the Goodyear Corporation, except, of course, Goldsmith himself. Not Goodyear, which lost $93 million in the "greenmail" it paid to fend off Goldsmith, or the stockholders or the company management, which must now figure out how to recover its substantial losses and still keep the company alive. The United States can expect a substantial increase in hostile foreign takeovers in the future—especially in view of the decline of the dollar.[16]

NEGOTIATE. RECOGNIZE THE U.S. BARGAINING POSITION, AND NEGOTIATE FROM STRENGTH.

There is too much fear in circulation that is based on the false assumption that foreign investors will not invest if the United States takes steps to remove the negative aspects of their investments. This fear is based on false or nonexistent information and leads to short-sighted policies. It powered the repeal of the unitary tax as states succumbed one by one to foreign investors' threats that they would move their plants to other states. Political leaders should remember that foreign investors are very anxious to invest in the United States, that they invest primarily for market share and profits, and that everything else is secondary. Once they learn what really motivates foreign investors, they will have far more latitude to act independently and in the country's interest.

COORDINATE A FOREIGN INVESTMENT STRATEGY.

The United States needs to develop a mechanism for coordinating state efforts to avoid giving away more resources than are necessary to attract foreign investment. At this point, the country is functioning as fifty separate countries, each negotiating its own trade and investment policies. States are not as strong as nation states, as this country found out over two hundred years ago; there is no way North Dakota can compete with Japan, West Germany, or even Singapore in the global marketplace.

DEMAND A LEVEL PLAYING FIELD.

At best, policymakers should identify exactly where foreign investors are given advantages over American investors—for example, some countries pay no taxes—and even out the playing field for Americans. It is also time to level the international playing field and demand a degree of reciprocity abroad in exchange for American hospitality to foreign investors. Even if it is legal, it is patently unfair for the Kuwaiti government to drill for oil on American soil if Americans are not accorded comparable rights in Kuwait. Laws, regulations, and policies that perpetuate these inequities should be analyzed with an eye toward revision where necessary.

Some have suggested linking investment policy to trade policy, since the two are linked in the minds of foreign investors and their governments. When the Japanese refused to allow U.S. construction companies to bid for the building of the Kansai airport, U.S. leaders should have taken a look at the negotiating possibilities offered by investment policy. In the trade area, negotiating from a position of strength has brought quick results. The European Community, for example, rapidly withdrew some of its protective tariffs in the winter of 1986–87 after President Reagan threatened tariffs on wine and cheese. Used sparingly, this could help toward the goal of breaking down barriers instead of waiting patiently for our trading partners to follow our free-trade and investment lead. As a future strategy, U.S. policymakers should follow their own trade model and press harder for multilateral solutions to investment issues. They could work through the GATT as well as the OECD.

LEARN FROM OTHER INDUSTRIALIZED COUNTRIES.

Other industrialized countries scrutinize foreign investment very carefully. What do they know that we don't? We look at the Japanese and the Germans, for example, with great admiration. We admire their economic miracles, their management skills, and their ability to coordinate competing interests. Most of all, we admire their ability to make government work for industry. Every industrialized country limits, to a greater or lesser extent, foreign investment in manufacturing plants, banks, farmland, real estate, and natural resources. All of these countries, under pressure from the United States, are relaxing many of their restrictions, but they still retain essential control over these precious resources and stall U.S. efforts at further reform.

Our major trading and investing partners also benefit from stricter ethics laws, which bar their government officials from engaging in the revolving-door practice of moving back and forth between their own government and foreign industries (or foreign governments). It is almost hopeless to look forward to tougher negotiations with foreign powers when our top officials go to work for foreign interests before the ink is dry on their resignation papers. As soon as Michael Deaver left the White House in 1985, a bevy of foreign governments, including Canada and Korea, signed up the services of his public relations firm, totaling over $2.5 million in contracts his first year out of office. Many others, like Deaver, leave the U.S. Trade Representative's office and other sensitive posts to share trade secrets and public policy with their new employers.

RECOGNIZE THAT CONTROLLING FOREIGN INVESTMENT DOESN'T HAVE TO MEAN RESTRICTING IT.

U.S. officials resist the thought of a government agency screening foreign investment because a screening process implies restricting foreign investment, and that would be bad for the economy. CFIUS, the Treasury-led group with official responsibility for screening controversial investments, has reflected this view: It meets rarely; has never, to anyone's knowledge, barred an undesirable investment from entering or remaining in the United States; and is most often referred to as a "paper tiger." For all practical purposes, CFIUS is defunct and should be replaced with another intergovernmental body with a firm mandate to evaluate foreign investment. If that body determines that a specific investment poses a serious threat to U.S. interests, then the proper government agency with responsibility for that area—farmland, natural resources, etc.—should follow through with measures to restrict that investment.

KEEP AN EYE ON THE BIG PICTURE.

What does all this investment really mean to the United States: to its competitiveness in the international community; to its ability to manage its affairs? Policymakers have a tendency to seize on the obvious and ignore the deeper message. In the case of the Bridgestone rescue, for example, why was Firestone allowed to fail? Was there any way the U.S. political and social system could have saved it? In the long run, is it better for the United States for Bridgestone or Firestone to corner the truck radial market? Bridgestone is 100 percent Japanese owned, its top management will remain totally Japanese, and an increasing percentage of its profits will return home.

Bridgestone's success was largely attributable to government intervention—both Japanese and American. In effect, the U.S. government is practicing industrial policy to lure foreign investors to its shores while resisting anything that looks like industrial policy for its own citizens. Bridgestone benefited from easy access to low-interest capital, while Firestone faced high interest rates; an under-valued currency, while the dollar was high; and favorable antitrust laws in an era of tighter U.S. enforcement.

There must be a reshifting of U.S. political resources, not to bail out failing companies but to do everything possible to ensure that U.S. companies enjoy the same benefits as their foreign competitors. This country cannot afford much longer to watch its own companies function at a disadvantage while luring foreign competitors to take their place. The U.S. cannot afford to practice free-market politics while the rest of the world practices intervention; its leaders must at least force changes in the practices of other countries until they formulate a more workable policy for themselves. The lines are now too starkly drawn between the hard-line free traders, ideologues who brook no interference with the forces of the marketplace, and those with absolute faith in government intervention as the panacea. It is time for the shadings: policies that take advantage of the best in both theories; policies that are forward looking, flexible, and tailored to the issue and the times.

Finally, responsible leaders must take a long, hard look at their country's growing dependence on foreign capital. It is too reminiscent of America's former dependence on foreign oil, and just as we shook ourselves loose from the OPEC cabal, we must reduce our craving for foreign money and practice more selectivity. The United States is sinking deeper and deeper into the condition of a developing country: importing capital when a few short years before it was the world's largest creditor nation. Advanced countries export capital, and that's the company this country should keep.

The forces of the international marketplace have begun to overwhelm America's capacity to deal with them. The surge of foreign investment is only one glaring example. The manner in which the nation's leaders respond will determine how we meet the most difficult economic challenge of our times: to retain U.S. sovereignty in the global economy.

EPILOGUE

The Future of Foreign Investment

Frank Fasi, the mayor of Honolulu, went to the state legislature in the late spring of 1988 and made an unprecedented request. Reflecting widespread public concern, Mr. Fasi sought legislation to prohibit the sale of residential real estate to foreign investors. This marked the first time in recent memory that a public official tried to block foreign investment—in contrast to the mayors and governors who spent hundreds of millions of dollars to woo overseas money—and it drew the national attention it deserved.

In Hawaii, where foreign investors—mostly Japanese—own two-thirds of the resort property as well as increasing blocks of prime residential and commercial real estate, the trend was more visible than it was in other parts of the country. A new class of speculators, capitalizing on the favorable yen-dollar ratio, found irresistible bargains throughout the state. Some of the bargain hunters attracted considerable publicity by conducting their shopping sprees in long white limousines, arriving unannounced at properties that caught their eye, and offering prices well above market rates. Many wealthy homeowners quickly succumbed to the opportunity to make a huge profit, but regretted it soon afterward. The "new homeless," as they were called, found the speculators had driven prices up so high that finding new homes proved unexpectedly difficult. Meanwhile, ordinary citizens protested the higher property taxes that followed this surge in land speculation.

What was happening in Honolulu was happening all over the country. By the fall of 1988, foreign investors owned 46 percent of the commercial property of downtown Los Angeles, 30 percent of downtown Houston, 33 percent of downtown Washington, and over 20 percent of Manhattan. National landmarks, such as the Watergate complex in the nation's capital, Arco Plaza in Los Angeles, and the U.S. Department of Justice building are now owned by foreign investors.[1] Lee Iacocca, the chairman of Chrysler, asked whether it was a good idea to lose control over so much real estate and become "a nation of tenants."

PUBLIC REACTIONS

Americans finally began to feel uneasy about the surge of foreign investments in the spring of 1988, and their concerns were reflected later that year in the presidential and congressional campaigns. Two national polls taken by *U.S. News & World Report* and Smick-Medley Associates indicated serious public concern. The Smick-Medley survey showed the public "restless and concerned" about growing foreign investment in the U.S., with 78 percent of those polled favoring a law to limit the extent of foreign investment in business and real estate. Both polls showed overwhelming public support for restricting foreign investment in cases affecting national security.

Why this sudden concern? Foreign investors had begun to act with unprecedented boldness, as reported foreign investment approached $2 trillion, a tenfold increase since 1974. Even this figure underestimates the true holdings of foreign investors, since many investors continue to take advantage of the loopholes in U.S. law, and use dummy corporations to hide their identities. Bolstered by the strong showing of the yen, deutsche mark, pound, and other currencies against the hapless dollar, foreign investments poured in at an unparalleled rate.

America's fire sale prices worked in tandem with lax enforcement of the antitrust laws during the Reagan years, fostering an environment even more conducive to hostile foreign takeovers than it was to U.S. raiders. Of seven major attempted takeovers in the fall of 1988, four were by British investors. Pillsbury was being raided by Grand Met, a British distillery. Farmers Group Inc., the nation's seventh largest insurance company, was acquired by Britain's B.A.T. Industries PLC. Robert Maxwell, the British publisher, acquired Macmillan. Koppers, a Pittsburgh-based construction company, was under siege by Beazer, a British company.

In the spring and summer of 1988, daily headlines tracked the surge of foreign takeover activity: the Campeau (Canadian) purchase of Federated Stores; the Bridgestone (Japanese) acquisition of Firestone's tire division, and the Saudi purchase of Texaco's oil refineries and marketing division. Even the People's Republic of China was getting into the act, purchasing a 50 percent stake in a California oil refinery and marketing operation, as well as timber interests in the Northwest and a lumber mill in New Jersey.[2]

Some Americans did not sit back passively and watch the export of their country's assets; on the contrary, they seized advantage of the opportunity to make some easy money. A leading investment banking firm in New York established a "Bargain Basement Committee" for the purpose of identifying vulnerable American assets for its foreign clients. Other firms followed suit and formed similar committees, with less colorful names. The more visible partners of these investment houses—some of them former Treasury, Commerce, and OMB officials—filled the editorial pages of the nation's newspapers with articles extolling the unalloyed benefits of foreign investment to the nation's well-being.

The nation's mayors and governors also accelerated their efforts to recruit foreign investment into their states. The most recent and controversial of these offerings involved Kentucky's victory in the competition over Toyota. The cost to Kentucky will approach $325 million by the year 2006, and includes the cost of land, highway improvements, site preparation, and education. The estimated benefits to the state are the employment of 3500 Kentuckians and a $100 million annual payroll. Former Governor Martha Layne Collins answered her political critics, who regarded the state's incentives as giveaways, by saying she'd "rather subsidize Toyota than subsidize unemployment."[3]

Foreign investors also made significant inroads into the securities industry. Nomura, the giant securities firm, purchased a 20 percent stake in Wasserstein-Perella, a firm famous for takeover activity. Nippon Life purchased a 13 percent stake in Shearson Lehman; Yasuda Mutual Life Insurance, an 18 percent stake in Paine Webber; and Yamaichi Securities, a 25 percent stake in the Lodestar Group.

The increasing foreign stake in the U.S. securities industry, while a natural by-product of the trend toward globalization, caused concern among those who feared a loss of sovereignty in the process. Some analysts suspected that foreign investors helped trigger black Monday. "The United States has lost control of its financial markets to foreigners and has run out of easy policy options to regain it," A. Gary Shilling, an economic consultant and portfolio strategist, warned in the Sunday financial section of

The New York Times. "The American financial tune is no longer being called in New York, but rather in Tokyo, London, and Frankfurt. In fact, this loss of control had a lot to do with the timing of the stock market crash last fall. Foreigners lost confidence in American economic policy and foreigners held all the important cards, panicked, and joined the rush to sell stocks."[4]

Foreign investors continued to finance the U.S. deficit, and now own 20 percent of the U.S. national debt. By mid-1988, the country's position as a debtor nation had worsened, with the current account deficit exceeding the $400 billion mark. In a major speech before the Economic Club of Washington, Felix Rohatyn spoke of the consequences of such shortsightedness: "We have now become the classic model for a failing economic power: increasing levels of foreign debt, a constantly depreciating currency, and a continuing negative trade balance regardless of currency levels. We are now going to add to this list a rapid rise in the level of U.S. assets owned abroad."[5]

Meanwhile, foreign purchases continued at a pace that far outstripped U.S. investments abroad. Several widely publicized foreign investments included the purchases of CBS Records, Smith-Corona Typewriters, and Standard Oil. Japanese investors now own six auto assembly plants and 150 auto parts suppliers making components for engines, transmissions, and heating and cooling systems. Experts predict that by 1990 there will be 300 Japanese auto parts manufacturers in the United States.

POLITICAL RESPONSES

A steady stream of headlines announcing foreign takeovers of real estate, companies, and U.S. debt underscored the message: The nation was selling off its assets faster than it was selling its products. The issue reached presidential and congressional campaigns, and led to three separate hearings on the 1988 trade bill that specifically addressed foreign investment.[6]

Governor Michael Dukakis and Senator Lloyd Bentsen, the Democratic presidential and vice-presidential candidates, warned that foreign investment was eroding America's economic and political independence. Mr. Dukakis told a rally in Hartford, Connecticut, that the nation must start "selling more American goods and services and buying back our own bonds and land and factories from the Japanese and the Europeans and the Saudis and the Kuwaitis . . . who have been buying them from us." In

Longview, Texas, he decried "foreign companies buying up real estate, buying up companies, buying up plants in this country."[7]

In a strategic blunder, Dukakis gave a major address on foreign investment while touring Moog Automotive, Inc., an Italian-owned company. "Maybe the Republican ticket wants our children to work for foreign owners, pay rent to foreign owners, and owe their future to foreign owners, but that's not the kind of future Lloyd Bentsen and I want for America," Mr. Dukakis said.

The Republicans responded with conventional wisdom, and said that foreign investment was a tribute to the American economy. George Bush went further, comparing Dukakis with the "Know-Nothing" movement of the nineteenth century, which fought immigration of Catholics to the United States. "He's turned to fear of foreigners," charged Bush.[8]

Accusations of "xenophobia," "protectionism," or even "racism" have increasingly been raised in an effort to discredit those who raised questions about the impact of foreign investment on trade policy. While some of these accusations are undoubtedly true—in Pittsburgh, local radio stations likened raider Brian Beazer with the British redcoats in the War of Independence, and newspapers reported the mayor threatening to scratch his eyes out if she met him—most of the charges have no basis in fact. It is easier to attack with clichés than to deal with substantive issues; it is a quick and effective way of dismissing problems that call for more thoughtful consideration.[9]

On Capitol Hill, always a good barometer of public sentiment, Congress overruled the objections of a small army of lobbyists and gave the president authority to bar any foreign investment that could jeopardize national security. The president previously could bar such investments only by declaring a state of national emergency, an action no president had ever taken. The administration reluctantly accepted this authority in the Exon-Florio amendment to the 1988 trade bill.

Congress also approved a bill vetoed by President Reagan that would have barred former high government officials, including former congressmen and their staffs, from working for foreign governments and foreign investors for one year after they left government service. Senator Strom Thurmond, South Carolina Republican, and the prime sponsor of this legislation, had been angered when a leading U.S. textile negotiator quit his job in the middle of negotiations and went to work for Hong Kong.

The new ethics in government act would probably have had

little impact on the growing influence of foreign investors and their American lobbyists. The loophole that allows foreign investors to run their own Political Action Committees would also have been invoked to ease their access and accelerate their impact: the notion that they are not foreign multinationals but U.S. companies, since their subsidiaries are incorporated in the United States. Similarly, the law firms and public relations companies representing Toshiba America, Inc., were not required to register with the Justice Department's Foreign Agent Registration Office, because Toshiba America is regarded as a U.S. corporation.

Senator John Heinz, Republican of Pennsylvania, estimated that Toshiba was able, in this way, to spend more than $9 million to weaken import sanctions levied against Toshiba products in the 1988 trade bill in retaliation for Toshiba's role in selling sensitive, high-tech, defense-related equipment to the Soviet Union. Toshsiba paid one law-lobbying firm $4.3 million. "The message of the Toshiba sanctions is that crime does pay," charged Heinz. "In all the twenty-one years I have been in office, I've never seen a lobbying campaign so orchestrated at so many levels," added Senator Jake Garn, Republican of Utah.[10]

The power of the foreign investors' lobbyists, which included a retinue of former highly placed U.S. government officials, meanwhile became manifest. In 1988, for example, "152 Japanese companies and government agencies have hired 113 firms for Washington representation," calculated Dr. Pat Choate, director of policy analysis for TRW, Inc. "For this representation and grass-roots activities they will pay more than $100 million— more than the combined budgets of the U.S. Chamber of Commerce, the National Association of Manufacturers, The Business Roundtable, the Committee for Economic Development, and the American Business Conference—the five most influential business organizations in Washington."[11]

Foreign investment also spawned the creation of a group called the Association of Foreign Investors in America. Foreign investors, who pay an annual membership fee of $10,000, were encouraged to join by the group's point man and chief counsel, Elliot Richardson. One of the country's most distinguished former public servants, Richardson served as Secretary of HEW, Defense and Commerce, as well as Attorney General and Ambassador to the Court of St. James. According to the group's executive director, Sam Rosenblatt, the list of investor members is secret.

These lobbyists, and dozens more, succeeded in defeating a measure that would have vastly improved the inadequate data collection on foreign investments. The Bryant amendment, as it was called, would have required foreign investors to provide more complete information on their identities and their holdings. The amendment was passed by the House of Representatives twice in 1988: first as part of the trade bill, and then as a freestanding bill in the waning days of the 100th Congress.

The battle over Bryant reflected the nation's rising concern over the impact of foreign investment on the American economy, and the willingness of congressional leaders to challenge the Reagan administration's firm laissez-faire stance on the issue. The Bryant amendment, along with a provision on plant closings, proved surprisingly resilient: both provisions were declared veto-bait by President Reagan, but clung stubbornly to the trade bill almost until the bitter end, when they were dropped.

The ultimate defeat of the Bryant amendment revealed the growing political muscle of foreign investors, along with their eagerness to draw on this strength even on such an abstruse and unthreatening issue as information collection. Members of Congress, along with key staff aides, reported that they had never been lobbied as hard on any trade or investment-related issue as they had been pressured on the Bryant amendment. Senator Tom Harkin, Democrat of Iowa, reflecting the experience of many of his colleagues, testified before the Senate Commerce Committee that a major foreign multinational corporation in his state called on him and threatened to move its plant to another state if he voted "wrong" on Bryant.

Another interesting development was the alliance between foreign and domestic multinational corporations on the Bryant lobbying effort. Backed by their governments, foreign investors convinced their U.S. counterparts to oppose the Bryant amendment, threatening unspecified retaliation in their countries. The battle over Bryant and the alliances it spawned was strongly reminiscent of the unitary tax campaign in California, when sixteen foreign governments and the multinationals they represented organized for a resounding victory over the state legislature, setting a pattern for foreign political influence that will strengthen with each success.

Foreign governments and foreign corporations expended a great deal of political capital in defeating the Bryant amendment, a decision that may well prove for several reasons to be a tactical error. Legislators and their staffs, for the most part, resented these unusually heavy-handed pressures, and they have long memories. Blatant threats may work on the state level, many said, but this was the U.S. Congress, where the pride, the backbones, and the egos were somewhat stronger. In addition, recent experience showed that information calms controversy: in the late 1970s, when Americans became concerned about foreign purchases of farmland, Congress passed legislation requiring the Department of Agriculture to collect information on an annual basis. Even though the information was inadequate—the law was riddled with loopholes enabling foreign investors to conceal their identities—the controversy quickly died down and was never revived.

The Bryant amendment will emerge again, as congressional interest in foreign investment continues to grow. The issue has a bipartisan base, with Democrats and Republicans expressing real concern and commitment to pursue the issue. The *Wall Street Journal* predicted that foreign investment would become "the political issue of the 1990s."[12] If that turns out to be true, and all signs point in that direction, it looks as if Congress, not the executive branch, will lead the way.

NATIONAL SECURITY

The gradual erosion of the nation's defense industrial base has been linked to laissez-faire policies toward foreign investment. When the Bryant amendment passed the House of Representatives as a freestanding bill on October 5, 1988, Representative Tom McMillen, Democrat of Maryland, raised the issue of national defense. Quoting former defense official Richard Perle, McMillen charged:

"We don't begin to know who owns what. There are security implications that are pointless to ignore. There are cases on the record where companies were acquired solely to acquire their technology."[13]

Examples abound. The manufacture of an advanced minicomputer by Kubota, Ltd., Japan's largest agricultural machinery company, traced the path of technology transfer through investment. "The design, the chips, and the software are all American, resulting from investments in some of the hottest start-up companies in Silicon Valley," reported David Sanger, in *The New York Times*. Kubota, which had never produced anything more complicated than a tractor, just assembled the computer from technology imported from its U.S. companies. "It's perfectly legal, even admirable, but it is also a little scary,'' said John P. Stern, head of the Tokyo office of the U.S. Electronics Association. What concerns analysts familiar with the issue is that Kubota's investments will accelerate the transfer of American supercomputer technology vital to the national defense and one of the few areas in which the U.S. retained a competitive edge.[14]

The Kubota case also debunks the view of those who scoff at the foreign challenge, arguing that in wartime America can always nationalize its foreign assets. That may be true, if a bit extreme; it is only valid, however, if the assets remain in the country, and if it isn't too late by the time the nation finds itself in a crisis. Kubota shows there is nothing to prevent foreign investors from shipping those assets abroad, just as there is no way to determine the hidden agendas of foreign investors until they emerge with new product lines.

National defense is the one area of foreign investment that has caused the executive branch to break ranks. Several months before the 1988 presidential election, the Defense Department sharply challenged the government's official enthusiasm for foreign investment with a report disputing the "most common view" that foreign investment benefits the U.S. because it creates jobs. That view, the Pentagon report declared, overlooked the fact that foreign owners tend to maintain control over critical manufacturing technologies—specifically, machine tools and electronics manufacturing equipment, such as semiconductors.

Most important, the Pentagon raised the issue of profits from foreign investments returning abroad, reinforcing the view of those who connect foreign investment with the nation's trade deficit. In language unusually strong for a government report, the Pentagon charged:

"The most common view is that the rapidly increasing level of foreign ownership is beneficial to the U.S. . . . This view overlooks economic issues such as the long-term impact on the current account of a continuing flow from the U.S. of repatriated profits and other fees. More importantly, it overlooks the fact that ownership tends to dictate the geographic location of the underlying technologies. Security concerns are not resolved by domestic manufacturing facilities that are dependent on technologies controlled by other nations."[15]

National defense includes many different industries, with wide variations in opinion about what kinds of investments compromise U.S. security interests. Foreign investment now accounts for 10 percent of the nation's manufacturing base, including most of the consumer electronics and concrete industries. The food industry is rapidly being acquired by foreign investors and, judging from the publicity surrounding the Pillsbury takeover, generating controversy.

The transportation and energy industries are also attracting considerable attention in the discussion over national security. British Petroleum now owns Standard Oil of Ohio, which gives it control over the lion's share of Alaska's five-billion-barrel Prudhoe Bay Oil reserve. British Petroleum was itself the target of an acquisition by the Kuwaiti government, which owned 28 percent of the stock of British Petroleum. Unlike U.S. policymakers, however, the British do not confuse self-preservation with protectionism. Faced with a clear threat from their Kuwaiti partners, the British forced them to divest a large share of their holdings.

Nor do the Japanese allow global rhetoric to impede their carefully defined vision of their national interest. When U.S. negotiators, after years of failure, finally convinced the Japanese to open their markets to U.S. beef and citrus products, Japanese investors quickly purchased Florida citrus groves and western cattle ranches and beef processing plants. "The whole point in opening up the Japanese market was for American producers to be able to sell here (in Japan)," said Bill Cody, director of Oregon's Japan Representative Office in Tokyo. "It's not a question of needing Japanese capital to develop an industry. We have an industry."[16]

Of all the recent acquisitions, the rapid expansion of foreign ownership of banking assets gives even the staunchest advocates some cause for concern. In one year's time, the percentage of U.S. banking assets owned by foreign investors rose from 16 to nearly 21 percent in 1988. In New York, the nation's financial capital, over 50 percent of all industrial and commercial loans are made by foreign-owned banks. Since banks play a key role in setting economic policies, and are also a great source of information on commercial and technological trends, critics fear this trend could further erode U.S. control over its own destiny.

The rapid transfer of such key U.S. assets raises the question of whether any industries should retain a degree of U.S. ownership and control. Most nations place a ceiling on foreign ownership of industries they consider critical to their national security and economic well-being. Australia, for example, has a ceiling of 16 percent on foreign ownership of its banking assets. Most industrialized countries place ceilings of some kind on high-tech industries, real estate, banking, and communications.

Many critics in and out of Congress believe the surge of foreign investment in the United States has reached a point requiring a full-scale national debate. Are there any industries in which Americans must retain a degree of control, or, in this global economy, is there no distinction between foreign and American ownership of the nation's assets?

Has laissez-faire brought us to the brink of a new international order in which the U.S. will lose a dimension of its economic and political sovereignty? Is such a change inevitable, and is America powerless to mute its impact? Or does the U.S. still have the imagination, resourcefulness, and determination that created this great nation, and made it the envy of the world and the target of foreign investors in the first place?

Bethesda, Maryland
November 1988

APPENDIX A

Brief Early History of Foreign Investment in the United States

Foreign investment has always played an active, vital role in the economic development of the United States. It poured into the country from earliest colonial times and continued to accelerate throughout the industrial revolution. Foreign capital contributed to the building of canals and railroads as well as factories and mines. By the end of the nineteenth century, America had outstripped its rivals to become the world's leading manufacturing nation, deeply in debt to foreign investors—mainly the British and continental Europeans—but rapidly overtaking its creditors in terms of industry growth and potential.

Then, as now, the British were the major foreign investors, beginning in colonial times by providing most of the capital for the colonies' four most important industries: iron, shipbuilding, tobacco, and naval supplies. Independence did not stem the flow of British investment, which continued for the next two hundred years.

The founding fathers recognized the benefits of foreign investment and immediately created an environment that assured its future welcome. Alexander Hamilton, then secretary of the treasury, issued the "Report on Manufactures," which set forth his government's policy. Foreign investment should be encouraged, he wrote, because it would permit "an increased amount of productive labor and useful enterprise to be set to work."

The rapid increase in foreign investment reflected Hamilton's influence and the country's receptivity. By 1828, the United Kingdom held 25 percent of the entire U.S. debt; and in the 1830s, the majority of the nation's cotton plantations were mortgaged to London investors. Dutch and French investors were also instrumental in sustaining the country during its early years of independence. Dutch banks helped float the debt in 1791 and 1803, while European money backed President Jefferson's purchase of the Louisiana Territory. British and European money was also largely responsible for funding the construction of the Erie Canal and other waterways as well as the nation's extensive railway system.

Foreign capital, combined with foreign management and technological expertise, was instrumental in fueling American growth. In the early part of the nineteenth century, nearly one-quarter of all business equity holdings was controlled by foreign investors. Although there were very few direct acquisitions of U.S. businesses and industries before the Civil War, foreign investors were well represented in cattle, banking, mining, brewing, finance, insurance, and oil production. Copper mining in Utah, for example, was controlled by British and French firms. The country also owed the rapid development of its infrastructure to foreign investors: in addition to financing the canals, overseas shareholders owned one-quarter of all railroad securities by 1853 and one-third by 1890.

Nothing seemed to discourage foreign investment; wars, depressions, and natural disasters acted only as temporary deterrents. Even the Tariff of 1842, designed to protect the nation's infant industries from foreign competition, encouraged foreign investors, who felt better about the United States as a protected economy.

U.S. leaders acted on the assumption that debt was a necessary component of national growth and began early to accumulate a foreign debt that was staggering. Europeans held half of the entire debt of the federal government by 1807 and one-half of all federal and state debts and securities and one-quarter of all municipal debts and securities by 1845. Concerned about the magnitude of the nation's foreign debt, the House of Representatives decided to investigate the issue. In 1843, the House issued a report estimating that of a total of $231.6 million worth of state bonds, about $150 million were owned by foreign investors. Two-thirds of Pennsylvania's $36 million debt, for example, was held abroad. Alarmed by their mounting debts, many states began to pass laws restricting the ability of state governments to borrow.

Within a few years, the nation's foreign debt suddenly became a much riskier proposition for Europeans than Americans. Until that period, European investors had always felt relatively secure in their purchases of state bonds, assuming that the states could always raise taxes to pay off their debts. They did not anticipate that during the financial crisis of the late 1830s and early 1840s nine states would default and stop paying interest on their loans. Florida, Mississippi, and Michigan went even further and repudiated all or part of their debts. In 1841, even the Bank of the United States defaulted, with 60 percent of its $33 million in stock held by European investors. By 1847, except for Mississippi, Florida, and Arkansas, all the states that had defaulted had resumed interest payments on their bonds or had reached compromises with their creditors.

The Europeans finally concluded that the United States was a poor credit risk and were ready to retreat until the sudden discovery of gold in California in 1849 renewed their interest. The emphasis began to shift in the period from the Civil War to World War I, with the first real influx of direct investments matching the traditional portfolio investments. The U.S. economy was becoming more and more attractive to European investors, who felt they could profit from the country's rapidly expanding domestic market (attributable to immigration flows), decline in transportation costs, and plentiful labor supply. In addition, this period of history was known for the free movement of capital and technology throughout the world. The United States and Australia were viewed as developing nations, while Germany and Great Britain, benefiting from expanded national savings, found themselves with a surplus of capital to invest.

Another important factor also emerged at this time to encourage foreign direct investment: as Americans developed their own industrial capability, they became less dependent on imports. Facing a stiff new competitor in a newly industrialized United States, European manufacturers began to practice "defensive investment" as a last resort to protect their export markets. This led to the creation of the giant multinationals, which emerged from 1870 to 1914 and included Lever Brothers, J. & P. Coats, and English Sewing Cotton from the United Kingdom and Siemens, Nestlé, and Royal Dutch Shell from continental Europe.

Americans also began to invest abroad during this period and to develop their own technology. The cotton gin revolutionized the textile industry, along with other inventions and processes that helped the country's progress toward rapid industrialization. By the 1880s, the United States was the world's leading industrial nation, with 29 percent of the world's total manufacturing output.

Foreign investment continued to pour in unabated until the outbreak of World War I. Foreign capital was crucial in the development of the West: in financing the westward expansion of the railroads and providing credit for land purchases. Huge chunks of western real estate were bought by British and European investors; in fact, American land agents journeyed abroad to stimulate further real estate purchases. Fearful of foreign control of agricultural land, half of the states passed laws in the 1890s restricting foreign ownership in farmland. These laws were virtually unenforceable, and foreigners continued to buy land, aided by the states themselves, who often reimbursed foreign investors with state land when they couldn't pay off their bonds.

By World War I, the United States was the world's leading debtor nation: European direct investments in the United States totaled $17 billion, while outward investment was only $3.5 billion. The war reversed the total investment picture. Many investments were eliminated by the end of the war: Great Britain was forced to liquidate at least 70 percent of its investments to finance the war, while all German-controlled subsidiaries were seized by the United States when it entered the war in 1917. After the war, the United States became a creditor nation for the first time in history, maintaining that position until 1985, when the country reverted back to debtor status.

Bibliography

Background sources for Appendix A include the following:

Adler, Dorothy R., and Muriel E. Hidy, eds. *British Investment in American Railways, 1834–1898.* Charlottesville, Va.: The University Press of Virginia, 1970.

Buckley, Peter J., and Brian R. Roberts. *European Direct Investment in the U.S.A. Before World War I.* New York: St. Martin's Press, 1983, chap. 3, pp. 20–42.

Cohen, Benjamin J. *The Question of Imperialism—The Political Economy of Dominance.* New York: Basic Books, 1973.

Fry, Earl H. *The Politics of International Investment.* New York: McGraw-Hill, 1983.

———. *The Financial Invasion of the U.S.A.: A Threat to American Society?* New York: McGraw-Hill, 1980.

Lebergott, Stanley. *The Americans: An Economic Record.* New York: W. W. Norton & Co., 1984.

Ratchford, B. U. *American State Debts.* Durham, N.C.: Duke University Press, 1941.

Solomon, Robert. *The United States as a Debtor in the 19th Century.* Washington, D.C.: The Brookings Institution, 1985.

APPENDIX B

TABLE 1

Major Political Action Committees of U.S. Corporations Wholly Owned by Foreign Companies

POLITICAL ACTION COMMITTEE	FOREIGN INVESTOR	AMOUNT RAISED	AMOUNT SPENT
Shell Oil Energy	Royal Dutch Shell, Netherlands, Britain	$191,433	$186,770
Seagrams Alcoholic beverages	Seagram Co. Ltd., Canada	173,608	162,524
Hoffman-La Roche Drugs	Hoffman-La Roche, Switzerland	74,716	66,404
Ciba-Geigy Drugs	Ciba-Geigy, Canada	72,101	80,995
Santa Fe International Oil and drilling	Kuwait Petroleum	66,429	70,108
Hardee's Fast foods	Imasco Ltd., Canada	51,360	42,600
Budd Co. Railroad equipment	Thyssen, A.G., West Germany	32,961	35,300

SOURCE: Federal Election Commission and *The New York Times*, December 30, 1985. Figures show amounts raised and contributed to 1984 congressional campaigns; some companies carried over money from the 1982 campaign.

TABLE 2

Major Political Action Committees of U.S. Corporations Wholly Owned by Foreign Companies (1986 Congressional Campaigns)

FOREIGN INVESTOR	NATIONALITY	AMOUNT SPENT
Joseph E. Seagram & Sons	Canada	$168,953
Shell Oil Company	Netherlands	160,200
Brown and Williamson	United Kingdom	111,575
Ciba-Geigy Corp.	Switzerland	89,300
McDermott, Inc.	Panama	83,250
Marine Midland Bank	Hong Kong	73,432
Santa Fe International	Kuwait	71,750

SOURCE: Congressional Research Service and the Federal Election Commission.

APPENDIX C

Federal Government Data Collection Efforts

Over two dozen federal agencies in the executive branch collect information on foreign investment in the United States. These are listed below, with brief descriptions of their data collection, followed by the major statutes that govern their work. The final section discusses the data gaps resulting from inadequacies in the laws and their implementation.

FEDERAL AGENCIES

Department of Commerce

Has major responsibility for data collection for foreign direct investment: investment resulting from foreign ownership or control of 10 percent or more equity interest in a U.S. business. All other foreign investment is categorized as portfolio investment, which is tracked primarily by the Treasury Department.

BUREAU OF ECONOMIC ANALYSIS (BEA)

Has the primary responsibility for conducting statistical surveys for foreign direct investment. These surveys are published annually in the *Survey of Current Business* and include estimates of U.S. affiliates' balance sheets and income statements; external financial position; property, plant and equipment; employment and employee compensation; U.S. merchandise trade; research-and-development expenditures; and U.S. land owned and leased. Foreign direct investment is only part of the BEA's work; the agency's primary mission is to compile and analyze capital inflows for balance-of-payments and gross-national-products accounts.

When a foreign investor purchases a direct interest in a U.S. business, the BEA collects information on the ownership of the investment, its cost, and selected financial data, including percentage of voting shares and total equity interest, identification of the foreign owner, and whether the foreign owner is government owned or controlled.

Data on transactions between U.S. affiliates and their foreign parent companies are collected on a quarterly basis. These data are used by the agency in preparation for its balance-of-payments accounts and reports on the international investment position of the United

States. Financial and operating data are collected on an annual basis. The BEA collects data by the following specific statistical surveys:

• BE-15 survey of foreign-owned U.S. businesses with total assets, net sales, or net income of $5 million or more.

• BE-13 report on a foreign acquisition, purchase, or establishment of a U.S. business or real estate (one time only, to be filed within forty-five days of the transaction).

• BE-14 report, related to BE-13, to be filed by the U.S. person who assists in the transaction covered by BE-13 or who enters into a joint venture with a foreign investor.

• Periodic benchmark surveys. These cover the direct investment position and related capital and income flows and a wide range of operating and financial data of U.S. affiliates of foreign direct investors (such as balance sheets, income statements, external financing, employment and compensation, merchandise trade, and other related data). Data from the 1980 benchmark survey are in *Foreign Direct Investment in the United States,* 1980. Data from the 1974 benchmark survey are in *Report to Congress, Foreign Direct Investment in the United States,* volume 2: Report of the Secretary of Commerce: Benchmark Survey, 1974. The next benchmark survey was conducted in 1987; benchmarks after 1987 will be taken every five years.

INTERNATIONAL TRADE ADMINISTRATION, OFFICE OF TRADE AND INVESTMENT ANALYSIS (OTIA)

Conducts research and analysis of global trends in international direct investment for purposes of monitoring and assessing the competitive position of the United States. Monitors foreign direct investment and reports on specific activities with implications for U.S. national interests to CFIUS, Committee on Foreign Investment in the United States, an interagency group. OTIA is restricted to collecting information from public sources, such as government records and secondary sources, including newspapers, magazines, and trade journals.

CENSUS BUREAU

Collects data on the operations of nearly all U.S. businesses, both foreign and domestically owned.

INVEST-IN-THE U.S.A.

Collects and provides information for the purpose of assisting prospective foreign investors.

Department of the Treasury

Treasury has major responsibility for foreign portfolio investment, defined as investment in which there is less than 10 percent direct or indirect foreign control or ownership of a U.S. business.

OFFICE OF INTERNATIONAL INVESTMENT

The Treasury Department is charged with two major reporting

requirements: (1) ongoing data collection on international portfolio capital flows (Treasury International Capital Reporting System) and (2) benchmark surveys every five years of foreign portfolio investment in U.S. securities.

COMPTROLLER OF THE CURRENCY

Collects data on foreign-owned banks.

INTERNAL REVENUE SERVICE (IRS)

Foreign investors must file annual information returns with the IRS documenting their ownership of U.S. real property. These reports, which are confidential, must include identification of ultimate beneficial owners.

Department of Agriculture

NATURAL RESOURCE ECONOMICS DIVISION, ECONOMIC RESEARCH SERVICE

Collects and publishes annually a report to Congress based on data on foreign investment in U.S. farmland and timberland.

The US. Trade Representative (USTR)

ASSISTANT TRADE REPRESENTATIVE FOR INTERNATIONAL INVESTMENT POLICY

This office has responsibility for policy matters regarding trade-related international investment issues. Under the direction of the Trade Act 1984, the USTR must collect information and publish an annual report to Congress on major investment barriers to U.S. outward investment.

Federal Reserve Banks

Collect international portfolio investment data that are published by the Treasury Department's Office of International Banking and Portfolio Investment.

Securities and Exchange Commission (SEC)

Receives reports from beneficial owners of more than 5 percent of the voting equity securities of publicly held U.S. companies. Owners must disclose their citizenship and ownership by filing forms "schedule 13(D)" or "schedule (G)" with the commission. In addition, all persons making tender offers that could result in ownership of more than 5 percent of the equity securities of a publicly held U.S. firm must disclose citizenship—among other data—at the time of the tender offer.

Department of Energy

Monitors foreign investment in the energy sector.

Interagency Groups

COMMITTEE ON FOREIGN INVESTMENT IN THE UNITED STATES (CFIUS)

Chaired by the assistant secretary of the treasury for international affairs, CFIUS is a monitoring body with authority to review foreign investments with major implications for U.S. national interests. Although it does not have the power to approve or disapprove foreign investments, it can (theoretically) focus the attention of the executive branch on potential trouble spots. Other members of the committee are assistant secretaries representing Commerce, State, the Council of Economic Advisers (CEA), and the Special Trade Representative. CFIUS was created by Executive Order 11858 in May 1975 under President Gerald Ford. Other agencies are invited to participate as issues arise.

INTERAGENCY COMMITTEE ON INTERNATIONAL INVESTMENT STATISTICS

Chaired by the Office of Management and Budget, this committee reviews the adequacy of existing data collection and makes recommendations for new information gathering programs.

TRADE POLICY COMMITTEE (TPC)

Chaired by the U.S. Trade Representative, the TPC has primary responsibility for bilateral investment treaties and investment issues, including performance requirements that have an impact on trade and investment. Ten cabinet-level agencies are represented, including the National Security Council.

CABINET COUNCIL ON ECONOMIC AFFAIRS (CCEA)

The highest-level group in the government with international direct investment policy-making responsibilities. Chaired by the secretary of the treasury, seven cabinet secretaries are included, plus the chairman of the CCEA and the Special Trade Representative.

Other Agencies

Data on foreign investment are also collected, to a lesser extent, by other federal agencies. They are:

1. Central Intelligence Agency
2. Commodity Futures Trading Commission
3. Department of Defense
4. Department of the Interior
5. Department of Justice
6. Federal Communications Commission
7. Federal Deposit Insurance Corporation
8. Federal Home Loan Bank Board
9. General Accounting Office
10. Federal Maritime Commission
11. Federal Reserve Board
12. Federal Trade Commission
13. Interstate Commerce Commission.

FEDERAL STATUTES AND EXECUTIVE ORDERS

Foreign Investment Study Act of 1974,
Public Law 93-479, October 26, 1974 (FISA)

Directed the secretary of commerce to conduct overall studies of foreign direct investment and the secretary of the treasury to conduct studies of foreign portfolio investment in the United States. The impetus behind this legislation was the fear that (1) investors from OPEC nations would use their newly acquired oil wealth to purchase U.S. industries and (2) the U.S. would not have sufficient data to monitor this new development.

Executive Order 11858, May 7, 1985

Created the interagency CFIUS and made the Department of Commerce the lead agency in the collection, monitoring, and reporting on foreign direct investment.

International Investment Survey Act of 1976,
Public Law 94-472, October 11, 1976,
and Amended Public Law 97-33, August 7, 1981

Requires the president to set up regular and comprehensive data collection and analysis programs (delegated to the secretaries of treasury and commerce), including surveys on foreign direct and portfolio investment; to publish reports and studies; and to conduct comprehensive benchmark surveys of foreign direct investment every five years. The act was amended in 1981 to allow a one-time exception for the benchmark surveys to be conducted seven years from the last benchmark survey in 1980.

Agricultural Foreign Investment Disclosure Act of 1978,
Public Law 95-460, October 14, 1978. (AFIDA)

Established a national system for monitoring foreign investment in U.S. farmland and timberland and for analyzing the data. AFIDA requires all foreign persons owning U.S. agricultural land to report their holdings to the secretary of agriculture. Exceptions are made for foreign investors holding less than ten acres if gross annual receipts do not exceed $1,000. In addition, the act requires all foreign owners with 5 percent or more interest in an agricultural entity to report their holdings.

Foreign Investment in Real Property Tax Act of 1980,
Public Law 96-499, December 5, 1980

Requires that all foreigners who acquired U.S. real property after July 18, 1980, to file an annual report with the IRS listing their holdings and appraised worth. If foreigners wish to avoid disclosure, they may establish an escrow account or security agreement to cover anticipated capital gains.

DATA GAPS: SELECTED PROBLEMS
IDENTIFIED BY SPECIFIC AGENCY

Department of Commerce
BUREAU OF ECONOMIC ANALYSIS

The data are collected and published in aggregate form. Names of specific investors and their companies are kept confidential, by law. No one can access this background information, even members of Congress and federal agencies, including offices in the Department of Commerce. Some statistical material is also withheld and can be identified by small capital Ds in parentheses throughout the charts. The reason: Even some aggregate statistical data can reveal trade secrets or privileged information about specific companies (see Appendix D).

Some critics fear that the BEA has missed some aggregate data, as well, due to loopholes in the law that preserved the anonymity of foreign investors. Before the BEA issued new rules (April 24, 1981) making investor anonymity more difficult, it was possible for a foreign investor to work through an intermediary and thus hide his identity. The new rules were encouraged, no doubt, by the Rosenthal Committee's hearings in 1980, which compared the BEA's charts with a list of holdings by investors from OPEC countries. Of eighty-two known OPEC investments, thirty-four could not possibly have fit into any of the BEA's categories; therefore, according to the committee's calculations, the agency missed at least thirty-four out of eighty-two foreign investments. The Rosenthal Committee concluded that the BEA had also understated by a significant amount the total assets owned by all foreign investors. The reason for this was that the BEA calculated only the "amount of funds brought into the United States to acquire property or other assets, and not the value of the assets purchased here, the money which was borrowed here, or the money raised here as equity."

OFFICE OF TRADE AND INVESTMENT ANALYSIS

This agency can compile its information only from public sources, such as newspapers, magazines, and government documents. It is prohibited from accessing the data collected by the BEA. In fact, the Department of Commerce feels so insecure about the data from this office that some of the OTIA's publications include the caveat that the Department of Commerce is not responsible for inaccuracies or information gaps.

U.S. Department of Agriculture

The act governing the USDA's foreign investment reporting contains a loophole that affects the accuracy of the data collection: the department is prohibited from investigating beyond three layers of incorporation, making it relatively easy for foreign investors to mask their identity as well as their nationality through dummy corporations.

Department of the Treasury

In order to attract increased investments in U.S. securities from the Middle East, Secretary of the Treasury William Simon agreed in 1975 to give investors from OPEC nations, primarily Kuwait and Saudi Arabia, preferential treatment by not disclosing investments from those nations on a country-by-country basis. Instead, the Treasury Department has published those investments under aggregate categories that mask the country of origin, such as Other Asia, Other Africa, and Middle East OPEC.

Securities and Exchange Commission

The SEC organizes its data under the name of the U.S. corporation. This means that each company would have to be checked separately to determine foreign ownership, a task so onerous as to limit the usefulness of SEC files for the purpose of data collection in this area of inquiry.

DATA GAPS: GENERAL PROBLEMS

Real Estate

No federal agency collects or analyzes data relating to urban and residential real estate.

Shortfall of Funds in the Current Account Balance

Known as "errors and omissions," $100 billion was missing from the 1979–83 tally. The figure in 1985 added up to $32 billion, or nearly the amount of that year's current account deficit. Critics attribute these shortfalls to inadequate data collection; defenders of the current system argue that these figures are insignificant and represent only a small fraction of the total amount of foreign investment in the country. Other observers say that the missing funds represent laundered money, an underground economy, or noncompliance by American or foreign-owned businesses that may be borrowing money secretly from overseas.

Bibliography

Material for Appendix C was collected from the following sources:

McNamara, Diane E. "Foreign Direct Investment in the United States: Disclosure Regulations." *Georgia Journal of International and Comparative Law,* vol. 12, spring 1982, pp. 193–207.

U.S. Congress, Committee on Energy and Commerce, Subcommittee on Telecommunications, Consumer Protection and Finance. "Disclosure of Foreign Investment in the United States." May 8, 1986, Washington, D.C.: U.S. Government Printing Office, 1986.

U.S. Congress, Committee on Government Operations. "The Adequacy of the Federal Response to Foreign Investment in the United States." August 1, 1980, Washington, D.C.: U.S. Government Printing Office, 1980.

U.S. Department of Commerce, International Trade Administration. "International Direct Investment—Global Trends and the U.S. Role." Washington, D.C.: U.S. Government Printing Office, August 1984.

APPENDIX D

TABLE 1

Nonbank U.S. Affiliates of Foreign Corporations—Selected Data, 1984

	Millions of dollars				Number of employees	Thousands of acres		Gross book value of property, plant, and equipment	Millions of dollars		
	Total assets	Sales	Net income	Employee compensation		Land owned	Mineral rights owned and leased		Expenditures for new plant and equipment	U.S. exports shipped by affiliates	U.S. imports shipped to affiliates
All industries	602,522	593,571	9,605	73,155	2,714,295	13,298	63,230	269,462	25,225	58,186	100,189
Mining	11,234	6,073	−354	1,314	32,603	634	4,873	9,526	452	796	174
Petroleum	70,547	71,820	3,096	4,916	125,441	1,018	40,961	70,247	5,205	1,313	6,272
Manufacturing	154,256	176,395	4,047	41,578	1,381,504	5,784	14,517	101,927	9,740	13,078	18,172
Food and kindred products	14,911	18,319	555	3,253	146,255	88	(P)	5,724	763	463	1,727
Chemicals and allied products	55,751	61,232	2,443	13,499	406,630	893	(P)	47,768	4,154	5,240	4,304
Industrial chemicals and synthetics	39,196	42,524	2,094	9,236	231,691	717	(P)	36,807	3,093	4,226	3,086
Drugs	5,015	5,162	17	1,497	48,236	14	0	2,919	359	348	425
Soap, cleaners, and toilet goods	3,832	5,372	198	991	29,513	4	0	1,552	262	190	189
Agricultural chemicals	6,493	6,987	−150	(P)	(P)	149	824	5,784	375	426	509
Other	1,216	1,187	−17	(P)	(P)	9	2	704	65	50	94
Primary and fabricated metals	20,795	23,534	−247	5,290	157,038	485	(P)	15,413	816	1,304	2,684
Primary metal industries	15,740	17,588	−193	3,351	95,738	476	(P)	12,160	516	957	2,354
Fabricated metal products	5,054	5,947	−54	1,939	61,300	9	0	3,253	300	347	330
Machinery	27,717	31,594	674	9,012	308,910	69	(P)	10,938	1,655	3,534	5,205
Machinery, except electrical	12,487	13,433	288	3,869	125,193	58	(P)	4,551	459	1,554	1,787
Electric and electronic equipment	15,230	18,160	386	5,143	183,717	11	(P)	6,386	1,196	1,981	3,418

TABLE 1
(Continued)

	Millions of dollars					Thousands of acres		Millions of dollars			
	Total assets	Sales	Net income	Employee compensation	Number of employees	Land owned	Mineral rights owned and leased	Gross book value of property, plant, and equipment	Expenditures for new plant and equipment	U.S. exports shipped by affiliates	U.S. imports shipped to affiliates
Other manufacturing	35,081	41,715	623	10,524	362,671	4,249	494	22,085	2,352	2,536	4,251
Textile products and apparel	1,896	2,596	64	647	34,624	11	0	1,109	101	69	141
Lumber, wood, furniture, and fixtures	1,226	1,091	-18	286	14,158	874	0	744	30	140	188
Paper and allied products	7,256	6,230	260	1,550	43,094	8	(D)	5,862	445	357	402
Printing and publishing	4,845	6,247	105	1,774	65,843	8	(D)	2,465	345	99	326
Rubber and plastics products	1,661	2,289	54	523	20,163	9	1	1,123	160	73	253
Stone, clay, and glass products	8,145	7,992	85	2,098	67,860	162	(D)	6,118	390	230	225
Transportation equipment	6,380	10,535	-26	2,404	65,699	6	(D)	3,044	607	1,149	1,948
Instruments and related products	1,729	2,421	-74	615	24,118	3	0	665	74	230	441
Other	1,943	2,315	26	628	27,112	10	(D)	954	199	189	326
Wholesale trade	67,954	228,220	1,822	8,146	287,365	313	(D)	15,485	1,823	40,539	72,478
Motor vehicles and equipment	16,876	55,715	1,500	1,949	62,221	(D)	(D)	4,648	600	1,255	29,311
Metals and minerals, except petroleum	10,769	51,540	-38	634	19,619	6	(D)	1,400	172	10,778	12,052
Other durable goods	24,267	57,771	290	3,560	126,484	(D)	33	4,738	724	1,876	19,903
Farm product raw materials	8,030	41,516	-30	756	26,345	59	9	1,910	96	22,888	5,295
Other nondurable goods	8,012	21,678	101	1,248	52,696	64	(D)	2,789	232	1,742	5,916
Retail trade	18,071	35,835	604	5,912	457,049	13	0	9,533	1,248	442	1,161
Food stores and eating and drinking places	6,813	19,846	206	2,838	238,579	5	0	4,403	612	13	17
Retail trade, nec	11,258	15,990	398	3,074	218,470	7	0	5,130	636	429	1,144
Finance, except banking	144,010	21,289	615	2,501	42,523	3	(D)	1,744	667	(D)	(D)
Insurance	55,719	21,623	-22	1,572	61,973	13	0	2,053	291	(D)	(D)
Real estate	54,274	11,797	446	576	27,192	2,515	106	42,607	4,003	(D)	(D)
Other industries	26,458	20,518	-652	6,640	298,645	3,006	(D)	16,345	1,797	(D)	(D)
Agriculture	2,205	947	-92	140	9,264	1,420	(D)	1,891	129	53	(D)
Forestry and fishing	251	83	-1	4	145	1,393	21	210	11	4	21
Construction	4,065	5,983	-65	1,284	42,915	21	1	1,454	149	64	(D)
Transportation	3,456	3,909	-6	1,638	53,100	108	(D)	2,352	176	(D)	(D)
Communication and public utilities	1,714	689	-94	201	9,460	6	2	1,310	199	(D)	(D)
Services	14,768	8,906	-394	3,374	183,741	58	(D)	8,529	1,133	169	9

(D)Suppressed to avoid disclosure of data of individual companies

*Less than $500,000 (±) or 500 acres.

SOURCE: Bureau of Economic Analysis, Department of Commerce, Survey of Current Business, May 1987.

TABLE 2

Capital Expenditures by Majority-Owned Foreign Affiliates of U.S. Companies, 1978–86

| | Percent change from preceding year | | | | | | | | | | Billions of dollars | | | | | | | | | | |
| | Actual expenditures | | | | | | Latest plans[1] | | Earlier plans[1] | | Actual expenditures | | | | | | | Latest plans[1] | | Earlier plans[1] | |
	1979	1980	1981	1982	1983	1984[1]	1985	1986	1984	1985	1978	1979	1980	1981	1982	1983	1984[1]	1985	1986	1984[1]	1985
Total	25	30	3	(*)	-18	-4	15	2	4	13	26.1	32.6	42.4	43.7	43.8	36.0	34.7	39.9	40.9	37.5	42.5
By industry																					
Mining	51	89	2	-47	-34	37	24	19	41	33	.4	.7	1.3	1.3	.7	.5	.6	.8	.9	.6	.8
Petroleum	16	34	-2	25	-21	-9	18	3	4	7	9.5	11.0	14.8	15.8	19.7	15.5	14.1	16.6	17.2	16.2	17.3
Manufacturing	29	27	-2	-13	-18	-2	16	1	6	22	12.0	15.4	19.5	19.2	16.8	13.7	14.0	16.2	16.5	14.5	17.7
Food and kindred products	25	29	-7	-5	-10	2	14	-5	10	21	.9	1.2	1.5	1.3	1.3	1.2	1.2	1.4	1.3	1.3	1.5
Chemicals and allied products	38	14	(*)	-6	-16	12	13	14	10	16	1.9	2.6	3.0	3.0	2.8	2.3	2.6	3.0	3.4	2.5	3.0
Primary and fabricated metals	11	-9	-9	-8	-3	12	-11	-27	20	-3	.6	.6	.9	.8	.9	1.0	1.0	.9	.6	1.1	1.0
Machinery, except electrical	31	18	-9	-4	-23	-15	14	10	3	19	3.6	4.7	5.6	5.1	4.9	3.8	3.2	3.7	4.0	3.4	4.1
Electric and electronic equipment	26	24	-10	-6	-23	25	-1	10	-4	18	.9	1.1	1.3	1.2	1.2	1.5	1.5	1.5	1.5	1.5	1.7
Transportation equipment	54	49	18	-33	-25	15	28	(*)	3	47	1.9	2.9	4.4	5.2	3.4	2.6	2.5	3.2	3.2	2.7	3.9
Other manufacturing	3	29	-13	-8	-23	15	27	-6	24	19	2.1	2.2	2.8	2.5	2.3	1.8	2.1	2.6	2.5	2.1	2.5
Trade	37	25	13	-11	-7	-6	12	-1	19	12	1.9	2.6	3.2	3.7	3.3	3.0	3.5	3.9	4.0	3.5	3.9
Finance (except banking), insurance, and real estate**	49	7	-13	4	-47	-6	11	-2	-18	12	.3	.3	.4	.4	.4	.4	.4	.2	.2	.2	.4
Other industries	22	28	5	-13	-4	-6	-5	-1	-3	35	1.8	2.1	2.7	2.9	2.5	2.4	2.3	2.1	2.1	2.3	2.3
By area																					
Developed countries	25	29	-2	-4	-16	(*)	15	3	8	12	19.8	24.8	31.9	31.3	30.0	25.3	25.3	29.1	29.8	27.2	30.5
Canada	20	29	-2	-9	-12	2	28	3	11	16	5.4	6.5	8.3	8.1	7.4	6.5	6.6	8.5	8.5	7.2	8.4
Europe	30	27	-4	-3	-15	-1	11	3	7	11	12.6	16.4	20.8	20.1	19.5	16.5	16.4	18.1	18.3	17.8	19.0
European Communities (9)	28	27	-9	-4	-11	-1	8	1	5	11	10.9	14.0	17.8	16.2	15.5	13.7	13.5	15.1	15.8	14.4	15.9
France	26	23	-9	(*)	-4	-4	12	6	-6	15	1.4	1.8	2.2	1.9	1.9	1.8	1.8	2.0	2.0	1.7	2.0
Germany	28	17	-15	-9	-4	-7	8	6	-1	20	2.6	3.4	3.9	3.1	3.1	2.8	2.8	3.1	3.1	2.9	3.5
United Kingdom	27	30	-6	-5	-20	10	11	8	3	3	4.7	6.0	8.0	7.5	7.1	5.7	6.1	6.7	7.3	6.5	6.7
Other	31	28	-8	-2	-4	-8	18	-4	17	15	2.2	3.4	3.7	3.4	3.3	3.2	2.9	3.5	3.3	3.2	3.7
Other	42	26	28	3	-30	-8	-8	-5	-6	-6	1.7	2.4	3.0	4.0	3.9	.6	2.9	2.6	2.5	2.1	3.1
Japan	15	42	-11	17	-33	21	24	11	19	34	.6	1.3	1.9	.8	.9	.6	.8	.9	1.0	.7	1.0
Australia, New Zealand, and South Africa**	7	40	22	-2	-28	-8	28	4	-2	35	1.2	1.3	1.8	2.2	2.2	1.6	1.5	1.9	1.9	1.6	2.1

TABLE 2 (Continued)

	Percent change from preceding year										Billions of dollars											
	Actual expenditures						Latest plans¹		Earlier plans²		Actual expenditures							Latest plans¹		Earlier plans²	
	1979	1980	1981	1982	1983	1984¹	1985	1986	1984	1985	1978	1979	1980	1981	1982	1983	1984¹	1985	1986	1984	1985
Developing countries	20	38	23	13	-20	-10	15	3	-2	17	5.5	6.6	9.0	11.1	12.5	10.1	9.1	10.4	10.7	9.8	11.5
Latin America	27	42	24	-8	-36	12	23	5	18	23	2.5	3.2	4.6	5.7	5.2	3.3	3.7	4.5	4.7	3.9	4.8
Other Africa	12	44	25	54	-23	-23	24	2	-14	18	.8	.9	1.3	1.6	2.5	1.9	1.5	1.8	1.9	1.6	1.9
Middle East	-27	-10	-24	40	3	-10	-6	-7	-10	-6	1.1	.8	.7	.5	.7	.8	.7	.6	.6	.7	.6
Other Asia and Pacific	52	47	33	23	(*)	-20	6	-2	-12	14	1.1	1.7	2.5	3.3	4.1	4.1	3.3	3.4	3.5	3.6	4.1
International	51	22	-8	-5	-45	-49	21	-17	-37	22	.8	1.2	1.5	1.4	1.3	.7	.4	.4	.4	.4	.5
Addenda: European Communities (10)⁴				-4	-11	-1	12	4	5	10				16.2	15.5	13.7	13.6	15.2	15.8	14.4	15.9
OPEC⁵	-2	13	14	46	-9	-32	12	2	-22	14	1.9	1.9	2.1	2.4	3.5	3.2	2.1	2.4	2.4	2.5	2.8

*Less than 0.5 percent (±).

1. Based on the BEA survey taken in June 1985.
2. Based on the BEA survey taken in December 1984.
3. European Communities (9) comprises Belgium, Denmark, France, Germany, Ireland, Italy, Luxembourg, Netherlands, and the United Kingdom.
4. European Communities (10) comprises European Communities (9) and Greece.
5. OPEC comprises Algeria, Ecuador, Gabon, Indonesia, Iran, Iraq, Kuwait, Libya, Nigeria, Qatar, Saudi Arabia, Venezuela, and the United Arab Emirates.

NOTE.—Estimates are for majority-owned nonbank foreign affiliates of nonbank U.S. parents.

SOURCE: Bureau of Economic Analysis, Department of Commerce, Survey of Current Business, September 1985.

TABLE 3

Nonbank U.S. Affiliates by Country and Industry of Ultimate Beneficial Owner—Selected Data, 1985

	Millions of dollars				Number of employees	Thousands of acres		Millions of dollars			
	Total assets	Sales	Net income	Employee compensation		Land owned	Mineral rights owned and leased	Gross book value of property, plant, and equipment	Expenditures for new plant and equipment	U.S. exports shipped by affiliates	U.S. imports shipped to affiliates
All countries, all industries	736,231	630,113	5,454	79,869	2,853,590	14,584	60,708	293,560	28,429	56,398	111,735
By country											
Canada	114,719	77,232	1,218	14,606	527,566	3,329	20,159	67,665	6,348	4,175	6,915
Europe	354,363	335,469	3,888	49,413	1,805,956	9,131	31,479	172,528	15,537	23,726	39,789
European Communities (10)	266,576	282,678	3,468	40,716	1,507,591	7,488	30,935	154,500	13,834	20,276	32,784
Belgium	5,915	7,545	133	765	39,395	119	(D)	4,551	404	132	988
Denmark	1,267	1,683	-15	339	18,744	(D)		646	58	56	443
France	29,956	43,705	-515	5,340	163,768	1,344	2,089	16,364	1,355	11,128	3,755
Germany	51,231	64,079	969	10,599	406,734	855	1,557	26,493	2,740	3,158	12,794
Greece	549	319	98	(D)	(D)	95	0	244	17	0	(D)
Ireland	917	2,125	-21	387	15,513	(D)	129	580	63	2	(D)
Italy	4,415	4,402	-304	481	13,620	80	410	2,318	377	963	810
Luxembourg	1,215	1,308	-20	(D)	(D)	22	(D)	665	87	70	397
Netherlands	57,901	46,651	1,425	6,248	213,038	450	10,042	43,969	3,425	1,672	4,446
United Kingdom	113,209	110,861	1,717	16,333	628,373	4,474	544	58,670	5,310	3,096	9,119
Other Europe	87,787	52,792	420	8,698	298,365	1,643		18,028	1,703	3,450	7,005
Austria	1,050	740	-229	104	3,812	40	0	508	35	48	228
Finland	1,117	(D)	(D)	(D)	(D)	2	0	570	117	17	51
Liechtenstein	1,785	(D)	(D)	(D)	(D)	608	0	1,171	35	14	81
Norway	818	804	-15	155	4,621	7	17	362	18	41	166
Spain	400	513	21	70	3,402	94	(D)	164	(D)	(D)	64
Sweden	8,309	11,622	156	1,549	51,876	11	(D)	2,641	382	453	3,233
Switzerland	73,898	34,451	456	6,077	198,593	876	323	12,515	1,080	2,847	2,781
Other	409	762	(D)	57	2,407	5	0	97	8	31	400
Japan	63,637	152,072	1,255	5,991	208,601	126	(D)	18,436	2,960	22,753	57,752
Australia, New Zealand, and South Africa	104,643	23,119	365	2,739	71,148	282	(D)	6,996	811	2,970	2,392
Latin America	16,164	17,071	-1,034	3,400	122,569	947	4,491	10,168	1,176	1,453	2,120
South and Central America	7,337	7,790	-201	1,636	46,877	717	193	4,736	442	726	1,259
Argentina	258	100	-4	6	283	30	(D)	176	29	7	(D)
Brazil	210	396	-14	14	430	8	(D)	57	6	109	97
Mexico	1,401	1,010	-29	119	3,764	274	(D)	882	130	60	358
Panama	4,103	4,254	-149	1,425	38,736	257	(D)	2,720	203	(D)	504
Venezuela	782	1,238	-3	34	1,751	88	5	487	46	5	(D)
Other	623	792	-2	39	1,913	61	0	414	27	(D)	219

TABLE 3
(Continued)

	Millions of dollars				Number of employees	Thousands of acres		Gross book value of property, plant, and equipment	Millions of dollars		
	Total assets	Sales	Net income	Employee compensation		Land owned	Mineral rights owned and leased		Expenditures for new plant and equipment	U.S. exports shipped by affiliates	U.S. imports shipped to affiliates
Other Western Hemisphere	8,788	9,281	−833	1,764	75,692	230	4,298	5,432	734	727	860
Bahamas	1,219	1,286	−118	202	12,107	38	(*)	670	87	(*)	124
Bermuda	2,255	3,894	−33	271	29,066	57	4,092	836	255	55	394
Netherlands Antilles	4,837	3,767	−690	1,187	29,457	109	200	3,673	367	(*)	336
United Kingdom Islands, Caribbean	451	315	8	96	4,827	23	0	233	22	8	5
Other	26	19	(*)	8	235	3	0	20	2	(*)	2
Middle East	59,261	9,246	−333	2,145	50,164	516	1,410	12,266	1,055	434	279
Israel	1,373	530	13	81	2,797	1	(*)	100	31	80	219
Other	57,888	8,716	−346	2,063	47,367	515	1,410	12,167	1,024	354	60
Kuwait	43,214	4,208	−319	1,107	20,532	379	(*)	6,951	474	(*)	0
Lebanon	1,053	692	−113	153	5,874	27	(*)	556	30	56	(*)
Saudi Arabia	12,106	3,276	97	696	16,180	97	(*)	3,415	406	206	(*)
United Arab Emirates	724	155	−6	20	936	3	0	700	33	(*)	(*)
Other	792	385	−5	88	3,845	9	0	545	82	4	(*)
Other Africa, Asia, and Pacific	9,115	9,614	−241	688	26,508	220	34	4,140	427	637	2,389
Other Africa	241	117	−23	22	1,234	44	21	218	10	15	5
Other Asia and Pacific	8,874	9,497	−218	666	25,274	177	13	3,923	408	623	2,383
Hong Kong	4,696	2,554	−79	436	16,972	113	13	2,433	253	49	527
Philippines	436	484	−25	37	767	5	0	120	20	21	180
South Korea	1,915	2,420	−69	80	2,889	3	0	188	33	531	1,503
Other	1,826	4,040	−45	113	4,646	58	(*)	982	101	22	174
United States	14,329	6,290	335	887	41,078	31	(*)	1,360	114	250	99
Addendum—OPEC	57,171	9,072	−229	1,871	41,031	576	(*)	11,770	968	292	93
By industry											
Government	64,029	22,076	−987	4,535	110,951	1,581	3,690	20,0⁰ᵃ	1,470	1,667	2,609
Individuals, estates, and trusts	86,664	80,106	383	10,438	464,210	7,152	2,084	43,386	3,673	9,535	4,893
Petroleum	70,163	55,515	1,737	4,717	109,825	939	35,643	70,241	4,987	1,580	5,535
Agriculture	833	4,405	−16	148	6,157	881	(*)	339	37	(*)	(*)
Mining	(*)	19,088	174	2,066	44,843	517	3,062	6,191	403	2,558	2,575
Construction	5,540	5,871	−58	991	32,218	33	8	2,268	215	33	295
Manufacturing	155,864	197,474	3,744	34,108	1,136,152	1,925	(*)	85,491	9,073	11,304	55,402
Transportation, communication, and public utilities	(*)	8,023	−83	2,311	74,141	215	(*)	6,452	828	265	719
Wholesale and retail trade	33,166	131,056	940	5,144	292,766	38	123	9,416	1,344	20,185	34,329
Banking	23,353	20,138	180	595	18,840	142	107	1,049	89	14	237
Holding companies	46,601	50,437	−1,167	10,032	361,446	737	3,466	24,534	2,823	7,120	4,109
Other finance and insurance	110,516	24,429	637	2,773	89,488	42	103	5,103	843	(*)	(*)
Real estate	23,223	6,632	78	521	23,876	364	(*)	17,184	2,472	(*)	58
Services	6,051	4,862	−108	1,490	88,677	18	(*)	1,804	171	272	261

ᵃSuppressed to avoid disclosure of data of individual companies.
*Less than $500,000 (±) or 500 acres.

SOURCE: Bureau of Economic Analysis, Department of Commerce, Survey of Current Business, May 1987.

TABLE 4

The 100 Largest Foreign Investments in the United States

Rank	Foreign investor	Country	US investment	% owned	Industry	Revenue (millions)	Net income (millions)	Assets (millions)
1	Seagram Co Ltd*	Canada	EI du Pont de Nemours*	23%	chemicals, energy	$29,239	$1,118.0	$25,140
			Joseph E Seagram & Sons	100	alcoholic beverages	1,810	247.0	5,792
						31,049		
2	Royal Dutch/Shell Group*	Netherlands/UK	Shell Oil	100	energy	20,477	1,650.0	26,528
			Scallop Corp	100	energy services			
			Billiton Exploration	100	metals	1,500E	NA	NA
			Billiton Metals	100	metals			
			Other companies	100	metals, coal			
						21,977E		
3	British Petroleum Plc*	UK	Standard Oil*	55	energy	13,002	308.0	18,330
			BP North America Inc	100	energy	4,871	194.1	3,470
						17,873		
4	Mitsui & Co Ltd*	Japan	Mitsui & Co (USA)	100	trading company	8,470E	30.1	2,918
			Alumax	45	aluminum	1,887	62.9	1,713
						10,357E		
5	B.A.T. Industries Plc*	UK	BATUS Inc	100	multicompany	5,087	164.0	4,517
	Imasco Ltd	Canada	Peoples Drug Stores	100	drug stores	1,327	NA	NA
			Imasco USA	100	fast food	1,094	NA	NA
	Eagle Star Holdings	UK	Eagle Star Insurance	100	insurance	61	−13.2	116
						7,569		
6	Tengelmann Group	Germany	Great A&P Tea*	53	supermarkets	6,615	56.1	1,664
7	Régie Nationale des Usines Renault	France	American Motors*	46	automotive	4,040	−125.3	2,001
			Mack Trucks*	42	automotive	2,063	−59.8	1,062
						6,103		
8	Nestlé	Switzerland	Carnation	100	food	2,500E	NA	NA
			Nestlé Enterprises	100	food, restaurants	2,500E	NA	NA
			Hills Brothers	100	coffee	415	NA	NA
			Alcon Laboratories	100	optical products	350E	NA	NA
			MJB	100	coffee	151	NA	NA
						5,916E		

Rank	Foreign investor	Country	US investment	% owned	Revenue (millions)	Net income (millions)	Assets (millions)
9	Beneficiaries of US Philips Trust*	Netherlands	North American Philips*	58	4,395	81.5	2,643
			Signetics	100	450E	NA	NA
					4,845E		
10	Volkswagenwerk AG*	Germany	Volkswagen of America	100	4,326	NA	NA
11	Unilever*	Netherlands	Lever Brothers	100	2,099	38.5	NA
			Thomas J Lipton	100	1,270	80.4	778
			National Starch & Chem	100	880	66.0	654
					4,249		
12	Hanson Trust Plc*	UK	Hanson Industries	100	1,850	110.9	1,261
			SCM	100	2,175	41.8	1,361
					4,025		
13	Bayer AG	Germany	Mobay Chemical	100	1,599	77.1	1,215
			Miles Laboratories	100	1,178	20.2	961
			Agfa-Gevaert	100	422	NA	NA
			Helena Chemical Company	100	410	NA	98
			Compugraphic Corp*	81	401	22.0	330
					4,010		
14	Bell Canada Enterpr*	Canada	Northern Telecom Inc*	100	2,878	NA	1,869
	Northern Telecom Ltd*	Canada	Great Lakes Transmission	50	287	25.2	373
	Trans Canada Pipeline*	Canada	Northern Border Pipeline	30	244	58.7	1,189
					3,409		
15	Anglo Amer of S Africa*	South Africa	Engelhard Corp*	30	2,264	42.7	936
	Minerals & Resources*	Bermuda	Inspiration Resources (US)*	60	1,056	291.4	731
	Charter Consol*	UK	National Mine Service*	51	62	18.4	NA
					3,382		
16	Générale Occidentale SA	France	Grand Union	100	2,612	20.5	592
	General Oriental	Br W Indies	Crown Zellerbach	100	592	NA	NA
					3,204		
17	Mitsubishi Corp*	Japan	Mitsubishi Intl Corp	100	2,950E	NA	NA
18	Electrolux AB*	Sweden	White Consolidated	100	1,946	34.1	1,140
			Dometic Inc	100	891	NA	439
					2,837		
19	Franz Haniel & Cie	Germany	Scrivner Inc	100	2,800	NA	NA
20	BASF Group	Germany	BASF Corporation	100	2,568	30.0	2,277

*Publicly traded in the U.S. in shares or ADRs. E Estimate. NA Not available.   Note: Some foreign investors in the list own U.S. companies indirectly through companies in italics.

Rank	Foreign investor	Country	US investment	% owned	Industry	Revenue (millions)	Net income (millions)	Assets (millions)
21	Group Bruxelles Lambert	Belgium	Drexel Burnham Lambert	26	finance	2,500	350.0E	33,051
22	Hongkong & Shanghai Banking Corp*	Hong Kong	Marine Midland Banks*	51	banking	2,495	125.1	23,386
23	Canadian Pacific Ltd*	Canada	Canadian Pacific Ltd USA	100	agricultural prods, minerals	774	NA	1,448
	AMCA Intl Ltd*		Soo Line Corp*	56	railroad	618	-8.7	1,138
		Canada	AMCA US	100	industrial machinery	1,096	NA	544
						2,488		
24	Crédit Suisse	Switzerland	First Boston*	34	investment banking	2,452	130.3	45,531
25	Petrofina SA	Belgium	American Petrofina*	82	energy	2,409	-10.2	1,817
26	Elf Aquitaine Group	France	Elf Aquitaine Inc	100	multicompany	2,215	NA	3,478
			Other companies	50-100	chemicals, drugs, bldg materials	165E	NA	NA
						2,380E		
27	CIBA-GEIGY Ltd	Switzerland	CIBA-GEIGY Corp	100	chemicals, drugs	2,363	NA	NA
28	Delhaize "Le Lion" SA	Belgium	Food Lion*	51	supermarkets	1,866	47.6	440
			Food Giant	100	supermarkets	482	-9.5	56
						2,348		
29	Total CFP	France	Total Petroleum Inc	100	energy	2,325	76.8	811
	Total Petrol NA Ltd*							
30	George Weston Ltd*	Canada	Eastern Fine Paper	100	paper products	438	NA	
			Interbake Inc	100	bakery			
			Stroehmann Bakeries	100	bakery			
	Loblaw Cos*	Canada	Peter J Schmitt	100	food wholesaling	1,657	NA	504
			National Tea	100	supermarkets			
						2,095		
31	Nippon Kokan*	Japan	National Steel	50	steel	2,082	-88.4	1,737
32	Imperial Chemical Industries Plc*	UK	ICI Americas	100	chemicals, drugs	1,600E	NA	NA
			Advanced Materials	100	chemicals	400	NA	NA
			ICI Specialty Chemicals	100	chemicals			
						2,000E		
33	Brascan Ltd*	Canada						
	Noranda Mines Ltd*	Canada	Noranda Inc*	100	aluminum	1,053	NA	1,404
	MacMillan Bloedel*	Canada	MacMillan Bloedel	100	forest products	946	NA	525
						1,999		

Rank	Foreign investor	Country	US investment	% owned	Industry	Revenue (millions)	Net income (millions)	Assets (millions)
34	Schlumberger NV*	Neth Antilles	Schlumberger Technology	100	oilfield sys, electronics	1,983	NA	2,664
35	Alcan Aluminium Ltd*	Canada	Alcan Aluminum	100	aluminum	1,957	42.0	1,110
36	Siemens AG*	Germany	Siemens Communication	100	telecommunications	1,862	−28.0	2,122
			Siemens Components	100	electronic components			
			Siemens Info Systems	100	office equipment			
			Siemens Medical Systems	100	medical equipment			
			Other companies	100	communications			
37	Rio Tinto-Zinc Plc*	UK	US Borax & Chemical	100	mining, chemicals	1,382	NA	1,087
			Penn Glass Sand	100	glass			
			Commonwealth Aluminum	35	aluminum			
	RTZ Pillar Ltd	UK	Indal US	61	building materials	406	NA	218
						1,788		
38	Dalgety Plc	UK	Martin-Brower Co	100	distribution	1,778	NA	3,140
			Modern Maid Food	100	food products			
			Pig Improvement Co	100	pig breeding			
39	Royal Insurance Plc*	UK	Royal USA	100	insurance	1,737	31.6	1,300
40	Hoechst AG*	Germany	American Hoechst	100	chemicals	1,660	5.7	1,300
41	Barclays Plc	UK	BarclaysAmericanCorp	100	financial services	501	35.2	3,391
			Barclays Bank NY	100	banking	1,121	9.7	11,218
			Barclays Bank Calif	100	banking			
						1,622		
42	Vendex International	Netherlands	Dillard Dept Stores*	44	retailing	1,601	66.9	862
43	Ahold NV	Netherlands	BI-LO	100	supermarkets	1,085	NA	NA
			Giant Food Stores	100	supermarkets	483	NA	NA
						1,568		
44	Henkel KGaA	Germany	Clorox	23	household products	1,055	86.1	778
			Loctite Corp	26	chemicals	231	NA	NA
			Henkel Corp	100	chemicals	209	NA	372
			Amchem Products	100	chemicals	54	NA	57
						1,549		
45	Thyssen Group	Germany	Budd Co	100	auto parts	1,377	NA	NA
			Transit America	100	railroad cars	158	NA	NA
						1,535		
46	Grand Metropolitan Plc*	UK	GrandMet USA	100	multicompany	1,486	81.1	1,481
47	BTR Plc*	UK	BTR Inc	100	energy, industrial equip	1,450E	NA	NA

*Publicly traded in the U.S. in shares or ADRs. E: Estimate. NA: Not available.

Note: Some foreign investors in the list own US companies indirectly through companies in italics.

Rank	Foreign investor	Country	US investment	% owned	Industry	Revenue (millions)	Net income (millions)	Assets (millions)
48	Volvo AB*	Sweden	Volvo White Truck	100	automotive	751	18.0	283
			Hamilton Oil Corp*	50	energy	275	26.5	974
			Clark Michigan Co	25	automotive	411	-15.0	272
						1,437		
49	Moore Corp Ltd*	Canada	Moore Business Forms	100	business forms	1,425	NA	824
50	Crownx	Canada	Crown Life Insurance	94	insurance	1,100E	34.0E	2,700E
			Extendicare Group	100	health care	210E	NA	NA
			Crowntek	100	information technology	74E	NA	NA
						1,384E		
51	Sun Life Assurance Co of Canada	Canada	Sun Life (US)	100	insurance	851	-4.1	2,084
			Suncan Equity Services	100	financial services			
			Sun Benefit Services	100	financial services			
			Mass Financial Services	100	financial services	500E	NA	3,700
						1,351E		
52	Genstar Corporation*	Canada	Genstar USA	100	bldg materials, RE dev	1,164	NA	1,051
			Genstar Mortgage	100	financial services	176	NA	448
						1,340		
53	Power Corp of Canada	Canada	Great-West Life Assur	96	insurance	1,317	13.7	3,904
54	Sanyo Electric Co Ltd*	Japan	Fisher Corp	70	audio equipment	866	NA	342
			Sanyo Manufacturing	74	electronics, appliances	389	2.0	150
			Sanyo E&E	48	electronics, appliances	48	NA	39
						1,303		
55	Daimler-Benz Group	Germany	Freightliner	100	automotive	1,302	NA	NA
56	Alusuisse	Switzerland	Consolidated Aluminum	100	aluminum	650E		
			Maremont	100	auto parts	465	-88.0	88.5
			Lonza	100	chemicals			
			Boxal	100	aluminum cans	186		
			Flexible Packaging	100	foil conversion			
						1,301E		
57	Ultramar Plc*	UK	Ultramar America Ltd	100	energy	1,299	NA	564
58	BOC Group Plc*	UK	BOC Group, Inc	100	gases	1,224	NA	NA
			Mountain Medical Equip*	52	medical equipment	36	2.2	NA
						1,260		

Rank	Foreign investor	Country	US investment	% owned	Industry	Revenue (millions)	Net income (millions)[1]	Assets (millions)
59	Commercial Union Assurance Plc	UK	Commercial Union Ins	100	insurance	1,250	-180.1	NA
60	Saban SA / Republic Holding SA	Switzerland / Luxembourg						
61	Montedison Group	Italy	Republic NY Corp*	33	banking	1,245	122.1	15,324
			Himont	86	chemicals	900	52.8	689
			Compo Industries	86	chemicals	168	-4.5	100
			Erbamont*	72	pharmaceuticals	163	8.5	175
						1,231		
62	Nationale-Nederlanden	Netherlands	Nationale-Nederlanden US	100	insurance	1,209	35.1	3,013
63	Manufacturers Life Insurance Co	Canada	Manufacturers Life Ins	100	insurance	1,200E	NA	NA
64	First City Financial Corp	Canada	HH Robertson*	21	construction	614	-32.0	391
			Scovill Inc	100	bldg materials, appliances	554	2.0	782
						1,168		
65	General Accident Fire & Life Plc	Scotland	Gen Accident Ins Amer	100	insurance	1,152	101.7	2,819
			Camden Fire Insurance	100	insurance			
			Penn General Insurance	100	insurance			
			Potomac Ins of Illinois	100	insurance			
66	Saint-Gobain	France	Certain Teed Corp*	57	building materials	1,110	53.4	763
67	Beecham Group Plc*	UK	Beecham	100	drugs, consumer prods	1,100	NA	1,100
			Beecham Cosmetics	100	cosmetics, fragrances			
			Beecham Home Improve	100	home improvement			
67	General Electric Plc*	UK	Picker International	80	medical equipment	700E	NA	NA
			AB Dick	100	office equipment	400E	NA	NA
						1,100E		
69	United Biscuits (Holdings) Plc	UK	Keebler	100	bakery	982	NA	NA
			Specialty Brands	100	food products	86	NA	NA
						1,068		
70	Sandoz Ltd	Switzerland	Sandoz United States Inc	100	multicompany	1,059	NA	NA
71	Lama Holdings	Mideast	Smith Barney	23	financial services	1,015	NA	NA
72	Roche/Sapac	Switzerland	Hoffmann-La Roche	100	drugs, chemicals	1,000E	NA	5,700
72	Kuwait Petroleum	Kuwait	Santa Fe Intl (KPC)	100	energy	1,000E	NA	NA

*Publicly traded in the U.S. in shares or ADRs. E: Estimate. NA: Not available.

Note: Some foreign investors in the list own U.S. companies indirectly through companies in italics.

Rank	Foreign investor	Country	US investment	% owned	Industry	Revenue (millions)	Net income (millions)	Assets (millions)
74	AEGON NV*	Netherlands	Life Investors*	81	insurance	888	44.0	2,138
			National Old Line	100	insurance	96	22.0	338
						984		
75	SNECMA	France	CFM International Inc	50	aviation	972	2.2	473
76	Bank of Tokyo Ltd*	Japan	California First Bank*	77	banking	550	25.6	5,401
			Bank of Tokyo Trust	100	banking	415	25.5	5,379
						965		
77	Canada Development Corp	Canada	Savin Corp*	67	office equipment	430	-102.7	223
			Other companies	100	energy	530	NA	482
						960		
78	Winterthur Swiss Insurance	Switzerland	Republic Finl Services	100	insurance	956	NA	1,200
79	Consolidated Gold Fields Plc*	UK	Newmont Mining*	26	mining	684	-36.4	2,085
			Gold Fields American	100	natural resources	261	-71.0	825
						945		
80	National Westminster Bank Plc	UK	Natl Westminster Bank US	100	banking	931	54.6	9,796
81	Bank of Montreal	Canada	Harris Bankcorp	100	banking	915	57.5	9,245
82	TBG Holdings NV	Netherlands	Electrical Sciences Inc	100	electrical products	900E	NA	NA
			InCom Packaging Inc	100	containers			
			Info Technology Group	100	electronic information			
			Metalink	100	metal products			
			Sterling Fluid Products	100	pumps			
83	Olympia & York Developments Ltd	Canada	Landmark Land*	25	recreation	228	15.3	1,653
	Trizec	Canada	Rouse*	20	property dev, banking	247	9.7	1,191
	Gulf Canada	Canada	Abitibi-Price	90	forest products	413	NA	194
						888		
84	NV AMEV	Netherlands	AMEV Holdings Inc	100	insurance	879	64.0	1,785
85	Fujitsu Ltd*	Japan	Amdahl Corp*	47	electronics	862	24.4	907
86	Honda Motor Co Ltd*	Japan	Honda of America Mfg	100	automotive	850E	NA	NA
87	Otto Versand	Germany	Spiegel Inc	100	catalog retailing	848	13.0	687
88	News Corporation Ltd*	Australia	News America	100	media	829	NA	1,277

Rank	Foreign investor	Country	US investment	% owned	Industry	Revenue (millions)	Net income (millions)	Assets (millions)
89	IFI International SA	Luxembourg	Moog Automotive	100	auto parts		NA	NA
			Chicago Rawhide	100	auto parts		NA	NA
			Incom International	100	industrial components	660E	NA	224
			RC Cement	20	cement	<u>160</u>E 820E		
90	Northern Foods Plc	UK	Prestige Foods	100	meat products	812	NA	224
			Keystone Foods	80	meat and poultry			
90	J Sainsbury Plc*	UK	Shaw's Supermarkets	21	supermarkets	812	11.3	152
92	Sobey Parties	Canada	Hannaford Brothers*	26	food distribution	807	14.4	220
93	Swiss Reinsurance Co	Switzerland	SwissRe Life Insurance	100	insurance	330	−55.6	787
			North Am Reinsurance	100	insurance	266	−51.1	681
			North Am Reassurance	100	insurance	105	−15.4	552
			Other companies	100	insurance	<u>106</u> 807	12.6	431
94	Broken Hill Proprietary	Australia	Utah International	100	energy, mining	600E	NA	NA
			Monsanto Oil Company	100	energy	<u>200</u>E 800E	NA	NA
95	Standard Chartered Bank Group	UK	Union Bank	100	banking	765	47.1	9,038
96	Pilkington Brothers Plc	UK	LOF Glass	100	glass	690	NA	375
			Other companies	25-100	electro-optics	<u>71</u> 761	NA	NA
97	Six European Banks	6 countries	European Amer Bancorp	100	banking	753	10.2	6,655
98	Johnson Matthey Plc	UK	Johnson Matthey Inc	100	printing, refining	750	7.3	431
99	Zurich Insurance Group	Switzerland	Zurich-American Ins	100	insurance	735	−19.6	1,463
100	Promodes	France	Red Food Stores	100	supermarkets	451		
			Houchens	100	supermarkets	208	8.9	165
			Prairie	100	supermarkets	<u>56</u> 715		

*Publicly traded in the U.S. in shares or ADRs. E. Estimate. NA. Not available.

Note: Some foreign investors in the list own U.S. companies indirectly through companies in italics.

SOURCE: *Forbes*, July 28, 1986. Reprinted by permission of *Forbes* magazine, July 28, 1986. © Forbes Inc., 1986.

TABLE 5
Employment of Nonbank U.S. Affiliates—1985

	All countries	Canada	Europe — Total	Europe — France	Europe — Germany	Europe — Netherlands	Europe — United Kingdom	Europe — Switzerland	Japan	Australia, New Zealand, and South Africa	Latin America	Middle East	Other Africa, Asia, and Pacific	United States	Addendum—OPEC
All industries	2,853,590	527,566	1,805,956	163,768	406,734	213,038	628,373	198,593	208,601	71,148	122,569	50,164	26,508	41,078	40,331
Mining	29,057	8,947	14,487	479	4,124	(P)	3,176	387	(P)	(P)	(P)	0	11	0	0
Petroleum	125,270	5,299	107,826	9,536	1,822	(P)	48,840	657	271	(P)	8,632	2,012	(P)	450	(P)
Manufacturing	1,438,882	285,836	941,278	90,872	250,754	91,855	313,679	114,967	71,819	30,601	69,238	9,383	9,182	21,545	4,006
Food and kindred products	151,272	(P)	115,347	5,362	657	3,713	68,440	(P)	4,533	879	924	2,083	(P)	(P)	(P)
Chemicals and allied products	429,690	(P)	299,007	6,513	165,290	22,410	54,782	42,352	3,968	6	(P)	(P)	(P)	0	(P)
Industrial chemicals and synthetics	231,611	(P)	116,738	4,636	48,745	11	38,036	(P)	850	6	8	(P)	(P)	0	(P)
Drugs	49,877	(P)	40,489	(P)	3,553	11	12,458	(P)	(P)	0	(P)	(P)	0	0	0
Soap, cleaners, and toilet goods	30,690	(P)	28,115	40	6,250	0	1,023	5,492	(P)	0	(P)	(P)	0	0	0
Agricultural chemicals	(P)	(P)	(P)	(P)	(P)	(P)	345	23	(P)	0	378	32	(P)	0	32
Other	(P)	497	(P)	103	(P)	(P)	2,920	231	43	6	0	0	(P)	0	(P)
Primary and fabricated metals	167,851	30,900	56,926	6,980	7,729	1,380	19,174	(P)	28,944	15,389	(P)	(P)	128	5,778	(P)
Primary metal industries	104,017	19,742	35,381	3,473	5,002	(P)	9,079	(P)	27,817	13,737	(P)	(P)	0	0	(P)
Fabricated metal products	63,834	11,158	21,545	3,507	2,727	(P)	10,095	2,205	1,127	1,652	(P)	(P)	128	5,746	0
Machinery	308,367	46,159	212,520	15,840	33,439	(P)	62,539	13,602	21,521	1,197	(P)	(P)	1,321	64	734
Machinery, except electrical	115,318	(P)	84,013	12,292	13,014	1,621	33,587	6,441	9,158	1,135	2,452	(P)	552	(P)	0
Electric and electronic equipment	193,049	(P)	128,507	3,548	20,425	(P)	28,952	7,161	12,363	62	(P)	(P)	769	(P)	734
Other manufacturing	381,702	72,142	257,478	56,177	43,639	(P)	108,744	14,883	12,853	13,130	9,974	(P)	4,830	(P)	362
Textile products and apparel	38,456	5,132	21,078	559	4,241	(P)	12,517	2,068	1,292	(P)	(P)	27	11	(P)	0
Lumber, wood, furniture, and fixtures	12,962	1,592	6,245	(P)	4,197	0	0	433	(P)	(P)	(P)	(P)	(P)	(P)	0
Paper and allied products	46,933	7,407	37,618	(P)	1,158	(P)	(P)	(P)	(P)	0	36	(P)	0	(P)	0
Printing and publishing	71,612	38,513	23,352	143	6,341	1,384	11,022	(P)	491	(P)	2,727	8	26	(P)	240
Rubber and plastics products	17,028	1,065	12,963	1,255	3,955	235	4,601	315	1,937	(P)	(P)	(P)	104	0	104
Stone, clay, and glass products	80,812	15,632	59,491	18,510	4,122	55	32,335	1,943	855	3,438	(P)	18	(P)	0	18
Transportation equipment	62,122	1,672	53,364	(P)	10,563	459	(P)	3,551	3,551	0	0	(P)	(P)	0	0
Instruments and related products	26,601	435	22,254	(P)	7,995	39	7,259	4,250	2,149	752	809	(P)	(P)	(P)	0
Other	25,176	694	21,113	2,669	1,067	(P)	11,195	1,638	1,261	(P)	(P)	11	2	0	0

TABLE 5 (Continued)

	All countries	Canada	Europe Total	Of which— France	Germany	Netherlands	United Kingdom	Switzerland	Japan	Australia, New Zealand, and South Africa	Latin America	Middle East	Other Africa, Asia, and Pacific	United States	Addendum— OPEC
Wholesale trade	296,144	21,869	167,345	29,569	51,206	5 105	40,697	12,772	91,864	2,527	3,057	4,407	4,869	206	4,600
Motor vehicles and equipment	71,634	(D)	46,223	(D)	21,436	16	10,386	(D)	21,026	(D)	147	(D)	469	0	(D)
Metals and minerals, except petroleum	20,570	(D)	9,322	(D)	2,724	(D)	2,377	(D)	6,788	(D)	666	275	66	0	(D)
Other durable goods	133,800	8,889	61,546	7,414	15,395	1,571	17,638	4,595	56,683	687	1,418	(D)	3,158	(D)	1,853
Farm product raw materials	20,006	220	15,018	10,467	74	354	563	(D)	4,612	(D)	(D)	0	0	(D)	0
Other nondurable goods	50,134	9,780	35,236	2,878	11,577	(D)	9,733	4,491	2,755	(D)	(D)	24	1,176	(D)	24
Retail trade	479,917	122,833	310,611	12,011	64,417	53,454	117,494	12,653	14,863	7,497	13,245	(D)	4,065	(D)	77
Food stores and eating and drinking places	256,270	81,806	166,730	(D)	(D)	(D)	39,516	7,382	2,803	0	0	5	(D)	(D)	5
Retail trade, nec	223,647	41,027	143,881	(D)	(D)	(D)	77,978	5,271	12,060	7,497	13,245	(D)	(D)	22	72
Finance, except banking	46,233	2,479	16,973	753	417	(D)	11,750	(D)	5,183	(D)	(D)	(D)	475	(D)	(D)
Insurance	69,217	9,850	46,554	278	3,024	11,581	23,854	7,149	(D)	15	0	0	0	(D)	0
Real estate	31,777	18,080	7,649	553	680	1 336	3,633	(D)	1,614	633	942	1,959	841	39	1,794
Other industries	337,093	52,373	193,233	19,717	30,290	7,855	65,250	45,928	22,701	18,628	26,248	14,682	6,962	2,266	12,682
Agriculture	9,742	244	5,768	537	1,041	330	1,976	1,370	1,659	0	1,235	427	(D)	7	297
Forestry and fishing	149	3	141	(D)	6	0	21	(D)	(D)	0	0	0	(D)	0	0
Construction	41,232	2,143	35,685	8,284	14,868	3,440	3,634	(D)	1,384	1,094	326	298	302	0	1
Transportation	58,940	18,163	24,575	2,025	2,025	1 206	(D)	13,779	6,329	497	780	497	2,160	0	64
Communication and public utilities	9,918	5,455	4,437	526	0	0	(D)	0	0	0	(D)	0	(D)	0	0
Services	217,112	26,365	122,627	9,620	12,350	2,879	50,740	26,867	13,329	(D)	23,880	13,460	4,232	(D)	12,320

(D)Suppressed to avoid disclosure of data of individual companies.

SOURCE: Bureau of Economic Analysis, Department of Commerce, *Survey of Current Business,* May 1987.

TABLE 6

Total Assets of Nonbank U.S. Affiliates—1985
[MILLIONS OF DOLLARS]

	All countries	Canada	Europe — Total	Of which — France	Germany	Netherlands	United Kingdom	Switzerland	Japan	Australia, New Zealand, and South Africa	Latin America	Middle East	Other Africa, Asia, and Pacific	United States	Addendum—OPEC
All industries	746,231	114,719	354,363	29,956	51,231	57,901	113,209	73,898	63,637	104,643	16,164	59,261	9,115	14,329	57,171
Mining	11,492	3,121	5,417	(¹)	1,483	(¹)	883	(¹)	(¹)	(¹)	11	0	3	14	0
Petroleum	76,481	5,173	66,352	(¹)	1,359	(¹)	25,604	559	712	689	2,157	694	(¹)	(¹)	798
Manufacturing	170,114	45,300	98,338	10,534	24,154	8,052	33,153	13,752	10,262	4,782	7,429	782	1,563	1,657	533
Food and kindred products	18,658	(¹)	(¹)	597	97	288	5,224	(¹)	504	86	(¹)	93	202	(¹)	(¹)
Chemicals and allied products	61,447	(¹)	(¹)	1,437	14,939	4,045	8,743	5,191	697	4	591	(¹)	17	0	(¹)
Industrial chemicals and synthetics	42,441	(¹)	(¹)	974	7,149	1,019	6,534	(¹)	288	0	2	0	0	0	(¹)
Drugs	5,780	(¹)	4,928	(¹)	413	6	1,793	(¹)	285	0	(¹)	0	0	0	0
Soap, cleaners, and toilet goods	4,622	(¹)	4,479	10	(¹)	0	109	516	(¹)	0	(¹)	4	0	0	4
Agricultural chemicals	6,833	(¹)	6,469	25	(¹)	0	77	3	(¹)	0	53	0	0	0	0
Other	1,771	61	1,259	(¹)	691	(¹)	230	24	(¹)	4	0	0	17	0	0
Primary and fabricated metals	22,275	4,243	7,355	729	960	114	2,920	1,196	4,210	3,172	(¹)	133	(¹)	429	(¹)
Primary metal industries	17,038	3,443	5,777	490	698	(¹)	(¹)	629	4,062	3,047	(¹)	(¹)	0	428	(¹)
Fabricated metal products	5,237	799	1,579	239	262	(¹)	(¹)	238	148	125	(¹)	0	17	1	0
Machinery	29,494	5,381	17,405	1,372	3,843	(¹)	5,569	1,196	2,634	111	(¹)	133	(¹)	18	29
Machinery, except electrical	12,542	(¹)	8,251	1,167	1,394	150	3,263	629	1,297	106	(¹)	(¹)	0	(¹)	0
Electric and electronic equipment	16,952	(¹)	9,154	205	2,449	(¹)	2,306	567	1,337	5	(¹)	(¹)	151	(¹)	29
Other manufacturing	38,240	6,399	26,056	6,400	4,314	(¹)	10,697	1,631	2,217	1,410	479	(¹)	702	(¹)	24
Textile products and apparel	2,385	273	1,283	29	282	(¹)	679	88	101	0	(¹)	(¹)	2	(¹)	0
Lumber, wood, furniture, and fixtures	1,275	130	891	(¹)	259	0	(¹)	(¹)	(¹)	(¹)	(¹)	13	(¹)	0	0
Paper and allied products	6,824	1,303	4,853	(¹)	174	(¹)	3,269	(¹)	580	0	8	(¹)	0	(¹)	0
Printing and publishing	6,205	2,894	2,234	11	687	141	1,027	(¹)	29	(¹)	203	(¹)	17	(¹)	13
Rubber and plastics products	1,512	51	1,196	112	489	(¹)	405	22	226	(¹)	17	0	0	(¹)	(¹)
Stone, clay, and glass products	9,408	(¹)	6,807	2,340	460	18	3,190	563	69	463	(¹)	0	186	(¹)	(¹)
Transportation equipment	6,592	(¹)	5,482	3,321	5	0	610	(¹)	747	0	0	0	0	(¹)	0
Instruments and related products	1,949	37	1,572	80	594	29	447	366	238	42	33	(¹)	(¹)	(¹)	0
Other	2,071	68	1,668	223	(¹)	6	(¹)	129	(¹)	(¹)	13	2	2	(¹)	0

TABLE 6 (Continued)

| | All countries | Canada | Europe | | | | | | Japan | Australia, New Zealand, and South Africa | Latin America | Middle East | Other Africa, Asia, and Pacific | United States | Adden-dum—OPEC |
			Total	France	Germany	Nether-lands	United Kingdom	Switzer-land							
Wholesale trade	76,367	3,863	33,583	5,762	9,962	822	8,546	2,318	34,135	469	904	948	2,190	275	610
Motor vehicles and equipment	20,921	(*)	9,856	(*)	5,389	2	1,283	(D)	10,165	(D)	(D)	(D)	324	0	(D)
Metals and minerals, except petroleum	11,392	710	2,784	410	650	(D)	725	(D)	7,208	164	213	182	132	0	(D)
Other durable goods	27,942	1,141	11,758	790	3,048	(D)	4,476	701	13,400	69	252	(D)	847	(D)	305
Farm product raw materials	7,240	73	4,394	(D)	8	82	536	897	2,686	(D)	(D)	(D)	0	(D)	6
Other nondurable goods	8,872	1,939	4,790	480	867	156	1,526	605	676	178	341	(D)	887	(D)	6
Retail trade	19,664	3,916	13,578	432	2,672	2,897	6,119	337	602	294	682	212	(D)	(D)	13
Food stores and eating and drinking places	7,563	2,067	5,129	246	(D)	(D)	(D)	75	281	0	0	3	(D)	(D)	3
Retail trade, nec	12,101	1,849	8,450	186	(D)	(D)	(D)	262	321	294	682	209	293	4	11
Finance, except banking	223,626	6,193	66,651	3,497	1,252	1,354	13,206	(D)	12,538	(D)	412	(D)	(D)	178	(D)
Insurance	67,449	21,590	33,279	343	4,184	8,440	11,920	(D)	(D)	(D)	329	0	9	(D)	0
Real estate	61,418	21,189	22,698	860	2,896	4,362	9,916	1,926	2,597	582	3,130	8,618	2,445	159	8,441
Other industries	29,620	4,374	14,467	3,620	3,268	790	3,862	1,741	2,160	(D)	1,112	(D)	628	192	(D)
Agriculture	2,272	79	1,422	166	387	41	277	351	97	(D)	454	(D)	41	6	180
Forestry and fishing	272	10	234	(D)	55	0	(D)	23	0	1	13	1	14	0	(D)
Construction	4,542	166	4,062	2,234	890	232	333	172	139	(D)	7	(D)	21	0	3
Transportation	4,266	1,931	1,467	137	116	111	507	476	(D)	(D)	(D)	12	127	9	4
Communication and public utilities	1,732	900	613	(D)	0	1	(D)	0	(D)	0	(D)	0	0	0	0
Services	16,536	1,288	6,669	976	1,821	405	2,154	720	1,425	915	560	5,077	425	178	(D)

(D) Suppressed to avoid disclosure of data of individual companies.

*Less than $500,000.

SOURCE: Bureau of Economic Analysis, Department of Commerce, Survey of Current Business, May 1987.

APPENDIX E

TABLE 1

Foreign Investment in the United States

State	Value of Foreign-Owned Property, Plants, and Equipment: 1981 (in billions)	Direct Jobs Resulting From Foreign Investment 1981	Direct Jobs Resulting From Foreign Investment 1983	Percent Change 1981–83
TX	$ 22.4	172,564	192,787	+ 11.7
CA	19.6	240,774	253,596	+ 5.3
AK	9.6	8,578	6,787	− 20.9
LA	8.2	45,718	49,396	+ 8.0
NY	7.1	204,393	217,150	+ 5.9
NJ	6.4	131,764	135,507	+ 2.8
NC	5.5	86,349	95,353	+ 10.4
IL	5.4	111,850	125,808	+ 12.5
FL	5.4	69,983	84,568	+ 20.8
PA	5.4	129,110	129,818	+ 0.1
SC	5.2	64,898	59,875	− 7.7
OH	5.0	97,018	121,667	+ 25.4
MI	4.1	65,070	66,745	+ 2.6
GA	4.0	73,742	86,014	+ 16.6
WV	3.9	34,835	33,179	− 4.8
TN	3.7	55,285	59,818	+ 8.2
AZ	2.9	29,396	25,828	− 12.1
VA	2.9	49,115	56,859	+ 15.8
MN	2.8	32,536	30,137	− 7.4
AL	2.8	26,501	30,711	+ 15.9
OK	2.6	24,459	27,821	+ 13.7

WA	2.3	25,329	28,646	+13.1
WI	2.2	59,666	63,797	+6.9
CO	2.2	23,961	29,701	+24.0
WY	2.0	4,070	3,833	−5.8
MD	2.0	43,900	44,792	+2.0
MO	1.9	31,123	37,191	+19.5
DE	1.8	35,340	34,688	−1.8
IN	1.8	44,881	47,269	+5.3
UT	1.8	17,188	13,776	−19.9
KY	1.8	25,366	28,750	+13.3
ME	1.6	17,692	21,675	+22.5
MA	1.6	52,578	66,098	+25.7
MS	1.4	10,905	13,515	+23.9
CT	1.2	40,128	40,135	—
MT	1.2	2,830	3,153	+11.4
HI	1.1	16,143	16,198	+0.3
IA	1.1	21,741	19,172	−11.8
ND	1.0	3,255	3,560	+9.4
NM	1.0	8,005	9,214	+15.1
KS	0.9	14,206	14,106	−0.7
OR	0.8	12,281	13,214	+7.6
AR	0.6	17,397	17,112	−1.6
NV	0.5	5,854	5,593	+4.5
NH	0.4	13,355	15,183	+13.7
NE	0.4	5,225	5,605	+6.8
RI	0.4	9,423	11,198	+18.8
VT	0.3	5,889	5,635	−4.3
ID	0.3	3,795	4,512	+18.9
SD	0.3	1,324	1,987	+30.1
U.S. Total	$180.0	2,343,115	2,536,553	+8.3

—indicates a less than 0.1 percent change

SOURCES: U.S. Department of Commerce, cited in *Business America*, May 27, 1985 (1981 Figures); U.S. Department of Commerce, Bureau of Economic Affairs, *Implications of Internationalization of the U.S. Economy*, January 14, 1986 (1983 figures).

TABLE 2

NASDA State Export Program Database State Appropriation, Staff and Foreign Office Comparison: FY84–FY86 Summary Table

STATE	International Budget (State Appropriation)			Number of Staff			Number of Foreign Offices		
	FY86	FY84	CHANGE	FY86	FY84	CHANGE	FY86	FY84	CHANGE
Alabama	$600,000	$600,000	—	18	14	+4	5	5	—
Alaska	790,000	n/a	n/a	11	n/a	n/a	2	1	+1
Arizona	477,900	200,000	+277,900	5	5	—	0	0	—
Arkansas	500,000	400,000	+100,000	11	9	+2	2	1	+1
California	5,700,000	460,000	+5,240,000	14	7	+7	0*	0	—
Colorado	220,000	150,000	+70,000	7	4	+3	2	0	—
Connecticut	625,000	350,000	+275,000	13	9	+4	2	0	+1
Delaware	75,000	n/a	n/a	1	n/a	n/a	0	1	—
Florida	1,586,700	725,000	+861,700	38	36	+2	3	2	+1
Georgia	1,296,200	904,500	+391,700	18	18	—	4	3	+1
Hawaii	225,000	200,000	+25,000	6	5	+1	0	0	—
Idaho	25,000	35,000	−10,000	.7	.5	+.2	0	0	—
Illinois	2,632,000	2,500,000	+132,000	31	31	—	5	4	+1
Indiana	675,800	560,000	+115,800	15	12	+3	3	3	+1
Iowa	500,000	369,800	+130,200	8	6	+2	2	2	+1
Kansas	132,000	82,000	+50,000	6	3	+3	1	0	+1
Kentucky	n/a	838,000	n/a	3	5.5	n/a	2	1	+1
Louisiana	300,000	n/a	n/a	n/a	n/a	n/a	1	1	—
Maine	n/a	n/a	n/a	n/a	.5	n/a	0	0	—
Maryland	1,400,000	n/a	n/a	18	n/a	n/a	2	2	—
Massachusetts	437,500	100,000	+337,500	7	5	+2	0	0	—
Michigan	1,966,600	1,480,600	+486,000	21	21	—	2	2	—
Minnesota	2,202,200	n/a	n/a	41	n/a	n/a	2	2	—

TABLE 2 (Continued)

STATE	International Budget (State Appropriation)			Number of Staff			Number of Foreign Offices		
	FY86	FY84	CHANGE	FY86	FY84	CHANGE	FY86	FY84	CHANGE
Mississippi	400,000	n/a	n/a	9	10	-1	0	0	—
Missouri	900,000	580,000	+320,000	13	10.5	+2.5	2	2.5	-.5
Montana	86,000	68,000	+18,000	1	1	—	1	0	—
Nebraska	n/a	275,000	n/a	2	5	-3	0	0	—
Nevada	160,000	n/a	n/a	.5	.5	n/a	0	0	—
New Hampshire	n/a	7,000	n/a	n/a	1	n/a	0	0	—
New Jersey	1,600,000	635,000	+965,000	10	10	—	0	1	—
New Mexico	n/a	125,000	n/a	n/a	3	n/a	0	5	—
New York	3,040,000	2,500,000	+540,000	38	37	+1	6	5	+
North Carolina	950,000	950,000	—	13	13	—	0	1	+
North Dakota	n/a	80,000	n/a	1	1	—	—	0	—
Ohio	2,500,000	1,900,000	+600,000	39	39	—	2*	2	—
Oklahoma	n/a	500,000	n/a	n/a	11	n/a	—	0	—
Oregon	739,000	529,800	+208,200	14.5	11	+3.5	4	4	-
Pennsylvania	845,000	n/a	n/a	20	12	+8	1	2	+
Rhode Island	275,000	326,500	-51,500	4.5	4.5	—	2	2	—
South Carolina	n/a	375,600	n/a	n/a	7	n/a	0	0	-
South Dakota	51,100	n/a	n/a	1	.5	+.5	0	0	—
Tennessee	575,000	575,000	—	3	3	—	—	—	—
Texas	253,000	308,300	-55,300	7	7	—	1	1	—
Utah	550,000	120,000	+430,000	8	6	+2	1	—	—
Vermont	n/a	n/a	—	n/a	.5	n/a	1	1	—
Virginia	900,000	900,000	—	14	14	—	2	2	—
Washington	1,940,000	n/a	n/a	10	n/a	n/a	0	—	—
West Virginia	n/a	n/a	n/a	1	.5	n/a	0	0	—
Wisconsin	725,000	535,000	+190,000	10	7	+3	2	1	+
Wyoming	355,000	n/a	n/a	3	n/a	n/a	0	0	—
TOTALS:	39,211,000	21,245,100		515.2	406.5		66	55.5	
AVERAGES:	980,275	590,142		12	9		1.3	1.1	

aCalifornia expects to open 2 offices in 1986.

*Ohio expects to open a 3rd office in 1986.

TABLE 3 — State Investment and Trade Recruitment Overseas

State	Total State International Appropriation	Investment Attraction	Number of Foreign Offices	Location of Foreign Offices
AL	$600,000	$222,000 (37%)	5	Bern, Munich, London, Tokyo, Seoul
AK	790,000	n/a	2	Tokyo, Hong Kong
AZ	477,900	238,950 (50%)	0	None
AR	500,000	250,000 (50%)	2	Brussels, Tokyo
CA	5,700,000	0	0*	Tokyo, London
CO	220,000	0	0	None
CT	625,000	312,000 (50%)	2	Frankfurt, Tokyo
DE	75,000	37,500 (50%)	0	None
FL	1,586,000	634,680 (40%)	3	London, Tokyo, Frankfurt
GA	1,296,200	998,074 (77%)	4	Brussels, Tokyo, Toronto, Seoul
HI	225,000	n/a	0	None
ID	25,000	0	0	None
IL	2,632,000	1,579,000 (60%)	5	Brussels, Osaka, Hong Kong, São Paulo (Brazil), Shenyang (China)
IN	675,000	304,110 (45%)	3	Tokyo, London, Brussels
IA	500,000	150,000 (30%)	2	Frankfurt, Hong Kong
KS	132,000	99,000 (75%)	1	Tokyo
KY	n/a	n/a	2	Tokyo, Southhampton, UK
LA	300,000	n/a	2	n/a
ME	n/a	n/a	0	n/a
MD	1,400,000	0	2	Brussels, Tokyo
MA	437,000	109,375 (25%)	0	None
MI	$1,966,000	$845,638 (43%)	2	Brussels, Tokyo
MN	2,202,000	550,550 (25%)	2	Oslo, Stockholm
MS	400,000	0	0	None
MO	900,000	540,000 (60%)	2	Tokyo, Dusseldorf
MT	86,000	n/a	0	None

TABLE 3 (Continued)

State	Total State International Appropriation	Investment Attraction	Number of Foreign Offices	Location of Foreign Offices
NE	n/a	n/a	0	None
NV	160,000	n/a	0	None
NH	n/a	n/a	0	None
NJ	1,600,000	640,000 (40%)	0	None
NM	n/a	n/a	0	None
NY	3,040,000	1,824,000 (60%)	6	Tokyo, London, Milan, Toronto, Montreal, Wiebaden
NC	950,000	570,000 (60%)	1	Dusseldorf
ND	n/a	n/a	0	None
OH	2,500,000	750,000 (30%)	2	Brussels, Taiwan
OK	n/a	n/a	1	n/a
OR	739,000	0	1	Tokyo
PA	845,000	591,500 (70%)	4	London, Tokyo, Frankfurt, Mexico City
RI	275,000	165,000 (60%)	1	Antwerp (Belgium)
SC	n/a	n/a	2	n/a
SD	51,000	12,775 (25%)	0	None
TN	575,000	488,750 (85%)	1	Mexico City
TX	253,000	126,500 (50%)	1	Tokyo
UT	550,000	110,000 (20%)	1	n/a
VT	n/a	n/a	2	Tokyo, Brussels
VA	900,000	720,000 (80%)	1	Tokyo
WA	1,940,000	n/a	0	None
WV	n/a	n/a	2	Frankfurt
WI	725,000	435,000 (60%)	0	None
WY	355,000	142,000 (40%)		

n/a indicates not available

*California opened two international offices in 1986

TABLE 4

Foreign Investment in the U.S. 1981

	Value of foreign-owned property, plants & equipment (in billions)	Direct jobs resulting from foreign investment
Texas	$ 22.4	172,564
California	19.6	240,774
Alaska	9.6	8,578
Louisiana	8.2	45,718
New York	7.1	204,393
New Jersey	6.4	131,764
North Carolina	5.5	86,349
Illinois	5.4	111,850
Florida	5.4	69,983
Pennsylvania	5.4	129,110
South Carolina	5.2	64,898
Ohio	5.0	97,018
Michigan	4.1	65,070
Georgia	4.0	73,742
West Virginia	3.9	34,835
Tennessee	3.7	55,285
Arizona	2.9	29,396
Virginia	2.9	49,115
Minnesota	2.8	32,536
Alabama	2.8	26,501
Oklahoma	2.6	24,459
Washington	2.3	25,329

State	%	Value
Wisconsin	2.2	59,666
Colorado	2.2	23,961
Wyoming	2.0	4,070
Maryland	2.0	43,900
Missouri	1.9	31,123
Delaware	1.8	35,340
Indiana	1.8	44,881
Utah	1.8	17,188
Kentucky	1.8	25,366
Maine	1.6	17,692
Massachusetts	1.6	52,578
Mississippi	1.4	10,905
Connecticut	1.2	40,128
Montana	1.2	2,830
Hawaii	1.1	16,143
Iowa	1.1	21,741
North Dakota	1.0	3,255
New Mexico	1.0	8,005
Kansas	0.9	14,206
Oregon	0.8	12,281
Arkansas	0.6	17,397
Nevada	0.5	5,854
New Hampshire	0.4	13,355
Nebraska	0.4	5,225
Rhode Island	0.4	9,423
Vermont	0.3	5,889
Idaho	0.3	3,795
South Dakota	0.3	1,324
U.S. total	**$180.0**	**2,343,115**

SOURCE: Commerce Department, cited in *Business America*, May 27, 1985

TABLE 5

Incentives Offered to Attract Major Automobile Plants[a]

Company and Location	Investment	Date of Completion	Estimated Annual Production	Estimated Employment	Direct Incentives	Indirect Incentives
Toyota Motor Corp. Scott County, Ky.	$800 million	1988	200,000	3,000	$15 m for land purchase $20 m for site prep. $10 m for skills center $33 m for job training $47 m for highway improvements Total: $125 million	Educational programs for Japanese employees and their families
Mazda/Ford Motor Flat Rock, Mich.	$450 million	Sept. 1987	240,000	3,500	$19 m for job training $4 m for road improvements $20 m low-interest loan for sewers & site improvements $500,000 small cities loan $1 m federal grant for sewers $3 m for rail spur $4.5 m for rail improvements	100 percent tax abatement for 14 years Mazda will pay $100,000 per year to city in lieu of taxes
Volkswagen AG East Huntington, Pa.	$200 million	1978	220,000 projected 90,000 actual	4,000–5,000 2,500 actual	$40 m low-interest loan $6 m loan from state $25 m for rail & highway Total: $71 million	Local tax abatements for 5 years VW makes payments in lieu of taxes.

Company and Location	Investment	Date of Completion	Estimated Annual Production	Estimated Employment	Direct Incentives	Indirect Incentives
Nissan Motor Co. Smyrna, Tenn.	$450 million $745 m actual	1983	120,000 projected 240,000 actual	2,600 3,100 actual	$7 m for job training $12 m for road improvements Total: $19 million	Local property tax abatements for 20 years Nissan makes payments in lieu of taxes
Honda of America Marysville, Ohio	$250 million $490 m actual	1982	150,000 projected 330,000 actual	2,000 3,300 actual	None: Ohio provided a $16.4 m grant to assist construction of nearby motorcycle plant (1979)	Property tax abatement on buildings.
General Motors[b] Springhill, Tenn.	$3.5 billion	1988	400,000 to 500,000	6,000	$20 m for job training $50 m for road improvements Total: $70 million	Local property tax abatements for 40 years GM will make payments in lieu of taxes
Mitsubishi/Chrysler Bloomington/ Normal, Ill.	$500 million	1988	180,000	2,500	$17.8 m for road improvements $11 m to buy plant site $11.4 m for water & sewer improvements $40 m for job training $3.1 m for roads, water, & sewers Total: $83.3 million	50% state property tax abatement for 10 years $14 m bonds to meet pollution control standards $8.6 m investment tax credit $8 m state sales tax credit $2.4 m savings on water & sewer fees $2 m local utility tax credit

a. Initial figures in production and employment columns are those projected at time decision to locate was made. Actual production and employment are indicated as such.

b. Tennessee did not offer incentives until after General Motors had decided on the Springhill location. General Motors has now scaled back its estimated production and employment.

SOURCE: Blaine Liner and Larry Ledebur, "Foreign Direct Investment in the United States: A Governor's Guide," National Governors' Association, Washington, D.C., 1987

APPENDIX F

Japan's investment in Tennessee

$1.1 Billion in Capital and Planned Investment
7,000 Employees
30 Companies

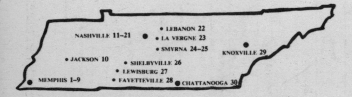

1. **Goh Shoji Company, Inc.**
2. **Gulf Coast Grain, Inc.**
3. **Mitsui and Company (U.S.A.), Inc.**
4. **Mitsui Grain Corporation**
5. NKC of America, Inc.
6. **Nisco Steel Services, Inc.**
7. **Nissan Industrial Equipment Company**
8. Sharp Manufacturing Company of America
9. **Toshiba Medical Systems**
10. Tabuchi Electric Company of America
11. **Chuetsu Metal, U.S.A., Inc.**
12. **Clarion Corporation of America**
13. Kagiya Trading Company Limited of America
14. Kohl-Madden Printing Ink Corporation
15. **Nissan Fire and Marine Insurance Company, Limited**
16. **Nissan Trading Corporation, U.S.A.**
17. Pearl International, Inc.
18. **Polychrome Corporation**
19. **Tsubakimoto Engineering of America, Inc.**
20. **Yasuda Fire and Marine Insurance Company**
21. **YKK USA, Inc.**
22. Toshiba America Inc.
23. Bridgestone Tire Manufacturing (U.S.A.), Inc.
24. **Nissan Motor Corporation in U.S.A.**
25. Nissan Motor Manufacturing Corporation U.S.A.
26. Calsonic Manufacturing Corporation
27. Kantus Corporation
28. Tennessee Fan Company
29. Matsushita Electronic Components Company
30. Komatsu America Manufacturing Corporation

Bold = Sales and/or Distribution (17)
Regular = Manufacturing (13)

APPENDIX G

TABLE 1

Summary of Foreign Bank Presence in the United States*

Date (YE)	Number of Foreign Banks	Number of Countries Represented	Number of U.S. Banking Offices						Total Assets of Foreign Bank Offices ($ Billion)	Share of U.S. Banking Market†
			Subsidiaries	Branches	Agencies	NYIC	EA/AC**	Total		
1973	61	22	27	32	62	3	0	124	$ 32.3	3.8%
1974	70	24	30	57	75	3	0	165	46.1	4.9
1975	77	26	33	65	82	4	0	184	52.4	5.3
1976	86	27	36	70	90	5	1	202	61.3	5.8
1977	116	28	35	98	113	5	2	253	76.8	6.4
1978	135	31	43	116	138	6	2	305	109.1	8.0
1979	153	33	42	132	163	6	2	345	149.6	9.9
1980	154	34	44	151	178	6	10	389	200.8	11.9
1981	186	41	46	193	185	7	23	454	251.2	13.5
1982	210	47	48	230	190	7	31	506	300.7	14.4
1983	230	53	54	265	187	8	34	548	331.9	14.7

*Includes data on U.S. banks and banking offices majority-owned (50%) by foreign banks.

**Edge Act or Agreement Corporations or branches of an Edge Act Corporation.

†Includes domestically-chartered commercial banks, branches and agencies of foreign banks, Edge Act and Agreement Corporations, and New York Investment Companies.

SOURCE: Federal Reserve Board Statistics; OCC analysis.

Appendix

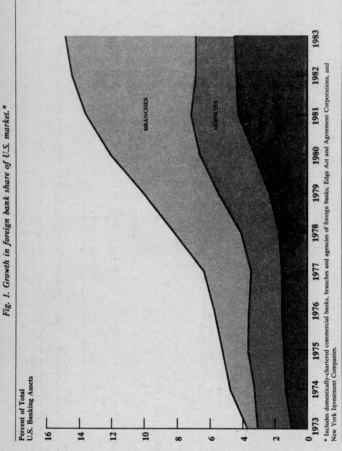

Fig. 1. Growth in foreign bank share of U.S. market.*

Percent of Total
U.S. Banking Assets

16
14
12
10
8
6
4
2
0

1973 1974 1975 1976 1977 1978 1979 1980 1981 1982 1983

BRANCHES

AGENCIES

* Includes domestically-chartered commercial banks, branches and agencies of foreign banks, Edge Act and Agreement Corporations, and New York Investment Companies.

SOURCE: Federal Reserve Board Statistics; OCC Analysis.

TABLE 2 — Foreign Bank Subsidiaries Among the Top 100 U.S. Banks December 31, 1983

Rank by Total Assets	U.S. Bank (location)	Foreign Bank Parent (home country)	Total Assets $ Billion	Form of Entry
12	Crocker National Bank (San Francisco)	Midland Bank Ltd. (U.K.)	23.0	Acquisition
13	Marine Midland Bank, N.A. (Buffalo, NY)	Hongkong & Shanghai Banking Corp. (Hong Kong)	22.6	Acquisition
30	Union Bank (Los Angeles)	Standard Chartered Bank Ltd. (U.K.)	7.9	Acquisition
32	National Westminster Bank USA (NYC)*	Standard Chartered Bank Ltd. (U.K.)	7.5	Acquisition
36	European-American B&TC (NYC)	European-American "Group"***	6.8	De Novo Acquirer
60	Bank of Tokyo Trust Co. (NYC)	Bank of Tokyo Ltd. (Japan)	4.5	De Novo
62	California First Bank (San Francisco)	Bank of Tokyo Ltd. (Japan)	4.3	De Novo Acquirer
82	Israel Discount Bank of NY (NYC)	Israel Discount Bank Ltd. (Israel)	3.4	De Novo
95	Bank Leumi Trust Co. (NYC)	Bank Leumi le-Israel (Israel)	3.0	De Novo Acquirer

*Formerly the National Bank of North America

**Banking "Group" is composed of Amsterdam-Rotterdam Bank (Netherlands), Creditanstalt-Bankverein (Austria), Deutsche Bank (W. Germany), Midland Bank (U.K.), Societe Generale de Banque (Belgium) and Societe Generale (France).

SOURCE: *American Banker* (March 16, 1984); OCC analysis.

TABLE 3   *Geographic Concentration of Foreign Banking Offices*
December 31, 1983

	Subsidiaries	Branches	Agencies	New York Investment Companies	Edge Act/ Agreement Corps.	Total No. of Offices	Percent of Total
New York	24	173	39	8	6	250	46%
California	26	17	96		2	141	26%
Florida	2		38		12	52	9%
Illinois	2	43			2	47	9%
Washington		11				11	2%
Georgia			11			11	2%
Texas					11	11	2%
Oregon		7				7	1%
Pennsylvania		6				6	1%
Massachusetts		5				5	1%
District of Columbia		3			1	4	1%
Hawaii			2			2	—
Louisiana	—	—	1	—	—	1	—
Total	54	265	187	8	34	548	100%

SOURCE: Federal Reserve Board statistics; OCC analysis.

How foreign role in U.S. economy has grown.
(Gone are days of business independence as Americans turn abroad)

Foreign Assets in U.S. Climb
End of 1985, by regions

	(In millions of dollars)	(Increase since 1984)
Western Europe	$515,032	21.9%
Latin America	$212,054	12.4%
Japan	$101,819	50.6%
Canada	$65,744	12.4%
Others	$165,158	5.7%

Source: U.S. Commerce Department

As Does Foreign Buying of Treasury Notes and Bonds
Net foreign purchases

	(In billions of dollars)	(As share of total purchases)
1986 (2Q)	$17	22%
1985	$29	19%
1984	$21.5	13%
1983	$5.4	4%

Source: U.S. Treasury Department

While Trade Patterns Shift

	Imports as a Share Of Domestic Consumption (1985 / 1981)		Exports as a Share Of Domestic Production (1985 / 1981)	
Radio and TV sets	63%	59%	8%	10%
Shoes	58%	33%	3%	2%
Machine tools	45%	25%	18%	20%
Semiconductors	40%	34%	32%	35%
Apparel	25%	12%	2%	2%
Steel mill products	24%	19%	1%	3%
Motor vehicles	20%	19%	2%	5%
Farm machinery	20%	13%	22%	23%
Photographic equipment	19%	15%	14%	16%
Computers	18%	7%	29%	29%
Construction machinery	16%	9%	21%	41%
Home appliances	15%	9%	6%	10%
Home furniture	14%	7%	1%	2%

SOURCE: U.S. Commerce Department, National Association of Manufacturers

Appendix

Foreign-Trade Balance Sinks

Includes goods, services and other transfers
(In billions of dollars)

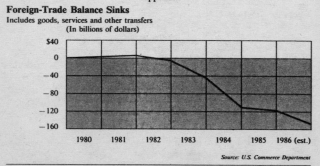

Source: U.S. Commerce Department

Nation Becomes a Debtor

International Investment Position of the U.S.
U.S. assets abroad less foreign assets in the U.S., at year-end
(In billions of dollars)

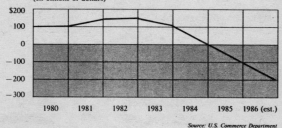

Source: U.S. Commerce Department

And Relative Economic Performance Lags

Gain in GNP from 1984 through the first quarter of 1986

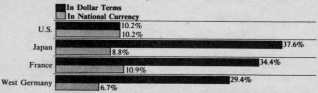

- In Dollar Terms
- In National Currency

	In Dollar Terms	In National Currency
U.S.	10.2%	10.2%
Japan	37.6%	8.8%
France	34.4%	10.9%
West Germany	29.4%	6.7%

SOURCE: International Monetary Fund, U.S. Federal Reserve Board, CM&M Group Inc. and Wall Street Journal, October 27, 1986.

APPENDIX I

The foreign side of U.S. treasury debt
(For each year figures are as of January 31: in billions of dollars)

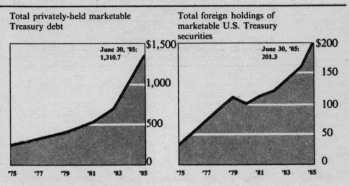

Total privately-held marketable
Treasury debt

June 30, '85:
1,310.7

$1,500
1,000
500
0

'75 '77 '79 '81 '83 '85

Total foreign holdings of
marketable U.S. Treasury
securities

June 30, '85:
201.3

$200
150
100
50
0

'75 '77 '79 '81 '83 '85

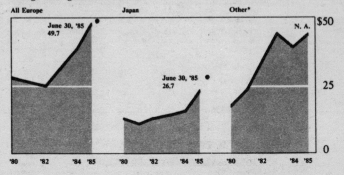

Foreign holdings of marketable U.S. notes and bonds

All Europe

June 30, '85
49.7

'80 '82 '84 '85

Japan

June 30, '85
26.7

'80 '82 '84 '85

Other*

N. A.

$50

25

0

'80 '82 '84 '85

*Mostly OPEC or oil-producing countries.
Source: Goldman Sachs, and U.S. Treasury Dept.
The New York Times/Nov. 7, 1985

TABLE 1

Estimated Net Capital Flight
cumulative flows during 1976–85
billions of dollars, minus sign indicates outflows

	Net direct investment inflows	Change in gross external debt	Current account balance*	Change in selected gross foreign assets**	Capital flight*** Total	1976–82	1983–85
Argentina	4	42	−15	−4	−26	−27	1
Bolivia	0	3	−2	−0	−1	−1	0
Brazil	20	80	−77	−13	−10	−3	−7
Chile	2	16	−16	−3	1	0	1
Colombia	2	10	−11	−2	0	0	0
Ecuador	1	7	−5	−1	−2	−1	−1
Mexico	11	75	−29	−3	−53	−36	−17
Peru	0	8	−6	−2	−0	1	−1
Uruguay	1	4	−3	−1	−1	−1	−0
Venezuela	−0	26	10	−5	−30	−25	−6
Subtotal	40	270	−154	−33	−123	−93	−30
India	0	22	−8	−5	−10	−6	−4
Indonesia	2	27	−15	−9	−5	−6	1
Korea	0	40	−22	−6	−12	−6	−6
Malaysia	9	19	−12	−4	−12	−8	−4
Nigeria	2	18	−15	4	−10	−7	−3
Philippines	1	23	−16	1	−9	−7	−2
South Africa	−2	16	2	2	−17	−13	−4
Thailand	2	17	−17	−1	−0	1	−1
Subtotal	14	181	−102	−18	−75	−52	−23
Total for 18 countries	54	451	−256	−51	−198	−145	−53

*Minus sign indicates deficit.

**Official reserve assets and other foreign assets of official monetary authorities plus foreign assets of commercial banks and certain other banking institutions. Minus sign indicates increase in foreign assets.

***Apparent change in other foreign assets (minus sign indicates increase) through residual capital flows measured as the counterpart of the sum of net direct investment inflows, change in gross external debt, current account balance, and change in selected gross foreign assets. Direct investment and current account data are taken from the reported balance of payments. Debt and asset changes are derived from estimated year-end outstandings in dollar terms.

Note: Due to rounding columns and rows may not add.

SOURCE: Morgan Guaranty Trust Company

APPENDIX J

TABLE 1

Investment Barriers by Country

COUNTRY	BARRIERS	COUNTRY	BARRIERS
Argentina	N/A	Kenya	F, L, N
Australia	A, B	Korea	N/A
Austria	N/A	Malaysia	C
Belgium	N/A	Mexico	A, B, C, D, F, K, N
Brazil	B, C, E, F, G	The Netherlands	N/A
Canada	D, G, H, I	New Zealand	N/A
Chile	N/A	Nigeria	N/A
China	D, E, G, J	Norway	N/A
Colombia	*, A, K	Pakistan	B, C, D, F, L
Denmark	N/A	Philippines	A, C, D, G, O
European Community	N/A	Portugal	L, P
Federal Republic of Germany	N/A	Singapore	N/A
Finland	N/A	South Africa	N/A
France	N/A	Spain	N/A
Greece	M	Sweden	N/A
Gulf Cooperation Council	N/A	Taiwan	B, D
India	C, D	Thailand	N/A
Indonesia	G	Turkey	N/A
Ireland	N/A	United Kingdom	N/A
Italy	N/A	Venezuela	*, B, D, G, K, L
Japan	N/A	Yugoslavia	N/A

Key: N/A: No investment barriers.
* *: Foreign investment regulations are covered by Decision 24 of the Cartagena Agreement governing foreign investment within Andean Pact nations. Decision 24 enacted a series of barriers to restrict foreign investment. None of the Andean Pact countries have complied fully with Decision 24.
* A: General foreign investment barriers (substantive and procedural restrictions).
* B: Local content requirements.
* C: Limitations on foreign equity participation.
* D: Export performance requirements.
* E: Restrictions on transferring earnings and capital.
* F: Price controls.
* G: Denial of national treatment to foreign-owned investments.
* H: Unreasonable entry restrictions.
* I: Discriminatory postal rates.
* J: Inadequate access to international arbitration.
* K: Patent and trademark law inadequacies.
* L: Restrictive licensing system.
* M: Controls over repatriating foreign capital and earnings.
* N: Rigid visa requirements.
* O: Prohibitions on land ownership.
* P: Restrictive quota system for distributors.

SOURCE: U.S. Office of the United States Trade Representative, *National Trade Estimate: 1986 Report on Foreign Trade Barriers* (Washington, D.C.: U.S. Government Printing Office, 1986).

Notes

1. Foreign Money

1. The White House, Executive Office of the President, Office of the Press Secretary, September 9, 1983.

2. The figure of $196 billion was calculated by the Commerce Department in 1974 and excluded foreign bank deposits abroad. By 1979, the Commerce Department's calculation had grown to $407 billion, and by 1983, $781.5 billion. Of that amount, foreign investments in government securities, stocks, and bonds had jumped from $153.9 billion to $646.1 billion. The figure of $1.5 trillion is the authors' estimate as of 1987, based on data collected for this study. Readers should bear in mind the inadequacy of existing data, presently collected by sixteen separate agencies, and significantly underreported in virtually all major categories. See Chapters 3–18. For an excellent analysis of the growth of foreign investment in the 1970s, see Earl Fry, *Financial Invasion of the United States*, New York: McGraw-Hill, 1980. For recent articles on foreign investment in the 1980s, see Marilyn Much, "The Foreign Invasion," *Industry Week*, February 23, 1987, pp. 37–40; and Jaclyn Fierman, "The Selling of America," *Fortune*, December 22, 1986, pp. 44–54.

3. The International Investment Survey Act of 1976, which directs the government to collect information on foreign investment, defines direct investment as the ownership or control, directly or indirectly, by a foreign person (defined as an individual, trust, corporation, association, corporation, or government) of 10 percent or more of a company. Portfolio investment includes all other holdings of U.S. assets, such as U.S. Treasury notes and bonds. See U.S. Department of Commerce, Bureau of Economic Analysis. *Foreign Direct Investment in the United States*, Washington, D.C.: U.S. Government Printing Office, 1983.

See Appendix D, Tables 1–6, and Appendix E, Table 1, for more specific data on foreign investments.

4. Britain leads with $43.8 billion; the Netherlands with $36.1 billion; Japan, $19.1 billion; Canada, $16.7 billion; West Germany, $14.4 billion; Switzerland, $11 billion; France, $6.3 billion; Kuwait, $4 billion; Australia, $2.7 billion; and Sweden, $2.4 billion. These figures are based on 1985 data and should be regarded—as with all official data—as underestimated.

5. James Sterngold, "Japanese Buying a Place on Wall Street—But Resentment Grows Over Lack of Reciprocity," *New York Times,* April 12, 1987, p. E26.

6. Cynthia Crossen, "Tales from the Dark Side: What a Market Crash Might Look Like," *Wall Street Journal,* April 21, 1987, p. 41.

7. See Appendix A for a brief historical sketch on the role of foreign investment in the United States.

8. U.S. Congress, Committee on Government Operations, "The Adequacy of the Federal Response to Foreign Investment in the United States," August 1, 1980, Washington, D.C.: U.S. Government Printing Office, 1980.

9. Jeff B. Copeland with Rich Thomas, "The U.S. Gets Foreign Aid," *Newsweek,* May 18, 1987, p. 58.

10. Alan Murray, "Foreign Central Banks Pick Up U.S. Bills," *Wall Street Journal,* May 18, 1987, p. 1.

11. Paul Blustein, "Dollar Looms Bigger in Fed's Decision at Risk of Recession," *Wall Street Journal,* May 19, 1987, p. 1.

12. U.S. Congress, Committee on Energy and Commerce, Subcommittee on Telecommunications, Consumer Protection, and Finance, "Disclosure of Foreign Investment in the United States," May 8, 1986, Washington, D.C.: U.S. Government Printing Office, 1986.

See also Appendix C for a discussion of the data gaps in government information-collecting activities.

13. Useful articles on the political and social ramifications of foreign investment include Martin Tolchin, "Foreigners' Political Roles in U.S. Grow by Investing," *New York Times,*

December 30, 1985, pp. A1 and A14; Andrew H. Malcolm, "Foreign Money Changing U.S. Social-Cultural Life," *New York Times*, December 31, 1985, pp. A1 and B4; and Barnaby Feder, "Foreign Money Spreading to All Walks of U.S. Life," *New York Times*, December 29, 1985, p. A1.

14. Jean-Jacques Servan-Schreiber, *The American Challenge*, New York: Atheneum, 1969, p. 4. Originally published as *Le Défi Américaine*, Paris: Editions Denoel, 1967.

15. Ibid., p. 9.

2. Trojan Horse or Gift Horse

1. The material for this section is drawn from interviews and from Martin Tolchin, "Foreigners' Political Roles in U.S. Grow by Investing," *New York Times*, December 30, 1985, pp. A1 and A14. For another article on foreign PACs, see Maxwell Glen, "The Foreign Connection," *National Journal*, July 26, 1986, pp. 1832–37.

2. See Chapter 8 for a more comprehensive discussion of the unitary tax.

3. The following analysis of the Sitka controversy is based on personal interviews and from a debate in the *Congressional Record*, October 17, 1985, vol. 131, no. 138, pp. S 13452–66.

4. U.S. General Accounting Office, "Farm Programs—Payments and Loans to Foreign Owners of U.S. Cropland," March 1987; and Ward Sinclair, "Foreigners Get U.S. Farm Subsidies," *Washington Post*, April 20, 1987, p. A13.

5. Eleanor Randolph, "Washington Times Hit by Resignations," *Washington Post*, April 15, 1987, p. A24.

6. U.S. Congress, Committee on Government Operations, "The Adequacy of the Federal Response to Foreign Investment in the United States," August 1, 1980, Washington, D.C.: U.S. Government Printing Office, 1980.

3. The New Wave

1. Jane Sneddon Little, "Foreign Direct Investment in New England," *New England Economic Review*, March/April, 1985, pp. 51–56.

2. John Herbers, "Study Sees States Moving to Achieve World Trade Ties," *New York Times*, August 5, 1985, p. A1. See also National Governors' Association, *States in the International Economy*, Committee on International Trade and Foreign Relations, August 4–6, 1985, pp. 28–30.

3. Jane Sneddon Little, "Foreign Direct Investment in the United States: Recent Locational Choices of Foreign Manufacturers," *New England Economic Review*, November/December 1980, p. 17.

4. *Business Week*, May 20, 1985, p. 156.

5. See Chapter 4 for more information on overseas state offices.

6. Their data were drawn on figures compiled in 1981. See Appendix E, Table 4, "Foreign Investment in the United States, 1981," U.S. Department of Commerce, cited in Dan Pilcher, "State Roles in Foreign Trade," *Business America*, May 27, 1985, p. 14.

7. See Chapter 11 for a further discussion of the controversy surrounding foreign acquisition of farmland and other real estate.

8. For an excellent discussion of the origins of Khashoggi's activities, see Kenneth C. Crowe, *America for Sale*, New York: Doubleday, 1978.

9. Ward Sinclair, "Aid for Irish Dairy Operation in Georgia Stirs Bitter Protest," *Washington Post*, April 12, 1986, pp. A1 and A8.

10. The section on cities and foreign investment is drawn from Martin Tolchin, "U.S. Cities Seeking Foreign Investing," *New York Times*, January 20, 1985, p. 17. Another comprehensive discussion can be found in Carol Steinbach and Neal R. Peirce, "Cities Are Setting Their Sights on International Trade and Investment," *National Journal*, April 28, 1984, pp. 818–22.

11. Martin Tolchin, "Some Governors Warn on Foreign Investment," *New York Times*, February 26, 1985, p. D19.

4. Baiting the Hook

1. See Chapter 8 for a fuller discussion of the unitary tax issue.

2. National Association of State Development Agencies (NASDA), "State Export Program Database," March 1986, p. 55. See also Appendix E, Tables 2 and 3.

3. See Appendix E, Table 1 for information on jobs relating to foreign direct investment, plus the value of foreign-owned property, plants, and equipment. See also National Association of State Development Agencies, *Directory of Incentives for Business Investment and Development in the United States; a State by State Guide*, Baltimore: Urban Institute Press, 1986.

4. For further information on state efforts and incentives, see Appendix E, Tables 2 and 3. Note that some of the data are not disaggregated for foreign investment activities as opposed to export promotion. Wherever possible, the data in the chapter will be separated. From NASDA State Export Program Database, March 1986.

5. David D. Driscoll, *Incentives to Foreign Direct Investment in the United States*, Congressional Research Service, Library of Congress, no. 81-76 E, March 19, 1981, p. 9. See also Appendix E, Tables 1–4. Another interesting work on state policy and foreign investment is John Kline's *State Government Influence in U.S. International Economic Policy*, Lexington, Mass.: D. C. Heath, 1983.

6. NASDA Database, op. cit. "State Appropriation, Staff and Foreign Office," Comparison: FY84–FY86, Summary Table.

7. The most common location for an Asian office is Tokyo, with twenty-two offices; European offices seem evenly divided between Belgium (ten offices) and Germany (nine offices). Brussels is a popular location for investors because it is also the headquarters for the European Community. See Appendix E, Tables 2 and 3.

8. California's $5.7 million international budget is by far the highest in the nation, $2 million more than New York's, the next highest state, which spends $3.04 million.

9. *Business Week*, May 20, 1985.

10. Michael R. Gordon, "With Foreign Investment at Stake, It's One State Against the Others," *National Journal*, October 18, 1980, p. 1746.

11. Driscoll, op. cit., p. 9. The list of incentives that follows in the text of the chapter is drawn, in part, from Driscoll's typology. See also, Appendix E, Table 5.

12. Ibid.

13. National Governors' Association, *States in the International Economy*, August 4–6, 1985, pp. 30–31.

14. Earl Fry, *Financial Invasion of the U.S.A.*, New York: McGraw-Hill, 1980, pp. 58–75.

15. Gordon, op. cit., p. 1746.

16. Ibid., p. 1747.

17. National Association of State Development Agencies, *Trade Monitor*, March 1986.

18. Gordon., op. cit., p. 1747.

19. The investment climate is determined by: logistical factors (ports, highways, railroads), labor factors (wages, available supply, unionization levels, skill levels and productivity, absenteeism, turnover, and work-stoppage rates), utility factors (availability and cost of water, energy, etc.), construction factors (availability and cost of land, construction costs), financial factors (types and levels of taxes, financial-assistance packages), and life-style factors (climate, recreational and educational facilities, cultural activities). See "The Impact of State Incentives on Foreign Investors' Site Selection," *Economic Review*, December 1981, pp. 36–42.

20. This is documented over and over again. The Arpan and Ricks study of foreign investment showed that incentives did not play a major role in site selection. Tong's study of investors ranked incentives in the bottom sixth of factors mentioned, and a study of Louisiana by Young and Kedia showed that with investments made through acquisitions, incentives played

no role at all. Another study of French firms ranked labor, transportation, and plant-site factors much higher than special incentives, while German investors in South Carolina rated labor conditions above all others. Ibid. See also Jeffrey S. Arpan and David Ricks, "Foreign Direct Investments in the United States and Some Attendant Research Problems," *Journal of International Business Studies,* spring 1974; H. M. Tong, *Plant Location Decision of Foreign Manufacturing Investors,* Ann Arbor: UMI Research Press, 1979; Bernard Imbert, *French Investment in the American Southeast,* report no. CS-10, Georgia World Congress Institute, Atlanta, Georgia, 1979.

21. Gordon, op. cit., p. 1748.

22. Driscoll, op. cit., p. 7.

23. Alex Kotlowitz and Dale D. Buss, "Costly Bait—Localities Giveaways to Lure Corporations Cause Growing Outcry," *Wall Street Journal,* September 24, 1986, pp. 1 and 27.

24. *Business Week,* July 21, 1986, p. 80.

5. Cherry Blossoms and Lift Trucks

1. See Appendix F, Figure 1, for Japanese investment in Tennessee. Although most of the material in this chapter is based on personal interviews, the following additional sources were used: *Business and Industrial Review,* Tennessee Department of Economic and Community Development, vol. 40, no. 2, April/May 1985; Thomas H. Rohan, "Dale Turnbull's Korean Lift Trucks," *Industry Week,* June 10, 1985, p. 62; Steven Greenhouse, "A Grim Era for Heavy Equipment," *New York Times,* September 22, 1985, p. F4; Dave Flessner, "Failure to qualify for grant likely to limit, delay Komatsu plant here," *Chattanooga Times,* October 4, 1985, p. Al; Dave Flessner, "Komatsu sees move as easing trade bars," *Chattanooga Times,* March 21, 1985; Dave Flessner, "Komatsu to begin work here within 3 months," *Chattanooga Times,* October 16, 1985, p. C1; Clyde Farnsworth, "Chattanooga Reviving Itself with Foreign Capital," *New York Times,* April 16, 1986, p. A23; Daniel F. Cuff, "Tennessee's Pitch to Japan," *New York Times,* February 27, 1985, pp. D1 and D6; and "Partners for Economic Progress, Statement of Objectives and Plans," *An Economic Development Plan for the Chattanooga Region,* March 1984.

2. A Foreign Trade Zone (FTZ) is a selected, enclosed, policed area in which goods may be brought into the United States without formal customs entry or payment of duty or excise taxes. Zones are operated as a public utility whose purpose is to encourage and facilitate international trade and increase employment. The Foreign-Trade Zone Act of 1934 created a board to review and approve applications for FTZs. According to the ITC and the GAO, the number of zones greatly increased from five subzones and thirteen general-purpose zones in the 1970s to thirty subzones and ninety-one general-purpose zones in 1983. In addition to autos and motorcycles, the primary products shipped from FTZs were microwave ovens, televisions, and petroleum derivatives. See *International Trade Reporter's U.S. Import Weekly*, Bureau of National Affairs, vol. 9, no. 24, March 21, 1984, p. 2.

3. Dave Flessner, "$20 million in bonds voted for Komatsu," *Chattanooga Times*, February 28, 1985.

6. Succeeding Where Firestone Failed

1. In December 1980, an American Deming Prize was established by the American Society for Quality Control and the New York–area branch of the American Statistical Association. An NBC White Paper on Productivity in June 1980 ("If Japan Can . . . Why Can't We?") brought Deming to public attention for the first time. For more information on Deming, his background, and on the quality control method, see Don Hellriegel and John W. Slocum, Jr., *Management*, Reading, Mass.: Addison-Wesley Publishing Co., pp. 690–94; William M. Ringle, "The American Who Remade 'Made in Japan,' " *Nation's Business*, February 1981, vol. 69, pp. 67–70; "Now Mr. Deming Is Lecturing Automakers," *Industry Week*, August 24, 1981, vol. 210, pp. 28–30; Joseph M. Callahan, "The Deming Era Arrives in Detroit," *Automotive Industries*, November 1981, vol. 161, pp. 45–47; and "Productivity on Prime Time," *Fortune*, July 28, 1980, vol. 102, pp. 34–35.

8. The "Juicing" of California

1. The preferred term for the unitary tax is "worldwide combination." Since the tax is more commonly referred to among political actors as the "unitary tax" and since the thrust of this chapter is an analysis of its political fortunes, the text will refer to the tax as the "unitary tax."

2. Robert Tannenwald, "The Pros and Cons of Worldwide Unitary Taxation," *New England Economic Review*, July/August 1984, p. 18.

3. The steel company in Minnesota, for example, could "quote an artificially high price for the coal, an ingredient of steel, in order to overstate the costs, and therefore understate the income, of the factory. The income of the mine would be overstated by the same amount. In this manner, the company could reallocate taxable income from high-tax Minnesota to low-tax North Dakota, reducing its overall state income tax liabilities." Ibid.

4. Senate Office of Research, "The Unitary Controversy," Issues Brief, Sacramento, California, December 1984.

5. *Container Corporation of America* v. *Franchise Tax Board*, 103 S. Ct. 2933 (1983).

6. Although they also filed suit just in case their legislative efforts failed. In 1986, sixteen nations filed suit in U.S. District Court in Chicago against the state of California, challenging its use of the tax on companies operating in this country that have foreign parents. (The *Container* case applied only to U.S. companies with foreign operations.) The suit was brought by Imperial Chemical Industries (a British company) and Alcan Aluminum Ltd. (Canadian).

7. Joint Legislative Budget Committee, California Legislature, "The 1985–86 Budget: Perspectives and Issues," Report of the Legislative Analyst, 1986, p. 118.

8. BNA International Trade Reporter, "Current Reports," vol. 2, January 23, 1985, p. 151.

9. Ibid.

10. Vincent W. Stove, "U.S. Unitary Tax Criticized in Australia," *Journal of Commerce*, March 12, 1984, p. 23B.

11. Tannenwald, op. cit., p. 22.

12. *Daily Commercial News*, August 28, 1984.

13. For an excellent discussion of California's "juice bills," see "The Juicing of California," *California Magazine*, February 1986, pp. 76–89.

14. The material in this subsection of the chapter is from Martin Tolchin, "With Lobbies in Full Cry, California Debates Repealing Multinational Tax," *New York Times*, February 18, 1986, p. B12.

15. Anne Swardson, "Unitary Tax Ban Sought by Reagan," *Washington Post*, November 9, 1985, pp. C1 and C8.

16. State of California, Governor's Office, Letter to Hon. Walter F. Mondale, U.S. Senate, Chairman, Senate Finance Subcommittee on State Taxation of Interstate Commerce, September 14, 1973.

17. California State Economic Development Commission, "The California Economic Development and Trade Update," vol. 2, no. 9, January 1986, p. 1.

18. *New York Times*, August 19, 1986, p. D14.

19. Other provisions of the bill include: Eligibility for selecting a water's-edge approach. Corporations that fall within the requirements of the "80–20" classification may elect the water's-edge formula. The "80–20" corporations have at least 80 percent of their payroll and property outside the United States or receive at least 80 percent of their income from foreign sources. See SB 85, Chapter 660 of the California Revenue and Taxation Code. See also Leonard W. Rothschild, Jr., "Worldwide Unitary Taxation: The End Is in Sight," *Journal of Accountancy*, December 1986, pp. 178–85.

20. Bill Curry, "Big U.S. and Foreign Firms Seek Repeal of Unitary Tax," *Los Angeles Times*, August 14, 1984.

21. Joint Budget Committee, Report of the Legislative Analyst, op. cit., p. 119.

22. Stuart Auerbach, "Trade with Pacific Rim Sets Off Second Gold Rush in California," *Washington Post*, April 29, 1984, pp. F1, F10; and Stuart Auerbach, "Asia Replaces Europe as Major Partner," *Washington Post*, April 22, 1984, pp. G1, G4–5.

9. Foreign-Owned U.S. Banks

1. CBS News Special, Newsmark, "Foreign Investment in America: Sales or Sellout?," March 31, 1979.

2. General Accounting Office, "Report by the Comptroller General of the United States," August 26, 1980, p. 6–1. Other sources used include: William Jackson, "Foreign Control of U.S. Banks: Changing the Bank Regulatory Climate," Congressional Research Service, August 17, 1979, Report No. 79–175 E; Roger M. Kubarych, *Foreign Exchange Markets in the United States*, New York: Federal Reserve Bank of New York, 1983; John E. Shockey and William B. Glidden, "Foreign-Controlled U.S. Banks: the Legal and Regulatory Environment," Staff Paper, Comptroller of the Currency, June 1980; William A. Longbrake, Melanie R. Quinn, and Judith A. Walter, "Foreign Ownership of U.S. Banks: Facts and Patterns," Staff Paper, Comptroller of the Currency, June 1980; Judith A. Walter, "Foreign Acquisitions of U.S. Banks: Motives and Tactical Considerations," Staff Paper, Comptroller of the Currency, June 1980; Thomas A. Loeffler and William A. Longbrake, "Prices Paid by Foreign Interests to Acquire U.S. Banks," Comptroller of the Currency, April 1981; and Judith A. Walter, "Supervisory Performance of Foreign-Controlled U.S. Banking Organizations," Comptroller of the Currency, June 1980.

3. Interview with James A. Houpt, financial analyst with the Federal Reserve Board, for 1986 data. For data from 1973 to 1983, see *Controller of the Currency Quarterly Journal*, September 1984, p. 6, and Appendix G, Tables 1–3 and Figure 1. See also James A. Houpt, "Foreign Ownership of U.S. Banks: Trends and Effects," *Journal of Bank Research*, vol. 14, no. 2, summer 1983, pp. 144–56.

4. Ibid.

5. U.S. Department of Commerce, International Trade Administration, September 1986.

6. Karene Witcher, "Foreign Banks Step Up Lending Competition in the U.S. and Abroad," *Wall Street Journal*, June 26, 1985, pp. 1 and 18.

7. Federal Reserve Board, "Structure Data for U.S. Offices of Foreign Banks by Country of Origin, as of 1985," 1986, pp. 2–66.

8. GAO, op. cit.

9. Ibid., p. 1–1.

10. Testimony before the House Subcommittee on Commerce, Consumer and Monetary Affairs, House of Representatives Committee on Government Operations, September 30, 1982.

11. GAO, op. cit., p. vi.

12. Ibid., p. 5–11.

13. Ibid., p. x.

14. Ibid., p. 6–1.

15. Ibid., p. 6–1.

16. Ibid., p. 8–1.

17. Ibid., p. 6–5.

18. Ibid., p. 6–7.

19. Ibid., p. 8–8.

20. Garn introduced S. 2193, "To Authorize the Comptroller of the Currency to Consider Reciprocity Among Other Factors in Acting on an Application by a Foreign Bank to Establish a Federal Branch or Agency, and for Other Purposes." At the hearing, witnesses testified on the lack of reciprocity toward U.S. banks in countries such as Australia, Mexico, Brazil, Venezuela, and Taiwan. Secretary of the Treasury Donald T. Regan opposed the imposition of reciprocity on the grounds that it would hurt international trade relationships, advocating "national treatment" instead. See U.S. Senate, Hearing before the Committee on Banking, Housing, and Urban Affairs, "National Treatment of Banks," Washington, D.C.: September 26, 1984. For a further discussion of reciprocity, see Chapters 16 and 17.

21. In 1986, the Federal Reserve Board allowed Sumitomo Bank Ltd. of Japan, the world's third-largest bank holding company, to invest in Goldman Sachs, a U.S. securities firm. Sumitomo will contribute up to 24.9 percent of Goldman Sachs's partners' equity in return for one-eighth of the firm's profits. This is the first time a foreign bank was permitted to

purchase a major part of a U.S. securities firm, casting another blow at the legal barriers between commercial banking and investment banking. Sumitomo had to promise it would exercise no operational control over Goldman Sachs.

22. GAO, op. cit., pp. 8–8.

23. *Wall Street Journal,* September 28, 1984, p. 33.

24. Ibid.

25. *Business Week,* August 6, 1984, p. 40.

10. The Kremlin's Banks in America

1. The material for this chapter is based mainly on extensive interviews and appeared initially in Martin Tolchin, "Russians Sought U.S. Banks to Gain High Tech Secrets," *New York Times,* February 16, 1986, p. 1. For a prior article on this subject, see *New York Times,* December 30, 1978, p. 25.

2. *United States of America* v. *Amos W. Dawe and Roger E. Dunbar,* U.S. District Court for the Northern District of California, Indictment, filed July 22, 1977, on counts of "conspiracy, misapplication of bank funds and aiding and abetting" (Title 18, U.S.C., Sections 371, 656 and 2). See also *Liew* v. *Breen,* 640 F.2d 1046 (1981); and In the High Court of Hong Kong, *The Queen* v. *Amos William Dawe,* Affidavit of Victor Vladimirovitch Gerashchenko.

3. James Bartholomew, "Moscow Narodny's Hidden Loss," *Far Eastern Economic Review,* September 29, 1978, pp. 57–58.

4. British Broadcasting Corporation, "Panorama," February 21, 1983, p. 12.

5. Ibid.

6. A study issued in 1985 by the Department of Defense, "Soviet Acquisition of Militarily Significant Western Technology—An Update."

7. U.S. Congress, Committee on Government Operations, "Federal Response to Criminal Misconduct and Insider Abuse in the Nation's Financial Institutions," October 4, 1984, Washington, D.C.: U.S. Government Printing Office, 1984.

11. Buying America

1. S. Livermore, *Early American Land Companies*, 1968, p. 25; and Gene Wunderlich, "Foreign Investment in U.S. Real Estate," U.S. Department of Agriculture, 1980.

2. A recent case illustrated this point. The attorney general of Oklahoma instituted suit on behalf of the state challenging a Canadian corporation's right to own land in the state. The Supreme Court of Oklahoma upheld the Canadian corporation on the grounds that once a foreign corporation has complied with "domestication procedures," it could be considered a "bona fide resident of the state" and no longer subject to restrictions on land ownership. See *State of Oklahoma* v. *Hillcrest Investments, Ltd.*, no. 54906, Supreme Court of Oklahoma, March 10, 1981 (Okl., 630 F. 2d 1253). A number of other restrictions by states on alien ownership run the gamut: some states do not allow foreign nationals to inherit property; others limit ownership only to certain nationalities; others place a ceiling on the amount of acreage. See Dale C. Schian, "State Laws Relating to the Ownership of U.S. Agricultural Land by Aliens and Business Entities," U.S. Department of Agriculture, May 1984.

3. Mahlon Apgar, IV, "The Changing Realities of Foreign Investment," *Development Review and Outlook*, Urban Land Institute, 1985, p. 381; and U.S. Department of Commerce, International Trade Administration, "International Direct Investment," August 1984.

4. Dan Dorfman, "On the Trail of Baby Doc," *New York* magazine, July 14, 1986, p. 19.

5. Apgar, op. cit., p. 381.

6. Ibid.

7. Ibid.

8. J. Peter DeBraal and T. Alexander Majchrowicz, "Foreign Ownership of U.S. Agricultural Land Through December 31, 1983," U.S. Department of Agriculture, 1984.

9. U.S. Department of Agriculture, "Close-up: Foreign Investment in U.S. Agriculture," *Farmline*, September 1981, p. 4.

10. J. Peter DeBraal and T. Alexander Majchrowicz, "Foreign Ownership of U.S. Agricultural Land Through December 31, 1984," U.S. Department of Agriculture, 1985. Information in this report indicated that forest land accounted for 51 percent of all foreign-owned acreage; cropland, 17 percent; pasture and other agricultural land, 27 percent; leaving 5 percent unreported. Investors from the United Kingdom, Canada, West Germany, the Netherlands Antilles, and Switzerland accounted for 70 percent of the foreign-held acreage.

11. J. Peter DeBraal, "Foreign Ownership of U.S. Farmland: What Does It Mean?" *The Farm and Food System in Transition*, Michigan State University, Cooperative Extension Service, 1984.

12. Martin Tolchin, "Britons' Buying Spree: Prime Real Estate," *New York Times*, January 17, 1986, p. A14; and Brian Kelly, "The British are Coming—Again," *Regardie's*, April 1984, p. 65.

13. Major British holdings in downtown Washington include the Army-Navy Club at Seventeenth and Eye Streets N.W. ($35 million); Demonet Building, Connecticut and M Streets ($40 million); 1200 Nineteenth Street ($40 million); 1100 Twentieth Street ($30 million); Walker Building, 1129 Twentieth Street ($22 million); 1020 Nineteenth Street ($35 million); 2001 L Street ($35 million); 1015 Eighteenth Street ($18 million); 122 C Street ($18 million); 1225 Connecticut Avenue ($34 million); and 816 Connecticut Avenue ($6 million). In addition, the Watergate complex is half owned by the British Coal Board Pension Fund, Mazza Gallerie is half owned by the British Petroleum Pension Fund, and the Electricity Supply Pension Fund is a major owner of L'Enfant Plaza. The British also have holdings in Georgetown and in the Maryland and Virginia suburbs.

14. "The Canadians Come Calling," *Time*, November 17, 1986, p. 68; Andrew Malcolm, "Buying Into America," *New York Times*, December 29, 1985, p. Al.

15. Hobart Rowen, "Japan Has Yen for U.S. Property," *Washington Post*, January 25, 1987, pp. Kl and K7; and "Japanese Firms Boost Purchases of Real Estate in U.S.," *Wall Street Journal*, October 20, 1986, p. 6. Currency fluctuations proved a bonanza for foreign investors from other countries as well

as Japan. The following are examples supplied by the Urban Land Institute, based on averages reported by the Frank Russell Co. Property Index: A U.S. investor who bought a piece of property in 1978 and sold it in 1984 would have had a 15.4 percent compound annual rate of return on his investment. If he were British, he would have earned 20.9 percent after his dollars were converted to pounds; a French investor would have earned 28.4 percent; an Italian, 30.3 percent; and a Mexican, 105 percent. See *Wall Street Journal*, January 30, 1985, p. 29.

16. Ibid.

17. *Salt Lake Tribune*, October 18, 1986, p. B1.

18. Wayne King, "Mexico's Money Crisis Imperiling Investments in U.S. Properties," *New York Times*, September 19, 1982, p. A1.

19. Wendy Swallow, "Registration Weighed for Foreign Investors," *Washington Post*, May 2, 1987, p. E1.

12. Capital Flight and Foreign Aid

1. U.S. Congress, *Congressional Record*, November 7, 1985, p. S-15126.

2. General Accounting Office, "The Philippines: Accountability and Control of U.S. Assistance," Briefing Report to Senator Edward M. Kennedy, May 1986. See also "The Philippines: Distribution and Oversight of U.S. Development and Food Assistance," Report to the Honorable Charles E. Schumer, November 1986.

3. Pete Carey, Katherine Ellison, and Lewis Simons, "How Top Filipinos Hide Fortunes Overseas," *San Jose Mercury News*, June 23, 1985, pp. 1A, 20A–21A; Pete Carey and Katherine Ellison, "Offshore Holdings Not Limited to Prominent Filipino Leaders," *San Jose Mercury News*, June 23, 1985, p. 21A; "Some Deals Sour, Legal Financial Troubles Plague Several Business Ventures in U.S.," *San Jose Mercury News*, June 23, 1985, p. 21A; "Wealthy Filipinos Find California Lucrative Territory For Investment," *San Jose Mercury News*, June 24, 1985, pp. 1A, 8A; "Conduits Help Filipinos Buy Real Estate," *San Jose Mercury News*, June 24, 1985, p.

9A; "Area Banks Are Favored Investments; Some Have Had Trouble," *San Jose Mercury News,* June 24, 1985, p. 9A; "Exiles Keep Tabs on Funds of Marcos's 'Cronies'," June 25, 1985, p. 10A; Lewis Simons, "Dollar Drains Link Unrest in the Philippines," *San Jose Mercury News,* June 25, 1985, pp. 1A, 10A.

4. Pete Carey, Katherine Ellison, and Lewis Simons, "Marcos's Nest Egg in the Philippines," *New Republic,* October 7, 1985, pp. 15–18

5. Steve Lohr, "Protests Increase in the Philippines," *New York Times,* August 14, 1985, p. A5.

6. *San Jose Mercury News,* op. cit.

7. Ibid., June 27, 1985.

8. Ibid.

9. Statement to the Subcommittee, January 21, 1986.

10. U.S. Congress, *Congressional Record,* February 3, 1986, p. H267.

11. Ibid.

12. Joe Conason, "Marcos Sells Manhattan," *Village Voice,* November 18, 1986, p. 14. See also William Bastone and Joe Conason, "Marcos Takes Manhattan—How the First Family of the Philippines and Their Friends Are Buying Up New York," *Village Voice,* October 15, 1985, pp. 17–20, 103.

13. Unions and Equal Employment

1. United Auto Workers, "Request for Interpretation of Specific Provisions on Employment and Industrial Relations in the *Guidelines for Multinational Enterprises,*" presented to the Committee on International Investment and Multinational Enterprises of the Organization for Economic Cooperation and Development, November 14, 1984, Appendix B, p. 10.

2. Testimony of L. Calvin Moore, vice-president, Oil, Chemical and Atomic Workers International Union, U.S. Congress, Hearing before the Subcommittee on Telecommunications,

Consumer Protection, and Finance of the Committee on Energy and Commerce, "Disclosure of Foreign Investment in the United States," May 8, 1986, pp. 157–67.

3. *Wall Street Journal*, December 27, 1985, p. 11.

4. Ibid.

5. United Auto Workers, op. cit.

6. Clyde Haberman, "Labor Peace Reigns and Unions Wither," *New York Times*, June 7, 1985, p. A2.

7. *Business Week*, May 13, 1985, p. 30.

8. *Business Week*, March 4, 1985, p. 54.

9. *Sumitomo Shoji Inc.* v. *Avagliano*, 457 U.S. 176, October 1981.

10. Moore, op. cit.

14. Brazil North

1. Grub is co-author, with Bryan L. Sudweeks, of *Foreign Direct Investment: Country Profiles and Cases*, Rockville, Md.: Mercury Press/Fairchild Publications, 1986.

2. For a discussion of debtor status from a multinational perspective, see John Dunning, *International Production and Multinational Enterprise*, London: George Allen & Unwin, 1981. For an interesting historical perspective on Brazil, see Cheryl Payer, *The Debt Trap: The International Monetary Fund and the Third World*, New York: Monthly Review Press, 1974.

3. Robert Samuelson, "Our Latin Loan Dilemma," *Newsweek*, April 16, 1984, p. 73.

4. Thomas O. Enders and Richard P. Mattione, *Latin America: The Crisis of Debt and Growth*, Washington, D.C.: The Brookings Institution, 1984.

5. Jorge G. Castaneda, "Mexico at the Brink," *Foreign Affairs*, vol. 64, no. 2, Winter 1985–86, pp. 287, 295.

6. Edward Cody, "Strings Tightening on Mexican Economy," *Washington Post*, September 1, 1986, pp. A1 and A30.

7. Christine A. Bogdanowicz-Bindert, "World Debt: the U.S. Reconsiders," *Foreign Affairs*, vol. 64, no. 2, winter 1985–86, p. 264.

8. Ibid.

9. Ibid., p. 266.

10. Harold Lever and Christopher Huhne, *Debt and Danger: The World Financial Crisis*, Boston, Mass: Atlantic Monthly Press, 1986.

11. See Dunning, op. cit.

12. Hobart Rowen, "Debtor Nation," *Washington Post*, September 22, 1985, p. F1 and F6.

13. The Institute for International Economics calculates that all indicators point to a trend line with an unpromising future: from $100 billion of U.S. debt in 1985 to $1 trillion in 1990. See Stephen Marris, *Deficits and the Dollar: The World Economy at Risk*, Washington, D.C.: Institute for International Economics, December 1985.

14. David Hale, "U.S. as Debtor: A Threat to World Trade," *New York Times*, September 22, 1985, p. F2.

15. For an excellent discussion of the U.S. international investment position, see Edward M. Bernstein, "The United States as an International Debtor Country," *Brookings Review*, fall 1985, pp. 28–36. See also Appendix H, for tables plotting the foreign role in the U.S. economy.

16. Throughout this chapter, the terms "debt" and "deficit" are used so frequently that the following definitions might be useful: A primary source of governmental revenue is borrowing, or the creation of *debt*. The public sector has several ways of creating and maintaining debt that are not available to the private sector, such as selling government bonds, mortgages, and treasury notes. Debt is a means of meeting a particular government situation, such as an economic crisis, or any situation creating an imbalance in the nation's treasury, which is known as a *deficit*. Technically, a deficit occurs when the volume of government expenditures exceeds the volume of revenues. A deficit budget provides the funda-

mental precondition for debt creation. In recent years, most of the debt was held internally, which meant that the U.S. government lent the money to itself. *Internal debt* was seen as a sign that the nation was economically strong enough to sustain the debt. *External debt* is money owed to foreign investors. See Bernard P. Herber, *Modern Public Finance*, Homewood, Ill.: Richard D. Irwin, Inc., 1983, pp. 102, 436–37, and 448–49.

17. See Chapters 16 and 17 for a discussion of reciprocity.

18. See the following sources for excellent historical background on foreign investment in the United States. (See also Chapters 1, 2, and Appendix A.) Alfred D. Chandler, *The Visible Hand: The Managerial Revolution in American Business*, Cambridge, Mass.: Belknap Press, 1977; Robert Solomon, "The United States as a Debtor in the 19th Century," unpublished monograph, Washington, D.C.: The Brookings Institution, 1985; and Earl H. Fry, *Financial Invasion of the U.S.A.*, New York: McGraw-Hill, 1980.

19. Jonathan Rauch, "Living With Deficits," *National Journal*, November 1, 1986, pp. 2627–30.

20. Ibid.

21. Craig S. Hakkio and Bryon Higgins, "Is the United States Too Dependent on Foreign Capital?" *Economic Review: Federal Reserve Bank of Kansas City*, June 1985, p. 36.

22. Martin Tolchin, "Foreign Capital Growth in U.S. Causes Concern," *New York Times*, April 1, 1985, p. D1. See also Alfred L. Malabre, Jr., "U.S. Grows Ever More Vulnerable to Foreign Influences," *Wall Street Journal*, October 27, 1986, p. 1.

23. U.S. Congress, Subcommittee on Telecommunications, Consumer Protection, and Finance, Committee on Energy and Commerce, "Disclosure of Foreign Investment in the United States," May 8, 1986, pp. 91–94, and pp. 81–90.

24. Peter T. Kilborn, "A Nation Living on Borrowed Money and, Perhaps, Time," *New York Times*, September 22, 1985, p. E5.

25. *National Journal*, op. cit., pp. 2627–30.

26. U.S. Congress, Testimony to the Senate Budget Committee, February 8, 1985.

15. Faustian Bargains

1. The White House, Executive Office of the President, Office of the Press Secretary, September 9, 1983.

2. U.S. House of Representatives, "Disclosure of Foreign Investment in the United States," Hearing before the Subcommittee on Telecommunications, Consumer Protection, and Finance, Committee on Energy and Commerce, 99th Cong., 2d sess., on H.R. 2582 and H.R. 4242, Serial no. 99–125, May 8, 1986, p. 91. Hereinafter known as the Bryant hearings.

3. The White House, op. cit.

4. Keith Schneider, "Financing U.S. Deficit Abroad," *New York Times*, November 7, 1985, pp. D1 and D8.

5. Department of the Treasury, "Treasury News," February 22, 1984.

6. Edward Cody, "Tax Dodgers Bask Under Caribbean Island Treaty," *Washington Post*, January 26, 1984, pp. A1 and A20.

7. Martha M. Hamilton, "Netherlands Antilles Declares War on Tax Proposal," *Washington Post*, April 22, 1984, p. G6.

8. Michael Quint, "Foreigners Flock to Note Sale," *New York Times*, October 25, 1984, p. D1.

9. Ibid.

10. Alan Murray and Michael R. Sesit, "Treasury Bonds to Give Secrecy to Foreigners," *Wall Street Journal*, August 17, 1984, pp. 1, 3.

11. Ibid.

12. *Wall Street Journal*, February 24, 1986. See also Appendix I, Figure 1.

13. *New York Times*, September 14, 1984, p. D2.

14. Bryant hearings, p. 51.

15. Ibid., pp. 179–80.

16. "LDC Capital Flight," *World Financial Markets*, Morgan Guaranty Trust Company of New York, March 1986, pp. 12–23. See also Appendix I, Table 1.

17. Ibid., pp. 14–15.

18. *Business Week*, September 24, 1984, p. 56.

19. Hobart Rowen, "Uncle Sam's Tax Haven," *Washington Post*, September 6, 1984, p. A21.

20. Ibid.

21. *Wall Street Journal*, August 17, 1984, p. 3.

22. *Business Week*, October 22, 1984.

23. Bryant hearings, p. 50.

24. Allan Sloane, "A Dangerous Addiction," *Forbes*, September 10, 1984, pp. 144–45.

25. Ibid.

26. Edward P. Foldessy and Tom Herman, "Analysts Fret Over Holding of Debt Issues by Foreigners," *Wall Street Journal*, February 24, 1985, p. 15.

27. Ibid.

28. George Anders and Art Pine, "U.S. Currency's Plunge Stirs Up Market Fears It May Drop Too Far," *Wall Street Journal*, April 25, 1986, pp. 1, 17.

29. Paul Craig Roberts, "A Minefield of Myths," *Business Week*, January 28, 1985, p. 18.

30. Lester Thurow, "America's Plunge Into the Debt Abyss," *New York Times*, September 3, 1985, p. A21.

16. The Perfect Host

1. The introductory examples are compiled from the following sources: Office of the U.S. Trade Representative, "National Trade Estimate: 1986 Report on Foreign Trade Barriers," Washington: U.S. Government Printing Office, 1986; Representative John Bryant, "The Foreign Investment Disclosure and Reciprocity Act," News Conference Statement, May 22, 1985; and U.S. General Accounting Office, "Mineral Leasing Act Reciprocity Provision—Implementation and Constraints," July 2, 1984. See Appendix J, Table 1 for specific investment restrictions on a country-by-country basis. For U.S. restrictions on foreign investment, see Michael Butler, "Restrictions on Foreign Investment in the U.S.," *National Law Journal*, January 10, 1983, pp. 46, 48.

2. Including limitations on the ownership of television stations, commercial airlines, and the maritime industry and requiring companies to get security clearances if they are involved in defense-related work. In the case of a national emergency, the president can impound foreign assets, as President Carter did when he seized Iranian assets during the hostage crisis in 1979. The Emergency Economic Powers Act, a legatee of legislation involving "trading with the enemy," formed the basis of his action.

3. Notwithstanding the data collected in the 1986 USTR report cited in footnote 1, which omits investment barriers in Japan, Korea, and the OPEC countries. For an interesting study of the legal and social barriers to investment in Japan, see Peter Reynolds, "Foreign Investment in Japan: The Legal and Social Climate," *Texas International Law Journal*, vol. 18, 1983, pp. 175–201.

4. The International Investment Survey Act of 1976 authorized the collection of information regarding foreign investment in the United States. The Bureau of Economic Analysis (BEA) of the Commerce Department prepares and administers the forms relating to the reporting requirements of the act. The information is treated as confidential. The BEA conducts a comprehensive survey once every five years, known as the benchmark survey. See 15 C.F.R. #806.7, and Appendix C.

5. "All South American countries except Argentina subjected at least 1/3 of U.S. affiliates to these requirements. Mexico's

percentage was 41%. In Africa, Egypt, Libya and Nigeria had requirements in 1/3 to 1/2 of the case. India's percentage was the highest in Asia and worldwide—60%.''

"By industry, U.S. affiliates in the mining industry were most often subject of performance requirements . . . 27% reported such constraints to investment. Manufacturing was next with 19% . . ."

"Affiliates manufacturing transportation equipment were most often affected—27% of the time. Electrical machinery and manufactured foods were next at 21%. . . . 16% of the petroleum industry." See Department of Commerce, International Trade Administration, Office of International Investment, Investment Policy Division, "The Use of Investment Incentives and Performance Requirements by Foreign Governments," October 1981.

6. Nicholas D. Christof, "Curbs Give Way to Welcome for Multinational Companies," *New York Times*, May 11, 1985, pp. 1, 33.

7. According to Wang Beiming, on why Americans are having such trouble with their investments in China—in marked contrast to the Japanese. See "Managers Journal," *Wall Street Journal*, September 29, 1986, p. 18.

8. Title III, International Trade and Investment Act. The "Danforth-Bentsen Reciprocity Bill to amend the Trade Act of 1974." The bill provides for "an annual accounting of major foreign barriers to U.S. exports of goods, services, and foreign direct investment . . . [it] broadens and strengthens section 301 of the Trade Act, particularly as it relates to foreign investment barriers." See *Congressional Record*, 98th Cong., 2nd sess., vol. 130, no. 132, Washington, D.C., October 9, 1984, p. 1; and *Congressional Record*, 98th Cong., 1st sess., vol. 129, no. 4—part III, January 26, 1983, pp. 1–7.

9. Ibid.

10. Ibid.

11. USTR, "Investment Incentives," op. cit.

12. U.S. House of Representatives, "Disclosure of Foreign Investment in the United States," Hearing before the Subcommit-

tee on Telecommunications, Consumer Protection, and Finance, Committee on Energy and Commerce, 99th Cong., 2d sess., on H.R. 2582 and H.R. 4242, serial no. 99–125, May 8, 1986.

13. The Foreign Agricultural Investment Disclosure Act requires public disclosure of purchases of farmland. It is relatively easy, however, to conceal the real purchaser and still remain within the law because of a loophole forbidding the government to look beyond four layers of incorporation. See Chapter 11 and Appendix C.

14. U.S. House of Representatives, "Disclosure of Foreign Investment," op. cit.

15. Ibid., pp. 92–93.

16. Ibid., p. 99.

17. *Congressional Record,* January 7, 1987, pp. H 151 and E 71.

18. The provisions of the Bryant provision of H.R. 3, as adopted in the House of Representatives on April 30, 1987, were:

I. *Contents of Registration*
For a "significant interest" of over 5 percent in a U.S. business or real estate property with assets over $5 million or annual sales over $10 million:
Foreign person's identity, nationality, address, industry.
Date interest acquired, size (%) and purchase price of interest.
Name, location, industry of U.S. property.
Terms and conditions of acquiring interest.
For a "controlling interest" of over 25 percent in a U.S. business enterprise with assets or annual sales over $20 million (additional contents):
English translation of public financial statements filed in home country.
With respect to the U.S. business enterprise—
(i) balance sheet, income statement, and statement of sales, assets, operating income, and depreciation by industrial segment;
(ii) location of U.S. facilities;
(iii) identity, nationality, and financial relation of directors and officers; and
(iv) significant civil litigation in which the business enterprise has been involved within the past year.

II. *Penalties for Failure to Comply*
Civil: Up to $10,000 per week late.
Criminal: Up to 1 year imprisonment, up to $10,000 fine, or both.
III. *Access to information*
  Available to public, indexed by name, nationality, and industry of foreign investor and by name, state, and industry of U.S. property.

19. *Congressional Record—House,* April 29, 1987, p. H 2822.

20. Ibid., p. H 2823.

21. Ibid., p. H 2848.

22. *Congressional Record—Senate,* July 17, 1987, p. S 510157.

23. Industrial Union Department AFL-CIO, Letter from Howard Samuel and David Mallino to members of Congress, April 28, 1987.

24. *Congressional Record—Senate,* July 17, 1987, pp. S 10154, S 10156.

25. Ibid., p. S 10158.

26. Ibid., p. S 10160.

27. Bruce Stokes, "Storming the Barricades," *National Journal,* May 17, 1986, pp. 1201–4.

28. Theodore H. Moran argues that investment barriers in developing countries have an insignificant effect on distorting investment flows. See, *Investing in Development: New Roles for Private Capital,* Washington, D.C.: Overseas Development Council, 1986.

29. Stokes, op. cit., p. 1201.

30. Kenichi Ohmae, *Triad Power,* New York: The Free Press, 1985.

31. Robert Christopher, *Second to None,* New York: Crown Books, 1986.

32. Robert L. Sharp, "A Rewarding Relationship—Prospects for U.S.-Japan Overseas Investment," *Speaking of Japan,* March 1985, vol. 5, no. 51, pp. 15–17.

33. William R. Cline, " 'Reciprocity': A New Approach to World Trade Policy," Washington, D.C.: Institute for International Economics, 1982, p. 21.

34. *Washington Post,* December 26, 1985, p. A19.

35. Ron Danielian, testimony before the Subcommittee on International Economic Policy and Trade, Committee on Foreign Affairs, House of Representatives, "Reciprocity and Foreign Investment," February 23, 1982.

36. Embassy of the United States of America, *Investment Climate Statement: Japan,* October 1984, p. 14.

37. Foreign Missions Bill. S. 854, Title II, Sec. 201 (c).

17. Coals to Newcastle

1. Mineral Lands Leasing Act (30 U.S.C. # 181), 1920. Except for the material cited in the following footnotes, additional sources on which this chapter is based include:

    General Accounting Office, Report to the Chairman, Subcommittee on Oversight and Investigation, Committee on Interior and Insular Affairs, House of Representatives, "Mineral Leasing Act Reciprocity Provision—Implementation and Constraints," July 2, 1984.

    James E. Horigan, "Foreign Participation in Domestic Oil and Gas Ventures," *Rocky Mountain Mineral Law Institute,* Proceedings of the 28th Annual Institute, vol. 28, July 22–24, 1982.

2. *Wall Street Journal,* January 10, 1983, p. 1.

3. U.S. Senate, Hearings before the Committee on Energy and Natural Resources, "Proposed Fiscal Year 1984 Budget Request," February 1–3, 1983, pp. 384–85.

4. Department of the Interior News Release, Office of the Secretary, March 10, 1983, and 48 Fed. Reg. 16348, April 15, 1983.

5. *Santa Fe Inter. Corp.* v. *Watt*, 591 F. supp. 929 (1984). U.S. District Court, Delaware. July 2, 1984.

6. The agency's interpretation of the act also indicated a relaxed interpretation of alien reciprocity; the provision has been invoked sparingly over the years. In the 1920s, for example, the Shell Oil company's leases were negotiated for five years by the State Department. The sticking point was nationality: the department wanted to establish that the company was Dutch not British.

7. It established a three-part reciprocity test and eliminated the department's list of reciprocal nations, substituting instead a list of nonreciprocal nations. See Office of the Secretary, Department of the Interior, "Procedures for Administering the Reciprocity Provision of the Mineral Lands Leasing Act of 1920," internal memorandum, May 7, 1982. Under the new procedures, the standards included:

   1. Requirements for an inquiry into whether the foreign country allows U.S. citizens to own stock in corporations that are not restricted from participation in a country's mineral resources on its public lands because of the U.S. citizen's stock ownership;
   2. If a country denies stock ownership, the Department of Interior must determine whether the foreign country allows other opportunities for investment or participation in the country's mineral resources;
   3. If a country does restrict investment in state-owned entities, the department must determine whether the discrimination exists against citizens or corporations of the U.S.

8. Secretary of the Interior, "Decision on the Status of Kuwait Under the Mineral Leasing Act of 1920" (U.S.C. #181 et seq.).

9. *Santa Fe* v. *Watt*, op. cit., note 18.

10. Jack Anderson and Joseph Spear, "All That Glitters Is Not U.S. Gold," *Washington Post*, April 28, 1987, p. B8.

18. Nine Myths That Govern Policy

1. U.S. House of Representatives Wednesday Group, "Backgrounder on Foreign Investment in the U.S.—Issues and Trends," March 21, 1980, p. 2.

2. Jeff B. Copeland et al., "Where the Jobs Are—Working for Japan Inc.," *Newsweek*, February 2, 1987, p. 43.

3. In 1983, Martin Feldstein, then chairman of the Council of Economic Advisers, said, "This year we suspect that half of all net investment in the U.S. will be financed by the inflow of foreign capital."

4. For example: to get around the European Community's tariff barrier on compact-disk players, the Sony Corporation set up a plant in the French Alsace. See, *Business Week*, July 21, 1986, p. 81.

5. Kiyohiko Fukushima, "Japan's Real Trade Policy," *Foreign Policy*, no. 59, summer 1985, p. 25.

6. See the Rosenthal hearings, U.S. Congress, Committee on Government Operations, "The Adequacy of the Federal Response to Foreign Investment in the United States," Washington: U.S. Government Printing Office, 1980.

7. *Newsweek*, op. cit.

8. James Sterngold, "A Nation Hooked on Foreign Funds," *New York Times*, November 18, 1984, p. F1.

9. Basco Eszeki, "Need for more data and controls on foreign investment debated," *Investment/USA*, Bureau of National Affairs, vol. 9, no. 5, May 1987, p. 18.

10. Harvey E. Bale, Jr., and David Walters, "Investment Policy Aspects of U.S. and Global Trade Interests," *Looking Ahead*, vol. 9, no. 1, January 1986, p. 2.

11. Robert B. Reich and Eric D. Mankin, "Joint Ventures with Japan Give Away Our Future," *Harvard Business Review*, vol. 86, no. 2, March/April 1986, pp. 78–86.

12. Edward Boyer, "Are Japanese Managers Biased Against Americans?" *Fortune*, September 1, 1986, pp. 72–75.

13. Cedric L. Suzman with J. Alexander Heslin, "An Evaluation of Current Trends in Foreign Direct Investment in the Southeast United States," monograph, Atlanta, Ga.: The Southern Center for International Studies, March 29, 1985, pp. 16–18.

14. Douglas Sease, "International Efforts Revive a Steel Factory Kaiser Had Shut Down," *Wall Street Journal*, June 4, 1985, p. 1.

15. William Safire, "Goodbye, Mr. Chips," *New York Times*, January 26, 1987, p. A35.

16. Other raiders include the Belzberg brothers of Canada, who took over Scovill, Inc., and Baron James E. Hanson of Great Britain, who built a $2.5 billion U.S. empire through takeovers. *Business Week*, March 4, 1985, p. 83. See also, Peter Gumbel and Douglas R. Sease, "Foreign Firms Build More U.S. Factories, Vex American Rivals," *Wall Street Journal*, pp. 1, 6.

19. Epilogue*

1. Linda M. Spencer, *American Assets: An Examination of Foreign Investment in the United States*. Washington, D.C.: Congressional Economic Leadership Institute, July 1988, p. 13.

2. Malcolm Gladwell, "China to Buy 50 Per cent Stake in U.S. Company's Oil Operation," *Washington Post*, August 4, 1988, p. D1.

3. John Yemma, "Kentucky Savors Bounty of Its Toyota Prize," *Christian Science Monitor*, September 26, 1988, p. 14.

4. A. Gary Shilling, "America's Financial Markets—Frankfurt and Tokyo Take Control," *New York Times*, September 11, 1988, p. F3.

5. Felix Rohatyn, Speech Before the Economic Club of Washington, January 26, 1988.

6. Senate Budget Committee, March 22, 1988; Senate Committee on Commerce, Science, and Transportation, March 24, 1988; and House Foreign Affairs Committee, Subcommittee on International Economic Policy and Trade, September 14, 1988.

*The authors gratefully acknowledge the research assistance of Dion Anderson for this chapter.

7. Andrew Rosenthal, "Dukakis Says Standard of Living Is Deteriorating," *New York Times*, October 4, 1988.

8. John Burgess, "Dukakis Keys in on Foreign Investment," *Washington Post*, October 13, 1988, p. C1.

9. "How Beazer Won the West," *Sunday Times* (of London), 12 June 1988.

10. Stuart Auerbach, "Toshiba Corp's. Costly Lobbying," *Washington Post*, October 13, 1988, p. C1.

11. Pat Choate, "Money Talks: How Foreign Firms Buy U.S. Clout," *Washington Post*, Outlook, June 19, 1988, p. C1.

12. Peter Gumbel and Douglas R. Sease, "Foreign Firms Build More U.S. Factories, Vex U.S. Rivals." *Wall Street Journal*, July 24, 1987, p. 1.

13. "Congressional Record," House of Representatives, October 5, 1988, p. H9589.

14. David Sanger, "U.S. Parts, Japanese Computer," *New York Times*, September 7, 1988, p. D1.

15. Department of Defense, "Bolstering Defense Industrial Competitiveness," Report to the Secretary of Defense by the Under Secretary of Defense (Acquisition), July 1988, pp. 30–31. See also, Department of Defense, Report of the 1988 Defense Science Board Study of The Defense Industrial and Technology Base, October 1988; and John H. Cushman, Jr., "Pentagon Is Urged to Be More Active in Economic Policy," *New York Times*, October 19, 1988, pp. A1 and D22.

16. Fred Hiatt, "Where's the (Japanese) Beef Industry?" *Washington Post*, pp. A1 and A10.

Bibliography

Books

Adler, Dorothy R., and Muriel E. Hidy, eds. *British Investment in American Railways 1834–1898*. Charlottesville, Va.: University Press of Virginia, 1970.

Aharoni, Y. *The Foreign Investment Decision Process*. Boston, Mass.: The Graduate School of Business Administration, Harvard University, 1966

Arendt, Hannah. *Imperialism*. New York: Harcourt, Brace and World, Inc., 1968.

Aubin, Henry. *City for Sale*. Toronto: James Lorimer & Company, 1977.

Bergsten, C. Fred, et al. *American Multinationals and American Interests*. Washington, D.C.: The Brookings Institution, 1978.

————. *The International Economic Policy of the United States: Selected Papers of C. Fred Bergsten, 1977–1979*. Lexington, Mass.: Lexington Books, 1980.

————. *The World Economy in the 1980s: Selected Papers of C. Fred Bergsten, 1980*. Lexington, Mass.: Lexington Books, 1981.

Bernstein, Marvin D., ed. *Foreign Investment in Latin America: Cases and Attitudes*. New York: Alfred A. Knopf, 1966.

Buckley, Peter J., and Brian R. Roberts. *European Direct Investment in the U.S.A. Before World War I*. New York: St. Martin's Press, 1982.

Chandler, Alfred D., Jr. *The Invisible Hand: The Managerial Revolution in American Business*. Cambridge, Mass.: Belknap Press, 1977.

Christopher, Robert. *Second to None*. New York: Crown Books, 1986.

Cline, William R. *"Reciprocity": A New Approach to World Trade Policy?* Washington, D.C.: Institute for International Economics, 1982.

Cohen, Benjamin J. *The Question of Imperialism—The Political Economy of Dominance and Dependence*. New York: Basic Books, 1973.

The Conference Board. *Foreign Investment in the United States: Policy, Problems and Obstacles*. New York: The Conference Board, Inc., 1974.

Crowe, Kenneth C. *America for Sale*. New York: Doubleday & Co., Inc., 1978.

Cushman, Robert F., and Herbert A. Morey, eds. *A Guide for the Foreign Investor: Doing Business in the U.S.A.* Homewood, Ill.: Dow Jones–Irwin, 1984.

Dunning, John H. *International Production and the Multinational Enterprise*. London: George Allen & Unwin, 1981.

Enders, Thomas O., and Richard P. Mattione. *Latin America: The Crisis of Debt and Growth*. Washington, D.C.: The Brookings Institution, 1984.

Fischer, W. Halder. *Technology Transfer as a Motivation for United States Direct Investment by European Firms*. Columbus, Ohio: Battelle Memorial Institute, Columbus Laboratories, 1977.

Franko, Laurence G. *European Business Strategies in the United States: Meeting the Challenge of the World's Largest Market*. Geneva, Switzerland S.A., September 1977.

Fry, Earl H. *Financial Invasion of the USA*. New York: McGraw-Hill Book Co., 1980.

————. *The Politics of International Investment*. New York: McGraw-Hill Book Co., 1983.

————, and Lee H. Radebaugh. *Regulation of Foreign Direct Investment in Canada and the United States*. Provo, Utah: Brigham Young University, David M. Kennedy International Center, 1983.

Goddin, C. Stewart, and Steven J. Weiss. *U.S. Banks' Loss of Global Standing*. Washington, D.C.: Strategic Analysis Division, Office of the Comptroller of the Currency, 1980.

Goldberg, Ellen S. *Analysis of Current Operations of Foreign-Owned U.S. Banks*. Washington, D.C.: Strategic Analysis Division, Office of the Comptroller of the Currency, 1980.

————. *Comparative Cost Analysis of Foreign-Owned U.S. Banks*. Washington, D.C.: Strategic Analysis Division, Office of the Comptroller of the Currency, 1980.

Grub, Phillip D., and Bryan L. Sudweeks. *Foreign Direct Investment: Country Profiles and Cases*. Rockville, Md.: Mercury Press/Fairchild Publications, 1986.

Hellriegel, Don, and John W. Slocum, Jr. *Management*. Reading, Mass.: Addison-Wesley Publishing Co., 1986.

Herber, Bernard P. *Modern Public Finance*. Homewood, Ill.: Richard D. Irwin Inc., 1983.

Hidi, Ralph W. *The House of Baring in American Trade and Finance: English Merchant Bankers at Work 1763–1861*. Cambridge, Mass.: Harvard University Press, 1949.

Hill and Knowlton, Inc. *The Foreign Investor in the American Marketplace*. New York, 1979.

Imbert, Bernard. *French Investment in the American Southeast*. Atlanta, Ga.: Georgia World Congress Institute, 1979.

Kindleberger, C. P., ed. *The International Corporation*. Cambridge, Mass.: M.I.T. Press, 1970.

Kline, John M. *International Codes and Multinational Business: Setting Guidelines for International Business Operations*. Westport, Conn.: Quorum Books, 1985.

————. *State Government Influence in U.S. International Economic Policy*. Lexington, Mass.: Lexington Books, 1983.

Kogut, Bruce, and Harbir Singh. *Entering the United States by Acquisition or Joint Venture: Cultural Characteristics*. Philadelphia, Pa.: Wharton School, Department of Management, 1985.

Krause, Lawrence B. *Evolution of Direct Foreign Investments: The United States and Japan*. Washington, D.C.: The Brookings Institution, 1973.

Kubarych, Roger M. *Foreign Exchange Markets in the United States*. New York: Federal Reserve Bank of New York, 1983.

Kuttner, Robert. *The Economic Illusion: False Choices Between Prosperity and Social Justice*. Boston, Mass.: Houghton Mifflin Co., 1984.

Lebergott, Stanley. *The Americans: An Economic Record*. New York: W. W. Norton & Co., 1984.

Lenway, Stephanie Ann. *The Politics of U. S. International Trade: Protection, Expansion and Escape*. Marshfield, Mass.: Pitman Publishing Inc., 1985.

Lever, Harold, and Christopher Huhne. *Debt and Danger: The World Financial Crisis*. Boston, Mass.: The Atlantic Monthly Press, 1985.

Longbrake, William, Melanie Quinn, and Judith Walter. *Foreign Ownership of U.S. Banks: Facts and Patterns*. Washington, D.C.: Strategic Analysis Division, Office of the Comptroller of the Currency, 1980.

McGrane, Reginald C. *Foreign Bondholders and American State Debts*. New York: Macmillan Company, 1935.

Makin, John H. *The Global Debt Crisis: America's Growing Involvement*. New York: Basic Books, Inc., 1984.

Marans, J. E., P. C. Williams, and J. P. Griffin. *Foreign Investment in the United States 1980: Legal Issues and Techniques*. Washington, D.C.: The District of Columbia Bar, 1980.

Mattione, Richard P. *OPEC's Investments and the International Financial System*. Washington, D.C.: The Brookings Institution, 1985.

Mommsen, Wolfgang J. *Theories of Imperialism*. Chicago: University of Chicago Press, 1977.

Moran, Theodore H. *Multinational Corporations: The Political Economy of Foreign Direct Investment*. Lexington, Mass.: Lexington Books, 1985.

National Association of State Development Agencies. *An Analysis of Innovative State Economic Development Financing Programs*. Washington, D.C.: NASDA, 1985.

———. *Directory of Incentives for Business Investment and Development in the U.S.: A State by State Guide*. Baltimore, Md.: Urban Institute Press, 1986.

———. *State Export Program Database*. Washington, D.C.: NASDA, 1986.

———. *Trade Monitor*. Washington, D.C.: NASDA, 1980.

National Governors' Association. *Governors of the American States, Commonwealths and Territories 1985: Biographical Sketches and Portraits*. Washington, D.C.: National Governors' Association, February 1985.

———. *States in the International Economy*. Washington, D.C.: National Governors' Association, 1985.

Ohmae, Kenichi. *Triad Power*. New York: The Free Press, 1985.

Overseas Development Council. *Investing in Development: New Roles for Private Capital.* Washington, D.C.: Overseas Development Council, 1986.

Partners for Economic Progress: Statement of Objectives and Plans, An Economic Development Plan for the Chattanooga Region. Chattanooga, Tenn.: 1984.

Payer, Cheryl. *The Debt Trap: The International Monetary Fund and the Third World.* New York: Monthly Review Press, 1974.

Perkins, Edwin J. *Financing Anglo-American Trade: The House of Brown, 1800–1880.* Cambridge, Mass.: Harvard University Press, 1975.

Pizer, Samuel, and Zalie Warner. *Foreign Business Investments in the United States.* Washington, D.C.: U.S. Department of Commerce, Office of Business Economics, 1962.

Platt, D. C. M. *Foreign Finance in Continental Europe and the United States, 1815–1870.* Boston, Mass.: George Allen & Unwin, 1984.

Poniachek, Harvey A. *Direct Foreign Investment in the United States.* Lexington, Mass.: Lexington Books, 1986.

Ratchford, B. U. *American State Debts.* Durham, N.C.: Duke University Press, 1941.

Richards, Timothy D. *The Guide to Foreign Investment in United States Real Estate.* New York: Van Nostrand Reinhold Company, 1984.

Roth, Allan R. *A Guide to Foreign Investment Under U.S. Law.* New York: Harcourt, Brace, Jovanovich, 1979.

Sargen, Nicholas, and Richard Segal. *Japan: The World's Number One Capital Exporter.* New York: Salomon Brothers, Inc., 1985.

Servan-Schreiber, Jean-Jacques. *The American Challenge.* New York: Atheneum, 1969.

Shockey, John E., and William B. Glidden. *Foreign-Controlled U.S. Banks: The Legal and Regulatory Environment.* Washington, D.C.: Strategic Analysis Division, Office of the Comptroller of the Currency, 1980.

Smith, W. Paul, and Steven J. Weiss. *Potential Acquisition Partners for Large U.S. Banks: The Discriminatory Effects of Law and Policy.* Washington, D.C.: Strategic Analysis Division, Office of the Comptroller of the Currency, 1980.

Sprague, Irvine H. *Bailout: An Insider's Account of Bank Failures and Rescues.* New York: Basic Books, Inc., 1986.

Staley, Sally J. *International Bond Manual: Japanese Yen,* 2nd ed. New York: Salomon Brothers, Inc., November, 1984.

Stanley, Timothy W., et al. *U.S. Foreign Economic Strategy for the Eighties.* Boulder, Colo.: Westview Press, 1982.

Sweezy, E., J. Baranson, and J. Hooper. *Field Survey to Assess Feasibility of Collection of Data for Analysis of Foreign Direct Investment and Technology Transfer.* Washington, D.C.: Institute of Public Administration, October 1980.

Tong, H. M. *Plant Location Decision of Foreign Manufacturing Investors.* Ann Arbor, Mich.: UMI Research Press, 1979.

Waldmann, Raymond, J. *Direct Investment and Development in the U.S.: A Guide to Incentive Programs, Laws and Restrictions.* Washington, D.C.: Transnational Investments, Ltd., 1979.

Walter, Judith A. *Foreign Acquisition of U.S. Banks: Motives and Tactical Consideration.* Washington, D.C.: Strategic Analysis Division, Office of the Comptroller of the Currency, 1980.

———. *Supervisory Performance of Foreign-Controlled U.S. Banking Organizations.* Washington, D.C.: Strategic Analysis Division, Office of the Comptroller of the Currency, 1980.

Weiss, Steven J. *The Competitive Balance Between Domestic and Foreign Banks in the U.S.* Washington, D.C.: Strategic Analysis Division, Office of the Comptroller of the Currency, 1980.

———. *Competitive Standards Applied to Foreign and Domestic Acquisitions of US. Banks.* Washington, D.C.: Strategic Analysis Division, Office of the Comptroller of the Currency, 1980.

———. *A Critical Evaluation of Reciprocity in Foreign Bank Acquisitions.* Washington, D.C.: Strategic Analysis Division, Office of the Comptroller of the Currency, 1980.

Wilkins, Mira. *Foreign Enterprise in Florida: The Impact of Non-U.S. Direct Investment.* Miami, Fla.: University Presses of Florida, 1979.

———. *New Foreign Enterprise in Florida.* Miami, Fla.: University Presses of Florida, 1980.

Worsham, John P. Jr. *Foreign Direct Investment in the United States: A Selected Bibliography.* Monticello, Ill.: Vance Bibliographies, 1980.

Zagaris, Bruce. *Foreign Investment in the U.S.* New York: Praeger Publishers, 1980.

Articles

Alexander, Charles P. "A Global Money Machine." *Time*, 14 January 1985, pp. 48–50.

Aliber, R. Z. "A Theory of Direct Foreign Investment." In C. P. Kindleberger, ed., *The International Corporation.* Cambridge: M.I.T. Press, 1970.

Anders, George, and Art Pine. "U.S. Currency's Plunge Stirs Up Market Fears It May Drop Too Far." *Wall Street Journal*, 25 April 1986, pp. 1, 17.

Anderson, Jack, and Joseph Spear. "All That Glitters Is Not U.S. Gold." *Washington Post*, 28 April 1987.

Anderson, Harry, et al. "The Kindness of Strangers." *Newsweek*, 27 February 1984, pp. 62–63.

Apgar, Mahlon IV. "The Changing Realities of Foreign Investment." *Development Review and Outlook*, Urban Land Institute, 1985.

Archiron, Marilyn, and Ronald Henkoff. "Braking in the Fast Lane." *Newsweek*, 27 August 1984, pp. 50–58.

"Are Foreign Partners Good for U.S. Companies?" *Business Week*, 28 May 1984, pp. 58–60.

Armstrong, Larry, et al. "Toyota's Fast Lane." *Business Week*, 4 November 1985, pp. 42–44.

Arpan, Jeffrey S., Edward B. Flowers, and David A. Ricks. "Foreign Direct Investment in the United States: The State of Knowledge in Research." *Journal of International Business Studies*, spring/summer 1981, pp. 137–54.

———, and David A. Ricks. "Foreign Direct Investments in the U.S. and Some Attendant Research Problems." *Journal of International Business Studies*, spring 1974, pp. 1–8.

———. "Regulation of Foreign Direct Investment in the United States: Quo Vasit, Quo Vasit." *Journal of Contemporary Business*, autumn 1977, pp. 99–119.

———. "The Impact of State Investors' Site Selections." *Federal Reserve Bank of Atlanta Economic Review*, December 1981, pp. 36–42.

———, and David A. Ricks. "The Impact on the U.S.A. of Investments Made by Foreign Firms." Allied Social Science Meetings, New York, December 1973.

Auerbach, Stuart. "Trade With Pacific Rim Sets Off Second Gold Rush in California." *Washington Post*, 29 April 1984, pp. F1, F10.

———. "Asia Replaces Europe as Major Partner." *Washington Post*, 22 April 1984, pp. Gl, G4–5.

Bach, Christopher L. "OPEC Transactions in the U.S. International Accounts, 1972–1977." *Survey of Current Business*, U.S. Department of Commerce, April 1978, pp. 21–32.

Bale, Harvey E., Jr., and David Walters. "Investment Policy Aspects of U.S. and Global Trade Interests." *Looking Ahead*, vol. IX, no. 1, January 1986.

Bangsberg, P. T. "U.S. Team Lobbies for Hong Kong Investment." *Journal of Commerce*, 29 March 1984, p. 3A.

Bartholomew, James. "Moscow Narodny's Hidden Loss." *Far Eastern Economic Review*, 29 September 1978, pp. 57–58.

Bartlett, Sarah, and Anthony Bianco. "Debt to the Danger Zone." *Business Week*, 4 August 1986, pp. 22–23.

Becker, William H. "Imperialism." In *Encyclopedia of American Economic History*. New York: Scribners, 1983, pp. 882–93.

Beiming, Wang. "Managers Journal." *Wall Street Journal*, 29 September 1986, p. 18.

Bell, R. "Foreign Investment in U.S. Properties." *Real Estate Review*, summer 1978, pp. 56–63.

Benzer, S. L. "Why Foreigners Are Buying Up So Much U.S. Real Estate." *Institutional Investor*, July 1977, pp. 88–91.

Bernstein, Aaron, et al. "Special Paper: Japan, U.S.A." *Business Week*, 14 June 1986, pp. 45–55.

Bernstein, Edward M. "The United States as an International Debtor Country." *The Brookings Review*, fall 1985, pp. 28–36.

Bianco, Anthony, and William Glasgall. "Wall Street and Tokyo Move a Little Closer." *Business Week*, 18 August 1986, pp. 38–39.

Bloomfield, Arthur T., and Richard C. Marston. "Policies for an OPEC Dollar Run." *Journal of Post Keynesian Economics*, spring 1981, vol. 3, no. 3, pp. 299–311.

Blustein, Paul. "Dollar Looms Bigger in Fed's Decision at Risk of Recession." *Wall Street Journal*, 19 May 1987, p. 1.

Bogdanowicz-Bindert, Christine A. "World Debt: The United States Reconsiders." *Foreign Affairs*, winter 1985/86, vol. 64, no. 2, pp. 259–73.

Bogert, Carroll, R. "America's Open Door." *The China Business Review*. September/October 1984, pp. 39–43.

Boyer, Edward. "Are Japanese Managers Biased Against Americans?" *Fortune*, 1 September 1986, pp. 72–75.

Brown, Warren. "Pact With Japanese Is Key Victory for Union." *Washington Post*, 26 November 1986, p. B2.

Brownstein, Vivian. "The World's Missing Billions." *Fortune*, 22 August 1983, pp. 154–55.

Buchanan, Ronald, and James R. Norman. "It's Don Mario to the Rescue at UPI." *Business Week*, 25 December 1985, p. 40.

Buell, Barbara. "The Muscular Yen Is Showing Investment Abroad." *Business Week*, 18 August 1980, pp. 50–51.

Bumpers, Donald L. "Foreign Direct Investment Trends in the Southwest." *Texas Business Review*, vol. 50, July/August 1982, pp. 205–8.

Butler, Michael. "Restrictions on Foreign Investments in the U.S." *National Law Journal*, 10 January 1983, pp. 46, 48.

Callahan, Joseph M. "The Deming Era: A New U.S. Industrial Revolution?" *Automotive Industries*, vol. 161, December 1981, p. 73.

———. "The Deming Era Arrives in Detroit." *Automotive Industries*, vol. 161, November 1981, pp. 45–47.

———. "Man Who Taught Japan Quality Now in Detroit." *Automotive Industries*, vol. 161, June 1981, pp. 34–35.

"The Canadians Come Calling." *Time*, 17 November 1986, p. 68.

Carey, Pete, Katherine Ellison, and Lewis Simons. "How Top Filipinos Hide Fortunes Overseas." *San Jose Mercury News*, 23 June 1985, pp. 1A, 20A–21A.

———. "Marcos's Nest Egg in the Philippines." *New Republic*, 7 October 1985, pp. 15–18.

Carey, Pete, and Katherine Ellison. "Offshore Holdings Not Limited to Prominent Filipino Leaders." *San Jose Mercury News*, 23 June 1985, p. 21A.

———. "Some Deals Sour, Legal Financial Troubles Plague Several Business Ventures in U.S." *San Jose Mercury News*, 23 June 1985, p. 21A.

———. "Wealthy Filipinos Find California Lucrative Territory for Investment." *San Jose Mercury News*, 24 June 1985, pp. 1A, 8A.

———. "Conduits Help Filipinos Buy Real Estate." *San Jose Mercury News*, 24 June 1985, p. 9A.

———. "Area Banks Are Favored Investments; Some Have Had Trouble." *San Jose Mercury News*, 24 June 1985, p. 9A.

————. "Exiles Keep Tabs on Funds of Marcos 'Cronies'." *San Jose Mercury News,* 25 June 1985, p. 10A.

Castaneda, Jorge G. "Mexico at the Brink." *Foreign Affairs,* vol. 64, no. 2, winter 1985, pp. 287–303.

Christelow, Dorothy B. "National Policies Toward Foreign Direct Investment." *Federal Reserve Bank of New York Quarterly Review,* vol. 4, winter 1979–80, pp. 21–32.

Christof, Nicholas D. "Curbs Give Way to Welcome for Multinational Companies." *New York Times,* 11 May 1985, pp. 1, 33.

Chrysler, K. M. "Japan's Dollars Come Home to Roost in U.S." *U.S. News & World Report,* 5 December 1983, p. 83.

Chung, William K., and Gregory G. Fouch. "Foreign Direct Investment in the United States in 1979." *Survey of Current Business,* U.S. Department of Commerce, August 1980.

————. "Foreign Direct Investment in the United States, 1977." *Survey of Current Business,* U.S. Department of Commerce, August 1978.

Cody, Edward. "Strings Tightening on Mexican Economy." *Washington Post,* 1 September 1986, pp. A1, A30.

————. "Tax Dodgers Bask Under Caribbean Island Treaty." *Washington Post,* 26 January 1984, pp. A1, A20.

"Colorado Legislators Offer Bill Replacing Unitary Tax with 'Water's Edge' Approach." *Bureau of National Affairs International Trade Reporter,* 23 January 1985, p. 151.

Conason, Joe. "Marcos Sells Manhattan." *Village Voice,* 18 November 1986, p. 14.

Conason, Joe, and William Bastone. "Marcos Takes Manhattan—How the First Family of the Philippines and Their Friends Are Buying Up New York." *Village Voice,* 15 October 1985, pp. 17–20, 103.

Conway, Carol. "Attacking The Trade Deficit: A Primer and a Proposal." *Southern International Perspectives,* February 1985, pp. 1–21.

Cook, Dan, and Maralyn Edid. "Why the UAW Can't Afford to Lose at Honda." *Business Week,* 2 December 1985, pp. 32–33.

Copeland, Jeff B., with Rich Thomas. "The U.S. Gets Foreign Aid." *Newsweek,* 18 May 1987, p. 58.

Copeland, Jeff B., et al. "Where the Jobs Are—Working for Japan Inc." *Newsweek,* 2 February 1987, pp. 42–48.

Corrigan, Richard. "Chrysler Going to Midwest for Japanese Car." *National Journal,* 20 April 1985, p. 872.

————. "Japan's Third Wave." *National Journal,* 20 April 1985, pp. 840–47.

Crossen, Cynthia. "Tales from the Dark Side: What a Market Crash Might Look Like." *Wall Street Journal,* 21 April 1987, p. 41.

Cuff, Daniel F. "Tennessee's Pitch to Japan." *New York Times,* 27 February 1985, pp. D1, D6.

Culbertson, John M. "The Folly of Free Trade." *Harvard Business Review,* September/October 1986, pp. 122–28.

Curry, Bill. "Big U.S. and Foreign Firms Seek Repeal of Unitary Tax." *Los Angeles Times,* 14 August 1984.

Danielian, Ron. "An Analysis: The U.S. as a Debtor Nation." *Journal of Commerce,* 13 January 1986.

Day, Charles R., Jr. "Looking For Trouble." *Industry Week,* 19 August 1985, pp. 30–32.

DeBraal, J. Peter. "Foreign Ownership of U.S. Farmland: What Does It Mean?" in *The Farm and Food System in Transition.* East Lansing, Mich.: Michigan State University, Cooperative Extension Service, 1984.

"Debt No Worry." *Industry Week,* 22 July 1985, p. 21.

Dentzer, Susan. "The Arab Banks in America." *Newsweek,* 20 January 1983, p. 61.

"Dr. Deming Shows Pontiac the Way." *Fortune,* 18 April 1983, p. 66.

Doerner, William R. "California's Political Gold Rush." *Time,* 3 February 1986, p. 24.

"The Dollar Run Scenario." *Fortune,* 29 October 1984, p. 6.

Donahue, Christine. "A Wily O'Reilly." *Forbes,* 4 June 1984, pp. 207–8.

Dorfman, Dan. "On the Trail of Baby Doc." *New York,* 14 July 1986, p. 19.

"Draining the Philippines." *San Jose Mercury News,* 27 June 1985, p. 1.

Dreyfack, Kenneth, and Marc Frons. "Bob Galvin's Angry Campaign Against Japan." *Business Week,* 15 April 1985, pp. 70–71.

"Drilling-Rig Demand Starts Slowing Down." *Business Week,* 11 January 1982, p. 37.

Edid, Maralyn. "The Chrysler Deal Dooms America's Cheap Small Cars." *Business Week,* 29 April 1985, p. 27.

Edwards, Franklin R. "Regulation of Foreign Banking in the United States: International Reciprocity and Federal-State Conflicts." *Columbia Journal of Transnational Law,* vol. 13, no. 2, 1974.

————, and Jack Zwick. "Foreign Banks in the United States—Activities and Regulatory Issues." *Columbia Journal of World Business,* spring 1975, pp. 58–73.

"European Banks Move In on the Foreign Action in Treasuries." *Business Week,* 30 July 1984, p. 52.

"European Community Contests State Unitary Taxation of Multinational Companies." *European Community News,* 12 December 1983.

Farnsworth, Clyde H. "Chattanooga Reviving Itself With Foreign Capital." *New York Times,* 16 April 1986, p. A23.

————. "Watchdog of U.S. Trade." *New York Times Magazine,* 14 September 1986, pp. 88–93.

Fedders, John M. "Interdependence and Cooperation: The Need for New Concepts to Police the International Capital Markets." Vienna, Austria: International Bar Association, 20th Biennial Conference, 4 September 1984.

————, et al. "Waiver By Conduct—A Possible Response to the Internationalization of the Securities Markets." *Journal of Comparative Business and Capital Markets Law,* vol. 6, 1984, pp. 1–54.

————, and Michael D. Mann. "The 'Waiver by Conduct' Concept—A Reply." *International Financial Law Review,* December 1984, pp. 10–11.

Feder, Barnaby. "Foreign Money Spreading to All Walks of U.S. Life." *New York Times*, 29 December 1985, p. A1.

Fierman, Jaclyn. "The Selling of America." *Fortune*, 22 December 1986, pp. 44–54.

Fischer, Barry M. "Canada's Foreign Investment Review Act as a Model for Foreign Investment Regulation in the United States." *Canada-United States Law Journal*, vol. 7, no. 1, 1984, pp. 61–91.

Flessner, Dave. "Failure to Qualify for Grant Likely to Limit, Delay Komatsu Plant Here." *Chattanooga Times*, 4 October 1985, p. A1.

———. "Komatsu to Begin Work Here Within Three Months." *Chattanooga Times*, 16 October 1985, p. C1.

———. "Twenty Million Dollars in Bonds Voted for Komatsu." *Chattanooga Times*, 28 February 1985.

Foldessy, Edward P., and Tom Herman. "Analysts Fret Over Holding of Debt Issues by Foreigners." *Wall Street Journal*, 24 February 1985, p. 15.

"Foreign Direct Investment in the U.S. Has Been Increasing Rapidly." *Inside World Trade*, 9 August 1985, p. 10.

"Foreign Holdings in U.S. Increase by 11 percent, U.S. Direct Investment Abroad Up by 9 Percent." *Bureau of National Affairs International Trade Reporter*, 2 July 1986, p. 872.

"Foreign Investments in U.S. at New High During 1981." *Business America*, 7 February 1983.

"Foreign Money: The Flow Becomes a Flood." *Business Week*, 13 February 1984, p. 44.

"Foreigners' Aid." *The Nation*, 3 March 1984, pp. 244–45.

Franko, Lawrence G. "Multinationals: The End of U.S. Dominance." *Harvard Business Review*, November/December 1978, pp. 93–101.

"Fujitsu Raises Its Rate in the U.S. Market." *Business Week*, 19 March 1984, p. 28.

Fukushima, Kiyohiko. "Japan's Real Trade Policy." *Foreign Policy*, no. 59, summer 1985, pp. 22–39.

Gareis, Robert J., and Jerome W. Jakurbik. "The United States Securities Credit Regulations: How They Affect Foreign Borrowers and Foreign Lenders in Acquisitions of U.S. Companies." *Journal of Comparative Corporate Law and Securities Regulation*, vol. 4, 1982, pp. 291–303.

Gelman, Eric, et al. "A Marriage of Convenience." *Newsweek*, 5 September 1984, pp. 75–76.

Glen, Maxwell. "The Foreign Connection." *National Journal*, 26 July 1986, pp. 1832–37.

Goddin, C. Stewart, and Steven J. Weiss. *U.S. Banks' Loss of Global Standing*. Strategic Analysis Division, Office of the Comptroller of the Currency, 1980.

Goldstein, Mark L. "Yamamoto's Rising Sun." *Industry Week*, 15 April 1985, pp. 63–64.

Gordon, Michael R. "With Foreign Investment at Stake, It's One State Against the Others." *National Journal*, 18 October 1980, pp. 1744–48.

Graham, E. M. "A Defensive Theory of Foreign Direct Investment and European Direct Investment in the United States." Sloan School of Management, Massachusetts Institute of Technology, 1976.

Gray, Christopher S. "More Than Exports." Business Week, 21 July 1986, pp. 22–57.

Greenhouse, Steven. "A Grim Era for Heavy Equipment." New York Times, 26 September 1985, p. F4.

Haberman, Clyde. "Labor Peace Reigns and Unions Wither." New York Times, 7 June 1985, p. A2.

Hakkio, Craig S., and Bryon Higgins. "Is the United States Too Dependent on Foreign Capital?" Economic Review: Federal Reserve Bank of Kansas City, June 1985, pp. 23–36.

Hale, David. "U.S. as Debtor: A Threat to World Trade." New York Times, 22 September 1985, p. F2.

Hamilton, Martha M. "Netherlands Antilles Declares War on Tax Proposal." Washington Post, 22 April 1984, p. G6.

Hampton, William J. "Mazda's Bold Embrace of the United Auto Workers." Business Week, 17 December 1984, p. 40.

Herbers, John. "Study Sees States Moving to Achieve World Trade Ties." New York Times, 5 August 1985, p. A1.

"Honda Announces Plans to Enlarge Ohio Plant, Study U.S. Car Engine Production." U.S. Import Weekly, 18 January 1984, p. 547.

Horigan, James E. "Foreign Participation in Domestic Oil and Gas Ventures." Rocky Mountain Mineral Law Institute, Proceedings of the 28th Annual Institute, vol. 28, 22–24 July 1982, pp. 969–1018.

Houpt, James A. "Foreign Ownership of U.S. Banks: Trends and Effects." Journal of Bank Research, vol. 14, no. 2, summer 1983, pp. 144–56.

Howenstine, Ned G. "Gross Product of U.S. Affiliates of Foreign Companies." Survey of Current Business, U.S. Department of Commerce, January 1979, pp. 28–36.

———. "Selected Data on the Operations of U.S. Affiliates of Foreign Companies, 1977." Survey of Current Business, U.S. Department of Commerce, July 1980, pp. 32–44, 55.

———. "U.S. Affiliates of Foreign Companies: Operations in 1982." Survey of Current Business, U.S. Department of Commerce, December 1984, pp. 26–40.

———. "U.S. Affiliates of Foreign Companies: Operations in 1983." Survey of Current Business, U.S. Department of Commerce, November 1985, pp. 36–39.

———. "U.S. Direct Investment Abroad in 1983." Survey of Current Business, U.S. Department of Commerce August 1984, pp. 18–25.

"How Overseas Investors are Helping to Reindustrialize America." Business Week, 4 June 1984, pp. 103–4.

"How the U.S. Deficit Squeezes Money Markets Abroad." Business Week, 6 August 1984, p. 38.

Hutton, Cynthia. "Are Japanese Managers Biased Against Americans?" Fortune, 1 September 1986, pp. 72–75.

"The Impact of State Incentives on Foreign Investors' Site Selection." *Economic Review*, December 1981, pp. 36–42.

International Investment Decision. "Benchmark Survey of Foreign Direct Investment in the United States, 1974." *Survey of Current Business*, U.S. Department of Commerce, May 1976, pp. 35–51.

———. "U.S. Business Enterprises Acquired or Established by Foreign Direct Investors in 1979." *Survey of Current Business*, U.S. Department of Commerce, January 1981, pp. 29–39.

"Invest in America's Cities." *American Perspective on U.S.-Japan Relations*, vol. 1, no. 6, December 1983.

Jackson, Robert C. "Foreign Investors Love New York." *Real Estate Review*, fall 1980.

"Japan Is Buying Its Way Into U.S. University Labs." *Business Week*, 24 September 1984, pp. 72–77.

"Japan Parries a Protectionist Thrust." *Business Week*, 11 April 1983, pp. 34–35.

"Japan's U.S. Plants Grow." *Industry Week*, 22 July 1985, p. 24.

"Japanese Companies Start to Flee the Unitary Tax." *Business Week*, 27 August 1984, pp. 30–31.

"Japanese Firms Boost Purchases of Real Estate in U.S." *Wall Street Journal*, 20 October 1986, p. 6.

"Japanese Ledger Shows Yen for Bigger U.S. Bank Account." *National Journal*, 9 March 1985, p. 560.

Johnson, Kathryn. "How Foreign Powers Play for Status in Washington." *U.S. News & World Report*, 17 June 1985, pp. 35–40.

"The Juicing of California." *California Magazine*, February 1986, pp. 72–89.

"June M. Collier." *Industry Week*, 15 October 1984, pp. 45–46.

Kapstein, Jonathan, et al. "Now Europe Is Hooked on Japanese Imports, Too." *Business Week*, 21 July 1986, pp. 80–81.

Kelly, Brian. "The British Are Coming—Again." *Regardie's*, April 1984, p. 65.

Kessler, Felix. "Overseas Investors Still Like U.S. Start-Ups." *Fortune*, 9 December 1985, p. 133.

Kilborn, Peter T. "A Nation Living on Borrowed Money and Perhaps Time." *New York Times*, 22 September 1985, p. E5.

Kline, John M. "The Expanding International Agenda for State Governments." *State Government*, vol. 57, no. 1, 1984, pp. 2–6.

"Komatsu Digs Deeper Into the U.S." *Business Week*, 1 October 1984, p. 83.

"Komatsu Locates in Chattanooga." *Business and Industrial Review: Tennessee*, vol. 40, no. 2, April/May 1985, pp. 1–3.

Koslow, Ralph. "Capital Expenditures by Majority-Owned Foreign Affiliates of U.S. Companies, 1985 and 1986." *Survey of Current Business*, vol. 65, no. 9, September 1985, pp. 22–27.

Kotlowitz, Alex, and Dale D. Buss. "Costly Bait—Localities' Giveaways to Lure Corporations Cause Growing Outcry." *Wall Street Journal*, 24 September 1986, pp. 1, 27.

Kraar, Louis. "A Big, Careful Singapore Fling." *Fortune*, 21 March 1983, pp. 90–92.

Krause, Lawrence B. "Evolution of Direct Foreign Investments: The United States and Japan," in J. B. Cohen, ed., *Pacific Partnerships: United States-Japan Trade*. Lexington, Mass.: D. C. Heath, 1972.

Kundrle, Robert T., and Davis B. Bobrow. "U.S. Policy Toward Foreign Direct Investment." *World Politics*, 6 April 1982, pp. 353–99.

Kuttner, Robert. "Zen and the Art of Trade Negotiation." *New Republic*, 12 and 19 August 1985, pp. 20–33.

"Kuwait Eyes Arco Refining." *The Oil Marketing Bulletin*, 18 February 1985, p. 1.

Laderman, Jeffrey M., et al. "The Epidemic of Insider Trading." *Business Week*, 29 April 1985, pp. 78–92.

Lall, Sanjaya, and N. S. Siddharthan. "The Monopolistic Advantages of Multinationals: Lessons from Foreign Investment in the U.S." *The Economic Journal*, vol. 92, September 1982, pp. 668–83.

"LDC Capital Flight," in *World Financial Markets*. New York: Morgan Guaranty Trust Company of New York, March 1986, pp. 12–23.

Leftwich, Robert. "Foreign Direct Investment in the United States, 1973." *Survey of Current Business*, U.S. Department of Commerce, August 1974, pt. 2, pp. 7–9.

———. "Foreign Direct Investment in the United States, 1962–71." *Survey of Current Business*, U.S. Department of Commerce, February 1973, pp. 29–40.

Lightburn, Jane. "New Wave of Arab Investment in U.S.?" *Saudi Business and Arab Economic Review*, 12 November 1984, p. 19.

Little, Jane Sneddon. "The Financial Health of U.S. Manufacturing Firms Acquired by Foreigners." *New England Economic Review*, July/August 1981, pp. 5–18.

———. "Foreign Direct Investment in New England." *New England Economic Review*, March/April 1985, pp. 46–57.

———. "Foreign Direct Investment in the United States: Recent Locational Choices of Foreign Manufacturers." *New England Economic Review*, November/December 1980, pp. 5–22.

———. "The Impact of Acquisition by Foreigners on Financial Health of U.S. Firms." *New England Economic Review*, July/August 1982, pp. 40–53.

———. "The Industrial Composition of Foreign Direct Investment in the U.S. and Abroad: A Preliminary Look." *New England Economic Review*, May/June 1984, pp. 38–47.

Lupo, Leonard A., and Gregory G. Fouch. "Foreign Direct Investment in the United States in 1975." *Survey of Current Business*, U.S. Department of Commerce, August 1976.

Madison, Christopher. "Is Japan Trying to Buy Washington or Just Do Business Capital Style?" *National Journal*, 9 October 1982, pp. 1710–14.

"Major Foreign Multinational Group Will Press States for Tax Concessions." *Inside U.S. Trade*, 22 June 1984, pp. 1–2.

Malabre, Alfred L. Jr. "U.S. Economy Grows Ever More Vulnerable to Foreign Influences." *Wall Street Journal*, 27 October 1987, p. 1.

Malcolm, Andrew H. "Foreign Money Changing U.S. Social-Cultural Life." *New York Times*, 31 December 1985, p. A1.

————. "Canada's New Economic Clout." *New York Times Magazine*, 17 February 1985, pp. 63–69.

Mantel, Ida May. "Foreign Direct Investment in the United States in 1974." *Survey of Current Business*, U.S. Department of Commerce, October 1975, pp. 36–42.

————. "Foreign Direct Investment in the United States, 1976." *Survey of Current Business*, U.S. Department of Commerce, October 1977, pp. 26–44.

Marcial, Gene G. "Polaroid's Parts Look Healthier Than the Whole." *Business Week*, 24 June 1985, p. 98.

McClenahen, John S. "Joint Ventures' Pitfalls." *Industry Week*, 28 October 1985, pp. 24–28.

————. "No U.S. Sales Boom." *Industry Week*, 24 June 1985, p. 29.

————. "Who Owns U.S. Industry?" *Industry Week*, 7 January 1985, pp. 30–34.

McNamara, Diane E. "Foreign Direct Investment in the United States: Disclosure Regulations." *Georgia Journal of International and Comparative Law*, vol. 12, spring 1982, pp. 193–207.

McSpadden, Stephen R. "U.S. Foreign Investment Policy: What Does the Future Hold in Congress?" *Investment U.S.A.*, vol. 3, no. 4, July 1981, pp. 10–12.

Melman, Seymour. "How the Yankees Lost Their Know-How." *Technology Review*, October 1983, pp. 57–64.

"Mexico: Containing the Debt Crisis." *Time*, 5 August 1985, p. 46.

"MidEast Insight." *MidEast Report*, 1 March 1985, p. 23.

"The Mighty Borrower." *The Economist*, 22 September 1984, pp. 15–16.

Mizrahi, David Tonfic. "Interview with Ghaith Rashad Pharaon." *MidEast Report*, 1 March 1985, pp. 2–6.

Moore, W. John. "Going Global." *National Journal*, 20 September 1986, pp. 2244–50.

Moskal, Brian S. " 'Greed Matches Need': Deal with Chrysler Can Only Help Me." *Industry Week*, 9 June 1986, pp. 21–22.

Much, Marilyn. "The Foreign Invasion." *Industry Week*, 23 February 1987, pp. 37–40.

Murray, Alan. "Japanese Automakers Forging Political Coalitions at Capital to Combat Protectionist Bills." *Congressional Quarterly*, 9 July 1983, pp. 1395–99.

————, and Michael R. Sesit. "Treasury Bonds to Give Secrecy to Foreigners." *Wall Street Journal*, 17 August 1984, pp. 1, 3.

Nau, Henry R. "Where Reaganomics Works." *Foreign Policy*, no. 57. winter 1984–85, pp. 14–37.

Nicholson, Tom, et al. "The Media-Mogul Invasion." *Newsweek*, 9 December 1985, p. 50.

"Nissan Makes a Stand in Dixie." *New York Times Magazine*, 10 September 1984, pp. 80–88.

"Now Dr. Deming is Lecturing Automakers." *Industry Week*, 24 August 1981, pp. 28–30.

"The 100 Largest Foreign Investments in the U.S." *Forbes*, 5 July 1982, pp. 115–26.

Oneal, Michael, and Robert Block. "Mayflower Rides a School Bus to Takeover Town." *Business Week*, 26 May 1986, p. 40.

Osborne, David. "Lobbying for Japan Inc." *New York Times Magazine*, 4 December 1983, pp. 133–39.

Patterson, Nicholas J. "Canada-U.S. Foreign Investment Regulation: Transparency Versions Diffusion." *Vital Speeches of the Day*, 15 May 1983, pp. 459–65.

Pauley, David, and Joseph Contreras. "Mexico's New Deal: Tyranny of the Weak?" *Newsweek*, 4 August 1986, pp. 38–39.

"Pearson: The Patrician of British Conglomerates Rolls up Its Sleeves in the U.S." *Business Week*, 22 October 1984, pp. 78–82.

"Pressure Mounting in California for Change in Unitary Method of Taxing Multinationals." *Bureau of National Affairs International Trade Reporter*, 6 March 1985, pp. 350–87.

"Productivity on Prime Time." *Fortune*, 28 July 1980, pp. 34–35.

"Protectionist Push Is Coming From the Top." *National Journal*, 27 April 1985, pp. 932–33.

Quint, Michael. "Foreigners Flock to Note Sale." *New York Times*, 25 October 1984, p. D1.

Ralozz, J. "Machine Tools: Symptom of America's Waning Competitive Edge." *Science News*, 12 March 1983, p. 168.

Randolph, Eleanor. "Washington Times Hit by Resignations." *Washington Post*, 15 April 1987, p. A24.

Rauch, Jonathan. "Living with Deficits." *National Journal*, 1 November 1986, pp. 2627–30.

Reich, Robert B. "Collusion Course." *New Republic*, 27 February 1984, pp. 18–21.

———, and Eric D. Mankin. "Joint Ventures with Japan Give Away Our Future." *Harvard Business Review*, vol. 86, no. 2, March/April 1986, pp. 78–86.

Reineman, G. Wendel. "Pursuing the Foreign Investor." *Real Estate Review*, summer 1980.

Reitter, John. "Recent and Future Trends in International Direct Investment." *Business America*, 6 August 1984, pp. 3–10.

Reuter, Madalyne, and Marianne Yen, eds. "The Urge to Merge." *Publishers Weekly*, 7 November 1986, p. 12.

Reynolds, Peter. "Foreign Investment in Japan: The Legal and Social Climate." *Texas International Law Journal*, vol. 18, 1983, pp. 175–201.

Rice, Faye. "America's New No. 4 Automaker—Honda." *Fortune*, 28 October 1985, pp. 30–33.

Ricks, David A., and Ronald L. Racster. "Restrictions on Foreign Owner-
    ship of U.S. Real Estate." *Real Estate Review*, spring 1980.

Ringle, William M. "The American Who Remade 'Made in Japan'." *Na-
    tion's Business*, February 1981, pp. 67–70.

Roberts, Paul Craig. "A Minefield of Myths." *Business Week*, 28 January
    1985, p. 18.

Rohan, Thomas M. "Dale Turnbull's Korean Lift Trucks." *Industry Week*,
    10 June 1985, pp. 62–64.

Ross, Stanford G. "United States Taxation of Aliens and Foreign Corpora-
    tions: The Foreign Investors Tax Act of 1966 and Related Develop-
    ments." *Tax Law Review*, March 1967, pp. 277–366.

Rossant, John. "Renault's New Surgeon May Not Cut Deep." *Business
    Week*, 20 May 1985, p. 77.

Rothschild, Leonard W., Jr. "Worldwide Unitary Taxation: The End Is in
    Sight." *Journal of Accountancy*, December 1986, pp. 178–85.

Rowen, Hobart. "Uncle Sam's Tax Haven." *Washington Post*, 6 September
    1984, p. A21.

———. "Japan Has Yen for U.S. Property." *Washington Post*, 25 January
    1987, pp. K1, K7.

Rudolph, Barbara. "Auto Suppliers." *Forbes*, 3 January 1983, pp.
    144–45.

Safire, William. "Goodbye, Mr. Chips." *New York Times*, 26 January 1987,
    A35.

St. Goar, Jinny. "Who's Next." *Forbes*, 19 December 1983, pp. 220–24.

Sametz, W., and J. Backman. "Why Foreign Multinationals Invest in the
    United States." *Challenge*, March/April 1974.

Samuelson, Robert J. "Our Latin Loan Dilemma." *Newsweek*, 16 April
    1984, p. 73.

Sanders, Sol W. "Reaganomics Is No Longer a Dirty Word in Europe."
    Business Week, 24 September 1984.

Sanford, Jonathan, and John Costa. "International Trends in the Regulation
    of Foreign Investment," Congressional Research Service, Library of
    Congress, March 1974.

"Saudi Influence at USC." *Boycott Report*, vol. 2, no. 9, September 1978,
    pp. 3–4.

Sease, Douglas. "International Efforts Revive a Steel Factory Kaiser Had
    Shut Down." *Wall Street Journal*, 4 June 1985, p. 1.

Securities Industry Association. "Foreign Activity in U.S. Securities." *For-
    eign Activity*, 6 February 1985.

Sharp, Robert L. "A Rewarding Relationship: Prospects for U.S.-Japan
    Overseas Investment." *Speaking of Japan*, vol. 5, no. 51, March
    1985, pp. 15–17.

Shea, Michael A. "U.S. Business Enterprises Acquired or Established by
    Foreign Direct Investors in 1985." *Survey of Current Business*, vol.
    66, no. 5, May 1986, pp. 47–54.

"The Shrinking World of U.S. Engineering Contractors." *Business Week*,
    24 September 1984, pp. 84–90.

Simon, W. Viana, and Robert S. Strauss. "Foreign Investment in America: Is It Helping or Hurting?" *Wall Street Journal*, 17 August 1982, p. 13.

Sinclair, Ward. "Aid for Irish Dairy Operation in Georgia Stirs Bitter Protest." *Washington Post*, 12 April 1986, pp. A1, A8.

———. "Foreigners Get U.S. Farm Subsidies." *Washington Post*, 20 April 1987.

Skilling, Kenneth. "Investment Control Bills Filed in Congress." *Commerce in Belgium*, 19 April 1983, p. 21.

Sloane, Allan. "A Dangerous Addiction." *Forbes*, 10 September 1984, pp. 144–45.

Smith, Lee. "Want to Buy a Japanese Company?" *Fortune*, 27 June 1983, pp. 106–9.

"Special Report on International Business: The 100 Largest Foreign Investments in the U.S." *Forbes*, 28 July 1986, pp. 200–6.

Spencer, Edson W. "Pacific Trade: A Level Playing Field?" *Industry Week*, 1 September 1986, p. 14.

"Spotlight in International Business: Special Report." *Forbes*, 4 July 1983, pp. 100–3; 106–10; 114; 118; 120; 124–26.

Spragins, Ellyn. "Stiffing the Foreigners." *Forbes*, 12 September 1983, p. 43.

Stauro, Barry. "Made in the U.S.A." *Forbes*, 22 April 1985, pp. 50–54.

Steinbach, Carol, and Neal R. Peirce. "Cities Are Setting Their Sights on International Trade and Investment." *National Journal*, 28 April 1984, pp. 818–22.

Stern, Richard L. "The Fed in the Middle." *Forbes*, 8 September 1986, pp. 32–33.

Sterngold, James. "Japanese Buying a Place on Wall Street—But Resentment Grows Over Lack of Reciprocity." *New York Times*, 12 April 1987, p. E26.

Stokes, Bruce. "Bill Brock Sees 'Damn Little Equity' in America's Trading Relationships." *National Journal*, 15 December 1984, pp. 2397–98.

———. "Lost Preeminence." *National Journal*, 20 April 1985, pp. 848–53.

———. "Storming the Barricades." *National Journal*, 17 May 1986, pp. 1201–4.

———. "U.S. Presses Japan to Open Up." *National Journal*, 5 July 1986, pp. 1671–72.

Stokes, Henry Scott. "Direct Investment Goes Both Ways." *Fortune*, 28 May 1984, p. 163.

"Strong Dollar Doldrums." *Forbes*, 2 July 1984, pp. 117–28.

"Supreme Court Declines to Rehear Case Upholding California's Unitary Tax." *U.S. Export Weekly*, 18 October 1983, p. 95.

Symonds, William C. "National Steel's New Game Plan Is Made in Japan." *Business Week*, 3 June 1985, p. 78.

Tannenwald, Robert. "The Pros and Cons of Worldwide Unitary Taxation." *New England Economic Review*, July/August 1984, pp. 17–28.

Tatum, John A. "National Economic Trends." *The Federal Reserve Bank of St. Louis*, September 1985.

Templeman, John, and Richard A. Melcher. "The View from Abroad: Bury America." *Business Week,* 3 December 1984, p. 88.

Terry, Edith, and Resa King. "Maybe the Belzbergs Should Stick to Raiding." *Business Week,* 9 December 1985, pp. 107–10.

Thomas, Rich. "How to Solve the Trade Problem." *Newsweek,* 12 January 1987, p. 40.

Thompson, Donald B. "Honeymoon? 'It's Over': Japanese Investments in U.S. Disillusioning." *Industry Week,* 23 June 1986, pp. 29–30.

Thurow, Lester. "America's Plunge into the Debt Abyss." *New York Times,* 3 September 1985, p. A21.

Tolchin, Martin. "Briton's Buying Spree: Prime Real Estate." *New York Times,* 17 January 1986, p. A14.

———."Foreign Capital Growth in U.S. Causes Concern." *New York Times,* 1 April 1985, p. D1.

———."Foreigners' Political Roles in U.S. Grow by Investing." *New York Times,* 30 December 1985, pp. A1, A14.

———."Foreign Role in Politics Is Questioned." *New York Times,* 8 January 1986, p. B7.

———. "With Lobbies in Full Cry, California Debates Repealing Multinational Tax." *New York Times,* 18 February 1986, p. B12.

———. "Russians Sought U.S. Banks to Gain High Tech Secrets." *New York Times,* 16 February 1985, p. 1.

———. "Some Governors Warn on Foreign Investment." *New York Times,* 26 February 1985, p. D19.

———. "U.S. Cities Seeking Foreign Investing." *New York Times,* 20 January 1985, p. 17.

"A Transatlantic Bidding War for the World's Savings." *Business Week,* 22 October 1984, pp. 38–39.

"Unitary Tax Melodrama Resumes in Sacramento." *The California Economic Development and Trade Update,* vol. 2, no. 9, January 1986, pp. 1, 3.

U.S. Department of Commerce. International Trade Administration. "Foreign Assets in the United States." *Survey of Current Business,* August 1959.

———. ———. "Foreign Investments-Summary and Analysis of Recent Census." *Survey of Current Business,* August 1960.

———. ———. "Foreign Investments in the United States." *Survey of Current Business,* September 1958.

U.S. Department of Commerce. "State Export Series: South Carolina." *Business America,* 15 October 1984, pp. 22–25.

"A U.S. Toolmaker Cozies Up to Its Former Foes." *Business Week,* 16 April 1984, p. 66.

"Utah Tax Commissioners Propose 'Water's Edge' Taxation of Multinational Firms." *Bureau of National Affairs International Trade Reporter,* 6 March 1985, p. 357.

Vamos, Mark N., et al. "Rupert Murdoch's Big Move." *Business Week,* 20 May 1985, pp. 104–8.

Waldmann, Raymond J. "A Guide to Foreign Investment in the U.S." *District Lawyer*, October/November 1979.

Wang, Penelope, et al. "The Dogfight Over Osaka Bay: Another Trade Dispute." *Newsweek*, 8 December 1986, p. 67.

Welch, C. M. "The Case for Federal Regulation of Foreign Bank Operations in the United States." *Columbia Journal of World Business*, winter 1975.

"What May Be Behind the Dollar's Latest Leap . . . and Why It Gave the Fed Room to Ease." *Business Week*, 24 September 1984, p. 26.

White, J. R. "How Foreign Money Buys U.S. Real Estate." *Appraisal Journal*, January 1979.

White, Theodore H. "The Danger from Japan." *New York Times Magazine*, 28 July 1985, pp. 18–59.

Willoughby, Jack. "Decision Time in Peoria." *Forbes*, 27 January 1986, pp. 36–84.

Yemma, John. "Buying Into America—Foreign Money Creates Jobs in the U.S., but Causes Concern." *Christian Science Monitor*, 10 March 1987, pp. 18–19.

Zagaris, Bruce. "The Agricultural Foreign Investment Disclosure Act of 1978: The First Regulation of Foreign Investment in U.S. Real Estate." U.S. Department of Agriculture.

Government Documents, Reports, and Testimony

Ahearn, Raymond. *U.S. Foreign Direct Investment Policy: Response to Foreign Government Investment Barriers and Distortions.* Washington, D.C.: Congressional Research Service, 8 January 1982.

———, and David Driscoll. *Executive Branch Organization to Formulate and Implement U.S. Foreign Trade and Investment Policy.* Washington, D.C.: Congressional Research Service, 25 August 1981.

Auley, Harriet, ed. "International Investment Policy," in *GIST.* U.S. Department of State: Bureau of Public Affairs, February 1985.

Ayittey, George B. N. "Summary of Written Testimony on 'The Foreign Investment Disclosure and Reciprocity Act.' " Bloomsburg, Pa.: Bloomsburg University, 8 May 1980.

Belli, R. David. "Foreign Direct Investment in the United States in 1983." *Survey of Current Business*, vol. 64, no. 10. Washington, D.C.: U.S. Department of Commerce, October 1984.

Bieber, Owen. "Statement Before the U.S. International Trade Commission Hearing on the Internationalization of the Automobile Industry and Its Effects on the U.S. Automotive Industry." Detroit, Michigan, 4 December 1984.

Bryant, John. News Conference Statement on "The Foreign Investment Disclosure and Reciprocity Act." 22 May 1985.

———. "The Foreign Ownership Disclosure Act." *Congressional Record*, 100th Cong., E71-72, 7 January 1987.

Buck, Stephen. *Arab Investment in the U.S.—Policies, Patterns and Politics.* U.S. Department of State, Foreign Services Institute, 26th sess., 1983–84, Executive Seminar in National and International Affairs.

Carlson, Ann, and Richard Dann. "The Unitary Controversy." *Senate Office of Research Issue Brief,* December 1984.

Cooper, William H. *Foreign Investments in the United States: Trends and Impact.* Washington, D.C.: Congressional Research Service, 10 September 1985.

DeBraal, J. Peter, and T. Alexander Majchrowicz. *Foreign Ownership of U.S. Agricultural Land Through December 31, 1984.* Washington, D.C.: U.S. Department of Agriculture, 1984.

———. *Foreign Ownership of U.S. Agricultural Land Through December 31, 1985.* Washington, D.C.: U.S. Department of Agriculture, 1985.

Dingell, John D. *Remarks to the National Press Club.* Washington, D.C., 18 March 1986.

Driscoll, David D. *Incentives to Foreign Direct Investment in the United States.* Washington, D.C.: Congressional Research Service, 19 March 1981.

"Foreign Direct Investment in the U.S.: Country and Industry Detail for Position and Balance of Payments Flows, 1984." *Survey of Current Business,* vol. 65, no. 8, August 1985, pp. 47–66.

Jackson, William. *Foreign Control of U.S. Banks: Changing the Bank Regulatory Climate.* Washington, D.C.: Congressional Research Service, 17 August 1979, report no. 79–175.

Loeffler, Thomas A., and William A. Longbrake. *Prices Paid by Foreign Interests to Acquire U.S. Banks.* Washington, D.C.: U.S. Comptroller of the Currency, 1981.

Longbrake, William A., Melanie R. Quinn, and Judith A. Walter. *Foreign Ownership of U S. Banks: Facts and Patterns.* Washington, D.C.: U.S. Comptroller of the Currency, June 1980.

McSpadden, Stephen R. "Testimony on the Impact of Foreign Investment in the U.S." Before the National Capital Area Chapter of the American Society for Public Administration. Washington, D.C., December 1982.

Rosenthal, Ben. "Report from Congressman Ben Rosenthal." Washington, D.C., October 1979.

Shockey, John E., and William B. Gidden. *Foreign-Controlled U.S. Banks: The Legal and Regulatory Environment.* Washington, D.C.: U.S. Comptroller of the Currency, June 1980.

State of California. "The 1985–86 Budget: Perspectives and Issues." Report of the Legislative Analyst to the Joint Legislative Budget Committee, pp. 115–27.

———. Economic Development Commission. "The California Economic Development and Trade Update," vol. 2, no. 9, January 1986, p. 1.

———. Governor's Office. Ronald Reagan. "Letter to Walter F. Mondale re: Federal Intervention in the Interstate Taxation Field." 14 September 1973.

————. Senate. David Roberti et al. "Letter to President Reagan re: Federal Preemption of State Tax Policy." 6 November 1985.

————. Senate Office of Research. "The Unitary Controversy." *Issues Brief*, Sacramento, Calif.: December 1984.

State of Florida. Department of Commerce. Bureau of International Trade and Development. *The Internationalization of Florida: The Bureau of International Trade and Development Perspective*. Tallahassee, Fla.: Florida Department of Commerce, 26 October 1984.

State of New York. Superintendent of Banks. *One Hundred Twenty-Ninth Annual Report*. Albany, N.Y.: New York Banking Department, 31 December 1979.

State of Virginia. Governor's Office. *Foreign Companies with Affiliations in Virginia, U.S.A.* Brussels, Belgium: State of Virginia European Office, February 1985.

U.S. Department of Agriculture. "Close-Up: Foreign Investment in U.S. Agriculture." *Farmline*, September 1981, p. 4.

————. Economics, Statistics and Cooperative Service. *Monitoring Foreign Ownership of U.S. Real Estate—Report to Congress*. Washington, D.C.: U.S. Government Printing Office, 1980.

————. *Foreign Investments in U.S. Real Estate*. Washington, D.C.: U.S. Government Printing Office, 1976.

U.S. Department of Commerce. *Foreign Direct Investment in the United States*, vols. 1–9: Report of the Secretary of Commerce to Congress. Washington, D.C.: U.S. Government Printing Office, 1976.

————. Bureau of the Census. *Selected Characteristics of Foreign-Owned U.S. Firms: 1981*. Washington, D.C.: U.S. Government Printing Office, 1983.

————. Bureau of Economic Affairs. *Implications of Internationalization of the U.S. Economy*. Washington, D.C.: U.S. Government Printing Office, 1980.

————. Bureau of Economic Analysis. *Current Reporting Requirements for Foreign Direct Investment in the United States*. Washington, D.C.: U.S. Government Printing Office, 1982.

————. ————. "The Net International Investment Position of the U.S. Decreased $43.6 Billion in 1983." Washington, D.C.: U.S. Government Printing Office, 1984.

————. Domestic and International Business Administration. *U.S. Taxation of Foreign Direct Investment in the United States*. Washington, D.C.: U.S. Government Printing Office, 1973.

————. ————. *Direct Investment Industry and Foreign Trade Classifications Booklet*. Washington, D.C.: U.S. Government Printing Office, 1983.

————. Bureau of Foreign and Domestic Commerce. *Foreign Investment in the United States*. Washington, D.C.: U.S. Government Printing Office, 1937.

————. ————. *Foreign Long-Term Investments in the United States 1937–39*. Economic Series no. 11. Washington, D.C.: U.S. Government Printing Office, 1940.

————. Industry and Trade Administration. *State Office Abroad.* Washington, D.C.: U.S. Government Printing Office, 1979.

————. Bureau of International Commerce. *Foreign Direct Investors in the United States.* Washington, D.C.: U.S. Government Printing Office, 1973.

————. ————. "Foreign Direct Investment in the United States." Conference Paper no. 6, 15 April 1969.

————. ————. *Invest in the U.S.A.: An Invitation from the President of the United States.* Washington, D.C.: U.S. Government Printing Office, 1969.

————. ————. *List of Foreign Firms with Some Interest/Control in American Manufacturing and Petroleum Companies in the U.S.* Washington, D.C.: U.S. Government Printing Office, 1976.

————. Office of International Finance, Investment and Services. *Summary of Foreign Investment Policies: A Survey of 35 Countries' Inward Investment Policy and Outward Investment Policy.* Washington, D.C.: U.S. Government Printing Office, 1981.

————. International Trade Administration. *A Local Impact Study of a Foreign Direct Investment in the United States: Noranda Aluminum Inc., New Madrid, Missouri.* Washington, D.C.: U. S. Government Printing Office, 1982.

————. ————. *Attracting Foreign Investment to the United States: A Guide for Government.* Washington, D.C.: U.S. Government Printing Office, 1981.

————. ————. *Bibliography on Foreign Direct Investment in the United States.* Washington, D.C.: U.S. Government Printing Office, 1981.

————. ————. *The Costs and Benefits of Foreign Investment from a State Perspective.* Washington, D.C.: U.S. Government Printing Office, 1982.

————. ————. *Direct Investment in the United States by Foreign Government-owned Companies, 1974–81.* Washington, D.C.: U.S. Government Printing Office, 1983.

————. ————. *Foreign Direct Investment in the United States: Completed Transactions, 1979–1982.* Washington, D.C.: U.S. Government Printing Office, 1983.

————. ————. *Foreign Direct Investment in the United States: 1982 Completed Transactions, 1982.* Washington, D.C.: U.S. Government Printing Office, 1984.

————. ————. *Foreign Direct Investment in the United States: 1983.* Washington, D.C.: U.S. Government Printing Office, 1984.

————. ————. *Foreign Direct Investment in the United States: 1985.* Washington, D.C.: U.S. Government Printing Office, 1986.

————. ————. *International Direct Investment: Global Trends and the U.S. Role.* Washington, D.C.: U.S. Government Printing Office, 1984.

————. ————. *Invest in the U.S.A.: A Guide for the Foreign Investor.* Washington, D.C.: U.S. Government Printing Office, 1981.

————. ————. "Investment Climate Statements: Major Trading and Investing Partners." Washington, D.C.: U.S. Government Printing Office, April 1981.

————. ————. *Quarterly Report on Foreign Direct Investment Activity in the United States.* Washington, D.C.: U.S. Government Printing Office, 1985.

————. ————. *The Use of Investment Incentives and Performance Requirements by Foreign Governments.* Washington, D.C.: U.S. Government Printing Office, 1981.

————. Office of Business Economics. *Foreign Business Investments in the United States.* Washington, D.C.: U.S. Government Printing Office, 1962.

————. ————. "Record Growth of Foreign Investments." *Survey of Current Business,* August 1957.

————. Office of Foreign Investment in the U.S. *Foreign Direct Investment in the United States: 1976 Transactions—All Forms, 1974–76 Acquisitions, Mergers and Equity Increases.* Washington, D.C.: U.S. Government Printing Office, 1977.

————. ————. *Foreign Direct Investment in the U.S. Food Industry, 1974.* Washington, D.C.: U.S. Government Printing Office, 1980.

————. ————. *Foreign Direct Investment in the U.S. Machinery Industry, 1974.* Washington, D.C.: U.S. Government Printing Office, 1980.

————. ————. *Foreign Direct Investment in the U.S. Primary and Fabricated Metal industries, 1974.* Washington, D.C.: U.S. Government Printing Office, 1980.

————. ————. *Foreign Direct Investment in the United States—1979 Transactions.* Washington, D.C.: U.S. Government Printing Office, 1980.

————. ————. *List of Foreign Direct Investment in the United States— Pending and Completed, 1977–1979.* Washington, D.C.: U.S. Government Printing Office, 1980.

————. Office of International Policy. *Foreign Direct Investment in the United States.* Washington, D.C.: U.S. Government Printing Office, 1980.

U.S. Congressional Budget Office. *The Federal Role in State Industrial Development Programs.* Washington, D.C.: U.S. Government Printing Office, 1984.

U.S. Department of Defense. *Soviet Acquisition of Militarily Significant Western Technology—An Update.* Washington, D.C.: U.S. Government Printing Office, 1985.

U.S. Embassy, Japan. *Investment Climate Statement: Japan.* Tokyo, Japan: Embassy of the United States of America, 1984.

U.S. Executive Office of the President. Office of the U.S. Trade Representative. *National Trade Estimate: 1986 Report on Foreign Trade Barriers.* Washington, D.C.: U.S. Government Printing Office, 1986.

————. ————. *A Preface to Trade.* Washington, D.C.: U.S. Government Printing Office, 1982.

————. President's Commission on Industrial Competitiveness. *Global Competitiveness: The New Reality*, vols. I and II. Washington, D.C.: U.S. Government Printing Office, 1985.

————. Press Release Statement by President Reagan re: *International Investment*. Washington, D.C.: Office of the Press Secretary, 9 September 1983.

U.S. Federal Energy Administration. Office of International Energy Affairs. *Foreign Ownership, Control and Influence on Domestic Energy Sources and Supply*. Report to Congress. Washington, D.C.: U.S. Government Printing Office, 1974.

U.S. Federal Register. *Decision on the Status of Kuwait Under the Mineral Lands Leasing Act of 1920*, vol. 48, no. 74, 15 April 1983, pp. 10348–49.

————. *Procedures for Administering Certain Alien Ownership Provisions of the Mineral Lands Leasing Act of 1920*, vol. 47, no. 123, 25 June 1982, pp. 27622–23.

U.S. Federal Reserve Board. Board of Governors. *Federal Reserve Bulletin*, vol. 67, no. 1, January 1981, p. A7.

————. "An Interview with James Houpt, financial analyst with the Federal Reserve Board for 1986 data." *Currency Quarterly Journal*, September 1984, p. 6.

————. *Structure Data for U.S. Officers of Foreign Banks by Country of Origin, as of 1985*. Washington, D.C.: U.S. Government Printing Office, 1986, pp. 2–66.

U.S. General Accounting Office. *Are OPEC Financial Holdings a Danger to U.S. Banks or the Economy?* Washington, D.C.: U.S. Government Printing Office, 1979.

————. *Changes Needed to Improve Government's Knowledge of OPEC Financial Influence in the United States*. Washington, D.C.: U.S. Government Printing Office, 1979.

————. *Collection of Data on Foreign Investment in U.S. Farmland*. Washington, D.C.: U.S. Government Printing Office, 1978.

————. *Considerable Increase in Banking in the U.S. Since 1972*. Washington, D.C.: U.S. Government Printing Office, 1979.

————. *Controlling Foreign Investment in National Interest Sectors of the U.S. Economy*. Washington, D.C.: U.S. Government Printing Office, 1977.

————. *Despite Positive Efforts, Further Foreign Acquisitions of U.S. Banks Should Be Limited Until Policy Conflicts Are Fully Addressed*. Washington, D.C.: U.S. Government Printing Office, 1980.

————. *Domestic Policy Issues Stemming from U.S. Direct Investment Abroad*. Washington, D.C.: U.S. Government Printing Office, 1978.

————. *Emerging Concerns Over Foreign Investment in the United States*. Washington, D.C.: U.S. Government Printing Office, 1975.

————. *Federal Systems Not Designed to Collect Data on All Foreign Investments in U.S. Depository Institutions*. Washington, D.C.: U.S. Government Printing Office, 1979.

————. *Foreign Direct Investment in the United States—The Federal Role.* Washington, D.C.: U.S. Government Printing Office, 1980.

————. *Foreign Investment in U.S. Agricultural Land—How It Shapes Up.* Washington, D.C.: U.S. Government Printing Office, 1979.

————. *Foreign Ownership of U.S. Farmland—Much Concern, Little Data.* Washington, D.C.: U.S. Government Printing Office, 1978.

————. *Impact of Foreign Direct Investments: Case Studies in North and South Carolina.* Washington, D.C.: U.S. Government Printing Office, 1976.

————. *Implementation of the Agricultural Foreign Investment Disclosure Act of 1978.* Washington, D.C.: U.S. Government Printing Office, 1979.

————. *Perspectives on Trade and International Payments.* Washington, D.C.: U.S. Government Printing Office, 1979.

————. *The Philippines: Accountability and Control of U.S. Assistance.* Washington, D.C., U.S. General Accounting Office, May 1986.

————. *Report by the Comptroller General of the U.S.* Washington, D.C.: U.S. Government Printing Office, 1980.

————. *Should Canada's Screening Practices for Foreign Investment Be Used by the U.S.?* Washington, D.C.: U.S. Government Printing Office, 1979.

————. *U.S. Role as Contracting Agent for the U.S.-Saudi Arabian Joint Commission on Economic Cooperation.* Washington, D.C.: U.S. Government Printing Office, 1984.

U.S. Submission to the General Agreement on Tariffs and Trade. U.S. National Study on Trade and Services. Washington, D.C.: U.S. Government Printing Office, 1984.

————. Committee on Energy and Commerce. *The Foreign Investment Control Act of 1981.* H.R. 3310, 97th Cong., 1st sess., 29 April 1981.

————. 98th Cong., 2nd sess., *Trade and Tariff Act of 1984.* Washington, D.C.: U.S. Government Printing Office, 1984.

————. ————. Subcommittee on Telecommunications, Consumer Protection, and Finance, "Disclosure of Foreign Investment in the United States," May 8, 1986. Washington, D.C.: U.S. Government Printing Office, 1986.

————. ————. *To Require Foreign Persons to Register Their Investments in the United States.* H.R. 312, 100th Cong., 1st sess., 7 January 1987.

————. Subcommittee on Commerce, Transportation and Tourism. Iacocca, L. A. "Prepared Remarks at a Hearing on The Federal Trade Commission and the GM-Toyota Decision's Effect on the U.S. Auto Industry," 8 February 1984.

————. Committee on Foreign Affairs. Subcommittee on Foreign Economic Policy. *Foreign Investment in the United States,* 29 January, 5 and 21 February 1974.

————. Subcommittee on International Economic Policy and Trade. Danielian, Ronald L. Statement before the Subcommittee on International Economic Policy and Trade. *Hearing—Reciprocity and Foreign Investment,* 23 February 1982.

————. ————. ————. Rosenthal, Benjamin S. "Statement on Foreign Investment in the United States," 23 September 1982.

————. ————. Subcommittee on Commerce, Consumer and Monetary Affairs. *Briefing Memorandum on the National Security Implications of Proposed Kuwait Takeover of Santa Fe International,* 23 November 1981.

————. ————. ————. McSpadden, Stephen R. "Memorandum to Benjamin S. Rosenthal on Possible Talking Points for Remarks on Arab Investment, Before the ADL's National Commission in New York City on 6 June 1982."

————. ————. ————. Rosenthal, Benjamin S. "Statements on OPEC Investment: What Should We Do About It?"

————. ————. *Federal Response to OPEC Country Investments in the United States,* Parts 1, 2 and 3. 97th Cong., 1st sess. Washington, D.C.: U.S., Government Printing Office, September, October, November, December 1981; April 1982.

————. ————. *The Adequacy of the Federal Response to Foreign Investment in the United States,* 96th Cong., 2nd sess., House Report No. 96–1216, 1 August 1980.

————. ————. *The Foreign Investment Reorganization Act of 1983.* HR 600, 98th Cong., 1st sess., 6 January 1983.

————. ————. *The Operations of Federal Agencies in Monitoring, Reporting on, and Analyzing Foreign Investments in the United States,* part 2. Washington, D.C.: U.S. Government Printing Office, 1979.

————. Committee on Interior and Insular Affairs. Subcommittee on Oversight and Investigation. U.S. General Accounting Office, Report to the Chairman, "Mineral Leasing Act Reciprocity Provision—Implementation and Constraints," Washington, D.C.: U.S. Government Printing Office, 1984.

————. Committee on Rules. "To Create a Joint Congressional Committee on Foreign Investment Control in the United States," H.R. 3311, 97th Cong., 1st sess., 29 April 1981.

————. Wednesday Group. *Backgrounder on Foreign Investment in the United States—Issues and Trends.* Washington, D.C.: U.S. Government Printing Office, 21 March 1980, p. 2.

U.S. Department of Housing and Urban Development. Office of Community Planning and Development. *The Impact of Foreign Direct Investment on U.S. Cities and Regions.* Washington, D.C.: U.S. Government Printing Office, 1979.

U.S. Department of Interior. *Decision on the Status of Kuwait Under the Mineral Lands Leasing Act of 1920 (30 USC 181 et seq.),* 10 March 1983.

————. *Secretarial Decision Paper: Procedures for Administering the Reciprocity Provision of the Mineral Lands Leasing Act of 1920 (30 USC 181).* 7 May 1982.

————. *Secretarial Decision Paper: Reciprocity Status of Canada,* Washington, D.C.: U.S. Government Printing Office, 1982.

————. "Watt Announces Kuwait Is Non-Reciprocal with United States in Mineral Leasing." News Release, 10 March 1983.

U.S. Department of Labor. Office of Foreign Economic Research. *Production Strategies and Practices of Foreign Multinationals in the United States, 1969.*

U.S. Library of Congress. Congressional Research Service. *Foreign Investment in U.S. Industry.* Issue Brief Number IB78091. Washington, D.C.: U.S. Government Printing Office, 1979.

U.S. President. Emergency Management Office, Coordinator of Inter-American Affairs Office. *Foreign Investment in the United States: History and Nature of Investments.* Washington, D.C.: U.S. Government Printing Office, 1944.

U.S. Securities and Exchange Commission. "Facilitation of Multinational Securities Offerings." *Federal Register,* vol. 50, no. 45. 7 March 1985, pp. 9281–84.

————. "Request for Comments Concerning a Concept to Improve the Commission's Ability to Investigate and Prosecute Persons Who Purchase or Sell Securities in the United States Markets from Other Countries." *Securities Regulation and Law Report,* vol. 16. 3 August 1984, pp. 1305–17.

U.S. Senate. Committee on Agriculture, Nutrition, and Forestry. *Foreign Investments in U.S. Agricultural Land.* Washington, D.C.: U.S. Government Printing Office, 1979.

————. Committee on Armed Services. Subcommittee on Preparedness. Cornell, Robert A. "Testimony Representing Department of Treasury's View of Foreign Direct Investment," 26 September 1984.

————. Committee on Commerce. Subcommittee on Foreign Commerce and Tourism. *Foreign Investment Legislation.* Washington, D.C.: U.S. Government Printing Office, 1975.

————. ————. ————. *Foreign Investment Review Act of 1974.* Washington, D.C.: U.S. Government Printing Office, 1974.

————. ————. ————. *Foreign Investments in the United States.* Washington, D.C.: U.S. Government Printing Office, 1974.

————. ————. ————. *Impact of Foreign Investment in the United States.* Washington, D.C.: U.S. Government Printing Office, 1973.

————. Committee on Foreign Relations. 97th Cong., 1st sess., *S. 854: To Promote the Orderly Conduct of International Relations by Facilitating the Operation of Foreign Missions in the U.S., Thereby Promoting the Secure and Efficient Operation of U.S. Missions Abroad.* Washington, D.C.: U.S. Government Printing Office, 1 April 1981.

————. Committee on Housing and Urban Affairs. Subcommittee on Securities of Banking. *Foreign Investment Act of 1975.* Washington, D.C.: U.S. Government Printing Office, 1975.

U.S. Temporary National Economic Committee. *Direct Foreign Investments in American Industry, 1937.* Monograph No. 6, Part 2. Washington, D.C.: U.S. Government Printing Office, 1941.

———. ———. *Foreign Portfolio Investment in the United States.* Report to Congress. Washington, D.C.: U.S. Government Printing Office, 1976.

———. Office of the Secretary. *Census of Foreign-Owned Assets in the United States.* Washington, D.C.: U.S. Government Printing Office, 1945.

———. *Report to Congress on Foreign Government Treatment of U.S. Commercial Banking Organizations.* Washington, D.C.: U.S. Government Printing Office, 1979.

———. ———. *Report on Foreign Portfolio Investment in the United States as of December 31, 1978.* Washington, D.C.: U.S. Government Printing Office, 1980.

———. *Summary of Federal Laws Bearing on Foreign Investment in the United States, June 1975.* Washington, D.C.: U.S. Government Printing Office, 1975.

———. *Taxation of Foreign Investment in U.S. Real Estate.* Washington, D.C.: U.S. Government Printing Office, 1979.

"U.S. Business Enterprises Acquired or Established by Foreign Direct Investors in 1984." *Survey of Current Business,* vol. 65, no. 5, May 1985, pp. 18–23.

U.S. United Nations Association. *The Global Repercussions of U.S. Monetary and Fiscal Policy.* New York: U.N. Association of America, 1984.

Walter, Judith A. *Foreign Acquisition of U.S. Banks: Motives and Tactical Considerations.* Washington, D.C.: U.S. Comptroller of the Currency, June 1980.

———. *Supervisory Performance of Foreign-Controlled U.S. Banking Organizations.* Washington, D.C.: U.S. Comptroller of the Currency, 1980.

Wertman, Patricia. "Investment Issues Between Canada and the United States." *Congressional Research Service Archival Issue Brief,* 29 June 1982.

Wilson, Arlene. *Foreign Investment in United States Industry.* Washington, D.C.: Congressional Research Service, 24 October 1983.

———. *The United States as a Net International Debtor.* Washington, D.C.: Congressional Research Service, 6 May 1985.

Winc, Kevin F. *Foreign Direct Investment in the United States: Patterns, Motives and Sources.* Washington, D.C.: Congressional Research Service, 29 May 1981.

Monographs, Reports, Court Cases, and Other Sources

Ames, Walter L. "Entering the Japanese Market via Acquisitions." *Japan Economic Institute Report,* 1985.

Asay, Michael R. "Internationalization of Future Markets: A National Response to Worldwide Economic Growth and Uncertainty." Speech given at the 1984 International Future Markets Conference, *Business Research International,* London, England, 24 February 1984.

Bale, Harvey E., Jr. "The United States Policy Toward Foreign Direct Investment." *Vanderbilt Journal of Transnational Law*, 1985 Symposium Issue, 1985.

———. *Foreign Investment Policy*. Cambridge, Mass.: Paper Presented at the NOMOS Project Seminar II, The Center for International Affairs, Harvard University, 24 May 1984.

British Broadcasting Corporation. "Panorama," 21 February 1983, p. 12.

Butler, Michael F. "U.S. Government Restrictions and Protections for Foreign Investment," Washington, D.C.: Andrews and Kurth,

CBS News Special: "Foreign Investment in America: Sales or Sellout?" 31 March 1979.

Container Corporation of America v. *Franchise Tax Board*, 103 S.Ct. 2933 (1983).

Georgia Department of Industry and Trade, *Annual Report of the International Division for 1984*, 1 January 1985.

Hervey, Jack L. "Foreign Investment in U.S. Business Increased in 1984." *Federal Reserve Bank of Chicago International Letter No. 549*, August 1985.

Japan Economic Institute. "Japan's Expanding U.S. Manufacturing Presence: 1984 Update." *Japan Economic Institute Report*, no. 6A, 15 February 1985.

———. "Recent Trends in U.S. Direct Investment in Japan." *Japan Economic Institute Report*, no. 23A, 15 June 1984.

———. "Regional Investment Promotion: The Kyushu Experience." *Japan Economic Institute Report*, no. 37A, 28 September 1984.

Japan Trade Center, New York. "Increased Americanization Effort Seen: Latest JETRO Survey of Japanese Manufacturers in the U.S." Press Release, 28 June 1984.

Johnson, Julius H., Jr. "Foreign Investment, Trade Imbalances, and the United States International Investment Position in 1985." Washington, D.C.: Unpublished Paper, 24 July 1986.

Lamm, Richard D. *List of Japanese Trade Barriers*. Denver, Colo.: State of Colorado, February 1985.

Levy, Joel H., and Marc D. Stern. "Petition for a Writ of Certiorari to the U.S. Ct. of Appeals of the D.C. Circuit," *American Jewish Congress* v. *U.S. Department of Treasury*, October Term 1983.

Liew v. *Breen*, 640 F. 2d 1046 (1981).

MacKnight, Susan. *Japan's Expanding Manufacturing Presence in the United States: A Profile*. Washington, D.C.: Japan Economic Institute of America.

Marris, Stephen. *Deficits and the Dollar: The World Economy at Risk*. Washington, D.C.: Institute for International Economics, December 1985.

Petition of Houdaille Industries, Inc., to the President of the United States through the Office of the United States Trade Representative for the exercise of Presidential Discretion. Authorized by Section 103 of the Revenue Act of 1971, 26 USC 48 (a) (7) (D), 3 May 1982.

Sakoh, Katsuro. "Japanese Investment in the U.S.: Creating Jobs and Narrowing the Trade Deficit." *Backgrounder*, no. 44. Washington, D.C.: The Heritage Foundation, Asian Studies Center, 16 April 1980.

Santa Fe Inter. Corp. v. *Watt*, 591 F. supp. 929 (1984). U.S. District Ct., Delaware, July 2, 1984.

Schaffer, William A. *The Economic Impact of Foreign Investment in Georgia.* Atlanta, Georgia: Georgia Institute of Technology, 1981.

State of Oklahoma v. *Hillcrest Investments, Ltd.* (Okla., 630 F. 2d 1253), March 1981.

Sumitomo Shoji America, Inc. v. *Avagliano*, 457 U.S. 176 (1982).

Suzman, Cedric L., and J. Alexander Heslin. *An Evaluation of Current Trends in Foreign Direct Investment in the Southeast United States.* Atlanta, Ga.: The Southern Center for International Studies, 29 March 1985.

The Conference Board. *Announcements of Foreign Investment in U.S. Manufacturing Industries 1978, 1983, 1984.* New York: The Conference Board, 1978, 1983, 1984.

Ukropna, James R. "Letter to Robert F. Burford, re: Public Comments Regarding the Status of Kuwait Under the Mineral Lands Leasing Act of 1920," Alhambra, Calif., 7 October 1982.

United States of America v. *Amos W. Dawe and Roger E. Dunbar.* U.S. Dist. Ct., N. Dist. Ct. Cal., July 1977.

Walinsky, Louis J. *Arab Investments and Influence in the United States.* New York: American Jewish Center, October 1978.

Index

ABOUT THE AUTHORS

Martin Tolchin is a prize-winning correspondent in the Washington bureau of *The New York Times*. **Susan J. Tolchin** is professor of public administration in the School of Government and Business Administration at George Washington University. Together they have written three previous books—*To the Victor: Political Patronage from the Clubhouse to the White House* (1971), *Clout: Womanpower and Politics* (1974), and *Dismantling America: The Rush to Deregulate* (1983).